Anonymous

The Clarendon Historical Society's Reprints

Series II. 1884 - 86

Anonymous

The Clarendon Historical Society's Reprints
Series II. 1884 - 86

ISBN/EAN: 9783337251871

Printed in Europe, USA, Canada, Australia, Japan

Cover: Foto ©ninafisch / pixelio.de

More available books at **www.hansebooks.com**

"INTER FOLIA FRUCTUS."

THE
CLARENDON
HISTORICAL SOCIETY'S
REPRINTS.

SERIES II.   1884—86.

"History is but the unrolled Scroll of Prophecy."
—James A. Garfield.

EDINBURGH:
PRIVATELY PRINTED FOR THE SOCIETY.

This edition is limited to 120 *large paper, and* 400 *small paper copies, for Subscribers only.*

INDEX.

	PAGE
I. The Journal of King Edward VI.,	1
II. Lex Talionis (1647),	87
III. Gallienus Redivivus (The Massacre of Glencoe), 1695	99
IV. The Declarations concerning the Birth of the Prince of Wales (1688),	129
V. Memoirs of the Chevalier de St. George (1712),	159
VI. The Remarkable Meeting at Windsor in the year 1648,	211
VII. A Dialogue between a Whig and a Jacobite (1716),	225
VIII. The Execution of Mary, Queen of Scots (1586),	251
IX. Twenty Lookes over all the Roundheads (1643),	263
X. Memoirs of George Leyburn (1722),	273
XI. The Character of a Modern Whig (1681),	355
XII. A Letter from General Monck and his Army to the Parliament (1659),	363

SUPPLEMENT.

Notes descriptive of a Curious Pack of Cavalier Playing Cards, (*circà* 1660), by Edmund Goldsmid, F.R.H.S., F.S.A., (Scot.) - 373

[*Illustrated with thirteen copper-plates, containing the 52 Cards* IN FACSIMILE.]

"INTER FOLIA FRUCTUS."

The Journal of King Edward's Reign,
written with his own Hand.

From the Original in the Cotton *Library.*
(Nero. c. 10.)

"History is but the unrolled scroll of Prophecy."
James A. Garfield.

Privately Printed
FOR THE CLARENDON HISTORICAL SOCIETY.
1884.

This Edition is limited to 120 *large paper and* 400 *small paper copies, issued only to members.*

The Journal of King Edward's Reign.*

THE Year of our Lord 1537, was a Prince born to King *Henry* the 8*th*, by *Jane Seimour* then Queen; who within few days after the Birth of her Son, died, and was buried at the Caſtle of *Windſor*. This Child was Chriſtned by the Duke of *Norfolk*, the Duke of *Suffolk*, and the Arch-Biſhop of *Canterbury*. Afterwards was brought up till he came to ſix Years old among the Women. At the ſixth Year of his Age he was brought up in Learning by Maſter Doćtor *Cox*, who was after his Almoner, and *John Cheeke* Maſter of Arts, two well-learned Men, who ſought to bring him up in learning of Tongues, of the Scripture, of Philoſophy, and all Liberal Sciences. Also *John Bellmaine* Frenchman, did teach him the *French* Language. The tenth Year not yet ended, it was appointed he ſhould be created Prince of *Wales*, Duke of *Cornwal*, and Count Palatine of *Cheſter:* At which time, being the Year of our Lord 1547, the ſaid King died of a Dropſie as it was thought. After whoſe death incontinent came *Edward* Earl of *Hartford*, and Sir *Anthony Brown* Maſter of the Horſe, to convoy this Prince to *Enfield*, where the Earl of *Hartford* declared to him, and his younger Siſter *Elizabeth*, the Death of their Father.

Here he begins anew again.

After the Death of King *Henry* the 8*th*, his Son *Edward*, Prince of *Wales*, was come to at *Hartford*, by the Earl of *Hartford*, and Sir *Anthony Brown* Maſter of the Horſe; for whom before was made great preparation that he might be created Prince of *Wales*, and after-

---

* The original is in the British Muſeum.

ward was brought to *Enfield*, where the Death of his Father was first shewed him; and the same day the Death of his Father was shewed in *London*, where was great lamentation and weeping: and suddenly he proclaimed King. The next day, being the   of   * He was brought to the *Tower* of *London*, where he tarried the space of three weeks; and in the mean season the Council sat every day for the performance of the Will, and at length thought best that the Earl of *Hartford*, should be made Duke of *Somerset*, Sir *Thomas Seimour* Lord *Sudley*, the Earl of *Essex* Marquess of *Northampton*, and divers Knights should be made Barons, as the Lord *Sheffield*, with divers others. Also they thought best to chuse the Duke of *Somerset* to be Protector of the Realm, and Governour of the King's Person during his Minority; to which all the Gentlemen and Lords did agree, because he was the King's Uncle on his Mothers side. Also in this time the late King was buried at *Windsor* with much solemnity, and the Officers broke their Staves, hurling them into the Grave; but they were restored to them again when they came to the *Tower*. The Lord *Lisle* was made Earl of *Warwick*, and the Lord Great Chamberlainship was given to him; and the Lord *Sudley* made Admiral of *England:* all these things were done, the King being in the *Tower*. Afterwards all things being prepared for the Coronation, the King being then but nine Years old, passed through the City of *London*, as heretofore hath been used, and came to the Palace of *Westminster*; and the next day came into *Westminster-Hall*. And it was asked the People, Whether they would have him to be their King? Who answered; Yea, yea: Then he was crowned King of *England*, *France*, and *Ireland*, by the Arch-Bishop of *Canterbury*, and all the rest of the Clergy and Nobles; and Anointed, with all such Ceremonies as were accustomed, and took his Oath, and gave a General Pardon, and so was brought to the Hall to Dinner on Shrove-sunday, where he sat with the Crown on his Head, with the Arch-Bishop of *Canterbury*, and the Lord Protector; and all the Lords sat at Boards in the Hall beneath, and the Lord Marshal's Deputy, (for my Lord of Somerset was Lord Marshal) rode about the Hall to make room; then came in Sir *John Dimock* Champion, and made his Challenge, and so the King drank to him, and he had the Cup. At night the King returned to his Palace at *Westminster*, where there was Justs and Barriers; and afterward Order was taken for all his Servants being with his Father, and being with the Prince, and the Ordinary and Unordinary were appointed. In the mean season Sir

---

* Blank in original.

Andrew Dudley, Brother to my Lord of *Warwick*, being in the *Paunfie*, met with the *Lion*, a principal Ship of *Scotland*, which thought to take the *Paunfie* without resistance; but the *Paunfie* approached her, and fhe fhot, but at length they came very near, and then the *Paunfie* fhooting off all one fide, burft all the overlop of the *Lion*, and all her Tackling, and at length boarded her and took her; but in the return, by negligence, fhe was loft at *Harwich-Haven*, with almoft all her Men.

In the month of *May died the French King called *Francis*, and his Son called *Henry*, was proclaimed King. There came alfo out of *Scotland* an Ambaffador, but brought nothing to pafs, and an Army was prepared to go into *Scotland*. Certain Injunctions were fet forth, which took away divers Ceremonies, and Commiffions fent to take down Images, and certain Homilies were fet forth to be read in the Church. Dr. *Smith* of *Oxford* recanted at *Pauls* certain Opinions of the Mefs, and that Chrift was not according to the Order of *Melchifedeck*. The Lord *Seimour* of *Sudley* married the Queen, whose name was *Katherine*, with which Marriage the Lord Protector was much offended.

There was great preparation made to go into *Scotland*, and the Lord Protector, the Earl of *Warwick*, the Lord *Dacres*, the Lord *Gray*, and Mr. *Brian*, went with a great number of Nobles and Gentlemen to *Barwick*; where the firft day after his coming, he muftered all his Company, which were to the number of 13000 Footmen, and 5000 Horfemen. The next day he marched on into *Scotland*, and fo paffed the *Peafe*; then he burnt two Caftles in *Scotland*, and fo paffed a ftreight of a Bridg, where 300 Scots Light-Horfemen fet upon him behind him, who were difcomfited. So he paffed to *Muffelburgh*, where the firft day after he came, he went up to the Hill, and faw the Scots, thinking them, as they were indeed at leaft, 36000 Men; and my Lord of *Warwick* was almoft taken, chafing the Earl of *Huntley*, by an Ambufh, but he was refcued by one *Bertivell*, with twelve Hagbutters on Horfeback, and the Ambufh ran away.

The 10*th* day of September, the Lord Protector thought to get the Hill, which the Scots feeing, paffed the Bridg over the River at *Muffelburgh*, and ftrove for the higher Ground, and almoft got it; but our Horfemen fet upon them, who although they ftayed them, yet were put to flight, and gathered together again by the Duke of *Somerfet*

---

* Should be *March*.

Lord Protector, and the Earl of *Warwick*, and were ready to give a new Onset. The Scots being amazed with this, fled theirwayes, some to *Edinburgh*, some to the Sea, and some to *Dalkeith*; and there were slain 10000 of them, but of Englishmen 51 Horsemen, which were almost all Gentlemen, and but one Footman. Prisoners were taken, the Lord *Huntley*, Chancellor of *Scotland*, and divers other Gentlemen; and slain of Lairds 1000. And Mr. *Brian*, *Sadler*, and *Vane*, were made Bannerets.

After this Battel *Broughtie-craig* was given to the Englishmen, and *Hume*, and *Roxburgh*, and *Heymouth*, which were Fortified, and Captains were put in them, and the Lord of *Somerset* rewarded with 500 *l*. Lands. In the mean season, *Stephen Gardiner* Bishop of *Winchester*, was, for not receiving the Injunctions, committed to Ward. There was also a Parliament called, wherein all Chaunteries were granted to the King, and an extream Law made for Vagabonds, and divers other things. Also the Scots besieged *Broughty-craig*, which was defended against them all by Sir *Andrew Dudley* Knight, and oftentimes their Ordnance was taken and marred.

Year II.

A Triumph was, where six Gentlemen did challenge all Comers, at Barriers, Justs, and Tournay; and also that they would keep a Fortress with thirty, with them against an hundred, or under, which was done at *Greenwich*.

Sir *Edward Bellingam* being sent into *Ireland* Deputy, and Sir *Anthony St. Leiger* revoked, he took *O-Canor*, and *O-Mor*, bringing the Lords that rebelled into subjection; and *O-Canor* and *O-Mor* leaving their Lordships, had apiece an 100 *l*. Pension.

The Scots besieged the Town of *Haddington*, where the Captain, Mr. *Willford*, every day made issues upon them, and slew divers of them. The thing was very weak, but for the Men, who did very manfully. Oftentimes Mr. *Holcroft* and Mr. *Palmer* did Victual it by force, passing through the Enemies; and at last the *Rhinegrave* unawares set upon Mr. *Palmer*, which was there with near a thousand and five hundred Horsemen, and discomfited him, taking him, Mr. *Bowes* Warden of the West-Marches, and divers other, to the number of 400, and slew a few. (Upon St. *Peter's* day the Bishop of *Winchester* was committed to the *Tower*.) Then they made divers brags, and they had the like made to them. Then went the Earl of *Shrewsbury* General of the Army, with 22000 Men, and burnt divers Towns and Fortresses, which the Frenchmen and Scots hearing, levied their Siege in the month of September; in the levying of which, there came one to *Tiberio*, who as then was in *Haddington*, and setting forth the weakness of the Town, told him, That all Honour was due to the Defenders, and none to the Assailers; so the Siege being levied, the Earl of *Shrewsbury* entred it, and victualled, and reinforced it. After his departing by night, there came into the Outer Court, at *Haddington*, 2000 Men armed, taking the Townsmen in their Shirts;

who yet defended them, with the help of the Watch, and at length, with Ordnance, iffued out upon them, and flew a marvellous number, bearing divers Affaults, and at length drove them home, and kept the Town fafe.

A Parliament was called, where an Uniform Order of Prayer was inftitute, before made by a number of Bifhops and learned Men gathered together in *Windfor*. There was granted a Subfidy, and there was a notable Difputation of the Sacrament in the Parliament-Houfe. Alfo the Lord *Sudley*, Admiral of *England*, was condemned to Death, and died in *March* enfuing. Sir *Thomas Sharrington* was alfo condemned for making falfe Coin, which he himfelf confeffed. Divers also were put in the *Tower*.

Year III.

HUME-CASTLE was taken by Night, and Treason, by the Scots. Mr. *Willford*, in a Skirmish, was left of his Men, fore hurt and taken. There was a Skirmish at *Broughty-craig*, wherein Mr. *Lutterell*, Captain after Mr. *Dudley*, did burn certain Villages, and took *Monsieur de Toge* Prisoner. The Frenchmen by night assaulted *Boulingberg*, and were manfully repulsed, after they had made Faggots with Pitch, Tar, Tallow, Rosin, Powder, and Wildfire, to burn the Ships in the Haven of *Bolein*, but they were driven away by the *Bollonors*, and their Faggots taken.

In Mr. *Bowes* Place, who was Warden of the West Marches, was put the Lord *Dacres*; and in the Lord *Gray's* Place, the Earl of *Rutland*; who after his coming entred *Scotland*, and burnt divers Villages, and took much Prey. The People began to rise in *Wiltshire*, where Sir *William Herbert* did put them down, over-run, and slew them. Then they rose in *Sussex*, Hampshire, Kent, *Gloucestershire*, Suffolk, *Warwickshire*, *Essex*, Hartfordshire, a piece of *Leicestershire*, *Worcestershire*, and *Rutlandshire*, where by fair Persuasions, partly of honest Men among themselves, partly by Gentlemen, they were often appeased; and because certain Commissions were sent down to pluck down Inclosures, they did rise again. The French King perceiving this, caused War to be proclaimed; and hearing that our Ships lay at *Jersey*, sent a great number of his Galleys, and certain Ships, to surprise our Ships; but they being at anchor, beat the French, that they were fain to retire with the loss of 1000 of their Men.

At the same time the French King passed by *Bullein* to *New-Haven*, with his Army, and took *Blackness*, by Treason, and the *Almain* Camp; which done, *New-Haven* surrendered. There were also in a Skirmish, between 300 English Footmen, and 300 French Horsemen, six Noblemen slain. Then the French King came with his Army to

Bollein, which they feeing, razed *Boulingberg* ; but becaufe of the Plague, he was compelled to retire, and *Chaftilion* was left behind, as Governour of the Army. In the mean feafon, becaufe there was a rumour that I was dead, I paffed through *London*.

After that they rofe in *Oxfordfhire*, *Devonfhire*, *Norfolk*, and *Yorkfhire*. To *Oxford*, the Lord *Gray* of *Wilton* was fent with 1500 Horfemen and Footmen, whofe coming, with the affembling of the Gentlemen of the Country, did fo abafh the Rebels, that more than half of them ran theirways, and other that tarried, were fome flain, fome taken, and fome hanged. To *Devonfhire*, the Lord Privy-Seal was fent, who with his Band, being but small, lay at *Honington*, whiles the Rebels befieged *Exeter*, who did ufe divers pretty Feats of War, for after divers Skirmifhes, when the Gates were burnt, they in the City did continue the Fire till they had made a Rampier within ; also after, when they were undermined, and Powder was laid in the Mine, they within drowned the Powder and the Mine, with Water they caft in ; which the Lord Privy-Seal having thought to have gone to inforce them a by-way, of which the Rebels having fpial, cut all the Trees betwixt St. *Mary Outrie* and *Exeter* ; for which caufe the Lord Privy-Seal burnt that Town, and thought to return home : The Rebels kept a Bridg behind his Back, and fo compelled him, with his fmall Band, to fet upon them, which he did, and overcame them, killing 600 of them, and returning home without any lofs of Men. Then the Lord *Gray*, and *Spinola*, with their Bands, came to him, and afterward *Gray*, with 200 of *Redding*, with which Bands he being reinforced, came to raife the Siege at *Exeter*, for because they had fcarcity of Victual ; and as he paffed from *Honington*, he came to a little Town of his own, whither came but only two ways, which they had reinforced with two Bullwarks made of Earth, and had put to the defence of the fame about 2000 Men ; and the reft they had laid, fome at a Bridg called *Honington-Bridg*, partly at a certain Hedg in a High-Way, and the moft part at the Siege of *Exeter*. The Rereward of the Horfemen, of which *Travers* was Captain, fet upon the one Bullwark, the **Waward** and Battail on the other ; *Spinola's* Band kept them occupied at their Wall : At length *Travers* drove them into the Town, which the Lord Privy-Seal burnt. Then they ran to a Bridg thereby, from whence being driven, they were in a Plain about 900 of them flain.

The next day they were met about other 2000 of them, at the entry of a High-Way, who firft defired to talk, and in the mean feafon fortified themselves; which being perceived, they ran theirways, and that same Night the City of *Exeter* was delivered of the Siege. After that they gathered at *Launston*, to whom the Lord Privy-Seal, and Sir *Will. Herbert* went, and overthrew them, taking their chief Heads and executing them. Neverthelefs some sailed to *Bridgwater*, and went about Sedition, but were quickly repreffed. Hitherto of *Devonshire*. At this time the Black Gally was taken. Now to *Norfolk*; The People fuddenly gathered together in *Norfolk*, and increafed to a great number, againſt whom the Lord Marquefs of *Northampton* was fent, with the number of 1060 Horfemen, who winning the Town of *Norwich*, kept it one day and one night; and the next day in the morning, with the loss of 100 Men, departed out of the Town, among whom the Lord *Sheffield* was flain. There were taken divers Gentlemen, and Servingmen, to the number of thirty; with which Victory, the Rebels were very glad; but afterward hearing that the Earl of *Warwick* came against them, they began to ſtay upon a ſtrong plot of Ground upon a Hill near to the Town of *Norwich*, having the Town confederate with them. The Earl of *Warwick* came with the number of 6000 Foot, and 1500 Horfemen, and entred into the Town of *Norwich*, which having won, it was fo weak that he could fcarcely defend it; and oftentimes the Rebels came into the Streets, killing divers of his Men, and were repulfed again; yea, and the Townfmen were given to Mifchief themfelves: So having endured their Affaults three days, and ſtopped their Victuals, the Rebels were conſtrained, for lack of Meat, to remove; whom the Earl of *Warwick* followed with 1000 Almains, and his Horfemen, leaving the Englifh Footmen in the Town, and overcame them in plain Battel, killing 2000 of them, and taking *Ket* their Captain, who in *January* following was hang'd at *Norwich*, and his Head hanged out; *Ket's* Brother was taken alfo, and punifhed alike. In the mean feafon *Chaſtilion* befieged the Peer of *Bolloin* made in the Haven, and after long Battery, 20000 fhot or more, gave affault to it, and were manfully repulfed; neverthelefs, they continued the Siege ſtill, and made often Skirmifhes, and falfe Affaults, in which they won not much. Therefore feeing they profited little that way, they planted Ordnance against the Mouth of the Haven that no Victual might come to it; which our Men feeing, fet upon them by night and flew divers Frenchmen, and difmounted many of their Peeces; neverthelefs the French came another time and planted their Ordnance toward the Sand-fide of the Sand-hills, and beat divers Ships of Victualers at the Entry of the Haven, but yet the Englishmen, at the King's Adventure, came into the Haven and refreshed divers times the Town. The Frenchmen seeing they could not that way prevail, continued their battery but smally, on which before they had spent 1500 Shot in a day, but loaded a Galley with Stones and Gravel, which they let go in the Stream to sink it; but or ere it funk, it came near to one Bank, where the Bulloners took it out, and brought the Stones to reinforce the Peer. Also at *Guines* was a certain Skirmish, in which there was about an 100 Frenchmen slain, of which some were Gentlemen and Noblemen. In the mean season in *England* rose great Stirs, like to increase much if it had not been well foreseen. The Council, about nineteen of them, were gathered in *London*, thinking to meet with the Lord Protector, and to make him amend some of his Disorders. He fearing his state, caused the Secretary, in My Name, to be sent to the Lords, to know for what Cause they gathered their Powers together; and if they meant to talk with him, that they should come in a peaceable manner. The next morning, being the 6th of *October* and *Saturday*, he commanded the Armour to be brought down out of the Armoury of *Hampton-Court*, about 500 Harnesses, to Arm both his and my men, with all the Gates of the House to be Rampeir'd, People to be raised: People came abundantly to the House. That night, with all the People, at nine or ten of the Clock of the night, I went to *Windsor*, and there was Watch and Ward kept every night. The Lords sat in open Places of *London*, calling for Gentlemen before them, and declaring the Causes of Accusation of the Lord Protector, and caused the same to be proclaimed. After which time few came to *Windsor*, but only Mine own Men of the Guard, whom the Lords willed, fearing the Rage of the People so lately quieted. Then began the Protector to treat by Letters, sending Sir *Philip Hobbey*, lately come from his Ambassage in *Flanders*, to see to his Family, who brought in his return a Letter to the Protector, very gentle, which he delivered to him, another to Me, another to my House, to declare his Faults, Ambition, Vain-Glory, entring into rash Wars in my Youth, negligent looking on *New-Haven*, enriching of himself of my Treasure, following of his own Opinion, and doing all by his own Authority, &c. Which Letters were openly read, and immediately the Lords came to *Windsor*, took him, and brought him through *Holborn* to the *Tower*. Afterward I came to *Hampton-Court*, where they appointed, by My consent, six Lords of the Council to be Attendant on Me, at least two and four

Knights; Lords, the Marquefs of *Northampton*, the Earls of *Warwick* and *Arundel*, the Lords, *Ruffel St. John*, and *Wentworth*; Knights, Sir *Andr. Dudley*, Sir *Edw. Rogers*, Sir *Tho. Darcy*, and Sir *Tho. Wroth*. After I came through *London* to *Weftminfter*. The Lord of *Warwick* made Admiral of *England*. Sir *Thomas Cheiney* fent to the Emperor for Relief, which he could not obtain. Mafter Wotton made Secretary. The Lord Protector, by his own Agreement and Submiffion, loft his Protectorfhip, Treafurefhip, Marfhalfhip, all his Moveables, and more, 2000 *l*. Land, by Act of Parliament. The Earl of *Arundel* committed to his Houfe, for certain Crimes of fufpicion againft him, as plucking down of Bolts and Locks at *Weftminfter*, giving of My Stuff away, &c. and put to fine of 12000 *l*. to be paid 1000 *l*. Yearly; of which he was after relieved.

Alfo Mr. *Southwell* committed to the *Tower* for certain Bills of Sedition, written with his Hand, and put to fine of 500 *l*. Likewife Sir *Tho. Arundel*, and fix, then committed to the *Tower* for Confpiracies in the Weft Places. A Parliament, where was made a manner to Confecrate, Priefts, Bifhops, and Deacons. Mr. *Paget* furrendring his Comptrolerfhip, was made Lord *Paget* of *Beaudefert*, and cited into the Higher Houfe by a Writ of Parliament. Sir *Anthony Wingfield*, before Vicechamberlain, made Comptroller. Sir *Thomas Darcy* made Vicechamberlaine. *Guidotty* made divers Errands from the Conftable of *France* to make Peace with us; upon which were appointed four Commiffioners to Treat, and they after long Debatement made a Treaty as followeth.

Anno 1549. *Mart.* 24.

Peace concluded between *England*, *France*, and *Scotland*; by our Englifh fide, *John* Earl of *Bedford*, Lord Privy Seal, Lord *Paget de Beaudefert*. Sir *William Petre* Secretary, and Sir *John Mafon*. On the French fide, *Monfieur de Rochepot*, *Monfieur Chaftilion*, *Guilluart de Mortier*, and *Boucherel de Sany*, upon thefe Conditions, That all Titles, Tribute, and Defences, fhould remain; That the Faults of one Man, except he be punifhed, fhould not break the League. That the Ships of Merchandize shall pafs to and fro: That Pirats shall be called back, and Ships of War. That Prifoners fhall be delivered of both fides. That we fhall not war with *Scotland*. That *Bollein*, with the pieces of New Conqueft, and two Bafilisks, two Demy-Cannons, three Culverines, two Demy-Culverins, three Sacres, fix Faulcons,

94 Hagbutts, a Crook, with Wooden Tailes, and 21 Iron Pieces; and *Lauder*, and *Dunglafs*, with all the Ordnance fave that that came from *Haddington*, fhall, within fix months after this Peace proclaimed, be delivered; and for that the French to pay 200000 Scutes within three days after the delivery of *Bollein*, and 200000 Scutes on our *Lady Day* in Harveft next enfuing; and that if the Scots raizd *Lauder*, and we fhould raze *Roxburg* and *Heymouth*. For the performance of which, on the 7th of *April*, fhould be delivered at *Guifnes* and *Ardres*, thefe Hoftages.

Marquefs *de Means*.	My Lord of *Suffolk*.
Monfieur *Trimoville*.	My Lord of *Hartford*.
Monfieur *D'anguien*.	My Lord *Talbot*.
Monfieur *Montmorency*.	My Lord *Fitzwarren*.
Monfieur *Henandiere*.	My Lord *Martavers*.
Vicedam de Chartres.	My Lord *Strange*.

Alfo that at the delivery of the Town, Ours fhould come home, and at the firft Payment three of theirs; and that if the Scots raze *Lauder* and *Dunglafs*, We muft raze *Roxburgh* and *Heymouth*, and none after fortify them, with comprehenfion of the Emperor.

25. This Peace, *Anno* 1550, proclaimed at *Calais* and *Bollein*.

29. In *London*, Bonefires.

30. A Sermon in Thankfgiving for Peace, and *Te Deum* fung.

31. My Lord *Somerfet* was delivered of his Bonds, and came to Court.

April.

2. The Parliament prorogued to the fecond day of the Term in *October* enfuing.

3. *Nicholas Ridley*, before of *Rochefter*, made Bifhop of *London*, and received his Oath.

Thomas Thirlby, before of *Weftminfter*, made Bifhop of *Norwich*, and received his Oath.

4. The Bifhop of *Chichefter*, before a vehement affirmer of Tranfubftantiation, did preach againft it at *Weftminfter* in the preaching place.

Removing to *Greenwich* from *Weftminfter*.

6. Our Hoftages paffed the Narrow Seas between *Dover* and *Calais*.

7. Monfieur *de Fermin*, Gentleman of the King's Privy Chamber, paffed from the French King by *England* to the Scotch Queen, to tell her of the Peace.

Journal of Edward the Sixth.

An Ambaffador came from *Guftave* the Swedifh King, called *Andrew*, for a furer Amity touching Merchandize.

9. The Hoftages delivered on both the fides, for the Ratification of the League with *France* and *Scotland*; for becaufe some said to Monfieur *Rochfort* Lieutenant, that Monfieur *de Guife*, Father to the Marquefs of *Means*, was dead, and therefore the delivery was put over a day.

8. My Lord *Warwick* made General Warden of the North, and Mr. *Herbert* President of *Wales*; and the one had granted to him 1000 Marks Land; the other 500; and Lord *Warwick* 100 Horfemen at the King's Charge.

9. Licences figned for the whole Council, and certain of the Privy Chamber to keep among them 2340 Retainers.

10. My Lord *Somerfet* taken into the Council. *Guidotti* the beginner of the talk for Peace, recompenfed with Knightdom, 1000 Crowns Reward, 1000 Crowns Penfion, and his Son with 250 Crowns Penfion.

Certain Prifoners for light Matters difmiffed; agreed for delivery of French Prifoners taken in the Wars. *Peter Vane* fent Ambaffador to *Venice*. Letters directed to certain Irifh Nobles, to take a blind Legat coming from the Pope, calling himself Bifhop of *Armagh*. Commiffions for the delivery of *Bulloin, Lauder,* and *Dunglafs*.

6. The *Flemings* Men of War would have paffed our Ships without vailing Bonet; which they feeing, fhot at them, and drove them at length to vail Bonet, and fo depart.

11. Monfieur *Trimaul*, Monfieur *Vicedam de Char*, and Monfieur *Henaudie*, came to *Dover*, the reft tarried at *Calais* till they had leave.

13. Order taken, that whofoever had Benefices given them, fhould preach before the King in or out of Lent, and every *Sunday* there should be a Sermon.

16. The three Hoftages aforefaid came to *London*, being met at *Debtford* by the Lord *Gray* of *Wilton*, Lord *Bray*, with divers other Gentlemen, to the number of 20, and Servingmen an 100, and fo brought into the City, and lodged there, and kept Houfes every Man by himfelf.

18. Mr. *Sidney* and Mr. *Nevel* made Gentlemen of the Privy Chamber. Commiffion given to the Lord *Cobham* Deputy of *Calais*, *William Petre* chief Secretary, and Sir *John Mafon* French Secretary, to fee the French King take his Oath, with certain Inftruction; and that Sir *John Mafon* should be Ambaffador Leigier.

Commiſſion to Sir *John* *Davies* and Sir *William Sharrington*, to receive the first Paiment, and deliver the Quittance.

19. Sir *John Maſon* taken into the Privy Council, and *William Thomas* made Clerk of the ſame.

Whereas the Emperors Ambaſſadors deſired leave, by Letters Patent that my Lady *Mary* might have Maſs; it was denied him. And where he ſaid we broke the League with him, by making Peace with *Scotland*, it was anſwered, That the French King, and not I, did comprehend them, ſaving that I might not invade them without occaſion.

10. *Lauther* being beſieged of the Scots, the Captain hearing that the Peace was Proclaimed in *England*, delivered it, as the Peace did will him, taking Sureties, that all the Bargains of the Peace ſhould be kept.

18. Monſieur *de Guiſe* died.

20. Order taken for the Chamber, that three of the Outer Privy-Chamber Gentlemen ſhould always be here, and two lie in the Palace, and fill the Room of one of the four Knights; that the Squires ſhould be diligent in their Office; and five Grooms ſhould be always preſent, of which one to watch in the Bed-Chamber.

21. The Marqueſs *de Means*, the Duke *de Anguien*, and the Conſtable's Son, arrived at *Dover*.

23. Monſieur *Trimoville*, and the *Vicedam* of *Chartres*, and Monſieur *Henaudy*, came to the Court, and ſaw the Order of the Garter, and the Knights, with their Sovereign, receive the Communion.

24. Certain Articles touching a ſtreighter Amity in Merchandize ſent to the King of *Sweeden*, being theſe.

First; *If the King of Sweden ſent bullion, he ſhould have our commodities and pay no Toll.*

Secondly; *He ſhould bring* Bullion *to none other Prince.*

Thirdly; *If he brought Ozymus, and Steel, and Copper,* &c. *he ſhould have our Commodities, and pay Cuſtom as an Engliſhman.*

Fourthly; *If he brought any other, he ſhould have free entercourſe, paying Cuſtom as a Stranger,* &c.

It was anſwered, to the Duke of *Brunſwick*, that whereas he offered Service with 10000 Men of his Land, that the War was ended; and for the Marriage of my Lady *Mary* to him, there was talk for her Marriage with the Infant of *Portugal*, which being determined, he should have anſwer.

25. Lord *Clinton* Captain of *Bulloin*, having ſent away before all his Men ſaving 1800, and all his Ordnance, ſaving that the Treaty did

referve, iffued out of the Town with thefe 1800, delivering it to Monfieur *Chaftilion*, receiving of him the fix Hoftages Englifh, an Acquittance for delivery of the Town, and fafe Conduct to come to *Calais*; whither when he came, he placed 1800 in the Emperors Frontiers.

27. The Marquefs *du Means, Count d' Anguien*, and the Conftable's Son, were received at *Black-Heath* by my Lord of *Rutland*, my Lord *Gray* of *Wilton*, my Lord *Gray*, my Lord *Lifle*, and divers Gentlemen, with all the Penfionaries, to the number of an hundred, beside a great number of Servingmen.

It was granted, that my Lord of *Somerfet* fhould have all his moveable Goods and Leafes, except thofe that be already given.

The King of *Sweden's* Ambaffador departed home to his Mafter.

29. The Count *d' Anguien*, Brother to the Duke of *Vendofme*, and next Heir to the Crown after the King's Children; the Marquefs *de Means*, Brother to the Scotch Queen; and Monfieur *Montmorency*, the Conftable's Son came to the Court. where they were received with much Mufick at Dinner.

26. Certain were taken that went about to have an Infurrection in *Kent*, upon *May* day following; and the Prieft, who was the chief Worker, ran away into *Effex*, where he was laid for.

30. *Dunglafs* was delivered as the Treaty did require.

May.

2. *Joan Boacher*, otherways called *Joan of Kent*, was burnt for holding, *That Chrift was not Incarnate of the Virgin* Mary; being condemned the Year before, but kept in hope of Conversion; and the 30th of *April*, the Bifhop of *London*, and the Bifhop of *Ely*, were to perfwade her, but she withftood them, and reviled the Preacher that preached at her Death.

The firft payment was payed at *Calais*, and received by Sir *Thomas Dennis*, and Mr. *Sharrington*.

4. The Lord *Clinton*, before Captain of *Bollein*, came to Court, where after Thanks, he was made Admiral of *England*, upon the Surrender of the Earl of *Warwick's* Patent; He was also taken into the Privy-Council, and promifed further Reward. The Captain alfo, and Officers of the Town, were promifed Rewards. Monfieur *de Brifay* paffed alfo by the Court to *Scotland*, where at *Greenwich* he came to the King, telling him, That the French King would fee that if he lacked any Commodity that he had, he wonld give it him; and likewise would the Conftable of *France*, who then bore all the Swing.

5. The Marquess *de Means* departed to *Scotland* with Monsieur *de Brisay*, to acquaint the Queen of the death of the Duke of *Guise*.

6. The Master of *Ayrskin*, and Monsieur *Morret's* Brother came out of *Scotland* for the Acceptation of the Peace, who after had Passport to go into *France*.

7. The Council drew a Book for every Shire, who should be Lieutenants in them, and who should tarry with Me; but the Lieutenants were appointed to tarry till *Chastilions*, *Sarcy*, and *Boucherels* coming, and then to depart.

9. Proclamation was made, That the Souldiers should return to Mansions; and the Mayor of *London* had charge to look through all the Wards, to take them and send them to their Countries.

The Debt of 30000 *l.* and odd Money, was put over an Year, and there was bought 2500 Cinquetales of Powder.

11. Proclamation was made, That all Wooll-winders should take an Oath that they would make good Cloth there, as the Lord Chancellor would appoint them, according to an Act of Parliament made by *Edward* the Third.

7. The Lord *Cobham*, the Secretary *Petre*, and Sir *John Mason* came to the French King to *Amiens*, going on his Journey, where they were received of all the Nobles, and so brought to their Lodgings, which were well dressed.

10. The French King took the Oath for the Acceptation of the Treaty.

12. Our Ambassadors departed from the French Court, leaving Sir *John Mason* as Legier.

14. The Duke of *Somerset* was taken into the Privy-Chamber, and likewise was the Lord Admiral.

15. It was appointed that all the Light-Horsemen of *Bollein*, and the Men of Arms, should be payed their Wages, and be led by the Lord Marquess of *Northampton*, Captain of the Pensioners; and all the Guard of *Bollein* under the Lord Admiral. Also that the chiefest Captains should be sent, with 600 with them, to the strengthning of the Frontiers of *Scotland*.

The comprehension of Peace with *Scotland* was accepted so far as the League went, and Sealed.

16. The Master of *Ayrskin* departed into *France*.
17. Removing from *Westminster* to *Greenwich*.
18. The French King came to *Bollein* to visit the Pieces lately deli-

vered to him, and to appoint an Order, and staying things there; which done he departed.

19. *Peter Vane* went as Ambassador to *Venice*, and departed from the Court with his Instructions.

20. The Lord *Cobham* and Sir *William Petre*, come home from their Journey, devering both the Oath, and the Testimonial of the Oath, witnessed by divers Noblemen of *France*: also the Treaty sealed with the Great Seal of *France*: and in the Oath was confessed, That I was Supream Head of the Church of *England* and *Ireland*, and also King of *Ireland*.

23. Monsieur *Chastilion*, and *Morier*, and *Boucherel*, accompanied with the Rhinegrave, *Dandelot* the Constable's second Son, and *Chenault*, the Legier, came to *Duresm* Place, where in their Journey they were met by Mr. Treasurer, and sixty Gentlemen, at *Woolwich*, and also saluted with great Peals, at *Woolwich*, *Deptford*. and the *Tower*.

24. The Ambassadors came to me presenting the Legier; and also delivering Letters of Credence from the French King.

25. The Ambassadors came to the Court, where they saw Me take the Oath for the Acceptation of the Treaty; and afterwards dined with Me: and after Dinner saw a Pastime of ten against ten at the Ridg, whereof on the one side were the Duke of *Suffolk*,, the Vicedam, the Lord *Lisle*, and seven other Gentlemen apparallel'd in Yellow. On the other, the Lord *Strange*, Monsieur *Henandoy*, and the eight other in blew.

26. The Ambassadors saw the baiting of the Bears and Bulls.

27. The Ambassadors, after they had hunted, sat with me at Supper.

28. The same went to see *Hampton-Court*, where they did Hunt, and the same night return'd to *Duresm-place*.

25. One that by way of Marriage had thought to assemble the People, and so make an insurrection in *Kent*, was taken by the Gentlemen of the Shire, and afterward punished.

29. The Ambassadors had a fair Supper made them by the Duke of *Somerset*; and afterward went into the *Thames*, and saw both the Bear hunted in the River, and also Wild-fire cast out of Boats, and many pretty Conceits.

30. The Ambassadors took their leave and the next day departed.

June.

3. The King came to *Shein*, where was a marriage made between the Lord *Lisle* the Earl of *Warwick*'s Son, and the Lady *Ann* Daughter to the Duke of *Somerset*; which done, and a fair Dinner made, and

Dancing finished, the King and the Ladies went into two Anti-Chambers made of Boughs, where first he saw six Gentlemen of one side, and six of another, run the course of the Field twice over. Their names here do follow.

    The Lord *Edward*.   Sir *John Apleby*, &c.*

And afterwards came three Masters of one side, and two of another whtch ran four Courses apiece. Their names be; †

Last of all came the *Regunete*, with three *Italians*, who ran with all the Gentlemen four Courses, and afterward fought at Tournay; and so after dinner returned to *Westminster*.

4. Sir *Robert Dudley* third Son so the Earl of *Warwick*, married Sir *John Robert's* Daughter; after which Marriage there were certain gentlemen that did strive who should first take away a Goofes Head which was hanged alive on two cross Posts.

5. There was Tilt and Tournay on foot, with as great staves as they run withal on Horseback.

6. Removing to *Greenwich*.

8. The Gests of My Progress were set forth, which were these; From *Greenwich* to *Westminster*, from *Westminster* to *Hampton-Court*, from *Hampton-Court* to *Windsor*, from *Windsor* to *Guilford*, from *Guilford* to *Oatland*, from *Oatland* to *Richmond*, &c.

Also the Vicedam made a great Supper for the Duke of *Somerset* and the Marquess of *Northampton*, with divers Masques and other Conceits.

9. The Duke of *Somerset*, Marquess of *Northampton*, Lord Treasurer, *Bedford*, and the Secretary Petre, went to the Bishop of *Winchester* to know to what he would stick. He made answer, That he would obey and set forth all things set forth by Me and my Parliament; and if he were troubled in Conscience, he would reveal it to the Council, and not reason openly against it.

The first Payment of the Frenchmen, was laid up in the *Tower* for all Chances.

10. The Books of my Proceedings were sent to the Bishop of *Winchester*, to see whether he would set his Hand to it, or promise to set it forth to the People.

11. Order was given for Fortifying and Victualling *Cales* for four months; and also Sir *Henry Palmer* and Sir —— *Alce*, were sent to the Frontiers of *Scotland*, to take a view of all the Forts there, and to report to the Council where they thought fit to fortify.

---

* Rest omitted.   † None given.

12. The Marquefs *de Means* came from *Scotland* in Poft, and went his way into *France*.

13. Commmiffions were figned to Sir *William Herbert*, and thirty other, to Intreat of certain Matters in *Wales*, and alfo Inftructions to the fame, how to behave himfelf in the Prefidentfhip.

14. The Surveyor of *Calais* was fent to *Calais*, firft to raze the Walls of *Risbank* toward the Sand-hills, and after to make the Wall maffy again, and the round Bullwark to change to a pointed one, which fhould run twenty foot into the Sea, to beat the Sand-hills, and to raze the Mount. Secondly, to view *Maubeug*, to make an high Bullwark in the midft, with Flankers, to beat through all the ftreight; and alfo four Sluces to make *Calais* haven better. Afterwards he was bid to go to *Guifnes*, where firft he fhould take away the three-corner'd Bullwark to make the outward Wall of the Keep, and to fill the fpace between the Keep and the faid outward Wall with the forefaid Bullwark, and to raife the Old Keep that it might defend the Town. Alfo he was bid to make *Parfon's* Bullwark, where it is now, round, without Flankers, both pointed, and alfo with fix Flankers to bear hard to the Keep.

Atwood and *Lambert* were fent to take view of *Allderney*, *Silly*, *Jernfey*, *Gernsey*, and the Ifle of *Gitto*.

The Duke of *Somerfet*, with five others of the Council, went to the Bifhop of *Winchefter*; to whom he made this anfwer; *I having deliberately feen the Book of* Common-Prayer, *although I would not have made it fo my felf, yet I find fuch things in it as fatisfieth my Confcience, and therefore I will both execute it my felf, and alfo fee other my Parifhioners to do it.*

This was fubfcribed by the forefaid Counfellors, that they heard him fay thefe words.

16. The Lord Marquefs, Mr. *Herbert*, the Vicedam, *Henaudie*, and divers other Gentlemen, went to the Earl of *Warwick's*, where they were honourably received; and the next day they ran at the Ring a great number of Gentlemen.

19. I went to *Debtford*, being bidden to Supper by the Lord *Clinton*; where before Supper I faw certain Men ftand upon the end of a Boat, without holding of any thing, and ran one at another, till one was caft into the Water. At Supper Monfieur *Vicedam* and *Henaudie* fupped with me. After Supper was there a Fort made upon a great Lighter on the *Thames* which had three Walls, and a Watch-Tower; in the midft of which Mr. *Winter* was Captain, with forty or fifty

other Souldiers in **Yellow and** Black. To the Fort **alfo** appertained a Gallery **of Yellow** Collour, with Men and Ammunition in it for defence **of the Caftle:** Wherefore there came four **Pinaces with their** Men in White, handfomely dreffed; which intending **to give affault** to the **Caftle, firft** drove away the Pinace, and after **with Clods, Squibs, Canes of** Fire-Darts made for the nonce, **and Bombards, affaulted the Caftle; and** at length came with their **Pieces, and burft the outer Walls of** the Caftle, beating them off the **Caftle into the fecond Ward, who after** iffued out and drove away the Pinaces, finking one of them, out **of which, all** the **Men** in it, being more than twenty, **leaped out** and fwam in the *Thames;* Then came the Admiral of the **Navy,** with three other Pinaces, and won the Caftle by Affault, and burft the top **of it** down, and took the Captain and under Captain. Then the Admiral went forth to take the Yellow Ship, and at length clafped with her, took her, and affaulted alfo her top, and won it alfo by compulfion, and fo returned home.

20. The Mayor of *London* caufed the Watches to be encreafed every night, becaufe of the great Frays, and alfo one Alderman to fee good Rule kept every night.

22. There was a privy fearch made through all *Suffex* for all Vagabonds, Gipfies, Confpirators, Prophefiers, all Players, and fuch like.

· 24. There were certain in *Effex* about *Rumford,* went about a **Conf**piracy, which were taken, and the Matter ftayed.

25. Removing to *Greenwich.*

23. Sir *John Yates,* Sheriff of *Effex,* went down with Letters to fee the Bifhop of *London's* Injunctions performed, which touched plucking down of Superaltaries, Altars, and fuch like Ceremonies and Abufes.

29. It was appointed that the *Germans* fhould have the *Auftin-Friars* for their Church to have their Service in, for avoiding of all Sects of *Anabaptifts,* and fuch-like.

17. The French Queen **was delivered of** a third Son, called *Monfieur d' Angoulefme.*

13. The Emperor departed from **Argentin** to *Augufta.*

30. *John Poynet* made Bifhop of *Rochefter,* and received his Oath.

July.

5. There was Mony provided to be fent into *Ireland,* for payment of the Souldiers there; and alfo Orders taken for the difpatch of the Strangers in *London.*

7. The Mafter of *Arskin* paffed into *Scotland* coming from *France.* Also the *French* Ambaffador did come before Me, firft after fhewing

the birth of *Monfieur d' Angoulefme*; afterward declaring, That whereas the French King had for my fake let go the Prifoners at St. *Andrews*, who before they were taken, had fhamefully murdered the Cardinal, he defired that all Scots that were Prifoners might be delivered. It was anfwered, That all were delivered. Then he moved for one called the Arch-Bifhop of *Glasgow*; who fince the Peace, came difguifed without Pafsport, and so was taken. It was anfwered, That we had no Peace with *Scotland*, fuch, that they might pafs our Countrey, and the Mafter of *Erskin* affirmed the same.

8. It was agreed that the 200 that were with Me, and 200 that were with Mr *Herbert*, should be sent into *Ireland*; Alfo that the Mint fhould be fet a work that it that it might coin 24000 *l*. a Year, and fo bear all my Charges in *Ireland* for this Year, and 10000 *l*. for my Coffers.

9. The Earl of *Warwick*, the Lord Treafurer, Sir *William Herbert*, and the Secretary *Petre*, went to the Bifhop of *Winchefter* with certain Articles figned by Me and the Council, containing the confeffing of his Fault, the Supremacy, the eftablifhing of Holy Days, the abolifhing of fix Articles, and divers other, whereof the Copy is in the Council Cheft; whereunto he put his hand, faving to the confeffion.

10. Sir *William Herbert* and Secretary *Petre* were sent unto him, to tell him, I marvelled that he would not put his hand to the Confeffion. To which he made anfwer, that he would not put his Hand to the Confeffion, for becaufe he was Innocent and alfo the Confeffion was but the Preface of Articles.

11. The Bifhop of *London* the Secretary *Petre*, Mr. *Cecil*, and *Goderick*, were commanded to make certain Articles according to the Laws, and to put in the Submiffion.

12. It was appointed, That under the Shadow of preparing for the Sea-Matters, there fhould be fent 5000 *l*. to the Proteftants to get their good Will.

14. The Bifhop of *Winchester* did deny the Articles that the Bifhop of *London* and the other had made.

13. Sir *John Yates* was fent into *Effex* to ftop the going away of the Lady *Mary*, becaufe it was credibly informed that *Scipperus* fhould fteal her away to *Antwerp*; divers of her Gentlemen were there, and *Scipperus* a little before came to fee the Landing-places.

16. It was appointed that the two hundred with the Duke of *Somerset*, and two hundred with the Lord Privy-Seal, and four hundred with Mafter *St. Legier*, fhould be fent to the Sea-Coaft.

17. It was agreed, that on *Wednesday* next, We should go in one day to *Windsor* and dine at *Sion*.

18. It was thought best that the Lord *Bowes* should tarry in his Wardenship still, and the Earl of *Warwick* should tarry here and be recompensed.

19. The Bishop of *Winchester* was sequestred from his Fruits for three months.

20. *Hooper* was made Bishop of *Glocester*. The Merchants were commanded to stay as much as they could their Vent into *Flanders*, because the Emperour had made many streight Laws against them that professed the Gospel.

21. A Muster was made of the *Boullonois*, who were fully payed for all past, and a month to come. Sir *John Wallop*, *Francis Hall* and Doctor *Coke*, were appointed Commissioners to appoint the Limits between Me and the French King.

23. Removing to *Windsor*.

22. The Secretary *Petre*, and the Lord Chancellour, were appointed to go to the Lady *Mary*, to cause her to come to *Oking*, or to the Court.

25. It was appointed that half the French King's Paiment should be bestowed on paying 10000 *l.* at *Calais*, 9000 *l.* in *Ireland*, 10000 *l.* in the North, 2000 *l.* in the Admiralty, so that every Crown might go for one of our Nobles.

27. Because the Rumour came so much of *Scipperus* coming, it was appointed that they of the Admiralty should set my Ships in readiness.

26. The Duke of *Somerset* went to set Order in *Oxfordshire*, *Sussex*, *Wiltshire*, and *Hampshire*.

28. The Lady *Mary*, after long communication, was content to come *Leez* to my Lord Chancellour, and then to *Hunsden*; but she utterly denied to come to the Court or *Oking* at that time.

31. The Earl of *Southampton* died.

14. *Andrew Dory* took the City of——in *Africa*, from the Pirat *Dragutte*, who in the mean season burnt the Country of *Genoa*.

8. The Emperour came to *Ausburgh*.

August.

4. Mr. *St. Legier* was appointed, by Letters Patents, to be Deputy there; and had his Commission, Instructions, and Letters to the Nobles of *Ireland* for the same purpose.

5. The same Deputy departed from the Castle of *Windsor*.

Journal of Edward the Sixth.

6. The Duke of *Somerset* departed to *Redding* to take an Order there.

7. It was appointed, that of the Mony delivered to Me by the French King, there should be taken 100000 Crowns to pay 10000 *l*. at *Calais*, 10000 in the North, and 2000 in the Admiralty, and 8000 in *Ireland*.

8. *Monsieur Henaudy* took his leave to depart to *Calais*, and so upon the Paiment, to be delivered Home; and *Tremoville* being sick, went in a Horse-Litter to *Dover*.

9. The French Ambassador came to *Windsor*, to sue for a Passport for the Dowager of *Scotland*; which being granted, so she came like a Friend; he required 300 Horse to pass, with 200 Keepers, which was not wholly granted, but only that 200 Horse, with an 100 Keepers in one Company, coming into this Realm, as should be appointed, should, without let, pass into *France*, and not return this way.

11. The *Vicedam* of *Chartres* shewed his Licence to tarry here, with a Letter written to the same purpose.

10. The Ambassadour of *France* departed not a little contented with his gentle Answers.

12. Removing to *Guilford*.

13. The Parliament was Prorogued to the 20*th* of *February* next following.

Mr. *Cook* Master of Requests, and certain other Lawyers, were appointed to make a short Table of the Laws and Acts that were not wholly unprofitable, and present it to the Board.

The Lord Chancellor fell sore sick, with forty more of his House, so that the Lady *Mary* came not thither at that time.

14. There came divers Advertisements from *Chamberlain*, Ambassadour with the Queen of *Hungary*, that their very Intent was to take away the Lady *Mary*, and so to begin an Outward War, and an Inward Conspiracy; insomuch that the Queen said *Scipperus* was but a Coward, and for fear of one Gentleman that came down, durst not go forth with his Enterprise to my Lady *Mary*.

16. The Earl of *Maxwell* came down to the North-Border with a good Power to overthrow the *Gremes*, who were a certain Family that were yielded to Me; but the Lord *Dacre* stood before his Face with a good band of Men, and so put him from his Purpose, and the Gentlemen, called *Gremes*, skirmished with the said Earl, slaying certain of his Men.

17. The Council appointed, among themselves, That none of

them should speak in any Man's behalf for Land to be given, Reversion of Offices, Leases of Manours, or extraordinary Annuities, except for certain Captains who served at *Bollein*, their answer being deferred till *Michaelmass* next.

18. A Proclamation that till *Michaelmass* all Strangers that sued for Pensions should go their way.

20. Removing to *Oking*.

15. The second Paiment of the French was paied, and *Henaudie* and *Tremoville* delivered.

21. 8000 *l.* of the last Payment was appointed to be payed to the Dispatch of *Calais*, and 5000 at the North.

24. 10000 *l.* was appointed to be occupied to win Mony to pay the next Year, pay the outward Pays; and it was promised that the Mony should double every month.

26. Removing to *Oatlands*.

27. *Andrea Doria* gave a hot Assault to the Town of ———— in *Africa* kept by the Pirat called *Drogute*, but was repulsed by the Townsmen.

29. The Pirat gave a hot Assault to *Andrea Dorea* by Night, and slew the Captain of *Thames*, with divers other notable Men.

31. The Duke *Maurice* made answer to the Emperour, That if the Council were not free, he would not come at it.

September.

2. *Maclamore* in *Ireland* before a Rebel, by the means of Mr. *Baberson*, surrendered himself and gave Pledges.

6. Mr *Wotton* gave up his Secretaryship, and Mr. *Cecil* got it of him.

8. Removing from *Nonsuch*.

13. Removing to *Oatlands*.

22. A Proclamation was set forth, by the which it was commanded; 1. That no kind of Victual, no Wax, Tallow, Candles, nor no such thing should be carried over, except to *Calais*, putting in Sureties to go thither. 2. That no Man should buy or sell the self-same things again except Broakers, who should not have more than ten quarters of Grain at once. 3. That all Justices should divide themselves into Hundreds, Rapes, and Wapentakes, to look in their Quarters what superfluous Corn were in every Barn, and appoint it to be sold at a reasonable price. Also that one of them must be in every Market to see the Corn brought. Furthermore, whoever shipped over any Thing aforesaid to the Parts beyond Sea, or *Scotland*, after eight days following the publication of the Proclamation, should forfeit his Ship, and

Journal of Edward the Sixth.

the Ware therein, half to the Lord of the Franchize, and half to the finder thereof; whoso bought to sell again after the day aforesaid, should forfeit all his Goods, Farms, and Leases, to the use, one half of the Finder, the other of the King; whoso brought not in Corn to Market as he was appointed, should forfeit 10 *l*. except the Purveyours took it up, or it were sold to his Neighbours.

25. Letters sent out to the Justices of the Peace for the due execution thereof.

18. *Andrea Doria* had a repulse from the Town of* in *Africa*, and lost many of his Men, and the Captain of *Thames*, and neverthelefs left not yet the Siege.

24. Order was given for the Victualing of *Calais*.

26. The Lord *Willoughby*, Deputy of *Calais*, departed and took his journey thitherward.

28. The Lord Treasurer sent to *London* to give Order for the preservation of the City, with help of the Mayor.

Whereas the Emperor required a Council, they were content to receive it, so it were free and ordinary, requiring also that every Man might be restored to his Right, and a general Peace proclaimed. They desired also, that in the mean season no Man might be restrained to use his fashion of Religion.

18. The Emperor made Answer, That the Council should be to the Glory of God, and Maintenance of the Empire at *Trent*; He knew no Title to any of his Territories, Peace he desired, and in the mean season would have them observe the Interim and last Council of *Trent*; he would also that they of *Breme* and *Hamburgh*, with their Associates, should leave their Seditions, and obey his Decrees.

21. *George* Duke of *Mecklenburgh* came with 8000 Men of War to the City of *Magdeburgh*, being Protestant; against whom went forth the Count of *Mansfield*, and his Brother, with 6000 Men, and eight Guns, to drive him from Pillage; but the other abiding the Battel, put the Count to flight, took his Brother Prisoner, and slew 3000 Men, as it is reported.

October.

4. Removing to *Richmond*.
5. The Parliament Prorogued to the 20*th* of *January*.
6. The French King made his entry into *Roan*.
10. It was agreed that *York*, Master of one of the Mints at the *Tower*, should make his Bargain with Me; viz. To take the Profit of

---
* *Afrodisium.*

Silver rifing of Bullion that he himfelf brought, fhould pay all my Debts, to the Sum of 1200000 *l.* or above, and remain accountable for the Overplus, paying no more but 6 *s.* and 6 *d.* the ounce, till the Exchange were equal in *Flanders*, and after 6 *s.* and 2 *d.* Alfo that he fhould declare all his Bargains to any fhould be appointed to overfee him, and leave off when I would: For which I fhould give him 15000 *l.* in Preft, and leave to carry 8000 *l.* over-Sea to abafe the Exchange.

16. Removing to *Weftminfter*.

19. Prices were fet of all kind of Grains, Butter, Cheefe, and Poultry-Ware, by a Proclamation.

20. The Frenchmen came to *Sandefield* and *Fins-wood*, to the number of 800, and there on my Ground did fpoil my Subjects that were relieved by the Wood.

26. The French Ambaffadour came to excufe the forefaid Men, faying, They thought it not meet that that Wood fhould be fpoiled of us, being thought and claimed as theirs, and therefore they lay there.

24. There were 1000 Men embarqued to go to *Calais*, and fo to *Guifnes*, and *Hammes*, *Rifhumbee*, *Newmanbridge*, the Caufie and the Bullwarks, with Victual for the fame.

November.

19. There were Letters fent to every Bifhop to pluck down the Altars.

20. There were Letters fent down to the Gentlemen of every Shire, for the obfervation of the laft Proclamation touching Corn, becaufe there came none to the Markets, commanding them to punifh the Offenders.

29. Upon the Letters written back by the fame, the fecond Proclamation was abolifhed.

December.

15. There was Letters fent for the taking of certain Chaplains of the Lady *Mary* for faying Mafs, which fhe denied.

19. *Borthwick* was fent to the King of *Denmark*, with privy Inftructions for the Marriage of the Lady *Elizabeth* to his Son.

20. There was appointed a Band of Horfemen divided amongft the Nobles.

An 100 to the Duke of *Somerfet*.
50 to my Lord Marq. *Northampton*.
Lord Marquefs of *Dorfet*. To the Earl of *Warwick*.
Earl of *Wiltfhire*.

Lord *Wentworth*. Lord Privy-Seal.
Lord Admiral.
Lord *Paget*. Mr. *Herbert*.
Mr. *Sadler*.
Mr. *Darcy*. Mr. Treafurer.

24. Removing to *Greenwich*.
26. Peace concluded between the Emperor and the Scots.

January.

6. The Earl of *Arundel* remitted of 8000 *l.* which he ought to have payed for certain Faults he had committed within 12 Years.

7. There was appointed, for becaufe the Frenchmen did go about practice in *Ireland*, that there fhould be prepared four Ships, four Barques, four Pinaces, and twelve Victualers, to take three Havens; of which two were on the South-fide toward *France*, and one in *James Cannes* the Scottifh Country, and alfo fend and break the forefaid Confpiracies.

10. Three Ships being fent forth into the Narrow Seas, took certain Pirats, and brought them into *England*, where the moft part was hanged.

27. Monfieur de *Lanfac* came from the French King by way of requeft, to ask that *Coumilis*, the fifhing of the *Tweed*, *Edrington*, the Ground debatable, and the Scotch Hoftages that were put here in the King my Father's days, fhould be delivered to the Scots, that they might be fuffered to Traffique, as though they were in Peace, and that all Intereft of the foresaid Houfes fhould be delivered to the Scots. Alfo that thofe Prifoners which were bound to pay their Ranfoms before the Peace laft concluded, fhould not enjoy the benefit of the Peace.

18. The Lord *Cobham* was appointed to be General Lieutenant in *Ireland*.

30. Letters written to Mr. *St. Lieger* to repair to tne South parts of *Ireland* with his Force.

February.

3. Mr. *Croftis* appointed to go into *Ireland*, and there with *Rogers* and certain Artificers, to take the Havens aforefaid, and begin fome Fortification.

5. Divers Merchants of *London* were fpoken withal for provifion of Corn out of *Danfick*, about 40000 Quarters.

10. *Mountford* was commanded to go to provide for certain proportions of Victual for the Ships that fhould go into *Ireland*.

11. Alfo for Provifion to be fent to *Barwick* and the North parts.

16. *Whaley* was examined, for perfwading divers Nobles of the Realm to make the Duke of *Somerfet* Protector at the next Parliament, and ftood to the denial, the Earl of *Rutland* affirming it manifeftly.

13. The Bifhop of *Winchefter*, after a long Trial, was depofed of his Bifhoprick.

20. Sir *William Pickering* Kt. was difpatched to the French King for Anfwer to *Monfieur de Lanfac*, to declare, That although I had right in the forefaid Places, yet I was content to furrender them, under Conditions to be agreed on by Commiffioners on both fides; and for the laft Articles I agreed without condition.

25. The Lord Marquefs *Dorfet* appointed to be Warden of the North-Borders, having three Sub-Wardens, the Lord *Ogle*, &c. in the Eaft, and the Lord *Coniers* in the Weft. Alfo Mr. *Auger* had the charge for victualling *Calais*.

28. The Learned Man *Bucerus* died at *Cambridg*; who was two days after buried in St. *Mary*'s Church at *Cambridg*; all the whole Univerfity, with the whole Town, bringing him to the Grave, to the number of 3000 Perfons. Alfo there was an Oration of Mr. *Haddon* made very eloquently at his Death, and a Sermon of* after that Mafter *Redman* made a third Sermon; which three Sermons made the People wonderfully to lament his Death. Laft of all, all the Learned Men of the Univerfity made their Epitaphs in his praife, laying them on his Grave.

March.

3. The Lord *Wentworth* Lord Chamberlain, died about ten of the Clock at Night, leaving behind him fixteen Children.

1. Sir *John York* made great lofs about 2000 *l.* weight of Silver, by Treafon of Englifh Men which he brought for Provifion of the Mints. Alfo *Judd* 1500, and alfo *Trefham* 500; fo the whole came to 4000 *l.*

February.

20. The Frenchmen came with a Navy of 160 Sail into *Scotland*, loaden with provifion of Grain, Powder, and Ordnance; of which fixteen great Ships perifhed on *Ireland* Coaft, two loaden with Artillery, and fourteen with Corn.

Alfo in this month the Deputy there fet at one, certain of the Weft Lords that were at variance.

March.

10. Certain new Fortifications were devifed to be made at *Calais*;

---

* Dr. *Parker*.

That at *Graveling* the Water should be let in in my Ground, and so should fetch a compass by the six Bulwarks to *Guisnes*, *Hammes*, and *Newnambridg* ; and that there should be a Wall of eight foot high, and six broad of Earth, to keep out the Water, and to make a great Marsh about the Territories of *Calais* 37 miles long. Also for Flankers at the Keep of *Guisnes*, willed to be made a three-cornered Bullwark at the Keep to keep it. Furthermore, at *Newmanbridg*, a massy Wall to the French-side there, as was a Green. Besides, at the West Gittie there should be another Gittie, which should defend the Victuallers of the Town always from Shot from the Sand-hills.

5. Mr. *Archer* had 2000 *l.* in Mony, wherewith he provided out of *Flanders* for *Calais* 2000 Quarters of Barley, 500 of Wheat.

18. The Lady *Mary*, my Sister, came to me to *Westminster*, where after Salutations, she was called, with my Council, into a Chamber ; where was declared how long I had suffered her Mass, in hope of her reconciliation, and how now being no hope, which I perceived by her Letters, except I saw some short amendment I could not bear it. She answered, That her Soul was God's, and her Faith she would not change, nor dissemble her Opinion with contrary doings. It was said I constrained not her Faith, but willed her not as a King to Rule, but as a Subject to obey ; and that her Example might breed too much inconvenience.

19. The Emperor's Ambassador came with a short Message from his Master of War, if I would not suffer his Cousin, the Princess, to use her Mass. To this was no answer given at this time.

20. The Bishops of *Canterbury*, *London*, *Rochester*, did consider to give licence to sin, was sin ; to suffer and wink at it for a time might be born, so all haste possible might be used.

23. The Council having the Bishops Answers, seeing my Subjects taking their vent in *Flanders*, might put the whole Realm in danger. The *Flemings* had Cloth enough for a Year in their hand, and were kept far under the danger of the Papists ; the 1500 Cinquetales of Powder I had in *Flanders*, the Harness they had for preparation of the Gendarmory, the goods my merchants had there at the *Woolfleet*, decreed to send an Ambassadour to the Emperor, Mr. *Wotton*, to deny the matter wholly, and perswade the Emperor in it, thinking, by his going, to win some time for a preparation of a Mart, convenience of Powder, Harness, &c. and for the Surety of the Realm. In the mean season to punish the Offenders, first of my Servants that heard Mass, next of hers.

24. Sir *Anthony Brown* sent to the *Fleet* for hearing Mass, with Serjeant *Morgan*, Sir *Clement Smith*, which a Year before heard Mass, chidden.

25. The Ambassadour of the **Emperor** came to have his Answer, but had none, saving that one should go to the Emperor within a month or two to declare the Matter.

22. Sir *William Pickering* came with great thanks from the French King.

27. Removing to *Greenwich*.

31. A Challenge made by Me, that I, with sixteen of my Chamber, should run at Base, Shoot, and run at the Ring with any seventeen of my Servants Gentlemen in the Court.

Mr. *Crofted* arrived in *Ireland*, and came to *Waterford* to the Deputy, consulting for Fortification of the Town.

April.

1. The first day of the Challenge at Base, or Running, the King won.

3 *Monsieur de Lansac* came again from the French King to go to *Scotland*, for appointing his Commissioners on the Scotch side, who were the French Ambassador in *Scotland*, the Bishop of* the Master of *Erskin*, &c.

Thomas Darcy made Lord *Darcy* of *Chich.* and Lord Chamberlain; for maintenance whereof he had given 100 Merks to his Heirs generally, and 300 to his Heirs Males.

6. I lost the Challenge of Shooting at Rounds, and won at Rovers.

7. There were apointed Commissioners on my side, either the Bishop of *Litchfield* if he had no Impediment, or *Norwich*, Mr. *Bowes*, Mr. *Bekwith*, and Sir *Thomas Chaloner*.

8. Sir *John Yates* made Vicechamberlain, and Captain of the Guard and 120 *l.* Land.

5. *Poinet* Bishop of *Rochester* received his Oath for the Bishoprick of *Winchester*, having 2000 Merk Land appointed to him for his Maintenance.

7. A certain *Arrian* of the Strangers, a **Dutch Man**, being excommunicated by the Congregation of his Countrymen, was after long disputation condemned to the Fire.

9. The Earl of *Wiltshire* had 50 more in my Lord Marquess *Dorset's* Place, Warden in the North, and my Lord of *Rutland* in my Lord *Wentworth's* Place other fifty.

---
* **Blank** in original.

10. Mr. *Wotton* had his Inftructions made to go withal to the Emperor, to be as Ambaffador Legier in Mr. *Morifon's* place, and to declare this Resolution, That if the Emperor would suffer my Ambaffadour with him, to ufe his Service, then I would his; if he would not suffer Mine, I would not fuffer his. Likewife, that my Sifter was my Subject, and fhould ufe my Service appointed by Act of Parliament.

Alfo it was appointed to make 20000 pound weight for necessity fomewhat bafer, to get gains 16000 *l.* clear, by which the debt of the Realm might by payed, the Country defended from any fudden Attempt, and the Coin amended.

11. Mr. *Pickering* had his Instructions and Difpatch to go into *France* as Ambaffadour Legier there, in Mr. *Mafon's* Place, who defired very much to come home; and Mr. *Pickering* had Inftructions to tell the French King of the appointing of my Commiffioners in *Scotland* aforefaid.

2. They of *Magdeburg* having in *January* laft paft taken in a conflict the Duke of *Mecklenhurg*, and three other Earls, did give an Onfet on Duke *Maurice*, by Boats on the River, when it overflowed the Country, and flew divers of his Men, and came home fafe, receiving a great portion of Victual into the Town.

15. A Confpiracy opened of the *Effex*-men, who within three days after minded to declare the coming of Strangers, and fo to bring People together to *Chelmsford*, and then to spoil the Rich Men's Houfes if they could.

16. Alfo of *Londoners*, who thought *Woodcock** to rife on *May*-day againft the Strangers of the City, and both the Parties committed to Ward.

23. The French King, and the Lord *Clinton*, chosen into the Order of the Garter, and appointed that the Duke of *Somerfet*, the Marquefs of *Northampton*, the Earl of *Wiltfhire*, and the Earl of *Warwick* fhould perufe and amend the Order.

24. The Lords fat at *London*, and banqueted one another this day, and three days after, for to fhew agreement amongft them, whereas Difcord was bruited, and fomewhat to look to the punifhment of Talebearers, and apprehending of evil Perfons.

25. A bargain made with the Foulcare for about 60000 *l.* that in *May* and *Auguft* fhould be payed for the defraying of it. 1. That the

---

* Here the fenfe is not perfect.

Foulcare should be put off for 10 in the 100. 2. That I should buy 12000 Marks weight, at 6 s. the ounce, to be delivered at *Antwerp*, and so conveyed over. 3. I should pay 100000 Crowns for a very fair Jewel of his, four Rubies marvelous big, one Orient and great Diamond, and one great Pearl.

27. *Mallet*, the Lady *Mary*'s Chaplain, apprehended and sent to the *Tower* of *London*.

30. The Lord Marquess of *Northampton* appointed to go with the Order, and further Commission of Treaty, and that in Post; having joined with him in Commission, the Bishop of *Ely*, Sir *Philip Hobbey*, Sir *William Pickering*, and Sir *John Mason* Knights, and two other Lawyers, *Smith* that was Secretary, &c.

May.

2. There was appointed to go with my Lord Marquess, the Earls of *Rutland*, *Worcester*, and *Ormond*; the Lords *Lisle*, *Fitzwater*, and *Bray*, *Barguenny*, and divers other Gentlemen, to the number of thirty in all.

3. The challenge at running at the Ring performed; at the which first came the King, sixteen Footmen, and ten Horsemen, in black Silk Coats, pulled out with white Taffety; then all the Lords, having three Men likewise apparelled; and all Gentlemen their Footmen in white Fustian, pulled out with black Taffety. The other side came all in yellow Taffety; at length the yellow Band took it thrice in 120 courses, and my Band touched often, which was counted as nothing, and took never, which seemed very strange, and so the Prize was of my Side lost. After that Tournay followed, between six of my Band and six of theirs.

4. It was appointed that there should be but four Men to wait on every Earl that went with my Lord Marquess of *Northampton*, three on every Lord, two on every Knight or Gentleman: Also that my Lord Marquess should in his Diet be allowed for the loss in his Exchange.

5. The Muster of the Gendarmoury appointed to be the first of *June* if it were possible, if not the 8*th*.

6. The Testourn cried down from 12 *d*. to 9 *d*. and the Groat from 4 *d*. to 3 *d*.

9. One *Stewart* a Scotchman meaning to poison the young Queen of *Scotland*, thinking thereby to get Favour here, was, after he had been a while in the *Tower* and *Newgate*, delivered on my Frontiers at *Caiais* to the French, for to have him punished there according to his deserts.

10. Divers Lords and Knights sent for to furnish the Court at the coming of the French Ambassadour, that brought hither the order of St. *Michael*.

12. A Proclamation proclaimed, to give warning to all those that keep any Farms, multitudes of Sheep, above the number limited in the Law, *viz.* 2000; decayed Tenements and Towns, Regratters, Forestalling Men that sell dear, having plenty enough, and put Plough Ground to Pasture, and Carriers over-Sea of Victual, that if they leave not these Enormities, they shall be streightly punished very shortly, so that they should feel the smart of it; and to command execution of Laws made for this purpose before.

14. There mustered before Me an hundred Archers, two Arrows apiece, all of the Guard; afterward shot together, and they shot at an inch Board, which some pierced quite, and stuck in the other Board; divers pierced it quite thorow with the Heads of their Arrows, the Boards being very well-seasoned Timber. So it was appointed there should be ordinarily 100 Archers, and 100 Halbertiers, either good Wrestlers, or casters of the Bar, or Leapers, or Runners, or tall Men of Personage.

15. Sir *Philip Hobbey* departed toward *France*, with ten Gentlemen of his own, in Velvet Coats and Chains of Gold.

16. Likewise did the Bishop of *Ely* depart with a Band of Men well furnished.

20. A Proclamation made that whosoever found a Seditious Bill, and did not tear and deface it, should be a partaker of the Bill, and punished as the Maker.

21. My Lord Marquess of *Northampton* had Commission to deliver the Order, and to treat of all things, and chiefly of Marriage for Me to the Lady *Elizabeth* his Daughter. First to have the Dote 12000 Marks a Year, and the Dowry at least 800000 Crowns. The Forfeiture 100000 Crowns at the most if I performed not, and paying that to be delivered; and that this should not impeach the former Covenants with *Scotland*, with many other Branches.

22. He departed himself in Post.

24. An Earthquake was at *Croidon* and *Blechinglee*, and in the most part of *Surrey*, but no harm was done.

30. Whereas before Commandment was given that 160000 *l.* should be Coined of three ounces in the Pound fine, for discharge of Debts, and to get some Treasure, to be able to alter all, now it was stopped, saving only 80000 *l.* to discharge my Debts, and 10000 Mark weight

that the *Foulcare* delivered in the laſt Exchange, at **four ounces** in the pound.

31. The **Muſters** defered till after *Midſummer*.

June.

2. **It** was appointed that I ſhould receive the Frenchmen that came hither at *Weſtminſter*, **where** was made preparation for the purpoſe, and **four** garniſh of **new Veſſels taken out** of Church Stuff, as Miters, **and** Golden Miſſals, and **Primers**, and **Croſſes**, and Reliques of *Pleſſay*.

4. Provision made in *Flanders* for **Silver** and Gold Plate, and Chains to be given to these Strangers.

7. A Proclamation set forth, that Exchange, or Re-exchange, ſhould be made under the Puniſhment **ſet forth** in King *Henry* the Seventh's Time, duly **to** be executed.

10. **Monſieur** *Mareſchal* departed from **the Court to** *Bulloigne* in Poſt, and ſo hither by Water in his Galleys and Foiſts.

In this Month, and the Month before **was** great **buſineſs for the City of** *Parma*, which Duke *Horatio** had delivered to the French King, for the **Pope aſcited him, as** holding it *in capite* of him, whereby he could **not alienate it without the** Pope's Will; but he came **not at his Day, for which cauſe the Pope** and Imperialiſts raiſed 8000 Men, **and took** a Caſtle on **the ſame** River ſide. Alſo the French King ſent *Monſieur de Thermes*, **who had been** his General in *Scotland*, with a great **piece** of his Gendarmory into *Italy*, **to** help Duke *Horatio*. Furthermore the **Turks** made great preparation **for** War, which ſome feared would **at length** burſt out.

21. I was elected of the Company **of St.** *Michael* in *France* by the French King and his Order.

13. Agreement made with the **Scots** for the Borders, between the Commiſſioners aforesaid, for both **the Parties.**

In this month *Dragute*, a **Pirat,** eſcaped (*Andrea Doria*, who had cloſed him in a Creek) by force **of his** Galley-Slaves, that digged another way into the Sea, and took **two of** *Andrea*'s Galleys that lay far into the Sea.

14. Pardon given to thoſe Iriſh Lords that would come in before a certain day limited by the Deputy; with Advertiſement to the Deputy to make ſharp War with thoſe that would reſiſt; and alſo ſhould adminiſter my Laws every-where.

---

* It ſhould be *Octavio*.

Journal of Edward the Sixth.

18. Becaufe of my Charges in Fortifications at *Calais* and *Barwick* fhould be payed, it was agreed, that befide the Debt of the Realm 80000 *l.* there fhould be 40000 *l.* coined, three ounces Fine, nine of Allay; and 5000 pound weight fhould be coined in a Standard of feven ounces Fine at the leaft.

17. *Soperantio* came as Ambaffadour from *Venice*, in *Daniel Barbaro*'s Place.

16. I accepted the Order of *Monfegnieur Michael* by promife to the French Ambaffadour.

17. My Lord Marquefs of *Northampton* came to *Nants* with the Commiffioners, and all thofe Noblemen and Gentlemen that came over-Sea with him.

20. Upon Advertifement of *Scipperus* coming, and rigging of certain Ships in *Holland*; alfo for to fhew the Frenchmen pleafure at their coming, all the Navy that lay in *Gillingham-water* was appointed to be rigged, and furnifhed with Ordnance, and lay in the river of *Thames*, to the intent, that if *Scippetus* came afterward, he might be met with, and at leaft the Frenchmen fhould fee the force of my Navy.

22. The Lady *Mary* fent Letters to the Council, marvelling at the Imprifonment of Dr. *Mallet*, her Chaplain, for faying of Mafs before her Houfhold, feeing it was promifed the Emperor's Ambaffadour fhe fhould not be molefted in Religion, but that fhe and her Houfhold fhould have the Mafs faid before them continually.

24. They anfwered, That becaufe of their Duties to King, Countrey, and Friends, they were compelled to give her anfwer, That they would fee, not only him, but alfo all other Mafs-Sayers, and breakers of Order, ftraitly punifhed. And that as for promife they had, nor would give none to make her free from the punifhment of the Law in that behalf.

18. *Chaftilion* came to my Lord Marquefs, and there banqueted him by the way at two times between *Nantes* and *Chafteau Brian*, where the King lay.

15. *Mendoza*, a Gentleman of the King's Chamber, was fent to him to conduct him to the Court.

19. My Lord Marquefs came to *Chafteau-Brian*, where half a mile from the Caftle there met him———* with an hundred Gentlemen, and brought him to the Court booted and fpur'd to the French King.

20. The French King was invefted with the Order of the Garter in

---

* Blank in original.

his Bed-Chamber, where he gave a **Chain** to the Garter worth 200 *l*. and his **Gown dreſſed with** Auglets worth **25** *l*. The Biſhop of *Ely* making **an Oration, and the Cardinal of** *Lorrain* making him **Anſwer.** At Afternoon the Lord **Marqueſs** moved the French **King** to the **Marriage of the Scots** Queen to be conſummate, for whoſe hearing **he appointed** two Commiſſioners.

21. The Cardinal of *Lorrain*, and **of** *Chaſtilion*, the Conſtable, the **Duke of** *Guiſe*, *&c.* were appointed Commiſſioners on the part of *France* who abſolutely denied the firſt motion for the Scotch Queen, ſaying, Both they had **taken** too much **Pains, and** ſpent too many Lives for her. Alſo **a concluſion was made for her** Marriage to the Dolphin. Then was proponed the Marriage **of the** Lady *Elizabeth*, the French King's eldeſt daughter; to which **they did most** chearfully aſſent. So after they agreed neither Party **to be bound in** Conſcience nor Honour, till ſhe were **twelve Years of Age and upwards.** Then they came to the Dote, **which** was firſt aſked 1500000 **Scutes of** *France*, at which they made **a mock; after** for *donatio propter nuptias*, they agreed that it ſhould **be as great as hath** been given by the King my **Father to** any Wife he had.

22. Our Commiſſioners came to 1400000 of Crowns, **which they** refuſed, then to a **Million,** which they denied; then **to 800000 Crowns, which they ſaid** they would not agree to.

23. Then our Commiſſioners aſked what they would offer? First they offered 100000 **Crowns, then** 200000, which they ſaid was the moſt, and more than ever was given. Then followed great Reaſonings, and ſhowing of Preſidents, but no nearer they would come.

24. **They went forward unto the** Penalties if the Parties miſliked, **after that the** King's Daughter were twelve and upwards, which the French offered 100000, 50000 **Crowns,** or promiſe, that ſhe ſhould **be** brought, **at her** Father's Charge, three months before ſhe were twelve, ſufficiently Jewelled and ſtuffed. Then bonds to be delivered alternately **at** *London*, and at *Paris*, **and ſo forth.**

26. The Frenchmen delivered the foreſaid anſwers written to my Commiſſioners.

July.

1. Whereas **certain Flemiſh** Ships, twelve Sail in all, ſix tall Men of War, looking for eighteen more Men of War, went to *Diep*, as it was thought, to take *Monſieur le Mareſchal* by the way; order was given, that ſix Ships being before prepared, with four Pinnaces and a Brigantine, ſhould go both to conduct him, and alſo **to** defend, if any thing

should be attempted against *England*, by carrying over the Lady *Mary*.

2. A Brigantine sent to *Diep*, to give knowledg to *Monsieur le Mareschal* of the *Flemings* coming; to whom all the *Flemings* vailed their Bonnet. Also the French Ambassador was advertised; who answered, That he thought him sure enough when he came into our Streams, terming it so.

2. There was a Proclamation signed for shortening of the fall of the Mony to that day; in which it should be proclaimed, and devised, that it should be in all places of the Realm within one day proclaimed.

3. The Lord *Clinton* and *Cobham* was appointed to meet the French at *Gravesend*, and so to convoy him to *Duresme-place*, where he should lie.

4. I was banqueted by the Lord *Clinton* at *Debtford*, where I saw the *Primrose* and the *Mary Willoughby* launched.

The Frenchmen landed at *Rie*, as some thought, for fear of the *Flemings* lying at the *Lands-end*, chiefly because they saw our Ships were let by the Wind that they could not come out.

6. Sir *Peter Mutas*, at *Dover*, was commanded to come to *Rie* to meet *Monsieur le Mareschal*, who so did; and after he had delivered his letters, written with Mine own Hand, and made my Recommendations he took orders for Horses and Carts for *Monsieur le Mareschal* in which he made such Provision as was possible to be for the suddain.

7. *Monsieur le Mareschal* set forth from *Rie*, and in his Journey Mr. *Culpepper*, and divers other Gentlemen, and their Men, to the number of 1000 Horse, well furnished, met him, and so brought him to *Maidston* that Night.

Removing to *Westminster*.

8. *Monsieur le Mareschal* came to Mr. *Bakers*, where he was very well feasted and banqueted.

9. The same came to my Lord *Cobhams* to Dinner, and at night to *Gravesend*.

Proclamation made that a Testourn should go at 9 *d.* and a Groat at 3*d.* in all Places of the Realm at once.

At this time came the Sweat into *London*, which was more vehement than the Old Sweat; for if one took cold, he died within three hours; and if he escaped, it held him but nine or ten hours at the most: also if he slept the first six hours, as he should be very desirous to do, then he roved, and should die roving.

11. It grew so much, for in *London* the 10*th* day there died 100 in

the Liberties, and this day 12o; and alfo one of my Gentlemen, another of my Grooms fell fick and died, that I removed to *Hampton-Court* with very few with Me.

The fame night came the Marefchal, who was faluted with all my Ships being in the *Thames*, fifty and odd, all with fhot well furnifhed, and fo with the Ordnance of the *Tower*. He was met by the Lord *Clinton* Lord Admiral, with forty Gentlemen, at *Gravefend*, and fo brought to *Durefme-place*.

13. Becaufe of the infection at *London*, he came this day to *Richmond*, where he lay with a great Band of Gentlemen, at least 400, as it was by divers efteemed, where that night he hunted.

14. He came to Me at *Hampton-Court* at nine of the Clock, being met by the Duke of *Somerfet* at the Wall-end, and fo conveied firft to Me; where after his Mafter's Recommendations and Letters, he went to his Chamber on the Queen's-fide, all hanged with Cloth of Arras, and fo was the Hall, and all my Lodging. He dined with Me alfo. After Dinner, being brought into an Inner-Chamber, he told Me, he was come, not only for delivery of the Order, but alfo for to declare the great Friendfhip the King his Mafter bore Me; which he defired I would think to be fuch to Me as a Father beareth to his Son, or Brother to Brother. And although there were divers perfuafions, as he thought, to diffuade Me from the King his Mafter's Friendfhip, and Witlefs Men made divers Rumours, yet he trufted I would not believe them. Furthermore, that as good Minifters on the Frontiers do great good, fo ill much harm. For which caufe he defired no Innovation fhould be made on things that had been fo long in controverfy by Hand-ftrokes, but rather by Commiffioners talk. I anfwered him, That I thanked him for his Order, and alfo his Love, &c. and I would fhew like Love in all Points. For Rumours, they were not always to be believed, and that I did fometime provide for the worft, but never did any harm upon their hearing. For Minifters, I faid, I would rather appeafe thefe Controverfies with words, than do any thing by force. So after he was conveyed to *Richmond* again.

17. He came to prefent the Order of *Monfeigneur Michael*; whereafter with Ceremonies accuftomed, he had put on the Garments, he, and *Monfieur Gye* likewife of the Order, came one at my right Hand, the other at my left to the Chappel, where-after the Communion celebrated, each of them kiffed my Cheek. After that they dined with Me, and talked after Dinner, and faw fome Paftime and fo went home again.

18. A Proclamation made againſt Regratters, and Foreſtallers, and the words of the Statute recited, with the Puniſhment of the Offenders. Also Letters were ſent to all Officers and Sheriffs for the executing thereof.

19. Another Proclamation made for puniſhment of them that would blow Rumours of abaſing and enhaunſing of the Coin to make things dear withal.

The ſame night *Monſieur le Mareſchal St. Andre* ſupped with Me ; after Supper ſaw a dozen courſes, and after I came and made Me ready.

20. The next Morning he came to Me to mine Arraying, and ſaw my Bed-Chamber, and went a hunting with Hounds ; and ſaw Me ſhoot, and ſaw all my Guards ſhoot together. He dined with Me, heard Me play on the Lute, Ride ; came to Me to my ſtudy, ſupped with Me, and ſo departed to *Richmond*.

19. The Scots ſent an Ambaſſador hither for receiving the Treaty, ſealed with the Great Seal of *England*, which was delivered him. Alſo I ſent Sir *Thomas Chaloner*, Clerk of my Council, to have the Seal of them, for Confirmation of the laſt Treaty at *Northampton*.

17. This day my Lord Marqueſs and the Commiſſioners coming to treat of the Marriage, offered by later Inſtructions 600000 Crowns, after 400000 *l*, and ſo departed for an hour. Then ſeeing they could get no better, came to the French Offer of 200000 Crowns, half to be paid at the Marriage, half ſix months after that.

Then the French agreed that her Dote ſhould be but 10000 Marks of Lawful Money of *England*.

Thirdly, It was agreed that, if I died, ſhe ſhould not have the Dote, ſaying, They did that for Friendſhips-ſake without preſident.

19. The Lord Marqueſs having received and delivered again the Treaty ſealed, took his leave, and ſo did all the reſt.

At this time there was a bickering at *Parma* between the French and the Papiſts, for *Monſieur de Thermes*, *Petro Strozi*, and *Fontivello*, with divers other Gentlemen to the number of thirty, with 1500 Souldiers, entered *Parma*, *Gonzaga* with the Emperors and Popes Band lay near the Town. The French made Sallies, and overcame, ſlaying the Prince of *Macedonia*, and the *Seigniour Baptiſta* the Pope's Nephew.

22. Mr. *Sidney* made one of the four chief Gentlemen.

23. *Monſieur le Mareſchal* came to Me, declaring the King his Maſters well-taking my readineſs to this Treaty ; and alſo how much his Maſter was bent that way. He preſented *Monſieur Bois Dolphine*

to be Ambaffador here, as my Lord **Marquefs** the 19th day did prefent Mr. *Pickering*.

26. *Monsieur le Marefchal* dined with Me. After **Dinner** faw the ftrength **of** the Englifh Archers. After he had fo done, **at his departure I gave him** a Diamond from my finger, worth, by estimation, 150 *l.* both for Pains, and alfo for my Memory. Then he **took his leave**.

27. He came **to a** hunting to tell me the News, **and** fhew the Letter his Mafter had fent him, and doubtlefs of *Monsieur Termes* and *Marignans* Letters, being Ambaffador with the Emperor.

28. *Monsieur le Marefchal* came to Dinner to *Hide-Park*, where there was a fair House made for **him, and he faw** the Courfing there.

30. He came to the Earl of *Warwick's*, **lay** there one night, and was well received.

29. He had his **Reward, being worth 3000** *l.* in Gold, of Currant Money. *Monsieur de Gye* 1000 *l. Monsieur Chenault* 1000 *l. Monsieur Movillier* 500 *l.* the Secretary 500 *l.* and the Bifhop *Peregrueux** 500 *l.*

August.

3. *Monsieur le Marefchal* departed to *Bolleign*, and had **certain of my** Ships to conduct him thither.

9. **Four and twenty Lords of** the Council met at *Richmond*, to commune of my Sister *Mary's* matter ; who at length agreed, That **it was not meet to be fuffered any** longer, making thereof **an** Inftrument **signed with** their Hands, and fealed, to be on Record.

11. The Lord **Marquefs, with the moft part of his Band, came home, and** delivered the Treaty Sealed.

12. Letters fent for *Rochester*, *Inglefield*, and *Walgrave* to come the 13*th* day, **but they** came not **till** another Letter was fent to them the 13*th* day.

14. My **Lord Marquefs's Reward was** delivered **at** *Paris*, worth 500 *l.* my Lord of *Ely's* 200. Mr. *Hobbey's* 150 ; the reft all about one fcantling.

14. *Rochefter*, &c. had commandment **neither** to hear nor to fuffer **any** kind of Service, but the Common and Orders fet forth at large by Parliament, and had a Letter to my Lady's Houfe from my Council for their Credit, another to her felf from me. Alfo appointed that I **fhould come and fit at Council** when great Matters were debating, or when I would.

This last month *Monsieur de Termes*, with 500 Frenchmen, came to

---

* *Perigueux.*

Journal of Edward the Sixth.

Parma, and entred safely; afterward certain issued out of the Town, and were overthrown, as *Scipiaro, Dandelot, Petro*, and others, were taken, and some slain; after they gave a Skirmish, entred the Camp of *Gonzaga*, and spoiled a few Tents, and returned.

15. Sir *Robert Dudley* and *Barnabe* sworn two of the six ordinary Gentlemen. The last month the Turks Navy won a little Castle in Sicily.

17. Instructions sent to Sir *James Croftes* for divers purposes, whose Copy is in the Secretary's hands. The Testourn cried down from 9 *d*. to 6 *d*. the Groat from 3 *d*. to 2 *d*. the 2 *d*. to 1 *d*. the Penny to an Half-penny, the Half-penny to a Farthing, &c.

1. *Monsieur Termes* and *Scipiaro* overthrew three Ensigns of Horse-men at three times; took one dispatch sent from *Don Fernando* to the Pope concerning this War, and another from the Pope to *Don Fernando*; Discomfited four Ensigns of Footmen; took the Count *Camillo* of *Castilion*, and slew a Captain of the Spaniards.

22. Removing to *Windsor*.

23. *Rochester*, &c. returned, denying to do openly the charge of the Lady *Mary's* House for displeasing her.

26. The Lord Chancellor, Mr. Comptroller, the Secretary *Petre*, sent to do the same Commission.

27. Mr. *Coverdale* made Bishop of *Exeter*.

28. *Rochester*, &c. sent to the *Fleet*.

The Lord Chancellor, &c. did that they were commanded to do to my Sister and her house.

31 *Rochester*, &c. committed to the *Tower*.

The Duke of *Somerset* taking certain that began a new Conspiracy for the destruction of the Gentlemen at *Okingam* two days past, executed them with Death for their Offence.

29. Certain Pinaces were prepared to see that there should be no conveyance over-Sea of the Lady *Mary* secretly done. Also appointed that the Lord Chancellor, Lord Chamberlain, the Vice-chamberlain and the Secretary *Petre* should see by all means they could, whether she used the Mass; and if she did that, the Laws should be executed on her Chaplains. Also that when I came from this Progress to *Hampton-Court*, or *Westminster*, both my Sisters should be with Me, till further Order were taken for this purpose.

September.

3. The French Ambassador came to declare, first how the Emperor wronged divers of his Masters Subjects and Vassals; arrested also his

Merchants, and did cloakedly begin War, for he besieged *Mirandula* round about with Forces he had made in the French King's Country. Also he stayed certain French Ships going a fishing to the *New-foundland*. Furthermore, he set out a dozen of Ships, which bragged they would take the Dowager of *Scotland*, which thing staied her so long at *Diep*. Whereupon his Master had taken the whole Fleet of *Antwerp*, conveying it to his Countrey into his Ports, by 20 Ships he had set forth under Baron *de la Garde*. Also minded to send more help to *Piedmont* and *Mirandula*. For this cause he defired that on my Coasts the Dowager might have safe passage, and might be secured by my Servants at the Sea-Coast if any chance should happen.

He was willed to put it in writing; he shewed how the Turks Navy, having spoiled a piece of *Sicily*, went to *Malta*, and there took an Isle adjacent called *Gozo*; from thence they went to *Tripoly*. In *Transilvania*, *Rosto-Bassa* was leader of the Army, and had spoiled it wholly.

In *Hungary* the Turks had made a Fort by the Mines to get them. *Magdeburg* was freshly victualled, and Duke *Maurice* came his way, being suspected that he had conspired with them there.

4. It was answered, to the French Ambassador, That the Dowager should in all my Ports be defended from Enemies, Tempest, and likewise also Thanks were given for the News.

5. The Emperor's Ambassador came to require, That my Sister *Mary's* Officers should be restored to their Liberty, and she should have her Mass till the Emperor was certified thereof.

It was answered, That I need not to answer except I list, because he spake without Commission, which was seen by the shortness of the time since the committing of her Officers, of which the Emperor could not be advertised. He was willed no more to move these Piques, in which he had been often answered, without Commission. He was answered, That the Emperor was by this time advertised, although the Matter pertained not to him. Also that I had done nothing but according to a King's Office herein, in observing the Laws that were so Godly, and in punishing the Offenders. The Promise to the Emperor was not so made as he pretended, affirmed by Sir *Philip Hobbey* being at that time their Ambassador.

6. Deliberation touching the Coin. *Memorandum*, That there were divers Standards nine ounces fine, a few eight ounces fine, as ill as four, because although that was fine, yet a Shilling was reckoned for two Shillings, six ounces, very many four ounces, many also three

ounces, 130000 *l.* now of late. Whereupon agreed that the Teſtourn being called to ſix Pence, four with help of ſix ſhould make ten fine, eight fine with help of nine, being fewer than thoſe of eight, ſhould make ten ounces fine, the two ounces of Allay ſhould quit the charges of Minting ; and thoſe of three-pence, being but few, ſhould be turned to a Standard of four of Farthings, and Half-pence, and Pence, for to ſerve for the poor People, becauſe the Merchants made no Exchange of it, and the Sum was not great. Alſo to bear the Charges, for becauſe it was thought that few or none were left of nine ounces fine, eight ounces were naught, and ſix ounces were two ways deviſed, one without any craft, the other was not fully ſix, of which kind was not a few.

9. A Proclamation ſet forth touching the Prices of Cattel, of Hogs, Pigs, Beeves, Oxen, Muttons, Butter, and Cheeſe, after a reaſonable price, not fully ſo good cheap as it was when the Coin was at the perfecteſt, but within a fifth part of it, or thereabouts.

10. I removed to *Farnham.*

12. A Proclamation ſet forth touching the Coin, That whereas it was ſo that Men for Gain melted down the Nine-pence Teſtourn continually, and the Six-pence ; alſo there ſhould no Perſon in any wiſe melt it down, upon pain to incur the Penalty of the Laws.

13. A Letter directed to the Lord Treaſurer, the Lord Great Maſter, and the Maſter of the Horſe, to meet at *London,* for the ordering of my Coin, and the paiment of my Debts ; which done, to return, and make report of their Proceedings.

11. War proclaimed in *Britain* between the Emperor and the French, in theſe terms, **Charles Roy d'Eſpaigne, et Duc de Milan,** leaving out Emperor.

10. Four Towns taken by the French Souldiers that were the Emperor's in *Piedmont Guerra :* from *Amiens* alſo the Emperor's Country there was ſpoiled, and 120 Caſtles or Fortreſſes taken.

Proclamation made in *Paris* touching the Bulls, that no Man ſhould go for them to *Rome.*

Other Ships alſo taken by *Prior de Capua* Merchants, to the number of a dozen ; *Prior de Capua* had 32 Gallies.

19. The French Ambaſſador ſent this News alſo, That the Turks had taken *Tripoly.*

20. The Secretary *Cecil,* and Sir *Philip Hobbey,* ſent to *London* to help the Lord Treaſurer, *&c.* in the Matters of the Biſhops of *Chicheſter, Worceſter,* and *Dureſme,* and examination of my Siſters Men.

18. Removing to *Windsor*.

20. The Lords at *London* having tryed all kinds of Stamping, both of the Fineness of 9, 8, 6, 4, and 3, proved that without any loss, but sufferable, the Coin might be brought to eleven ounces fine: For whereas it was thought before, that the Testourn was, through ill Officers and Ministers corrupted, it was tried, that it had the valuation just by eight sundry kinds of melting, and 400 *l.* of *Sterling* Mony, a Testourn being but Six-pence, made 400 *l.* 11 ounces fine of Mony *Sterling*.

22. Whereupon they reported the same, and then it was concluded that the Testourn should be eleven ounces fine, the proportion of the Pences according to the Gold; so that five Shillings of Silver should be worth five of Gold.

23. Removing to *Oatlands*.

24. Agreed that the Stamp of the Shilling and Six-pence should be on one side, a King painted to the Shoulders in Parliament-Robes, with a Chain of the Order. Five Shillings of Silver, and half five Shillings, should be a King on Horse-back, armed with a naked Sword hard to his Breast. Also that *York's* Mint, and *Throgmorton's* in the *Tower*, should go and work the fine Standard. In the City of *York* and *Canterbury* should the small Mony be wrought of a baser State. Officers for the same were appointed.

A piece of *Barwick* Wall fell, because the Foundation was shaken by working of a Bullwark.

28. The Lord Marquess of *Dorset* grieved much with the disorder of the Marches toward *Scotland*, surrendered the Wardenship thereof to bestow where I would.

27. The Wardenship of the North given to the Earl of *Warwick*. Removing to *Hampton-Court*.

28. Commissioners appointed for fitting on the Bishop of *Chichester* and *Worcester*; three Lawyers, and three Civilians.

10. The Imperialists took the Suburbs of *Heading*, and burnt them.

26. The Passport of the Dowager of *Scotland* was made for a longer time, till *Christmas*; and also if she were driven, to pass quietly by Land into *Scotland*.

20. Monsieur *d'Angoulesme* was born; and the Duke of *Vendosme* had a Son by the Princess of *Navarr* his Wife.

30. The Feast of *Michaelmass* was kept by Me in the Robes of the Order.

October.

1. The Commiffion for the making of five Shillings, half five Shillings, Groats, and Six-pences, eleven ounces fine, and Pence, with Half-pence, and Farthings, four ounces fine, was followed and figned.

5, *Jarnac* came in Poft for declaration of two things; the one, that the Queen had a third Son of which fhe was delivered, called *Le Duc d'Angoulefme*, of which the King prayed Me to be God-father. I anfwered, I was glad of the News, and that I thanked him for that I fhould be God-father, which was a token of good Will he bare me. Alfo that I would difpatch for the accomplifhment thereof, the Lord *Clinton* the Lord Admiral of *England*. He faid, he came alfo to tell a fecond Point of the good success of his Mafters Wars; He told how the laft month in *Shampaign*, befide *Sedan*, 1000 Horfe Imperialifts, with divers Hungarians, *Martin Vanroffy* being their Captain and Leader, entred the Country; and the Alarm came, the Skirmifh began fo hot that the French Horfe, about two or three hundred Men of Arms, came out and took *Vanroffy*'s Brother, and flew divers. Alfo how in *Piedmont*, fince the taking of the laft four Towns, three other were taken, *Monrechia*, *Saluges* and the Town of *Burges*. The Turks had come to *Naples*, and fpoiled the Country, and taken *Oftium* in the mouth of *Tyberis*. Alfo in *Sicily* he had taken a good Haven and a Town.

6. *Jarnac* departed, *having lying** in the Court under my Lodging. The Night before the Bifhops of *Worcefter* and *Chichefter* were depofed for Contempts.

7. There were appointed to go with the Lord Admiral, Mr. *Nevil*, Mr. *Barnabie*, Gentlemen of the Chamber; Sir *William Stafford*, Sir *Adrian Poinings*, Sir *John Norton*, Sir *John Teri*, Knights; and Mr. *Brook*.

8. Letters directed to the Captains of Gendarms, that they fhould mufter the 8*th* of *November*, being the *Sunday* after *Hallow-Eve* day.

11. *Henry* Marquefs of *Dorfet*, created Duke of *Suffolk*; *John* Earl of *Warwick*, created Duke of *Northumberland*; *William* Earl of *Wiltfhire*, created Marquefs of *Winchester*; Sir *William Herbert*, created Earl of *Pembrook*, and Lord of *Cardiff*; Mr. *Sidney*, Mr. *Nevil*, Mr *Cheek*, all three of the Privy-Chamber, made Knights; also Mr. *Cecil* one of the two Secretaries.

13. Proclamation figned touching the calling in of Teftourns and Groats, that they that lift might come to the Mint and have fine Silver of Twelve-pence for two Teftourns.

---

* *Sic.*

3. *Prior de Capua* departed the **French** King's Service, **and went** to his Order **of Knights** in *Malta*, partly for difpleafure **to the** Count *Villars* **the** Constable's Brother-in-Law, partly for **that** *Malta* was affailed often by the Turks.

7. Sir *Thomas Palmer* came **to the Earl** of *Warwick*, **since that time Duke of** *Northumberland*, to deliver **him** his Chain, being **a very fair** one (for every **Link** weighed **an ounce) to be** delivered **to** *Jarnac*, and fo to receive as much ; whereupon in my **Lords Garden** he declared a Confpiracy, How at **St.** *George's* **day laft,** my **Lord of** *Somerset*, who then was going to the North, **if the Mafter** of the Horfe, Sir *William Herbert*, had not affured **him** on **his Honour** that he fhould have no hurt, **went to** raife the People, **and the** Lord *Gray* went before to know **who were his Friends.** Afterward **a Device was** made to call the Earl **of** *Warwick* to a Banquet, with the Marquefs of *Northampton*, and divers **others, and to cut off their Heads.** Alfo he found a bare Company about them by the way to fet upon them.

11. He declared alfo, that **Mr.** *Vane* had **2000 men in readinefs** ; Sir *Thomas Arundel* had affured my Lord, that the *Tower* was fafe ; **Mr. Partridge** fhould raife *London*, and take the **Great Seal with the** Apprentices of *London* ; *Seymour* and *Hammond* fhould **wait upon him, and all the Horfe of the** Gendarms fhould be flain.

13. Removing to *Weftminfter*, becaufe it **was** thought this Matter might eafilier and furelier be difpatched there, **and** likewife all other.

14. **The** Duke fent for **the** Secretary *Cecil* to tell him he fufpected fome ill. Mr *Cecil* anfwered, **That** if he were not guilty, he might **be of good** courage ; if he were, **he** had nothing to fay, but to lament him. Whereupon the Duke fent him a Letter of Defiance, and called *Palmer*, who after denial **made of** his Declaration, was let go.

16. This morning none was **at** *Weftminfter* of the Confpirators. The first was **the** Duke, who came **later** than he was wont of himfelf. After Dinner **he** was apprehended. **Sir** *Thomas Palmer* on the Tarras walking there, *Hammond* paffing by **Mr.** Vice-chamberlain's Door, was called in by *John Piers* to make a match at Shooting, and fo taken. *Nudegates* was called **for as** from my **Lord** his Mafter, and taken ; likewife were *John Seimour* and *David Seimour*. *Arundel* alfo was taken, and the Lord *Gray* coming out of the Country. *Vane* upon two fendings of my **Lord** in the morning, fled at the firft fending ; he faid, My Lord was not ftout, and if he could get home, he cared for none of them all, he was fo ftrong. But after he was found by *John Piers* in a **Stable of his Mans** at Lambeth under the Straw.

These went with the Duke to the *Tower* this Night, saving *Palmer*, *Arundel*, and *Vane*, who were kept in Chambers here apart.

17. The Dutches, *Crane* and his Wife, with the Chamber-keeper, were sent to the *Tower* for devising these Treasons. *James Wingfield* also for casting of Bills seditiously; also Mr. *Partridge* was attaqued, and Sir *James Holcroft*.

18. Mr. *Banister* and Mr *Vaughan* were attaqued and sent to the *Tower*, and so was Mr. *Stanhope*.

19. Sir *Thomas Palmer* confessed that the Gandarms, on the Muster-day, should be assaulted by 2000 Footmen of Mr. *Vane*'s, and my Lord's hundred Horse; besides his Friends which stood by, and the idle People which took his part. If he were overthrown, he would run through *London*, and cry, **Liberty, Liberty,** to raise the Apprentices, and R; if he could, he would go to the *Isle of Wight*, or to *Pool*.

22. The Dowager of *Scotland* was by Tempest driven to Land at *Portsmouth*, and so she sent word she would take the benefit of the safe Conduct to go by Land and to see Me.

23. She came from *Portsmouth* to Mr. *Whites* House.

24. The Lords sat in the *Star-Chamber*, and there declared the Matters and Accusations laid against the Duke, meaning to stay the minds of the People.

25. Certain German Princes, in the beginning of this month, desired Aid in Cause of Religion 400000 Dollars, if they should be driven to make shift by necessity, and offered the like also, if I entred into any War for them; whereupon I called the Lords, and considered, as appeareth by a Scroll in the Board at *Westminster*, and thereupon appointed that the Secretary *Petre*, and Sir *William Cecil* another Secretary, should talk with the Messenger to know the matter precisely, and the Names of those would enter the Confederacy.

28. The *Dowager* came to Sir *Richard Cotton*'s House.

29. She came from Sir *Richard Cotton*'s to the Earl of *Arundel* to Dinner, and brought to Mr. *Brown*'s House, where met her the Gentlemen of *Sussex*.

30. She came and was conveied by the same Gentlemen to *Guilford*, where the Lord *William Howard*, and the Gentlemen of *Surrey* met her.

All this month the Frenchmen continued spoiling of the Emperor's Frontiers, and in a Skirmish at *Ast* they slew 100 *Spaniards*.

31. A Letter directed to Sir *Arthur Darcy* to take the charge of the

Tower, and to discharge Sir *John Markham* upon this, that without making any of the Council privy, he suffered the Duke to walk abroad, and certain Letters to be sent and answered between *David Seimour* and Mrs. *Poinings*, with other divers Suspicions.

17. There were Letters sent to all Emperors, Kings, Ambassadors, Noblemen, Men, and Chief Men, into Countries, of the late Conspiracy.

31. She came to *Hampton-Court*, conveied by the same Lords and Gentlemen aforesaid; and two miles and a half from thence, in a Valley, there met her the Lord Marquess of *Northampton*, accompanied with the Earl of *Wiltshire*, Son and Heir to the Lord High Treasurer; Marquess of *Winchester*; the Lord *Fitzwater*, Son to the Earl of *Suffex*; The Lord *Evers*, the Lord *Bray*, the Lord *Robert Dudley*, the Lord *Garet*, Sir *Nicholas Throgmorton*, Sir *Edward Rogers*, and divers other Gentlemen, besides all the Gentlemen Pensioners, Men of Arms and Ushers, Sewers and Carvers, to the number of 120 Gentlemen, and so she was brought to *Hampton-Court*. At the Gate thereof met her the Lady Marquess of *Northampton*, the Countess of *Pembrook*, and divers other Ladies and Gentlewomen, to the number of sixty; and so she was brought to her lodging on the Queen-side, which was all hanged with Arras, and so was the Hall, and all the other Lodgings of Mine in the House very finely dressed; and for this night, and the next day, all was spent in Dancing and Pastime, as though it were a Court, and great presence of Gentlemen resorted thither.

26. Letters were written, for becaufe of this Business, to defer the Musters of Gendarmory till the —* day of *December*.

November.

1. The Dowager perused the House of *Hampton-Court*, and saw some coursing of Deer.

2. She came to the Bishop's Palace at *London*, and there she lay, and all her Train lodged about her.

3. The Duke of *Suffolk*, the Earl of *Warwick*, *Wiltshire*, and many other Lords and Gentlemen were sent to her to welcome her and to say, on My behalf, That if she lacked any thing she should have it for her better Furniture; and also I would willingly see her the day following.

The 26*th* of *October*.

Crane confessed the most part, even as *Palmer* did before, and more

---
* Blank in original.

Journal of Edward the Sixth.

also, how that the place where the nobles should have been banqueted, and their Heads striken off, was the Lord *Paget*'s House, and how the Earl of *Arundel* knew of the Matter as well as he, by *Stanhop* who was a Messenger between them; also some part, how he went to *London* to get Friends once in *August* last, feigning himself sick. *Hammond* also confessed the Watch he kept in his Chamber at Night. *Bren* also confessed much of this matter. The Lord *Strange* confessed how the Duke willed him to stir me to marry his third Daughter, the Lady *Jane*, and willed him to be his Spie in all Matters of my Doings and Sayings, and to know when some of my Council spoke secretly with Me; this he confessed of himself.

November.

4. The Duke of *Suffolk*, the Lord *Fitzwater*, the Lord *Bray*, and divers other Lords and Gentlemen, accompanied with his Wife the Lady *Francis*, the Lady *Margaret*, the Dutchesses of *Richmond* and of *Northumberland*, the Lady *Jane* daughter to the Duke of *Suffolk*; the Marquess of *Northampton* and *Winchester*; the Countesses of *Arundel*, *Bedford*, and *Huntingdon*, and *Rutland*; with 100 other Ladies and Gentlewomen went to her, and brought her through *London* to *Westminster*. At the Gate there received her the Duke of *Northumberland*, Great Master, and the Treasurer, and Comptroller, and the Earl of *Pembrook*, with all the Sewers, and Carvers, and Cup-bearers, to the number of thirty. In the Hall I met her, with all the rest of the Lords of my Council, as the Lord Treasurer, the Marquis of *Northampton*, &c. and from the outer-Gate up to the Presence-Chamber, on both sides, stood the Guard. The Court, the Hall, and the Stairs, were full of Servingmen; the Presence-Chamber, Great-Chamber, and her Presence-Chamber, of Gentlemen. And so having brought her to her Chamber, I retired to Mine. I went to her to Dinner; she dined under the same Cloth of State, at my left Hand; at her rereward dined my Cousin *Francis*, and my Cousin *Margaret*; at Mine sat the French Ambassadour. We were served by two Services, two Sewers, Cupbearers, Carvers, and Gentlemen. Her Master *Hostel* came before her Service, and my Officers before Mine. There were two Cupboards, one of Gold four Stages high, another of massy Silver six Stages: In her great Chamber dined at three Boards the Ladies only. After Dinner, when she had heard some Musick, I brought her to the Hall, and so she went away.

5. The Duke of *Northumberland*, the Lord Treasurer, the Lord Marquess of *Northampton*, the Lord Privy-Seal, and divers others, went

to see her, and to deliver a Ring with a Diamond, and two Nags, as a Token from Me.

6. The Duke of *Northumberland*, with his Band of a hundred, of which forty were in Black-Velvet, white and black Sleeves, sixty in Cloth, the Earl of *Pembrook* with his Band, and fifty more, The Earl of *Wiltshire*, with 58 of his Father's Band, all the Pensioners, Men of Arms, and the Country, with divers Ladies, as my Cousin *Margaret*, the Dutchesses of *Richmond* and *Northumberland*, brought the Queen to *Shoreditch*, through *Cheap-side* and *Cornhill*; and there met her Gentlemen of *Middlesex* an 100 Horse, and so she was conveied out of the Realm, met in every Shire with Gentlemen.

8. The Earl of *Arnndel* committed to the *Tower*, with Master *Stroadly*, and St. *Alban* his Men, because *Crane* did more and more confess of him.

7. A Frenchman was sent again into *France*, to be delivered again to the eight Frenchmen at the Borders, because of a murder he did at *Diep*, and thereupon he fled hither.

14. Answer was given to the *Germans*, which did require 400000 Dollars, if need so required, for maintenance of Religion.

First, that I was very well inclined to make Peace, Amity, or Bargain with them I knew to be of mine Religion ; for because this Messenger was sent only to know my Inclination and Will to enter, and not with full Resolution of any Matters.

Secondly, I would know whether they could get unto them any such strength of other Princes as were able to maintain the War, and to do the Reciprogue to Me if need should require ; and therefore willed those three Princes, Duke *Maurice* of *Saxon*, the Duke of *Mecklenburgh*, and the Marquess *John* of *Brandenburgh*, from which he was sent, to open the matter to the Duke of *Prussia*, and to all Princes about them, and somewhat to get the good Will of *Hamburgh*, *Lubeck*, *Bremen*, &c. shewing them an inkling of the matter.

Thirdly, I would have the matter of Religion made more plain, lest when War should be made for other Quarrels, they should say it were Religion.

Fourthly, He should come with more ample Commission from the same States to talk of the sum of Mony, and other Appurtenances. This Answer was given, lest if I assented wholly at the first, they would declare mine Intent to the Stadts and whole Senates, and so to come abroad, whereby I should run into danger of breaking the League with the Emperor.

16. The Lord Admiral took his leave to go into *France* for chriften-
ing of the French King's Son.

18. *Foffey*, Secretary to the Duke *Maurice*, who was here for matter
above-fpecified.

20. A Proclamation appointed to go forth, for that there went one
before this time, that fet prices of Beef, Oxen, and Muttons, which
was meant to continue but to *November*; when-as the Parliament
fhould have been to abbrogate that, and to appoint certain Commiffioners to caufe the Grafiers to bring to the Market, and to fell at prices
reafonable. And that certain Overfeers fhould be befides to certify of
the Juftices doings.

23. The Lord Treasurer appointed High-Steward for the Arraign-
ment of the Duke of *Somerfet*.

At this time Duke *Maurice* began to fhew himfelf a Friend to the
Proteftants, who before that time had appeared their Enemy.

21. The forefaid Proclamation proclaimed.

17. The Earl of *Warwick*, Sir *Henry Sidney*, Sir *Henry Nevil*, and Sir
Henry Yates, did challenge all Commers at Tilt the third of *January*,
and at Tornay the fixth of *January*; and this challenge was proclaimed.

28. News came that *Maximilian* was coming out of *Spain*, nine of
his galleys with his Stuff, and 120 Gennets, and his Treafure, was
taken by the French.

24. The Lord Admiral entred *France*, and came to *Bulloign*.

26. The Captain of *Portfmouth* had word and commandment to bring
the Model of the Caftle and Place, to the intent it might be fortified,
becaufe *Baron de la Gard* had feen it, having an Engineer with him,
and as it was thought had the Plott of it.

30. 22 Peers and Nobles, befides the Council, heard Sir *Thomas
Palmer*, Mr. *Hammond*, Mr. *Crane*, and *Nudigate*, fwear that their Con-
feffions were true; and they did fay, that that was faid without any
kind of compulfion, Force, Envy, or Difpleasure, but as favourably to
the Duke as they could fwear to with fafe Confciences.

24. The Lord Admiral came to *Paris*.

December.

1. The Duke of *Somerfet* came to his Trial at *Weftminfter-Hall*; The
Lord-Treafurer fat as High-Steward of *England*, under the Cloth of

State, on a Bench between two Posts, three degrees high. All the Lords to the number of 26, viz.

Dukes.	Huntingdon.	Evers.
	Rutland.	Latimer.
Suffolk.	Bath.	Bourough.
Northumberland.	Sussex.	Souch.
	Worcester.	Stafford.
Marquess.	Pembrook.	Wentworth.
	Vis. Hereford.	Darcy.
Northampton.		Sturton.
	Barons.	Windsor.
Earls.		Cromwell.
	Burgaveny.	Cobham.
Derby.	Audley.	Bray.
Bedford.	Wharton.	

These sat a degree under, and heard the Matter debated.

First, After the Indictments were read, five in number, the Learned Counsel laid to my Lord of *Somerset*, *Palmer's* Confession. To which he answered, That he never minded to raise the North, and declared all the ill he could devise of *Palmer*, but he was afraid for Bruites, and that moved him to send to Sir *William Herbert*. Replied it was again, that the worse *Palmer* was, the more he served his purpose. For the Banquet, he swore it was untrue, and required more Witnesses. Whence *Crane's* Confession was read, He would have had him come Face to Face. For *London*, he meant nothing for hurt of any Lord, but for his own Defence. For the Gendarmoury, it were but a mad matter for him to enterprise with his 100 against 900. For having Men in his Chamber at *Greenwich*, confessed by *Partridg*, it seemed he meant no harm, because when he could have done harm he did it not. My Lord *Strange's* Confession, he swore it was untrue, and the Lord *Strange* took his Oath it was true. *Nudigate's*, *Hammond's*, and *Alexander Seimour's* Confessions he denied, because they were his Men.

The Lawyers rehearsed, how to raise Men at his House for an ill Intent, as to kill the Duke of *Northumberland*, was Treason, by an Act, *Anno tertio* of my Reign, against Unlawful Assemblies, for to devise the Death of the Lords was Felony. To mind resisting his attachment was Felony; To raise *London* was Treason, and to Assault the Lords was Felony. He answered, He did not intend to raise *London*, and swore, that the Witnesses were not there. His assembling of Men was but for his own defence. He did not determine to kill the Duke of *Northumberland*, the Marquefs, &c. but fpoke of it, and determined after the contrary, and yet feemed to confefs he went about their Death.

The Lords went together. The Duke of *Northumberland* would not agree that any fearching of his Death fhould be Treafon. So the Lords acquitted him of High-Treafon, and condemned him of Treafon Fellonious, and fo he was adjudged to be hang'd.

He gave thanks to the Lords for their open Trial, and cried Mercy of the Duke of *Northumberland*, the Marquefs of *Northampton*, and the Earl of *Pembrook*, for his ill meaning againft them, and made fuit for his Life, Wife, Children, Servants, and Debts, and fo departed without the Ax of the *Tower*. The People knowing not the Matter, fhouted half a dozen of times fo loud, that from the Hall-Door it was heard at *Charing-Crofs* plainly, and rumours went that he was quit of all.

The Peace concluded by the Lord Marquefs, was ratified by Me before the Ambaffadour, and delivered to him Signed and Sealed.

3. The Duke told certain Lords that were in the *Tower*, that he had hired *Bertivill* to kill them; which thing *Bertivill* examined on, confeffed, and fo did *Hammond* that he knew of it.

4. I faw the Mufters of the new Band-men of Arms; 100 of my Lord Treafurers; 100 of *Northumberland*, 100 *Northampton*, 50 *Huntingtoun*, 50 *Rutland*, 120 of *Pembrook*, 50 *Darcy*, 50 *Cobham*, 100 Sir *Thomas Cheyney*, and 180 of the Penfioners and their Bands, with the old Men of Arms, all well-armed Men; fome with Feathers, Staves, and Penfils of their colours; fome with Sleeves and half-Coats; fome with Bards and Staves, &c. The Horfes all fair and great, the worft would not have been given for lefs than 20 *l*. there was none under fourteen handfull and an half the moft part, and almoft all Horfes with their Guider going before them. They paffed twice about St. *James*'s Field, and compaffed it round, and fo departed.

15. Then were certain Devices for Laws delivered to my Learned Council to Pen, as by a Schedule appeareth.

18. It was appointed I fhould have fix Chaplains ordinary, of which two ever to be prefent, and four always abfent in preaching: one Year two in *Wales*, two in *Lancafhire* and *Darby*; next Year two in the Marches of *Scotland*, two in *Yorkfhire*; the third Year, two in *Devonfhire*, two in *Hampfhire*; fourth Year, two in *Norfolk* and *Effex*, and two in *Kent* and *Suffex*, &c. Thefe fix to be *Bill, Harle, Perne, Grindall, Bradford*.*

---

* The other name dafht.

20. The Bishop of *Duresme* was for concealment of Treason written to him, and not disclosed at all till the Party did open him, committed to the *Tower*.

21. *Richard* Lord *Rich* Chancellor of *England*, considering his sickness, did deliver his Seal to the Lord-Treasurer, the Lord great Master, and the Lord Chamberlain, sent to him for that purpose, during the time of his sickness, and chiefly of the Parliament.

5. The Lord-Admiral came to the French King, and after was sent to the Queen, and so conveied to his Chamber.

6. The Lord Admiral christned the French King's Child, and called him, by the King's commandment, *Edward Alexander*. All that day there was Musick, Dancing, and Playing with Triumph in the Court; but the Lord Admiral was sick of a double *Quartane*, yet he presented *Barnabe* to the French King, who took him to his Chamber.

7. The Treaty was delivered to the Lord-Admiral, and the French King read it in open Audience at Mass, with Ratification of it. The Lord Admiral took his leave of the French King, and returned to *Paris* very sick.

The same day the French King shewed the Lord Admiral Letters that came from *Parma*, how the French Men had gotten two Castles of the Imperialists; and in the defence of the one, the Prince of *Macedonia* was slain on the Walls, and was buried with triumph at *Parma*.

22. The Great Seal of *England* delivered to the Bishop of *Ely*, to be Keeper thereof during the Lord *Rich*'s sickness.

The Band of 100 Men of Arms, which my Lord of *Somerset* of late had, appointed to the Duke of *Suffolk*.

23. Removing to *Greenwich*.

24. I began to keep Holy this *Christmass*, and continued till *Twelve-tide*.

26. Sir *Anthony St. Legier*, for Matters laid against him by the Bishop of *Dublin*, was banished my Chamber till he had made answer, and had the Articles delivered him.

28. The Lord Admiral came to *Greenwich*.

30. Commission was made out to the Bishop of *Ely*, the Lord Privy-Seal, Sir *John Gates*, Sir *William Petre*, Sir *Robert Bowes*, and Sir *Walter Mildmay*, for calling in my Debts.

January.

1. Orders were taken with the Chandlers of *London*, for selling their Tallow-Candles, which before some denied to do; and some were punished with Imprisonment.

3. The Challenge that was made in the laſt Month, was fulfilled. The Challengers were.
>Sir *Henry Sidney.*
>Sir *Henry Nevel.*
>Sir *Henry Gates.*
>
>Defendants.

The Lord *Williams.*	Mr. *Digby.*
The Lord *Fitzwater.*	Mr. *Warcop.*
The Lord *Ambroſe.*	Mr. *Courtney.*
The Lord *Roberts.*	Mr. *Knolls.*
The Lord *Fitzwarren.*	The Lord *Bray.*
Sir *George Howard.*	Mr. *Paſton.*
Sir *William Stafford.*	Mr. *Cary.*
Sir *John Parrat.*	Sir *Anthony Brown.*
Mr. *Norice.*	Mr. *Drury.*

Theſe in all ran ſix Courſes a-piece at Tilt againſt the Challengers, and accompliſhed their Courſes right-well, and ſo departed again.

5. There were ſent to *Guiſnes* Sir *Richard Cotton,* and Mr. *Bray,* to take view of *Calais, Guiſnes,* and the Marches; and with the advice of the Captain and Engineers, to deviſe ſome amendment, and thereupon to make me Certificate, and upon mine anſwer to go further to the Matter.

4. It was appointed, that if Mr. *Stanhop* left *Hull,* then that I ſhould no more be charged therewith, but that the Town ſhould take it, and ſhould have 40 *l.* a Year for the repairing of the Caſtle.

2. I received Letters out of *Ireland,* which appear in the Secretary's Hand, and thereupon the Earldom of *Thowmount* was by Me given from *O-Brians* Heirs, whoſe Father was dead, and had it for term of Life, to *Donnas* Baron of *Ebrecan,* and his Heirs Males.

3. Alſo Letters were written of Thanks to the Earls of *Deſmond* and *Clanrikard,* and to the Baron of *Dunganan.*

3. The Emperor's Ambaſſador moved me ſeveral times that my Siſter *Mary* might have Maſs, which with no little reaſoning with him was denied him.

6. The foreſaid Challengers came into the Tournay, and the foreſaid Defendants entred in after, with two more with them, Mr. *Terill,* and Mr. *Robert Hopton,* and fought right well, and ſo the Challenge was accompliſhed.

The ſame night was firſt of a Play, after a Talk between one that was called *Riches,* and the other *Youth,* whether of them was better.

After some pretty Reasoning, there came in six Champions of either side.

On *Youth*'s side came.

My Lord *Fitzwater*.
My Lord *Ambrose*.
Sir *Anthony Brown*.
Sir *William Cobham*.
Mr. *Cary*.
Mr. *Warcop*.

On *Riches* side.

My Lord **Fitzwarren**.
Sir *Robert Stafford*.
Mr. *Courtney*.
Digby.
Hopton.
Hungerford.

All these fought two to two at **Barriers** in the Hall. Then came in two apparelled like *Almains*, the Earl of *Ormond* and *Jaques Granado*, and two came in like Friars, but the *Almains* would not suffer them to pass till they had fought; the Friars were Mr. *Drury* and *Thomas Cobham*. After this followed two Masques, one of Men, another of Women. Then a Banquet of 120 Dishes. This day was the end of *Christmass*

7. I went to *Debtford* to dine there, and broke up the Hall.

8. Upon a certain Contention between the **Lord** *Willowby*, and Sir *Andrew Dudley* Captain of *Guisnes*, for their Jurisdiction, the Lord *Willowby* was sent for to come over, to the intent the Controversy might cease, and Order might be taken.

12. There was a Commission granted to the Earl of *Bedford*, to Mr. Vicechamberlain, and certain others, to call in my Debts that were owing Me, and the days past; and also to call in these that be past when the days be come.

17. There was a Match run between six Gentlemen of a side at Tilt.

Of one Side.

The Earl of *Warwick*.
The Lord **Roberts**.
Mr. *Sidney*.
Mr. **Novel**.
Henry Gates.
Anthony Digby.

Of the other Side.

The Lord *Ambrose*.
The Lord *Fitzwater*.
Sir *Francis Knollis*.
Sir *Anthony Brown*.
Sir *John Parrat*.
Mr. *Courtney*.

These wan by four Taintes.

18. The French Ambassador moved, That We should destroy the Scotch part of the Debatable Ground as they had done Ours. It was answered: 1, The Lord **Coniers** that made the Agreement, made it none otherwise but as it should stand with his Superiour's Pleasure:

whereupon the fame Agreement being mifliked, becaufe the Scotch part was much harder to overcome, word was fent to ftay the Matter. Neverthelefs the Lord *Maxwell* did, upon malice to the Englifh Debatables, over-run them; whereupon was concluded, That if the Scots will agree it, the Ground fhould be divided; if not, then fhall the Scots wafte their debatablers, and we Ours, commanding them by Proclamation to depart.

This day the Stiliard put in their Anfwer to a certain Complaint that the Merchant-Adventurers laid againft them.

19. The Bifhop of *Ely*, *Cuftos Sigilli*, was made Chancellor, becaufe as *Cuftos Sigilli*, he could execute nothing in the Parliament that fhould be done, but only to Seal ordinary things.

21. Removing to *Weftminfter*.

22. The Duke of *Somerfet* had his Head cut off upon *Tower-hill*, between eight and nine a Clock in the morning.

16. Sir *William Pickering* delivered a Token to the Lady *Elizabeth*, a fair Diamond.

18. The Duke of *Northumberland* having under him 100 Men of Arms, and 100 Light-Horfe, gave up the keeping of 50 Men at Arms to his Son the Earl of *Warwick*.

23. The Seffions of Parliament began.

24. *John Grefham* was fent over into *Flanders*, to fhew to the *Foul-care*, to whom I owed Mony, that I would defer it; or if I paied it, pay it in Englifh, to make them keep up their French Crowns, with which I minded to pay them.

25. The Anfwer of the Stiliard was delivered to certain of my Learned Council to look on and overfee.

27. Sir *Ralph Vane* was condemned of Felony in Treafon, anfwering like a Ruffian.

Paris arrived with Horfes, and fhewed how the French King had fent Me fix Cortalls, two Turks, a Barbary, two Gennets, a ftirring Horfe, and two littles* Mules, and fhewed them to Me.

29. Sir *Thomas Arundel* was likewife caft of Felony in Treafon, after long controverfie, for the Matter was brought in Trial by feven of the Clock in the morning.

28. At noon the Inqueft went together; they fat fhut up in a Houfe together, without Meat or Drink, becaufe they could not agree all that Day and all that Night.

29. This day in the morning they did caft him.

---
* *Sic.*

February.

2. There was a King of Arms made for *Ireland*, whose Name was *Ulster*, and his Province was all *Ireland*; and he was the fourth King of Arms, and the first Herauld of *Ireland*.

The Emperor took, the last month and this, a Million of pounds in *Flanders*.

It was appointed that Sir *Philip Hobbey* should go to the Regent, upon pretence of ordering of Quarrels of Merchants, bringing with him 63000 *l.* in French Crowns to be paid in *Flanders* at *Antwerp*, to the *Schortz* and their Family, of Debts I owed them, to the intent he might dispatch them both under one.

5. Sir *Miles Partridge* was condemed of Felony for the Duke of *Somerset*'s Matter, for he was one of the Conspirators.

8. Fifty Men at Arms appointed to Mr. *Sadler*.

9. *John Beaumont*, Master of the *Rolls*, was put in Prison for forging a false Deed from *Charles Grandon* Duke of *Suffolk*, to the Lady *Ann Powis*, of certain Lands and Leases.

10. Commission was granted out to 32 Persons, to examine, correct, and set forth the Ecclesiastical Laws.

The Persons Names were these.

The **Bishops**.	The **Divines**.	**Civilians**.
Canterbury.	*Taylor* of *Lincoln.*	Mr. Secretary *Petre.*
Ely.	*Tylor* of *Hadlee.*	Mr. Secretary *Cicil.*
London.	Mr. *Cox*, Almoner.	Mr. *Traherne.*
Winchester.	Sir *John Cheek.*	Mr. *Red.*
Exeter.	Sir *Anthony Cook.*	Mr. *Coke.*
Bath.	*Petrus Martyr.*	*May*, Dean of *Pauls.*
Glocester.	*Joannes Alasco.*	*Skinner.*
Rochester.	*Parker* of *Cambridge.*	

Lawyers.

Justice *Broomley.*	*Goodrick.*	*Lucas.*
Justice *Hales.*	*Stamford.*	*Gawdy.*
Gosnald.	*Carel.*	

10. Sir *Philip Hobbey* departed with somewhat more Crowns than came to 53500 and odd Livers, and had authority to borrow, in my Name, of *Lazarus Tuker* 10000 *l.* Flemish, at 7 *per Cent.* for six months, to make up the Pay, and to employ that that was in Bullion, to bring over with him; also to carry 3000 Merks weight upon a Licence the Emperor granted the Scheitz which they did give me. After that to

Journal of Edward the Sixth.

depart to *Bruges*, where the Regent lay, and there to declare to he the griefs of my Subjects.

11. There was delivered of Armour, by *John Gresham* Merchant, 1100 pair of Corslets and Horsemen-harnesses, very fair.

14. It was appointed that the *Jesus* of *Lubeck*, a Ship of 800 Tun, and the *Mary Gouston* of 600 Tun, should be let out for a Voyage to Merchantmen for a 1000 *l*. they at the Voyage to *Levants-end* to answer the Tackling, the Ship, the Ordnance, Munition, and to leave it in that case they took it. Certain others of the worst of my Ships were appointed to be sold.

9. A Proclamation was made at *Paris*, that the Bands of the *Dolphine*, the Duke of *Vendosme*, the Count *d'Anguien*, the Constable of *France*, the Duke *de Guise*, and *d'Aumale*, the Count *de Sancerres*, the Mareschal S. *Andrew*, *Monsieur de Jarnac* and *Tavennes*, should, the 15th day of *March*, assemble at *Troyes* in *Champaign* to resist the Emperor. Also that the French King would go thither in Person, with 200 Gentlemen of his Houshold, and 400 Archers of his Guard.

16. The French King sent his Secretary *de Lausbespine* to declare this Voyage to him,* and to desire him to take pains to have Mr. *Pickering* with him to be a Witness of his Doings.

19. Whereupon it was appointed, that he should have 2000 Crowns for his Furnishment, besides his Diet, and *Barnabe* 800.

20. The Countess of *Pembrook* died.

18. The Merchant-Adventurers put in their Replication to the Stiliards Answer.

23. A Decree was made by the Board, that upon knowledg and information of their Charters they had found : First, That they were no sufficient Corporation. 2. That their Number, Names, and Nation, was unknown. 3. That when they had forfeited their Liberties, King *Edward* the 4th did restore them on this condition, That they should colour no Strangers Goods, which they had done. Also that whereas in the beginning they shipped not past 8 Clothes, after 100, after 1000, after that 6000; now in their Name was shipped 44000 Clothes in one Year, and but 1100 of all other Strangers. For these Considerations sentence was given, That they had forfeited their Liberties, and were in like case with other Strangers.

28. There came Ambassadors from *Hamburgh*, and *Lubeck*, to speak on the behalf of the Stiliard Merchants.

* This is imperfect.

29. A Flemming would have searched the *Falcon* for Frenchmen, the *Falcon* turned, shot off, boarded the Fleming, and took him.

Paiment was made of 63500 *l*. Flemish to the *Foulcare*, all saving 6000 *l*. which he borrowed in French Crowns by Sir *Philip Hobbey*.

March.

2. The Lord of *Burgaveny* was committed to Ward for striking the Earl of *Oxford* in the Chamber of presence.

The Answer for the Ambassadours of the Stiliard was committed to the Lord Chancellor, the two Secretaries, Sir *Robert Bowes*, Sir *John Baker*, Judge *Montague*, *Griffith* Solicitor, *Gosnald*, *Goodrick*, and *Brooks*.

3. It was agreed, for better dispatch of things, certain of the Council, with others joined with them, should over-look the Penal Laws, and put certain of them in execution. Others should answer Suitors; Others should oversee my Revenues, and the Order of them; also the superfluous Paiments heretofore made. Others should have Commission for taking away superfluous Bullwarks.

First, Order was given for defence of the Merchants to send four Barques and two Pinaces to the Sea.

4. The Earl of *Westmoreland*, the Lord *Wharton*, the Lord *Coniers*, Sir *Tho. Palmer*, and Sir *Tho. Chaloner*, were appointed in Commission to meet with the Scotch Ambassadors, for equal division of the Ground that was called the *Debatable*.

6. The French Ambassador declared to the Duke of *Northumberland* how the French King had sent him a Letter of Credit for his Ambassadry. After delivery made of the Letter he declared how Duke *Maurice* of *Saxony*, the Duke of *Mecklenburgh*, the Marquess of *Brandenburgh*, the Count of *Mansfield*, and divers other Princes of *Germany*, made a League with his Master Offensive and Defensive; the French to go to *Strasburg*, with 30000 Footmen, and 8000 Horsemen; the *Almains* to meet with them there the 25*th* of this month, with 15000 Footmen and 5000 Horsemen. Also the City of *Strasburgh* had promised them Victual, and declared how the French would send me Ambassadors to have Me into the same League. Also that the Marquess of *Brandenburg*, and Count of *Mansfield*, had been privately conveied to the French King's Presence, and were again departed to leavy Men; and he thought by this time they were in the Field.

10. He declared the same thing to Me in the same manner.

9. It was consulted touching the Marts, and it was agreed that it was most necessary to have a Mart in *England* for the enriching of the same to make it the more famous, and to be less in other Mens danger,

Journal of Edward the Sixth.

and to make all things better cheap, and more plentiful. The time was thought good to have it now, becaufe of the Wars between the French King and the Emperor. The places were the meeteft, *Hull* for the Eaft parts, *Southampton* for the South Parts of *England*, as appeareth by two Bills in my Study. *London* alfo was thought no ill place, but it was appointed to begin with the other two.

11. The Bills put up to the Parliament were over-feen, and certain of them were for this time thought meet to pafs and to be read, other of them for avoiding tedioufnefs to be omitted, and no more Bills to be taken.

15. Thofe that were appointed Commiffioners for the Requefts, or for the execution of Penal Laws, or for overfeeing of the Courts, received their Commiffions at my Hand.

18. It was appointed, that for the paiment of 14000 *l*. in the end of *April*, there fhould be made an Anticipation of the Subfidy of *London*, and of the Lords of my Council, which fhould go near to pay the fame with good Provifion.

20. The French Ambaffador brought me a Letter of Credit from his Mafter, and thereupon delivered me the Articles of the League betwixt the Germans and him, defiring Me to take part of the fame League; which Articles I have alfo in my Study.

23. The Merchants of *England* having been long ftaied, departed, in all about 60 Sail, the Woolfleet, and all to *Antwerp*. They were countermanded becaufe of the Mart, but it was too late.

24. Forfomuch as the Exchange was ftayed by the Emperor to *Lions*, the Merchants of *Antwerp* were fore afraid; and that the Mart could not be without Exchange, liberty was given to the Merchants to exchange and rechange Mony for Mony.

26. *Henry Dudley* was fent to the Sea with four Ships, and two Barks, for defence of the Merchants, which were daily before robbed; who, as foon as he came to the Sea, took two Pirats Ships and brought them to *Dover*.

28. I did deny after a fort, the Requeft to enter into War, as appeareth by the Copy of my Anfwer in the Study.

29. To the intent the Ambaffador might more plainly underftand My meaning, I fent Mr. *Hobbey* and Mr. *Mafon* to him, to declare him mine intent more amply.

31. The Commiffioners for the Debatable of the Scotch fide, did deny to meet, except a certain Caftle, or Pile, might be firft razed;

whereupon Letters were sent to stay our Commissioners from the Meeting till they had further word.

10. Duke *Maurice* mustered at *Artnstas* in *Saxony* all his own Men, and left Duke *August*, the Duke of *Anhault*, and the Count of *Mansfield*, for defence of his Country, chiefly for fear of the *Bohemians*. The Young *Lansgrave*, *Reiffenberg*, and others, mustered in *Hassen*.

14. The Marquess *Albert* of *Brandenburgh* mustered his Men two leagues from *Erdfort*, and after entered the same, receiving of the Citizens, a Gift of 20000 Florins; and he borrowed of them 60000 Florins, and so came to *Steinfurt*, where Duke *Maurice* and all the German Princes were assembled.

April.

2. I fell sick of the Measels and Small Pox.

4. Duke *Maurice*, with his Army came to *Augusta*; which Town was at first yielded to him, and delivered into his Hands, where he did change certain Officers, restored their Preachers, and made the Town more free.

5. The Constable, with the French Army, came to *Metz*, which was within two days yielded to him, where he found great provision of Victuals, and that he determined to make the Staple of Victual for his Journey.

8. He came to a Fort wherein was an Abbey called *Gocoza*, and that Fort abide 80 Cannon-shot; at length came to a Parley, where the Frenchmen got in and won it by Assault, slew all, saving 115, with the Captain, whom he hanged.

9. He took a Fort called *Maranges*, and razed it.

12. The French King came to *Nancy* to go to the Army, and there found the Duchess and the young Duke of *Lorrain*.

13. The *Mareschal St. Andrew*, with 200 Men of Arms, and 2000 Foot-men, carried away the young Duke, accompanied with few of his old Men toward France, to the *Dolphin*, which lay at *Rhemes*, to the no little discontentation of his Mother the Dutchess. He fortified also divers Towns in *Lorrain*, and put in French Garisons.

14. He departed from *Nancy* to the Army which lay at *Metz*.

7. *Monsieur Senarpon* gave an overthrow to the Captain of St. *Omers*, having with him 600 Foot-men, and 200 Horse-men.

15. The Parliament broke up, and because I was sick, and not able to go well abroad as then, I signed a Bill containing the Names of the Acts which I would have pass; which Bill was read in the House. Also I gave Commission to the Lord Chancellor, two Arch-Bishops,

two Bishops, two Dukes, two Marquesses, two Earls, and two Barons, to dissolve wholly this Parliament.

18. The Earl of *Pembrook* surrendered his Mastership of the Horse, which I bestowed on the Earl of *Warwick*.

19. Also he left 50 of his Men of Arms, of which 25 were given to Sir *Philip Hobbey*, and 25 to Sir *John Gates*.

21. It was agreed that Commissions should go out for to take certificate of the superfluous Church Plate to Mine use, and to see how it hath been embezeled.

The French Ambassador desired, That forasmuch as it was dangerous carrying of Victual from *Bolleyn* to *Ard* by Land, that I would give licence to carry by Sea to *Calais*, and from *Calais* to *Ard*, in my Ground.

22. The Lord *Paget* was degraded from the Order of the Garter for divers his Offences, and chiefly because he was no Gentleman of Blood, neither of Father-side nor Mother-side.

Sir *Anthony St. Leiger*, which was accused by the Bishop of *Dublin* for divers brawling Matters, was taken again into the Privy-Chamber, and sat among the Knights of the Order.

23. Answer was given to the French Ambassador, that I could not accomplish his Desire, because it was against my League with the Emperor.

24. The Order of the Garter was wholly altered, as appeareth by the new Statutes. There were elected Sir *Andrew Dudley*, and the Earl of *Westmoreland*.

26. *Monsieur de Couriers* came from the Regent, to desire that her Fleet might safely, upon occasion, take harbour in my Havens. Also he said, he was come to give order for redressing all Complaints of our Merchants.

25. Whereas it was appointed that the 14000 *l*. that I owed in the last of *April*, should be paied by the anticipation of the Subsidy of *London*, and of the Lords, because to change the same over-Sea, was loss of the sixth part of the Mony I did so send over. Stay was made thereof, and the paiment appointed to be made over of 20000 *l*. Flemish, which I took up there 14 *per Cent*. and so remained 6000 *l*. to be paid there the last of *May*.

30. Removing to *Greenwich*.

28. The Charges of the Mints were diminished 1400 *l*. and there was left 600 *l*.

18. King *Ferdinando*, *Maximilian* his Son, and the Duke of *Bavaria*,

came to *Linx*, to treat with Duke *Maurice* for a **Peace**; where *Maurice* declared his **Griefs**.

16. Duke *Maurice*'s Men received an overthrow at *Ulms*; Marquefs *Albert* fpoiled the Country, and gave them a day to answer.

31. A **Debt** of 14000 *l.* was paied to the *Foulcare*.

May.

1. The **Stilyard-men** received their Anfwer; which was, to confirm the former **Judgment** of my Council.

2. A **Letter** was fent to the *Foulcare* from my Council to this effect; That I have paied 63000*l.* Flemifh in *February*, and 14000 in *April*, which came to 77000*l.* Flemifh, which was a fair Sum of Mony to be paid in one Year, chiefly in this **bufy World**, whereas it is moft necef- fary to be had for Princes. Befides this, That it was thought Mony fhould not now do him fo much pleafure as at another time peradven- ture. Upon these confiderations **they had advised Me** to pay but 5000 *l.* of the 45000 I now owe, and fo put over the reft according to the **old Intereft 14** *per Cent.* with which they defired him to take patience.

4. *Monfieur de Couriers* received his Anfwer, which was, **That I had long ago given order that the** Flemifh Ships fhould not **be molefted in my Havens, as it** appeareth, becaufe Frenchmen chafing **Flemings into my Havens, could not get** them becaufe **of the refcue they had, but that** I thought **it not** convenient to have **more Ships to come into my Havens** than **I could well rule and govern.** Alfo a note of divers **Complaints** of my Subjects was delivered to him.

10. Letters were fent to **my** Ambaffadors, That they fhould move to the Princes of *Germany*, **to the** Emperor, and to the French King, **That if this** Treaty came **to any effect** or end, I might be compre- hended in the fame.

Commiffion was given **to Sir *John*** Gates, Sir *Robert Bowes*, the Chancellor **of the** Augmentation, Sir *Walter Mildmay*, Sir *Richard Cotton*, to fell **fome** part of the Chauntry Lands, and of the Houfes, for the paiment of my Debts, which **was** 251,000 *l. Sterling* at the leaft.

Taylor, Dean of *Lincoln*, was made Bifhop of *Lincoln*.

Hooper, Bifhop of *Glocefter*, was made Bifhop of *Worcefter* and *Glocefter*.

Story, Bifhop of *Rochefter*, was made Bifhop of *Chichefter*.

Sir *Robert Bowes* was appointed to be made Mafter of the *Rolls*.

Commandment was given **to** the Treafurers, that nothing of the **Subsidy fhould** be difburfed **but** by Warrant from the Board ; and **likewife for** our *Lady-day* Revenues.

14. The Baron of the *Exchequer*, upon the furrender made by Juftice *Lecifter*, was made Chief-Juftice, the Attorney Chief-Baron, the Sollicitor-General Attorney, and the Sollicitor of the Augmentation, *Cofnold*, General-Sollicitor, and no more Sollicitor to be in the Augmentation Court. Alfo there were appointed eight Serjeants of the Law againft *Michaelmafs* next coming.

Gaudy.
Stamford.
Carell, &c.

16. The Mufter was made of all the Men at Arms faving 50 of Mr. *Sadlers*, 25 of Mr. Vicechamberlains, and 25 of Sir *Philip Hobbey's*, and alfo of all the Penfioners.

17. The Progrefs was appointed to be by *Dorchefter* to *Pool* in *Dorfetfhire*, and fo through *Salifbury* homeward to *Windfor*.

18. It was appointed Mony fhould be cried down in Ireland after a Pay, which was of Mony at *Midfummer* next; in the mean feafon the thing to be kept fecret and clofe. Alfo the Pirry, the Mintmafters, taking with him Mr. *Brabazon*, chief Treafurer of the Realm, fhould go to the Mines and fee what profit may be taken of the Oar the *Almains* had digged in a Mine of Silver; and if it would quit coft, or more, to go forward withal, if not, to leave off and difcharge all the *Almains*.

Alfo that of 500 of the 2000 Souldiers there being, fhould be cut off, and as many more as would go and ferve the French King, or the Emperor, leaving fufficient at Home, no Fortifications to be made alfo yet for a time, in no place unfortified; and many other Articles were concluded for *Ireland*.

20. Sir *Richard Wingfield, Rogers,* and ————* were appointed to view the State of *Portfmouth*, and to bring again their Opinions concerning the fortifying thereof.

4. The French King having paffed the Straits of *Lorrain*, came to *Savern* four miles from *Strafburg*, and was victualled by the Country, but denied paffage through their Town.

21. Anfwer came from the *Foulcare*, That for the deferring of 30000 *l.* parcel of 45 Troas, he was content; and likewife *August Pyfo*, he might have paied him 20000 *l.* as foon as might be.

22. It was appointed, that forafmuch as there was much diforder on the Marches on *Scotland*-fide, both in my Fortifications of fome Places, and negligent looking to other Forts, the Duke of *Northumber-*

---

* Blank in original.

land, general Warden thereof, should go down and view it, and take order for it, and return home with speed.   Also a pay of 10000 *l.* to go before him.

23. It was appointed that these Bands of Men of Arms should go with me this Progress.

Lord Treasurer	30	Lord Admiral	15
Lord Great Master	25	Lord *Darcy*	30
Lord Privy-Seal	30	Lord *Cobham*	20
Duke of *Suffolk*	25	Lord *Warden*	20
Earl of *Warwick*	25	Mr. Vicechamberlain	15
Earl of *Rutland*	15	Mr. *Sadler*	10
Earl of *Huntingdon*	25	Mr. *Sidney*	10
Earl of *Pembrook*	50		

26. It was appointed that *Thomas Gresham* should have paied him out of the Mony that came of my Debts 7000 *l.* for to pay 6800 *l.* the last of the month, which he received the same Night.

28. The same *Thomas Gresham* had 9000 *l.* paid him toward the paiment of 20000 *l.* which the *Foulcare* required to be paied at the Pass-mart, for he had taken by Exchange from hence 5000 *l.* and odds, and 10000 *l.* he borrowed of the *Scheits*, and ten of *Lazarus Tukkar*. So there was in the whole 25, of which was paid the last of *April* 14, so there remained 11000, and 9000 *l.* which I now made over by Exchange, which made 20000 *l.* to pay the *Foulcare* with.

30. I received Advertisement from Mr. *Pickering*, that the French King went from *Savern* to *Aroumasshes*, which was yielded to him; from this to *Leimsberg*, and so towards *Spires*, his Army to be about 20000 Footmen, and 8000 Horsemen, well appointed, besides Rascals. He had with him 50 pieces of Artillery, of which were 26 Cannons, and six Organs, and great number of Boots.   From *Leimsberg*, partly doubting Duke *Maurice*'s meaning, partly for lack of Victual; and also because he had word that the Regent's Army, of which were Guides the Count *de Egmont*, *Monsieur de Rie*, **Martin** *Vanrouse* and the Duke of *Holest*, to the number of 16000 Footmen, and 6000 Horsemen, had invaded *Champaign*, and fortified *Aschenay;* he retired homeward till he came to *Striolph*, and there commanded all unprofitable Carriage and Men should depart to *Chalons*, and sent to the Admiral to come to him with 6000 *Swissers*, 4000 Frenchmen, 1500 Horsemen, and 30 pieces of Ordnance, meaning, as it was thought, to do some enterprise about **Luxemberg**, or to recover *Aschenay* which the Regent had fortified.

There died in this Journey 2000 Men for lack of good Victual; for eight days they had but Bread and Water, and they had marched 60 Dutch miles at the leaft, and paft many a Streight, very painfully and labourfomly.

19. Duke *Maurice* coming from *Aufpurg* in great haft, came this day to the firft Paffage called the *Clowfe*, which the Emperor had caufed to be ftrongly fortified and victualled, a paffage through an Hill, cut out artificially in the way to *Infpurg*, and there was a ftrong Bulwark made hard by it, which he wan, after a long fight within an hour and an half by Affault, and took and flew all that were within. And that Night he marched through that Hill into a Plain, where he looked for to fee twelve Enfigns of *Lanfknights* of his Enemies, but they retired to the fecond Streight, and yet divers of them were both flain and taken; and fo that Night he lodged in the Plain, at the entry of the fecond Paffage, where there were five Forts and one Caftle, which with Ordnance flew fome of Duke *Maurice*'s Men.

20. This morning the Duke of *Mecklenburg*, with 3000 Footmen, caft a Bridg over a River five miles beneath the Sluce, and came and gave Affault behind the Sluce, and Duke *Maurice* gave Affault in the Face, and the Country-men of *Tirol*, for hate of the *Spaniards*, helped Duke *Maurice*, fo that five Forts were won by Affault, and the Caftle yielded upon condition to depart, not to serve in three months after the Emperor. In this Enterprise he flew and took 3000 and 500 Perfons, and 23 pieces of Artillery, and 240000 S.

The Emperor hearing of this, departed by Night from *Infbpruk*, forty miles that Night in Poft; he killed two of his Gennets, and rode continually every Night, firft to *Brixinium*; and after, for doubt of the Cardinal of *Ferrara*'s Army, turned to *Villucho* in *Carinthia*. The 30*th* of *May*, tarrying for the Duke *d'Alva*, who fhould come to him with 2000 Spaniards, and 3000 Italians that came from *Parma*. Alfo the Emperor delivered Duke *Frederic* from Captivity, and fent him through *Bohemia* into *Saxony*, to raife a Power against Duke *Maurice*'s Nephew.

22. Duke *Maurice*, after that *Hala* and divers other Towns about *Infbpruk* in *Tirol* had yielded, came to *Infbpruk*, and there caufed all the Stuff to be brought to the Market-place, and took all that pertained to Imperialifts as confifcate, the reft he fuffered the Townfmen to enjoy. He took there fifty pieces of Ordnance, which he conveied to *Aufburg*, for that Town he fortified, and made it his Staple of Provifion.

Certain **Things** which the Commiſſioners for the Requeſts ſhall not meddle withal.

Firſt, Suits for Lands.

Secondly, **Suits for** Forfeits, amounting to more than 40 *l.* value.

Thirdly, **Suits for** Penſions.

Fourthly, Reverſions of Farms, which have more than **one Year to come.**

Fifthly, Leaſes of Manours.

Sixthly, **Leaſes for** more than **21 Years.**

Seventhly, **No** offices of ſpecial **Truſt** in Reckonings of Mony, as Cuſtomers, Comptrollers, **Surveyors, Receivers,** Auditors, Treaſurers, and Chancellors, *&c.* to be given **otherwiſe** than *durante beneplacito.* Alſo all Mint-Maſters, and others that **have a** doing in the Mint, and ſuch-like. The Biſhops, **Judges,** and other Officers of Judgment, *quam diu ſe bene geſſerit.* Balliwicks, Stewardſhips, keeping of Parks and **Houſes,** *&c.* to be granted during Life.

Eighthly, Suits **for forgivement of Debts.**

Ninthly, Releaſing of **Debts to be paid.**

Tenthly, **Suits for Mony, to** the intent to pay **Debts they owe elſe**where.

Eleven, Suits **to buy Land.**

Twelve, **Suits for Licenſes, to** carry over Gold, Silver, Lead, Leather, **Corn,** Wood, *&c.* that be things unlawful.

Thirteen, Unreſidence **upon Beneſices.**

They ſhall meddle with Baliewicks and Stewardſhips, during Leaſes for **21 Years;** Forfeits under 40 *l.* Receiverſhips, Woodwardſhips, **Surveyorſhips,** *&c.* during **pleaſure.** Inſtalments of days for Debts. To thoſe Gentlemen that **have** well-ſerved, Fee-Farms to them and their Heirs **Males** of their **Body, paying** their Rent, and diſcharging the Annuities **due to** all Officers touching the ſame. Keeping of Houſes and **Parks,** ordinary Offices, **as Yeomen of** the Crown, the Houſhold **Offices,** *&c.*

June.

2. Sir *John Williams,* who was committed to the *Fleet* for diſobeying a Commandment given **to** him for not paying any Penſions, without not making my Council **privy,** upon his ſubmiſſion was delivered out of Priſon.

4. *Beaumont* Maſter of the *Rolls,* did confeſs his Offences, who in his Office of Wards had **bought** Land with my Mony, had lent it, and kept it from Me, to the value of 9000 *l.* and above, more than

this twelve month, and 11000 in Obligations, how he being Judg in the *Chancery* between the Duke of *Suffolk* and the Lady *Powis*, took her Tittle, and went about to get it into his Hands, paying a Sum of Mony, and letting her have a Farm of a Manour of his, and caufed an Indenture to be made falfly, with the old Duke's counterfeit Hand to it; by which he gave these lands to the Lady *Powis*, and went about to make twelve Men perjured. Alfo how he had concealed the Felony of his Man to the Sum of 200 *l.* which he ftole from him, taking the Mony into his own hand again. For thefe Confiderations he furrendered into my Hands all his Offices, Lands, and Goods, moveable and unmoveable, toward the paiment of this Debt, and of the Fines due to thefe particular Faults by him done.

6. The Lord *Paget*, Chancellor of the Dutchy, confeffed how he, without Commiffion, did fell away my Lands and great Timber-Woods; how he had taken great Fines of my Lands, to his faid particular Profit and Advantage, never turning any to my Ufe or Commodity; how he made Leafes in Reverfion for more than 21 Years. For these Crimes, and other-like recited before, he furrendred his Office, and fubmitted himself to those Fines that I or my Council would appoint to be levied of his Goods and Lands.

7. *Whaley*, Receiver of *York-fhire*, confeffed how he lent my Mony upon Gain and Lucre; how he paied one Years Revenue over, with the Arrearages of the laft; how he bought mine own Land with my own Mony; how in his Accompts he had made many falfe Suggeftions; how at the time of the fall of Mony, he borrowed divers Sums of Mony, and had allowance for it, after by which he gained 500 *l.* at one crying down, the whole Sum being 2000 *l.* and above. For thefe and fuch-like Confiderations he furrendred his Office, and fubmitted to Fines which I or my Council fhould affign him, to be levied of his Goods and Lands.

8. The Lords of the Council fat at *Guild-Hall* in *London*, where in the prefence of a thoufand People, they declared to the Mayor and Brethren their floathfulnefs in fuffering unreafonable prices of Things and to Craftfmen their willfulnefs, &c. telling them, That if upon this Admonition they did not amend, I was wholly determined to call in their Liberties as confifcate, and to appoint Officers that fhould look to them.

10. It was appointed that the Lord *Gray* of *Wilton* fhould be par- doned of his Offences, and delivered out of the *Tower*.

Whereas Sir *Philip Hobbey* fhould have gone to *Calais* with Sir

Richard Cotton, and *William Barnes* Auditor, it was appointed Sir *Anthony St. Legier*, Sir *Richard Cotton*, and Sir *Thomas Mildmay*, fhould go thither, carrying with them 10000 *l.* to be received out of the *Exchequer*.

Whereas it was agreed that there fhould be a **Pay now** made to *Ireland* of 5000 *l.* and then the Mony to be cried down, it was appointed that 3000 weight which I had in the *Tower*, fhould be carried thither, and coined at 3 **Denar.** fine; and that incontinent the Coin fhould be cried down.

12. Becaufe *Pirry* tarried here for the Bullion, *William Williams* Effay-Mafter was put in his place, to view the Mines with Mr. *Brabazon*, or him whom the **Deputy** fhould appoint.

13. *Banefter* and *Crane*, the one for his large confeffion, the other becaufe little Matter appeared againft him, were delivered out of the *Tower*.

16. The Lord *Paget* was brought into *Star-Chamber*, and there declared effectuoufly his fubmiffion by word of Mouth, and delivered it in writing.

Beaumont who had before made his Confeffion in writing, began to deny it again; but after being called before my Council, he did confefs it again, and there acknowleged a Fine of his **Land**, and figned an Obligation in furrender of all his Goods.

17. *Monfieur de Couriers* took his leave.

2. The French **King** won the Caftle of *Rohdemae*. Certain Horfemen of the Regents came and fet upon the **French** King's Baggage, and flew divers of the Carriers, but at length, with fome lofs of the Frenchmen, they were compelled to retire. The French King won *Mount St. Ann*.

4. The French King came to *Deuvillars*, which was a ftrong Town, and befieged it, making three Breaches.

12. The **Town** was yielded to him, with the Captain. He found in it 2500 **Footmen**, 200 Horfemen, 63 great Brafs-pieces, 300 Hagbuts of Croke, much victual, and much Ammunition, as he did write to his Ambaffador.

19. It was appointed that the Bifhop of *Durham*'s Matter fhould ftay till the end of the Progrefs.

20. *Beaumont* in the *Star-Chamber* confeffed, after a little fticking upon the Matter, his Faults, to which he had put to his Hand.

22. It was agreed that the Bands of Men of Arms, appointed to Mr. *Sidney*, Mr. *Vicechamberlain*, Mr. *Hobbey*, and Mr. *Sadler*, fhould not be furnifhed, but left off.

Journal of Edward the Sixth.

25. It was agreed, that none of my Council should move Me in any Suit of Land for Forfeits above 20 *l.* for Reversion of Leases, or other extraordinary Suits, till the State of my Revenues were further known.

15. The French King came to a Town standing upon the River of *Mosa*, called *Yvoire*, which gave him many hot Skirmishes.

18. The French King began his Battery to the Walls.

14. The Townsmen of *Mountmedy* gave a hot Skirmish to the French, and slew *Monsieur de Toge*'s Brother, and many other Gentlemen of the Camp.

12. The Prince of *Salerno*, who had been with the French King to treat with him touching the Matter of *Naples*, was dispatched in Post with this Answer, That the French King would aid him with 13000 Footmen, and 1500 Horsemen in the French Wages, to recover and conquer the Kingdom of *Naples*; and he should marry, as some said, the French King's Sister, Madam *Margaret*. The Cause why this Prince rebelled against the Emperor, was, partly the uncourteous handling of the Viceroy of *Naples*, partly ambition.

The Flemings made an Invasion into *Champaign*, in so much that the *Dolphin* had almost been taken; and the Queen lying at *Chalons*, sent some of her Stuff toward *Paris*.

Also another Company took the Town of *Guise*, and spoiled the Country.

22. *Monsieur de Tallie* was sent to raise the Arrierbands and Legionars of *Picardy* and *Champaign*, to recover *Guise*, and invade *Flanders*.

27. Removing to *Hampton-Court*.

30. It was appointed that the Statds should have this Answer, That those Clothes which they had bought to carry over to the Sum of 2000 Clothes and odd, should be carried at their old Custom, so they were carried within six weeks; and likewise all Commodities they brought in till our *Lady-day* in Term next, in all other Points, the old Decree to stand, till by a further Communication the Matter should be ended and concluded.

The Lord *Paget* was licensed to tarry at *London*, and there-abouts, till *Michaelmass*, because he had no Provision in his Country.

26. Certain of the Heraulds, *Lancaster* and *Portcullis*, were committed to Ward, for counterfeiting *Clarencieux* Seal to get Mony by giving of Arms.

23. The French King having received divers Skirmishes of the Townsmen, and chiefly two: in the one, they slew the French Light-

horfe, lying in a Village by the Town ; in the other, they entred into the Camp, and pulled down Tents ; which two Skirmifhes were given by the Count of *Manffield* Governour of the Town. And the Duke of *Luxemburg* and his 300 Light-horfe, underftanding by the Treafon of four Priefts, the weakeft part of the Town, fo affrighted the Townfmen and the Flemifh Souldiers, that they by threatnings, compelled their Captain the Count, that he yielded himfelf and the Gentlemen Prifoners, the Common-Souldiers to depart with white Wands in their Hands. The Town was well Fortified, Victualled, and Furnifhed.

24. The Town of *Mountmedy* yielded to the French King, which before had given a hot Skirmifh.

July.

4. Sir *John Gates* Vicechamberlain was made Chancellor of the Dutchy.

7. Removing to *Oatlands*.

5. The Emperor's Ambaffador delivered the Regent's Letter, being of this effect; That whereas I was bound by a Treaty with the Emperor, made *Anno* Dom. 1542, at *Dotrecht*, That if any Man did Invade the two Countries, I fhould help him with 5000 Footmen, or 700 Crowns a day during four Months, and make War with him within a Month after the Requeft made ; and now the French King had invaded *Luxemberg*, defiring my Men to follow the effect of the Treaty.

7. The Names of the Commiffioners was added, and made more, both in the Debts, the Surveying of the Courts, the Penal Laws, &c. and becaufe my Lord Chamberlain, my Lord Privy-Seal, Mr. Vicechamberlain, and Mr. Secretary *Petre*, went with Me this Progrefs.

8. It was appointed that 50 poundweight of Gold fhould be coined after the new Standard, to carry about this Progrefs, which maketh 150 *l. Sterling.*

9. The Chancellor of the *Augmentation* was willed to furceafe his Commiffion, given him in the third Year of our Reign.

3. *Monfieur de Boffy,* Grand Efcuyer to the Emperor, was made General of the Army in the *Low-Countries,* and *Monfienr de Prat* over the Horfemen.

10. It was appointed here, that if the Emperor's Ambaffador did move any more for Help or Aid, this Anfwer fhould be fent him by two of my Council, That this Progrefs-time my Council was difperfed, I would move by their Advife, and he muft tarry till the Matter were

concluded, and their Opinions heard. Also I had committed the Treaty to be confidered by divers learned Men, &c. And if another time he would press Me, then anfwer to be made, That I trufted the Emperor would not wifh Me, in thefe young Years, having felt them fo long, to enter into them. How I had Amity fworn with the French King, which I could not well break; and therefore if the Emperor thought it fo meet, I would be a Mean for a Peace between them, but not otherwife. And if he did prefs the Treaty, laftly to conclude, That the Treaty did not bind Me which my Father had made, being againft the profit of my Realm and Country; and to defire a new Treaty to be made between Me and the Emperor in the laft Wars. He anfwered, That he marvelled what We meant, for we are bound, quoth the Emperor, and not You. Also the Emperor had refufed to fulfil it divers times, both in not letting pafs Horses, Armour, Ammunition, &c. which were provided by Me for the Wars. As alfo in not fending Aid upon the Forraging of the Low-Country of *Calais*.

12. A Letter was written to Sir *Peter Meutas*, Captain of the Ifle of *Jerfey*, both to command him that *Divine Service* may there be ufed as in *England*; and alfo that he take heed to the Church Plate that it be not ftollen away, but kept fafe till further Order be taken.

9. The French King came to the Town *Aveins* in *Hainault*, where after he had viewed the Town, he left it, and befieged a Pile called *Tirlokbut*; the Bailiff of the Town perceiving his departure, gave the Onfet on his Rereward with 2000 Footmen, and 500 Horfemen, and flew 500 Frenchmen. After this, and the winning of certain Holds of little force, the French King returned into *France*, and divided his Army into divers good Towns to reft them, becaufe divers were fick of the Flux, and fuch other Difeafes, meaning fhortly to increafe his Power, and fo to go forward with his Enterprife.

12. *Frederick* Duke of *Saxony* was releafed from his Imprifonment, and fent by the Emperor into his own Country, to the great rejoicing of all the Proteftants.

5. The Emperor declared, That he would none of thefe Articles to which Duke *Maurice* agreed, and the King of the *Romans* alfo. The Copy of them remaineth with the Secretary *Cecil*.

Marquefs *Albert* of *Brandenburg* did great harm in the Country of *Franconia*, burnt all Towns and Villages about *Norimberg*, and compelled them to pay to the Princes of his League 200,000 Dollars, ten of the faireft pieces of Ordnance, and 150 Kintalls of Powder. After that he went to *Frankfort*, to diftrefs certain Souldiers gathered there for the Emperor.

15. Removing to *Guildford*.

20. Removing to *Petworth*.

23. The Anfwer was made to the Emperor's Ambaffador, touching the Aid he required, by Mr. *Wotton*, and Mr. *Hobbey*, according to the firft Article *supra*.

24. Becaufe the number of Bands that went with Me this Progrefs made the Train great, it was thought good they fhould be fent home, fave only 150 which were pickt out of all the Bands. This was, becaufe the Train was thought to be near 4000 Horfe, which were enough to eat up the Country, for there was little Meadow nor Hay all the way as I went.

25. Removing to *Londre*, Sir *Anthony Brown's* Houfe.

27. Removing to *Halvenaker*.

30. Whereas it had been before devifed, that the New Fort of *Barwick* fhould be made with four Bulwarks; and for making of two of them, the Wall of the Town fhould be left open on the Enemies fide a great way together, (which thing had been both dangerous and chargeable) it was agreed the Wall fhould ftand, and two Slaughter-houfes to be made upon it to fcour the outer Courtins; a great Rampier to be made within the Wall, a great Ditch within that, another Wall within that, with two other Slaughter-Houfes, and a Rampier within that again.

26. The Flemings entred in great numbers into the Country of *Terovenne*; whereupon 500 Men of Arms arofe of Frenchmen, and gave the Onfet on the Flemings, overthrew them, and flew of them 1435, whereof were 150 Horfemen.

31. It was appointed, on my Lord of *Northumberland's* Requeft, that he should give half his Fee to the Lord *Wharton*, and make him his Deputy-Warden there.

Auguft.

2. Removing to *Warblington*.

3. The Duke of *Guife* was fent into *Lorrain*, to be the French King's Lieutenant there.

4. Removing to *Waltham*.

8. Removing to *Portfmouth*.

9. In the morning I went to *Chaterton's* Bullwark, and viewed alfo the Town; at afternoon went to fee the Store-houfe, and there took a Boat and went to the wooden Tower, and fo to *Hafelford*. Upon viewing of which things, it there was devifed two Forts to be made upon the entry of the Haven; one where *Ridley's* Tower ftandeth,

upon the Neck that maketh the Camber; the other upon a like Neck ſtanding on the other fide the Haven, where ſtood an old Bullwark of Wood. This was deviſed for the ſtrength of the Haven. It was meant, that that to the Town-fide ſhould be both ſtronger and larger.

10. *Henry Dudley* who lay at *Portſmouth*, with a warlike Company of 140 good Soldiers, was ſent to *Guiſnes* with his Men, becauſe the Frenchmen aſſembled in theſe Frontiers in great numbers.

Removing to *Tichfield*, the Earl of *Southampton*'s Houſe.

14. Removing to *Southampton*.

16. The French Ambaſſador came to declare how the French King meant to ſend one that was his Lieutenant in the Civil Law, to declare which of our Merchants Matters have been adjudged on their ſide, and which againſt them, and for what Conſideration.

16. Removing to *Beuleu*.

The French Ambaſſador brought News how the City of *Siena* had been taken by the French-ſide on St. *James*'s day, by one that was called the Count *Perigliano*, and other Italian Soldiers, by Treaſon of ſome within the Town; and all the Gariſon of the Town, being Spaniards, were either taken or ſlain. Alſo how the *Mareſchal Briſac* had recovered *Saluzzo*, and taken *Verucca*. Alſo how *Villebone* had taken *Turnaham* and *Mountreville* in the Low-Countrey.

18. Removing to *Chriſt-Church*.

21. Removing to *Woodlands*.

In this month, after long Buſineſs, Duke *Maurice* and the Emperor agreed on a Peace, but Marqueſs *Albert* of *Brandenburg* would not conſent thereto, but went away with his Army to *Spires* and *Worms*, *Colen* and *Treves*, taking large ſums of Mony of all Cities which he paſſed, but chiefly of the Clergy. Duke *Maurice*'s Souldiers perceiving Marqueſs *Albert* would enter into no Peace, went almoſt all to the Marqueſs's Service; among which were principal the Count of *Manſ-felt*, Baron *Haydeke*, and a Colonel of 3000 Footmen, and 1000 Horſe-men, called *Reiffenberg*; So that of 7000 which ſhould been ſent into *Hungary* againſt the Turks, there remained not 3000. Alſo the Duke of *Wittenberg* did ſecretly let go 2800 of the beſt Souldiers in *Germany*, to the Service of Marqueſs *Albert*, ſo that his Power was now very great.

Alſo in this month the Emperor departing from *Villachia*, came to *Inſbruk*, and ſo to *Monaco*, and to *Auguſta*, accompanied with 8000 Spaniards, and Italians, and a little Band of a few ragged *Almains*. Alſo in this month did the Turks win the City of *Tameſino*, in *Tranſil-*

vania, and **gave** a Battel to the **Chriſtians**, in which **was** ſlain Count *Pallavicino*, and **7000** Italians and Spaniards. Alſo in **this** Month did the Turks Navy take the Cardinal **of** *Trent*'s two Brethren, and ſeven Gallies, and had in chaſe 39 other. Alſo **in this** month did the Turks **Navy Land** at *Terracina* in the Kingdom of *Naples*; and the Prince of *Salerno* ſet forward with 4000 Gaſcoins, and 6000 Italians; **and the** Count *Perigliano* brought to his Aid 5000 Men of thoſe that were at the Enterpriſe **of** *Siena*. Alſo the *Mareſchal Briſac* won a **Town** in **Piedmont** called *Buſſac*.

24. Removing to *Saliſbury*.

26. Upon **my** Lord of *Northumberland*'s return **out of the** North, it **was** appointed for the better ſtrengthening **of the** Marches, that no one Man ſhould **have** two offices; **and that** Mr. *Sturley*, Captain of *Barwick*, ſhould leave the **Wardenſhip** of the Eaſt Marches to the Lord **Evers**; and upon the **Lord Coniers** reſignation, the Captainſhip of the Caſtle of *Carliſle* was appointed to Sir ——— *Gray*, and the Wardenſhip of the Weſt-Marches to Sir *Richard Musgrave*.

27. Sir Richard *Cotton* made Comptroller of the Houſehold.

28. Removing **to** *Wilton*.

30. Sir **Anthony** *Archer* was appointed to be Marſhal of *Calais*, **and** Sir *Edward Grimſton* Comptroller of *Calais*.

22. The Emperor **being at** *Auguſta*, did baniſh two Preachers **Pro-****teſtants** out of *Auguſta*, **under** pretence that they preached ſeditiouſly, and left *Mecardus* the chief Preacher, and ſix other Proteſtant Preachers in the Town, giving the Magiſtrates **leave** to chuſe others in their place **that** were baniſhed.

29. The Emperor cauſed eight Proteſtant Citizens of the Town to be baniſhed, of them that went **to** the Fair at *Lintz*, under pretence, that they taking Marqueſs *Albert*'s **part**, would not abide his Preſence.

September.

2. Removing to *Wotiſſunt*, my **Lord** *Sandes* Houſe.

5. **Removing to** *Wincheſter*.

7. From thence to *Baſing*, my Lord Treaſurer's Houſe.

10. And ſo to *Donnington*-Caſtle beſides the Town of *Newbery*.

12. And ſo to *Reading*.

15. To *Windſor*.

16. *Stuckley* being lately arrived out of *France*, declared, how that the French King being wholly perſuaded that he would never return again into *England*, becauſe he came away without leave, upon the apprehenſion of the Duke of *Somerſet* his old Maſter, declared to him

his Intent, That upon a Peace made with the Emperor, he meant to befiege *Calais*, and thought furely to win it by the way of *Sandhills*, for having *Ricebank* both to famifh the Town, and alfo to beat the Market-Place; and asked *Stuckley*'s Opinion: When *Stuckley* had anfwered, he thought it impoffible. Then he told him that he meant to Land in *England*, in an Angle thereof about *Falmouth*, and faid, the Bullwarks might eafily be won, and the People were papiftical; alfo that *Monfieur de Guife* at the fame time fhould enter into *England* by *Scotland*-fide, with the Aid of the Scots.

19. After long reafoning it was determined, and a Letter was fent in all hafte to Mr. *Morifon*, willing him to declare to the Emperor, That I having pity, as all other Chriftian Princes fhould have, on the Invafion of Chriftendom by the Turk, would willingly join with the Emperor, and other States of the Empire, if the Emperor could bring it to pafs in fome League againft the Turk and his Confederates, but not to be aknown of the French King, only to fay, That he hath no more Commiffion, but if the Emperor would fend a Man into *England*, he fhould know more. This was done on intent to get fome Friends. The Reafonings be in my Defk.

21. A Letter was fent only to try *Stuckley*'s Truth to Mr. *Pickering*, to know whether *Stuckley* did declare any piece of this Matter to him. *Barnabe* was fent for home.

23. The Lord *Gray* was chofen Deputy of *Calais* in the Lord *Willowby*'s place, who was thought unmeet for it.

24. Sir *Nicholas Wentworth* was difcharged of the Porterfhip of *Calais* and one—*Cotton* was put into it. In confideration of his Age, the faid Sir *Nicholas Wentworth* had 100*l.* Penfion.

26. Letters were fent for the difcharge of the Men of Arms at *Michaelmafs* next following.

27. The young Lords Table was taken away, and the Mafters of Requefts, and the Serjeants of Arms, and divers other extraordinary Allowances.

26. The Duke of *Northumberland*, the Marquefs of *Northampton*, the Lord Chancellor, Mr. Secretary *Petre*, and Mr. Secretary *Cecil*, ended a Matter at *Eaton*-College, between the Mafter and the Fellows; and alfo took order for the amendment of certain fuperfluous Statutes.

28. Removing to *Hampton-Court*.

29. Two Lawyers came from the French King to declare what things had paffed with the Englifhmen in the King's Privy-Council;

what and why **againſt** them, and **what was now** in doing, and **with** what diligence. Which when they had eloquently declared, they were referred to *London*, where there ſhould ſpeak **with** them Mr. Secretary **Petre**, Mr. *Wotton*, and Sir *Thomas Smith*; whereby then was declared the **Griefs of** our Merchants, which came to **the** Sum of 50000 *l.* **and upwards;** to which they **gave little** anſwer, **but that they would** make Report when they came home, becauſe **they had yet no Commiſſion, but only to declare** us the Cauſes of things **done.**

The firſt day of this month the Emperor departed from *Auguſta* towards *Ulmes*; and thanking the Citizens for their stedfasſt ſticking to him in theſe perrilous Times, he paſſed by them to *Straſburg*, accompanied only with 4000 Spaniards, 5000 Italians, 12000 Almains, and 2000 Horſmen, and thanking alſo them of *Strasburg* for their goodwill they bore him, that they would not let the French King come into their Town, he went to *Weyſenberg*, and ſo to *Spires*, and came thither the 23*d* of this month. Of which the French King being advertiſed, ſummoned an Army to *Metz*, and went thitherward himſelf; ſent a Pay of three months to Marqueſs *Albert*, and the Rhinegrave and his Band; alſo willing him to ſtop the Emperor's Paſſage into theſe Low-Countries, and to fight with him.

27. The Matter of the Debatable was agreed upon, according to the laſt inſtructions.

26. Duke *Maurice*, with 4000 Footmen and 1000 Horſemen, arrived at *Vienna* againſt the Turks.

21. Marqueſs *Hans* of *Brandenburg*, came with an Army of 13000 Footmen, and 1500 Horſemen, to the Emperor's Army; and many Almain Souldiers encreaſed his Army wonderfully, for he refuſed none.

October.

3. Becauſe I had a pay of 48000 *l.* to be paid in *December*, and had as yet but 14000 beyond Seas to pay it withal, the Merchants did give me a Loan of 40,000 *l.* to be paid by them the laſt of *December*, and to be repaied again by Me the laſt of *March*. The manner of levying this Loan was of the Clothes, after the rate of 20*s.* a Cloth, for they carried out at this Shipping 40000 Broad-Clothes. This Grant was confirmed the 4*th* day of this month, by a company aſſembled of 300 Merchant-Adventurers.

2. The Bullwarks of Earth and Boards in *Eſſex*, which had a continual allowance of Souldiers in them, were diſcharged, by which was ſaved preſently 500 *l.* and hereafter 700 or more.

4. The Duke *D'Alva*, and the Marquefs of *Margina*, fet forth with a great part of the Emperor's Army, having all the Italians and Spaniards with them, toward *Treves*, where the Marquefs *Albert* had fet ten Enfigns of Launce-Knights to defend it, and tarried himfelf with the reft of his Army at *Landaw* befides *Spires*.

6. Because Sir *Andrew Dudley*, Captain of *Guifnes*, had indebted himfelf very much by his Service at *Guifnes*; alfo becaufe it fhould feem injurious to the Lord *Willowby*, that for the Contention between him and Sir *Andrew Dudley*, he fhould be put out of his Office, therefore it was agreed, That the Lord *William Howard* fhould be Deputy of *Calais*, and the Lord *Gray* Captain of *Guifnes*.

Alfo it was determined that Sir *Nicholas Sturley* fhould be Captain of the new Fort at *Barwick*, and that *Alex. Brett* fhould be Porter, and one *Roksby* fhould be Marfhal.

7. Upon report of Letters written by Mr. *Pickering*, how that *Stuckley* had not declared to him, all the while of his being in *France*, no one word touching the Communication afore fpecified; and declared alfo how Mr. *Pickering* thought, and certainly advertifed, that *Stuckley* never heard the French King fpeak no fuch word, nor never was in credit with him, or the Conftable, fave once, when he became an Interpreter between the Conftable and certain Englifh Pioneers, He was committed to the *Tower* of *London*.

Alfo the French Ambaffador was advertifed how we had committed him to Prifon, for that he untruly flandered the King our good Brother, as other fuch Runnagates do daily the fame. This was told him, to make him fufpect the Englifh Runnagates that be there. A like Letter was fent again to Mr. *Pickering*.

8. *Le Seigneur de Villandry* came in Poft from the French King with this Meffage. Firft, That although Mr. *Sidney's* and Mr. *Winter's* Matters, were juftly condemned; yet the French King, becaufe they both were my Servants, and one of them about me, was content *gratuito* to give Mr. *Sidney* his Ship, and all the Goods in her; and Mr. *Winter* his Ship, and all his own Goods. Which Offer was refufed, saying, We required nothing *gratuito*, but only Juftice and Expedition. Alfo *Villandry* declared, That the King his Mafter, wifhed that an Agreement were made between the Ordinances and Cuftoms of *England* and *France* in Marine Affairs. To which was anfwered, that our Ordinances were nothing but the Civil Law, and certain very old Additions of the Realm; That we thought it reafon not to be bound to any other Law than their old Laws, which had

been of long time continued, and no fault found with them. Also *Villandry* brought forth two new Proclamations, which for things to come were very profitable for *England*, for which he had a Letter of Thanks to the King his Master. He required also Pardon and Releasement of Imprisonment for certain Frenchmen taken on the Sea-Coast. It was shewed him they were Pirats: Now some of them should by Justice be punished, some by Clemency pardoned; and with this Dispatch he departed.

11. *Horne* Dean of *Durham* declared a secret Conspiracy of the Earl of *Westmoreland*, the Year of the apprehension of the Duke of *Somerset*, How he would have taken out Treasure at *Midleham*, and would have robbed his Mother, and sold 200 *l*. Land; and to please the People, would have made a Proclamation for the bringing up of the Coin, because he saw them grudg at the fall. He was commanded to keep this Matter close.

6. Mr. *Morison*, Ambassador with the Emperor, declared to the Emperor the Matter of the Turks before specified; whose Answer was, He thanked us for our gentle Offer, and would cause the Regent to send a Man for the same purpose, to know our further meaning in that behalf.

11. Mr. *Pickering* declared to the French King, being then at *Rhemes*, *Stuckley's* Matter of Confession, and the Cause of his Imprisonment: Who after protestation made of his own good Meaning in the Amity, and of *Stuckley's* Ingratitude toward him, his lewdness and ill-demeanour, thanked Us much for this so gentil an uttering of the Matter, that we would not be led with false Bruites and Tales.

The Bishop *Tunstal* of *Durham* was deprived of his Bishoprick.

In this month *Monsieur de Rue*, *Martin Rossen*, and an Army of Flemings, while the French had assembled his Men of War in *Lorrain* had sent the Constable to the Army, which lay four leagues from *Verdun*, the Duke *de Guise* with 7000 Men to *Metz*, and the *Mareschal St. Andrew* at *Verdeun*, razed and spoiled, between the River of *Some* and *Osse*, many Towns, as *Noyon*, *Roy*, *Chamy*; and Villages, *Nelle*, *Follambray*, a new built House of the King's, &c. insomuch that the French King sent the Admiral of *France* to help the Duke of *Vendosme* against that Army.

There was at this time a great Plague that reigned in sundry parts of *France*, of which many Men died.

20. A Man of the Earl of *Tyrones* was committed to the *Tower*, because he had made an untrue Suggestion and Complaint against the

Deputy and the whole Council of *Ireland*. Also he had bruited certain ill Bruites in *Ireland*, how the Duke of *Northumberland*, and the Earl of *Pembrook* were fallen out, and one againſt another in the Field.

17. The Flemings, and the Engliſhmen that took their parts, aſſaulted by Night *Hamletue;* the Engliſhmen were on the Walls, and ſome of the Flemings alſo ; but by the cowardiſe of a great part of the Flemings, the Enterprize was loſt, and many Men ſlain. The number of the Flemings were 4000, the number of the men within *Hambletue* 400. The Captain of this Enterpriſe was *Monſieur de Vandeville* Captain of *Gravelin*.

6. *Monſieur de Boiſſey* entred *Treves* with a Flemiſh Army, to the number of 12000 Footmen, and 2500 Horſemen, Burgunions, without any reſiſtance, because the Enſigns there left by Marqueſs *Albert* were departed ; and thereupon the Duke *d' Alva*, and the Marqueſs of *Marion*, marched toward *Metz* ; the Emperor himſelf, and the Marqueſs *Hans* of *Brandenburg*, hauing with him the reſt of his Army, the ninth day of this month departed from *Landaw* towards *Metz*. *Monſieur de Boiſſey's* Army also joined with him at a place called *Swayburg*, or *Deuxpont*.

23. It was agreed, that becauſe the State of *Ireland* could not be known without the Deputy's preſence, that he ſhould, in this dead time of the year, leave the governance of the Realm to the Council there for the time, and bring with him the whole State of the Realm, whereby ſuch order might be taken, as the ſuperfluous Charge might be avoided, and alſo the Realm kept in quietneſs, and the Revenue of the Realm better and moſt profitably gathered.

25. Whereas one *George Paris* an Iriſhman, who had been a practiſer between the Earl of *Deſmond* and other Iriſh Lords, and the French King, did now, being weary of that Matter, practiſe means to come home, and to have his old Lands in *Ireland* again. His Pardon was granted him, and a Letter written to him from my Council, in which he was promiſed to be confidered and holpen.

There fell in this month a great Contention among the Scots, for the *Kers* flew the Lord of *Balcleugh*, in a Fray in *Edinburgh;* and as ſoon as they had done, they aſſociated to them the Lord *Home* and all his Kin : But the Governour thereupon ſummoned an Army to go againſt them ; but at length, because the Dowager of *Scotland* favoured the *Kers* and *Homes*, and ſo did all the French Faction, the French King having alſo ſent for 5000 Scotch Footmen, and 500 Horſemen for his Aid in thefe Wars, the Governour agreed the 5000 Footmen under the leading of the Earl of *Caffils;* and 500 Light-Horfemen, of which the *Kers* and the *Homes* fhould be Captains, and go with such hafte into *France,* that they might be in fuch place as the French King would appoint them to ferve in, by *Chriftmafs,* or *Candlemafs* at the furtheft. And thus he trufted to be well rid of his moft mortal Enemies.

27. The Scots hearing that *George Paris* practifed for Pardon, committed him to Ward in *Striveling*-Caftle.

25. *Monfieur de Rue* having burnt in *France* eighteen leagues of length, and three leagues in breadth ; having pillaged, and facked, and razed the fair Towns of *Noyon, Roy, Nelle,* and *Chamy,* the King's new Houfe of *Follambray,* and infinite other Villages, Bullwarks, and Gentlemens Houfes in *Champaign* and *Picardy,* returned into *Flanders.*

23. The Emperor in his Person came to the Town of *Metz* with his Army, which was reckoned 45000 Footmen, as the Bruit went, and 7000 Horfemen. The Duke *d' Alva* with a good Band went to view the Town ; upon whom iffued out the Souldiers of the Town, and flew of his Men about 2000, and kept him play till the main force of the Camp came down, which caufed them to retire with lofs. On the French Party was the Duke of *Nemours* hurt on the Thigh. There was in the Town as Captain, the Duke of *Guife;* and there were many other great Lords with him, as the Prince of *Rochfurion,* the Duke *de Nemours,* the Vicedam of *Chartres, Pietro Stozzy, Monfieur Chaftilion,* and many other Gentlemen.

November.

5. *Monfieur de Villandry* returned to declare, how the King his Mafter did again offer to deliver four Ships againft which Judgment has paffed. He said, the King would appoint Men to hear our Merchants at *Paris,* which fhould be Men of the beft fort. He said likewife, how the King his Mafter meant to mend the Ordinance, of which Amendment he brought Articles.

7. Thefe Articles were delivered to be considered by the Secretaries.

9. Certain were thought to be fought out by feveral Commiffions ; *viz.* Whether I were juftly answered of the Plate, Lead, Iron, *&c.* that belonged to Abbeys ? Whether I were juftly anfwered the Profit of Alome, Copper, Fuftians, *&c.* which were appointed to be fold ? and of fuch Land as the King my Father fold, and such-like Articles.

12. *Monsieur Villandry* received anfwer for the firft Article, as he did before, How I meant not by taking freely fo few, to prejudice the rest. For hearing of our Merchants Matters at *Paris*, by an inferior Council, We thought both too dilatory after thefe long Suits, and also unreafonable, becaufe the inferior Council would undoe nothing (though caufe appeared) which had been before judged by the higher Council. And as for the New Ordinances, we liked them in effect as ill as their Old, and defired none other but the Old accuftomed ones which have been ufed in *France* of late Time, and to be yet continued between *England* and the *Low-Country*. Finally, we defire no more Words, but deeds.

4. The Duke *d' Aumail* being left in *Lorrain*, both to ftop the Emperor's Provifion, to annoy his Camp, and to take up the Straglers of the Army, with a Band of 400 Men of Arms, which is 1200 Horfe, and 800 Light-Horfe, hearing how Marquefs *Albert* began to take the Emperor's part, fent firft certain Light-Horfe to view what they intended. Thofe Avan-Couriers lighted on a Troop of 500 Horfe-men, who drove them back till they came to the Duke's Perfon; Whereupon the Skirmifh grew fo great, that the Marquefs with 12000 Footmen, and 1000 Horfemen, came to his Mens fuccours, fo the Duke's Party was difcomfited, the Duke himfelf taken and hurt in many places; *Monfieur de Roan* was alfo flain, and many other Gen-tlemen flain and taken. This Fight was before *Toul*, into which Fort efcaped a great part of the Light-Horfe.

6. *Heading* Town and Caftle was taken by the *Monfieur de Reux*; The Caftle was reckoned too well ftored of all things, and rendred either by Cowardice or Treafon. The Battery was very fmall, and not fuitable. The moft was, that the Captain, *Monfieur Feulis*, was, with one of the firft fhots of the Cannon, flain, and his Lieute-nant with him.

In this month *Ferdinando Gonzaga* befieged St. *Martins* in *Piedmont*.

18. There was a Commiffion granted out to Sir *Richard Cotton*, Sir *John Gates*, Sir *Robert Bowes*, and Sir *Walter Mildmay*, to examine the account of the fall of Mony, by the two Proclamations.

20. The Lord *Ogle* leaving the Wardenfhip of the Middle Marches, becaufe my Lord *Evers* Land lay there, he was made Deputy-Warden there, with the Fee of 600 Merks; and Sir *Thomas Dacres* of the Eaft Marches, with the Fee of 500 Merks.

24. *Thomas Grefham* came from *Antwerp* hither, to declare how *Monfieur de Langie*, Treafurer to the Emperor, of *Flanders*, was fent to

him from the Regent with a certain Pacquet of Letters which the Burgonions had taken in *Bullonois*, coming from the Dowager of *Scotland*: The Effect whereof was, How she had committed *George Paris* the Irish-man to Prison, because she had heard of his meaning to return into *England*; how she had found the Pardon he had, and divers other Writings; and how she had sent *O-Coners's* Son into *Ireland*, to comfort the Lords of *Ireland*. Also he shewed certain Instructions, *Anno* 1548, upon the Admiral's fall, given to a Gentleman that came hither, That if there were any here of the Admiral's Faction, he should do his uttermost to raise an Uproar.

29. Henry *Knowls* was sent in Post into *Ireland* with a Letter, to stay the Deputy, if he met him, in *Ireland*, because of the Business; and that he should seem to stay for his own Affairs, and prolong his going from Week to Week, lest it be perceived. Also he had with him certain Articles concerning the whole state of the Realm, which the Deputy was willed to answer.

30. There was a Letter of Thanks written to the Regent, and sent to Mr. Chamberlain, to deliver for the gentle Overture made to *Thomas* Gresham by the Treasurer *Langie*. He was also willed to use gentle words in the delivery of the Letters, wishing a further Amity: And for recompence of her Overture, to tell her of the French King's practice, for 5000 Scotch Footmen, and 500 Horsemen. And also how he taketh up by Exchange at *Lubeck* 100000 *l.* whereby appeareth some meaning that way the next Spring.

20. The Lord *Paget* was put to his Fine of 6000 *l.* and 2000 *l.* diminished to pay it within the space of—Years, at days limited.

Here the Journal ends, or if more was written by the King, it is lost.

Finis.

"Inter folia fructus."

LEX TALIONIS;

OR,

A Declamation against Mr Challener,

THE CRIMES OF THE TIMES AND THE MANNERS OF
YOU KNOW WHOM.

1647.

"History is but the Unrolled Scroll of Prophecy."
—James A. Garfield.

PRIVATELY PRINTED
FOR THE CLARENDON HISTORICAL SOCIETY.

1885.

This edition is limited to 120 *large paper and* 400 **small paper copies,** *for* Subscribers only.

LEX TALIONIS;

OR,

A Declamation
against
Mr Challener,

THE CRIMES OF THE TIMES, AND
THE MANNERS OF YOU
KNOW WHOM.

In quo quis peccat, in eo punitur.
—— *Nec Lex est justior ulla,*
Quam necis artifices arte perire sua.

Judges I. vers. 7.

" *And Adonibezek said, As I have done, so God hath requited me.*

Printed in the Yeare, 1647.

A
Declamation against Mr Challener,

THE CRIMES OF THE TIMES, AND THE MANNERS OF YOU KNOW WHOM.

WHAT *Cicero* said to *Cataline*, and his confederates in their Conspiracie, I say the same to Master *Challener*, that hee may tell it to his companions in the covenant,—

Quousq, tandem abutére patientiâ nostrâ?

It must never be forgotten how those venerable women came in simplicity of heart to the Parliament at *Westminster* to sue for Peace.

It must never be forgotten to all Posterity in what measure those innocent Women were dealt withall by you; some being cruelly wounded, some most barbarously slaine.

Will not the bloud of my Lord of *Stafford;* nor the bloud of my Lord of *Canterbury;* nor the bloud of *Tomkins* and *Challener;* nor the bloud of *Yeomans* and *Boucher;* nor all the innocent bloud of so many thousands, which have been sacrificed in these late intestine broyles, provoke you to seeke Peace, nor invite you to embrace Peace, when it is so freely offered unto you. O *Tempora!* O *Mores!*

In the sharp language of *Cicero* I did begin with you, in the blunt honestie of *Cato* I intend to proceed.

As the base and spungie offal of man (being the common sewer of indigested excrements) can by no means returne backe any nourishment into the more nobler part, the stomache, from whence it first received it; no more can the body possibly subsist and live without the influence **and distillation from its** native and proper **head.**

And **as in the bodies Natural, so in** Politick, King *Charles* is the **essential head, of our Politique** Body. **He** is the true **Lord and owner of these his Kingdomes by** right of Inheritance. **He** holds his **title in Fee-simple, by the blessed** *Tenour in Capite,* **from God Almighty, who is** *Lord Paramount* **of all. To** God alone is the **King onely** obliged **to pay his Homage, and** oweth not the smallest *quitrent* whatsoever **to** my Lord Chancellor of *Scotland,* his *Machivillian* eloquence, nor to Mr *Challener* his home-spun slovenly malice.

It is **a** bold assertion between **you** both, **to** enter into a saucy dispute **about** the disposing of **the sacred person of the** King, as if he were a Child, a Ward, or an Ideot. When God can beare him witnesse, Hee hath more Wit, more Judgement, and more Honestie in Him, **then any of** you all, or all of you together.

Here **let me interpose** with my short, **and true definition of him, both as he is a man, and** as he is our King : **As he is a man, me thinks I** heare my **Saviour saluting** him, as he did *Nathanael, Behold a man indeed in whom there is no guile.* And **all the world** that knows him must acknowledge with the poet, He is *Homo intiger vita, sceleris*q. *purus,* and I wish to God, from my heart I could say the same of any of you.

Now **as** he is our King, how can both Houses, as M. *Challener* saith, **or how** can both kingdoms, as my Lord Chancellor of *Scotland* would have it, dare to take upon them to dispose of him, who hath under God the sole disposall of us all, with this limitation, with the joynt consent, and wholesome advice of the honest and great Councell of each kingdome, and this is both Law and Gospell.

Inconsistent **and** incompatible are two very good words, if rightly applyed, but I am bound to beleeve the Devill himselfe did work very strongly upon Master Challener's weaknesse, rather than that his owne naturall *genius* could be possest with such malignancy of spirit as to make so wilde, so **base,** and so ungodly an application of them both.

I **had** almost forgotten that remarkable badge of your through Reformation, I meane your Covenant, and the two notorious Committees **of** both kingdoms : Give me leave to tell you what your

Covenant was at first, and what it now is; It was at first by vertue of Inchantment, a lowsie thread-bare *Scotch* Chaplin, who growing wearie of the slender stipend of a bare *Scotch* mark *per annum* came over into England to seek its further Advancement, where it became a Sub-preacher, and so rendering itselfe incapable of holy Orders, did take upon it to preach and teach on its own accord.

The first attempt by which this covenant sought to ingratiate itself into the people, was by consummating a marriage betwixt the two Committees of both Kingdomes. The march was privately contracted in the close Committee, and afterwards solemnly published by legislative power, which marriage being thus accomplished without the approbation of his matie, without the Licence of our Church, and without the consent of our Laws, I doubt not it may easily be made null by a bill of divorce, and for the farther punishment of this Inchanted Chaplaine your Covenant, let it be banished out of this Kingdome for ever, and let it be consigned to the utmost part of Scotland, there to pine and waste itself away upon its owne dunghill, or else let it be presently torne in pieces, in remembrance of the dispite which was lately done to the King's broad Seal in the presence of both Houses.

And whereas Mr Challener saith, the Houses are accomptable to none but God Almighty, I must answer him with these few questions.

Who called or caused you to be a Parliament? Was it not by the Soveraigne power of the King?

Who convened the House of Commons together? Was it not the free suffrages, and elections of the people? Can the servants be greater then their Masters?

Did the King and we conferre this trust and authority upon you, thus to lord it over us? I tell you nay; for unlesse you speedily returne unto your wonted Allegiance to his Maiestie, and your dutifull affections towards us, both he and wee shall suddainly call you to a strict accompt.

Read over the Chronicles, where you shall find two Knights of the Shire were called to an accompt by the Counties, for which they had formerly served in Parliament; and both of them were hanged up for their labours.

What, are you so transported and puffed up with pride by reason of your many successes you have lately gotten in your new Modell of

War? Must you needs stand upon your tiptoes, and think you dance in a net? Doe but tell me of one Ordinance you have made which speakes the least sillable tending to a Reformation?

The King hath made an absolute Reformation of all abuses done under his Government, and like a gracious Prince gave us a Trienniall Parliament to boote. But a Trienniall Parliament will not serve your turnes, you must needs have an everlasting Parliament, *quis talia fando temperet a lacrimis;* for with horror I speak it, as you have handled the matter, nothing stands so much in neede of a thorough Reformation as your everlasting Parliament. For if the King and you should be reconciled to-morrow; and that He and you should joyn together to governe us by an everlasting Parliament: We whose Ancestors have ever been the freest subjects under Heaven should be come the meer'st slaves upon the face of the earth.

Beware of *Lex talionis.*

To explain my selfe, I never did heare nor read of any Prince, any great man, nor any great body of a Councell, dare to do any act illegall or extrajudiciall. But God Almighty did either retaliate with his owne immediate vengeance, or else they were met withall by the knowne laws of the Land, in a condigne punishment.

Sir *John Hotham* and his son have tasted of the one already; and take you heed least some, if not all of you, doe not at last feele the smart of the other.

Felix quem faciunt aliena pericula cautum.

To prevent the like ensuing dangers which must needs fall upon our heads, I will give you these three remarkable examples of *Lex Talionis.*

1. In the dayes of K. *Henry* the 8. the Lord Chancellor *Cromwell* perswaded the King, that by vertue of his prerogative, he might put any man to death, and bring it to tryall at law afterwards, and did not the same *Lex talionis* light upon him, when he was the onely man that did so?

2. *Barnavill*,[*] the Chiefe Advocate of *Holland*, and one of the States, conceived a displeasure against a younker, and nothing would serve his turne (though it were in his owne cause) but corporall punishment. The priviledge of the Gentleman's birth was pleaded by his lawyers; notwithstanding *Barnavill* being prevalent with the Board of States, perswaded them: It would be an addition to their greatnesse

---

[*] Barneveld.

to make a President in this kinde, and so a President was made, and the Gentleman was whipt.

Not long after a competition grew betwixt the Prince of *Orange*, and great *Barnavill*, wherein the Prince, having the Military party of his side, got the better of him, so that *Barnavill* was confined; and by that same rule of *Barnavill's* formerly made a President, to whip that Gentleman, a President was made to cut off his head; ther's *Lex talionis* for him.

3. My Lord of *Strafford*, when he was Sir *Thomas Wentworth*, and oracle of the House of Commons, perswaded them, that there was no other way to cut off the Duke of *Buckingham*, but by accusing him of States suggestions, under the name of high Treason; by which meanes if they could once sequester him from the King's elbow by confinement; He doubted not but accusations would come enough against him, to his further destruction, and did not the same *Lex talionis* light upon him. *Jam proximus ardet Ucaligon*. It is high time, then, for every man severally, and all of us together joyntly, to looke about us, Least *Lex talionis* overtake us.

The degenerate House of Lords have altogether declined their true fountain of Honour, the King, from whose cleare streames they had wont to suck both their honour and honestie, by his vertuous example. And these pittifull Lords, having throwne themselves into Mire and Muddy Affections of the Common Rabble, are now glad to drink of the puddle water of Scorne, and Contempt from the meanest Rascalls; Ther's *Lex talionis* in part for them.

The adulterate House of Commons have so deviated from the honest principles and integrity of their ancestors, and having left their righteous middle way; in which they had wont to walke in; Tire themselves out with halting between two cripples, two contraries of extreames: for which their black consciences, they are forc'd to sit down, some leaning to the Presbyterian madnesse on the one side; some to the Independent folly on the other; Ther's *Lex talionis* in part for them.

The proud Metropolis of this Kingdome, the City of *London* of all other escape Scot-free, for this Citie hath beene from the beginning the venerable Bawd of all the Parliament's designes. It hath fed them with million upon million, upon the publike faith, by which meanes it manifesteth itselfe to be the chiefe fomenter of this unnaturall War, and the grand Abettor in this unhappy difference betwixt King and people.

It is still fresh in memorie, how this City sent forth its spurious scum in multitudes to cry downe Bishops, roote, and branch, who like sholes of Herrings, or swarmes of Hornets, lay hovering about the Court with lying Pamphlets, and scandalous Pasquills, untill they forc'd the King from his throne, and banisht the Queene from his Bed, and afterwards out of his Kingdome; besides this Citie still continues to this day dancing attendance with their Traine bands, to guard the causelesse feares, and jealousies of both Houses: they **come** creeping with their Petitions to them, whom they might command: would they but command their Bands to stay at home, they may **thank** themselves for all the delayes, and denyalls, they have received.

What guerdon hath this City got for all its costs and paine? I will tell it, This citie is stiled in the world's opinion, the *Parliament's Asse*, on whose backe the members of both Houses ride at pleasure, laying on load upon load, what they think fit. Now good City, if you must continue still to be an Asse learne of your Predecessor. *Balaam's* Asse, and tell your great masters, they have gone astray, tell them so freely, for they dare not beate you for it as *Balaam* did.

Oh my poore countrey, miserable countrey, wretched countrey, **that** hath these five years past in innocence, drunk of the bitter cup, the dregs whereof is reserved in store by *Lex talionis* for the stupid, senselesse city of *London*. *If thou hadst known, even thou, at least in this thy day, the things which belong unto thy peace! but now they are hid from thine eyes.* Luk. 19, vers. 42.

Much might be said concerning the Prince Elector, but little shall serve the turne, *Si ingratum dixeris, omnia.* He hath gotten the repute of late to become a precious babe of grace, by his princely faculty of snuffing up the back breath of the Reverend Synod, and in a blind devotion takes it for incense. He, good man, not considering his Royal Unkle, nor his owne peculiar interest, which we might justly challenge to him else in *Germany*, but contents himselfe here with my Lord *Peter's* whole estate.

Hitherto have we seen what hath betyded others, and we cannot chuse but fore-see what must betide us, unlesse we betake ourselves to a speedy and preventing Remedy; Loe here it is.

(1.) Let all things be restored in *Statu quo prius*.

(2.) Let the *Scots* in the name of God, or the Devill that sent them goe home.

(3.) **Let** King *Charles* (**in** spite of Mr *Challener*) with honour and safety **come** home, that every one of us may live quietly at home, and this I am sure is very consistent with the honour of God, and very compatible with the safety and tranquillity of the nation.

Salus Regis, et Salus Reipublicae are not only twins, but *Gemini*, inseparable and individuall; Cursed be those that have hitherto divided them, and blessed be they who seek to cement, and re-unite them together.

Three things have been the bane of Monarchie.
1. First, Weekely Lectures.
2. Corporations.
3. Trained-bands.

And Three Things will be the baine of Anarchy.
1. First, your New Modell of Religion.
2. Your New Modell of Government.
3. Your New Broad Scale.

Let three things be undone by you which have undone us all, and the King shall grant us three things in lieu of them, which shall re-make us.

The Three Things to be undone by You.
1. First, Let your Close Committee, and *Legislative* Power which sits in the Chaire thereof (contrary to Law) be damn'd for ever.
2. Let all the Cavaleers be freed from their illegall Sequestrations.
3. Let your black Propositions which you lately sent to the King be recal'd back, and burnt by the Hangman.

Three things which the King is to doe.
1. That His Majestie will be pleased to renew, ratifie, and enlarge our Petition of Right.
2. That he will grant you an *Act of oblivion*.
3. That he will re-marry His Royall Prerogative, and *Magna Charta* together. *Then seeke peace, and ensue it, and the God of peace will grant it.* Now that we may avoid those numbers three, which we find to be ominous, and embrace those numbers three which are propitious; Let us apply ourselves to that blessed number three which is in Heaven: and let not your illiterate Synod dare to meddle with that any more, by any audacious disputation; but rather let us all appeale to him, by an humble Adoration: That so that blessed Trinitie in unitie may grant Peace to every man's conscience in particular, Peace to the whole Kingdome in generall, and Peace and joy eternall to us hereafter.

Farewell Mr Challener.

A Letter to the Army.

How can you expect an Act of Indemnity? *So long as* **the King** *remaines in* **Captivity,** *the Parliament cannot grant it unto you, for they cannot* **give it to** *themselves.*

How can you expect money? when you know the Parliament **hath been so prodigall in the distribution of such** *large Proportions to one* **another,** *that they have little left to reward you withall.*

Is it liberty of conscience you speak for? **That** *you know rests onely in the* **Kings breast.**

Restore the King **to** *the Throne againe, and all these things shall be added to you.*

If you neglect this faire opportunitie, the vengeance of **God** *shall dogge you at the heeles. Instead of a Trophie for all your Victories, you shall render your-* **selves slaves to the** *Presbyterian Bondage, who like the* Egyptian Task- masters **shall compell you to make** Brick **in their full tale,** *and without giving you stubble.*

To whom then will you fly for succour? **God will abominate** *you, and will not help* **you;** *man (especially)* Englishmen) *will scorne you, and laugh* **at your** *misery.*

Behold, I have **set** this day before your eyes, *Honour,* and *Dishonour,* being the two **sole** Rewards of all humane Actions. Consider this **timely,** and be wise.

Be it unto you according to your **merit.**

Finis.

"Inter Folia Fructus."

GALLIENUS REDIVIVUS;

OR,

Murther Will Out, &c.,

BEING A TRUE ACCOUNT OF THE

DE-WITTING OF GLENCOE, GAFFNEY, &c.

"History is but the Unrolled Scroll of Prophecy."
—James A. Garfield.

PRIVATELY PRINTED
FOR THE CLARENDON HISTORICAL SOCIETY.
1885.

This edition is limited to 120 large paper and 400 small paper copies, for Subscribers only.

GALLIENUS REDIVIVUS;

OR,

Murther Will Out, Etc.,

Being a True Account of the

DE-WITTING

OF

GLENCOE, GAFFNEY, &c.

They gave out that the design of their Coming was to introduce Liberty, and depose Tyrants: But having gain'd the Power, They did so Tyrannize Themselves, That the Reign of Former Oppressors seem'd a Golden Age, if compar'd with the Arbitrariness and Exaction of these pretended Deliverers; which made the Sicilians think them much more happy, who Expir'd in Servitude, than those who liv'd to see such a Dismal Freedom.

—*Plutarch. Life of Timoleon.*

Printed at Edinburgh, in the Year 1695.

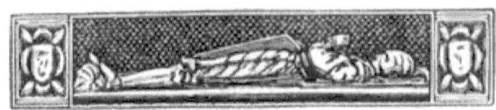

A Letter from a Gentleman in Scotland to his Friend at London, who desir'd a Particular Account of the Business of Glenco.

EDINBURGH, *April*. 20*th* 1692.

SIR,

THE Account you desir'd of that strange and surprizing Massacre of *Glenco* take as follows :—

Mac-jan Mac-donald, Laird of *Glenco*, a Branch of the *Mackdonalds*, one of the greatest Clans (or Tribes) in the North of *Scotland*, came with the most considerable Men of his Clan to Coll. *Hill*, Governour of *Fort William* at *Inverlochy*, some few days before the Expiring of the time for receiving the Indemnity appointed by Proclamation, which as I take it, was the First of *January* last, entreating he would administer unto him the *Oaths* which the foresaid Proclamation requir'd to be taken ; that so submitting himself to the Government, he might have its Protection. The Colonel receiv'd him with all Expressions of Kindness ; nevertheless shifted the administring the *Oaths* to him, alledging that by the Proclamation it did not belong to him, but to the Sheriffs, Bailyffs of Regalities, and Magistrates of Burghs, to administer them. *Mac-jan* Complaining that by this *Disappointment* he might be wrong'd, the Time being now near the Expiring, and the Weather so extreme, and the ways so very bad, that it was not possible for him so soon to reach any Sheriff, &c. got from Coll. *Hill*, under his Hand, his Protection ; and withal he was assur'd, that no Orders from the Government against him should be put in Execution, until he were first advertis'd, and had time allow'd him to apply himself to King or Council for his

103

Safety. But the better to make all sure, (tho' this might have seem'd Security enough for that time) with all dispatch imaginable he posted to *Inverary*, the Chief Town of *Argyleshire*, there he found Sir *Collin Campbel* of *Arakinlis*, Sheriff of that Shire, and crav'd of him the Benefit of the Indemnity, according to the Proclamation, he being willing to perform all the Conditions requir'd. Sir *Collin* at first scrupled to admit him to the Oaths, the Time which the Proclamation did appoint being elapsed by one day, alledging it would be of no use to him then to take them: But *Mac-jan* represented that it was not his Fault, he having come in time enough to Colonel *Hill*, not doubting but he could have administred the Oaths to him, and that upon his refusal he had made such hast to *Inverary*, that he might have come in time enough, had not the extremity of the Weather hinder'd him; and even as it was, he was but one day after the Time appointed; and that would be very unbecoming the Government to take Advantage of a Man's coming late by one Day, especially when he had done his utmost to have come in time. Upon this, and his threatning to protest against the Sheriff for the Severity of this Usage, he administred to him and his Attendants the Oaths, *Mac-jan* depending upon the Indemnity granted to those who should take them; and having so done, he went home, and lived quietly and peaceably under the Government, till the day of his Death.

In *January* last, a Party of the Earl of *Argile's* Regiment came to that Country: the Design of their coming was then suspected to be to take course with those who should stand out, and not submit, and take the Oaths. The Garison of *Inverlochy* being throng'd, and *Glenco* being commodious for quartering, as being near that Garison, those Soldiers were sent thither to Quarter; they pretended they came to exact Arrears of Cess and Hearth-Money, (a Tax never known in *Scotland*, until laid on by the Parliament, 1690, after the Parliament of *England* had eas'd themselves of it;) e'er they entred *Glenco*, that Laird, or his Sons, came out to meet them, and asked them if they came as Friends or as Enemies? The Officers answer'd as Friends; and gave their Paroll of Honour, that they would do neither him nor his Concerns any harm; upon which he welcom'd them, promising them the best Entertainment the Place could afford. This he really perform'd, as all the Soldiers confess. He and they lived together in mutual Kindness and Friendship fifteen days or thereabouts; so far was he from fearing any Hurt from them. And the very last Day of his Life he spent in keeping Company with the

Massacre of Glencoe.

Commander of that Party, Capt. *Campbell* of *Glenlyon*, playing at Cards with him till 6 or 7 at Night, and at their parting mutual Protestations of Kindness were renew'd. Some time that very day, but whether before or after their parting, I know not, Capt. *Campbell* had these Orders sent him from Major *Duncanson*, a Copy whereof I here send you.

"BALLACHOLIS, *Feb.* 12. 1692.
"SIR,
"You are hereby ordered to fall upon the Rebels the *Mac-Donalds* of *Glenco*, and put all to the Sword under 70. You are to have especial Care, that the Old Fox and his Sons do upon no account escape your Hands; You are to secure all the Avenues, that no Man escape : This you are to put in Execution at five a Clock in the Morning precisely, and by that time or very shortly after it, I'll strive to be at you with a stronger Party ; If I do not come to you at five, you are not to tarry for me, but to fall on. *This is by the King's SPECIAL COMMAND*, for the Good and Safety of the Country, that these Miscreants may be cut off, Root and Branch. See that this be put in Execution without Feud or Favour, else you may expect to be Treated as not true to the King or Government, nor a Man fit to carry Commission in the King's Service. Expecting you will not fail in the fulfilling hereof, as you love your self. I subscribe these with my Hand,
"ROBERT DUNCANSON.

"For Their Majesties Service, to Capt. *Robert Campbell* of *Glenlyon*."

Duncanson had receiv'd Orders from Lieutenant Collonel *Hamilton*, which were as follows.

"Ballacholis, Feb. 12, 1692.
"SIR,
"Per Second to the Commander in Chief, and my Collonel's Orders to me, for putting in Execution the Service commanded against the Rebels in Glenco, wherein you, with the Party of the Earl of Argyle's Regiment under your Command are to be concern'd:

You are therefore forthwith to order your Affairs so, as that the several Posts already assign'd you, be by you and your several Detachments fallen in Action with, precisely by five a Clock to morrow Morning, being Saturday; at which time I will endeavour the same with those appointed from this Regiment for the other Places. It will be most necessary you secure those Avenues on the South side, that the Old *Fox*, nor none of his Cubs get away. The Orders are that none be spar'd, from 70, of the Sword, nor the Government troubled with Prisoners. This is all, until I see you. From

"Your humble Servant,

"JAMES HAMILTON.

"Please to order a Guard to secure the Ferry, and the Boats there; and the Boats must be all on this side the Ferry, after your Men are over.

"For their Majesties Service, for Major *Robert Duncanson*, of the Earl of Argyle's Regiment."

The Soldiers being disposed five or three in a House, according to the Number of the Family they were to Assassinate, had their Orders given them secretly. They had been all receiv'd as Friends by those poor People, who intended no Evil themselves, and little suspected that their Guests were design'd to be their Murtherers. At 5 a Clock in the Morning they began their bloody Work, Surpris'd and Butcher'd 38 Persons, who had kindly receiv'd them under their Roofs. *Mac-jan* himself was Murther'd, and is much bemoan'd; He was a stately well-favour'd Man, and of good Courage and Sense: As also the Laird *Archintrikin*, a Gentleman of more than ordinary Judgment and Understanding, who had submitted to the Government, and had Coll. *Hill's* Protection in his Pocket, which he had got three Months before. I cannot without Horror represent how that a Boy about Eight Years of Age was murthered; he seeing what was done to others in the House with him, in a terrible Fright run out of the House, and espying Capt. *Campbell*, grasp'd him about the Legs, crying for Mercy, and offering to be his Servant all his Life. I am informed Capt. *Campbell* inclined to spare him; but one *Drummond*, an Officer, barbarously run his Dagger through him, whereof he died immediately. The rehearsal of several Particulars and Circumstances of this Tragical Story, makes it appear most doleful; as that *Mac-jan* was killed as he was drawing on his Breeches, standing before his Bed, and

Massacre of Glencoe.

giving Orders to his Servants for the good Entertainment of those who murthered him; While he was speaking the Words, he was shot through the Head, and fell dead in his Ladies Arms, who through the Grief of this and other bad Usages she met with, died the next day. It is not to be omitted, that most of those poor People were killed when they were asleep, and none was allowed to pray to *God* for Mercy. Providence ordered it so, that that Night was most boisterous; so as a Party of 400 Men, who should have come to the other End of the *Glen*, and begun the like work there at the same Hour, (intending that the poor Inhabitants should be enclosed, and none of them escape) could not march at length, until it was 9 a Clock, and this afforded to many an Opportunity of escaping, and none were killed but those in whose Houses *Campbell* and *Glenlyon's* Men were Quartered, otherwise all the Male under 70 Years of Age, to the number of 200, had been cut off, for that was the Order; and it might have been easily executed, especially considering that the Inhabitants had no Arms at that time; for upon the first hearing that the Soldiers were coming to the *Glen*, they had conveyed them all out of the way: For though they relyed on the promises which were made them for their Safety; yet they thought it not improbable that they might be disarmed. I know not whether to impute it to difficulty of distinguishing the difference of a few Years, or to the fury of the Souldiers, who being once glutted with *Blood*, stand at nothing, that even some above Seventy Years of Age were destroyed. They set all the Houses on Fire, drove off all the Cattle to the Garison of *Inverlochy*, viz. 900 Cows, 200 Horses, and a great many Sheep and Goats, and there they were divided amongst the Officers. And how dismal may you imagine the Case of the poor Women and Children was then! It was lamentable, past expression; their Husbands and Fathers, and near Relations were forced to flee for their Lives; they themselves almost stript, and nothing left them, and their Houses being burnt, and not one House nearer than six Miles; and to get thither they were to pass over Mountains, and Wreaths of Snow, in a vehement Storm, wherin the greatest part of them perished through Hunger and Cold. It fills me with horror to think of poor stript Children and Women, some with Child, and some giving Suck, wrestling against a Storm in Mountains, and heaps of Snow, and at length to be overcome, and give over, and fall down, and die miserably.

You see in *Hamilton's* Order to *Duncanson*, there's a special Caution,

*That the Old Fox **nor none** of his **Cubs** should escape;* and in *Duncanson's* Order to Capt. *Campbell* of *Glenlyon, That the old Fox **nor none of his Sons escape;*** but notwithstanding **all** this wicked Caution, it pleas'd God that **the** two **young** gentlemen, *Mac-jan's* Sons escap'd: For it happen'd that the younger of these Gentlemen trusted **little** to the **fair** promises of *Campbell*, and had **a** more watchful eye over him than his Father or Brother, who suffered themselves by his reiterated Oaths **to be** deluded into **a belief of his** Integrity: He having a strong Impression on **his** Spirit, that **some** mischievous *Design* was hidden under *Campbell*'s specious *Pretences*, it made him, after the rest were in Bed, remain in a retired Corner, where he had an advantagious Prospect into their Guard. About midnight perceiving several Souldiers to enter it, this encreased his Jealousy; so he went and communicated his Fears **to his Brother,** who could not for a long time be perswaded there was any bad *Design* against them, and asserted, **That** what he had seen, was not a doubling their Guards in order to any ill design, but that being in **a strange place**, and at a distance from the Garison, **they were to** send out **Centinels far** from the *Guard*, and because **of the Extremity** of the Weather relieved them often, and the Men **he saw could be** no more but these. Yet he persisting to say, That they **were not** so secure, but that it was fit to acquaint their Father with what he had seen, he prevailed with his Brother to **rise**, and go with **him to** his Father who lay in a Room contiguous to **that they** were in. Though what the younger **Son** alledged made no great Impression on **his** Father, yet he allowed his Sons to try what **they** could discover. **They** well knowing all Skulking places there, **went and hid** themselves near **to a** Centinel's Post, where instead of one **they** discovered **eight or ten** Men; this made them more inquisitive, **so** they crept **as near as** they could without being **discovered, so** near that they **could hear** one say to his Fellows, That **he liked not this Work,** *and that had **he** known of it he would have been very unwilling to **have** come there; but that **none**, except their Commanders, knew **of it until within a quarter of an hour.*** The Soldier added, That he was willing to fight against the Men of the *Glen*, but it was base to murder them. But to all this was answered, *All the blame be on such as gave the Orders; we are free, being bound to obey our Officers.* Upon hearing of these words the young Gentlemen retired as quickly and quietly as they could towards the House, to inform their Father of what they had heard; **but** as they came nigh to it, they perceived it surrounded, and heard Guns discharged, **and** the People shrieking; whereupon, being unarm'd, and totally unable to rescue their Father, they preserved their own Lives in hopes yet to serve their King and Country, and see Justice done upon those Hell-Hounds, treacherous Murtherers, the *Shame* of their Country, and *Disgrace* of Mankind.

I must not forget to tell you, That there were two of these officers who had given their Paroll of Honour to *Mac-jan*, who refused to be concerned in that *Brutal Tragedy*, for which they were sent Prisoners to *Glasco*, where if they remain not still, I am sure they were some Weeks ago.

Thus, Sir, in obedience to your Commands, I have sent you such Account as I could get of that monstrous and most inhuman Masssacre of the Laird of *Glenco*, and others of his *Clan*. You desire some Proofs of the truth of the Story; for you say there are many in *England* who cannot believe such a thing could be done, and publick Justice not executed upon the Ruffians: For they take it for granted, that no such order could be given by the Government; and you say they will never believe it without a downright Demonstration. Sir, As to the Government, I will not meddle with it; or whether these Officers who murdered *Glenco*, had such Orders as they pretended from the Government; the Government knows that best, and how to vindicate their own Honour, and punish the Murtherers who pretended their authority, and still stand upon it. But as to the Matter of Fact of the murder of *Glenco*, you may depend upon it, as certain and undeniable. It would be thought as strange a thing in *Scotland* for any Man to doubt of it, as of the death of my Lord *Dundee*, or with you that the Duke of *Monmouth* lost his Head. But to put you out of all doubt, you will e'er long have my Lord *Argyle*'s Regiment with you in *London*, and there you may speak with *Glenlyon* himself, with *Drummond* and the rest of the Actors in that dismal Tragedy; and on my Life, there is never a one of them will deny it to you; for they know that it is notoriously known all over *Scotland*, and it is an Admiration to us that there should be any one in *England* who makes the least doubt of it. Nay, *Glenlyon* is so far from denying it, that he brags of it, and justifies the Action publicly: He said in the Royal Coffee-House in *Edinburgh*, that he would do it again; nay, That he would stab any man in *Scotland* or in *England*, without asking the Cause, if the King gave him Orders, and that it was every good Subject's duty so to do; and I am credibly inform'd, that *Glenlyon* and the rest of them have address'd themselves to the Council for a Reward for their good Service, in destroying *Glenco*, pursuant to their Orders.

There is enough of this mournful Subject: If what I have said satisfy you not, you may have what farther Proof, and in what manner you please to ask it.

Sir,

Your Humble Servant, &c.

N.B. That the Gentleman to whom this Letter was sent, did on *Thursday, June* 30. 1692. when the Lord *Argyle*'s Regiment was quartered at *Brentford*, go thither, and had this Story of the Massacre of *Glenco* from the very Men who were the Actors in it: *Glenlyon* and *Drummond* were both there. The Highlander who told him the Story, expressing Guilt which was visible in *Glenlyon*, said, *Glenco* hangs about *Glenlyon* Night and Day, and you may see him in his Face. I am told likewise that Sir *John Lowther* refused to accept of the Place of Lord Advocate of *Scotland*, unless he might have liberty to prosecute *Glenlyon*, and the rest of the Murtherers of *Glenco*, which not being granted, *James* Stuart (who was forfeited for Treason by K. C. 2. and since Knighted by K. W.) has now the Place.

GALLIENUS REDIVIVUS;

OR,

Murther Will Out, &c.

THE fore going Account of the Barbarous Massacre of Glenco, was Printed in the year 1692. in the Answer to Dr. King's Book of the State of Protestants in Ireland: And all the Reception it met with among many here in England, was, That it was a Jacobite Story, on purpose to Reflect upon the Government, and that there was no such thing: But this is now confuted by the Proceedings of the Parliament in Scotland, this Summer Session, 1695. Wherein they have voted the killing of the Glenco-men to be a Murther; and yet have acquitted Sir Thomas Levingston, and Collonel Hill, who gave the Orders for Killing of them. Why? Because their Orders were but pursuant to the Instructions they had from Court. Where will this Lodge the Murther? The Design, it is well enough known, is to put it upon Sir John Dalrymple, commonly call'd Maister of Stair, one of the Secretaries for Scotland, because he is not so Fiery a Presbyterian as the other Secretary, James Johnston, who hath it by Inheritance to love Crown and Mitre alike; and to have a just Reward for it. But Dalrymple is only a Libertine, or Latitudinarian, One of the modern No-Religion, who are indifferent to All, so they be troubled with none. Therefore he cares not whether Episcopacy or Presbytery, or what else is set up, provided the People be easy with it.

Now it being known to all the World, That the Pretence of the Inclinations of the People in Scotland, which was made the Groundwork for abolishing Episcopacy, and setting up Presbytery there, was a mere **Sham**, contriv'd by this Johnston, and the BIGOT Presbyterian Party **in** Scotland; who **were** all put in Power, **in** the beginning of **this** Revolution; and **set on** the Barbarous Rabbling of the Episcopal Clergy in the West of Scotland, that **they might cry out,** The Inclinations of the People were against Episcopacy: And having, by these and other Arts (which are fully related **in Print**) Pack'd, and then surpriz'd the first Convention, or meeting of **Estates**, to Abolish Episcopacy: They dare not have a new Parliament (as **in** England) but keep on the same Convention (only changing the name into that of a Parliament) **to this** day: Because no Free Parliament can be had in Scotland, which **would** not the first day, spue out Presbytery, and Re-Establish **their much more** belov'd Episcopacy, and the People showing **great Un-easiness** under their present Establishment (which hath been **trick'd** and forc'd **upon** them), all the Craft and Violence of the Regnant Presbytery, assisted by Acts of Parliament, and all the Countenance of the Government, having not yet been able to **O**ust the Episcopal Clergy in the North, and other parts of Scotland, **or** prevail with the People to admit of, or **almost** give Civil Treatment **to** the Presbyterian Ministers **sent** to them, **tho'** Establish'd by Law. The Presbyterian Interest standing there upon so slender a bottom, their **Juncto** think it not safe to have a Man of **Dalry**mple's Latitude in Religion, in so eminent a Post, and near their **King;** lest he should follow **the** Inclinations of the People, in GOOD EARNEST, and Call a New Parliament there, which would ruine all **their** Measures: **Therefore ways** and means **must** be used to **Remove him;** and leave Johnston and the Presbyterian Faction in the **sole** Possession **of** the Court. At length, this of Glenco was pitched upon; which was so Odious, They knew their King durst not own it: And therefore they would throw it upon Dalrymple, who was Secretary, and attended when the instructions were sent for that Bloody Murther. And thereby **too,** They would seem to take off the Odium from their King; This was their pretence; and they had proof enough against Dalrymple: But how that Clear'd his Master will be seen.

They produced Nine Letters of Dalrymple's (of which I have Copies) concerning the Massacre of Glenco. And I shall have occasion **to** mention them hereafter; I will now set down their

Massacre of Glencoe.

several Dates, and Directions; and quote them to save repetition, only by their Number, Letter i. ii. iii. &c. The two first are directed to Lieutenant Collonel Hamilton, and bear Date, on the 1st, and the other the 3d. Decemb. 1691. The 4 next are to Sir Thomas Levingston of these several Dates, 7, 9, 11 and 16 of January 169½. Then follow two more to Collonel Hill, of the 16th and 30th of the same Month; And lastly one of the 30th Ditto, to Sir Thomas Levingston. It seems very strange that K. W. would suffer these Letters to be exposed to the Parliament in Scotland, being most of them wrote by his Order, enlarging upon, and enforcing the Execution of Instructions, sent with them for the Massacre of Glenco, &c. And the Regard which his Dear Presbyterians, and his Favourite Johnston, in particular, had to his Honour, was very slender, when, to compass their Ends, they load him so fouly, that they might load Dalrymple too. Johnston says, No, But that he foreseeing (because some say of his own Contriving) that the Parliament (who are most of them his Creatures, to their Honour be it spoken) would fall upon the Business of Glenco; and that they must be, at least seemingly Gratified in it, otherwise that it might obstruct the Money-Bills, did therefore, advise his Master to send down a Commission to men of his own choosing, to enquire into the affair of Glenco; but withal to give secret Instructions to his Commissioner, to keep up the said Commission, unless the Parliament should enter upon that Business. And if they did, then to produce the said Commission, to shew his Majesty's Innocence, by his Care to have it Examined; and withal, it would take the Examination of it out of the hands of Parliament Committees, who might not manage so dextrously, as those of his own naming.

Things being thus stated, and the necessary Orders given, it is vilely suspected, that Johnson procured the Matter to be started in Parliament, whereby, at once, to get rid of his Rival Secretary, and Root up the interest of any, who had but an indifferency towards Episcopacy at Court; though to the utter Shipwrack of his Master's Honour, to be Recorded for all Posterities (as if it were inseperable from some Constitutions to betray those they serve, even though they wish them well, and must stand and fall with them.) For considering the inflence Johnston had in that Parliament, and that they have never yet oppos'd his Will in any thing; and that he has been able to suppress the least Murmur, or Hint, that looked towards Glenco, when the Fact was New Committed; and the Horror of it fresh and **Bleeding**; and now for three years after: I say, It is not supposed by **men who** understand that **Parliament, that it** could have been brought upon **the** Stage, when it **was almost dead and** forgotten, if the hand **of Joab had** not been in it: but let him look to that. **I have only** to add, as a Completion **of the** fore-going Narrative, that **I can** from unquestionable Vouchers, give the Reader an Account of **the Orders from Court** to Sir Thomas Levingston, and Collonel Hill, **which** are not in the Letter that goes before; and when the Reader **is told that Hamilton** (whose Order to Duncanson is inserted) had his **Order from** Levingston, **and** Collonel **Hill**; then he has the whole **thread,** *viz.* **W. R.'s Order to** Levingston and **Hill**; Levingston and **Hill to Hamilton;** Hamilton to Duncanson; **and** Duncanson to Glenlyon, who was the butcher.

You find in the Gazettes **Two Sett of Instructions, one** of the **11th, the other of the 16th Jan. 169½ and I will** give you an **Account of them both.** Those of the 11th did expressly Order **FIRE and SWORD, [these were the words]** against all the **Highland-Clans,** who had **not taken** the Oaths. **After they were** sent away, my Lord Carmarthen **(now** Leeds) being **told of** it, by Dalrymple (as I am informed) did **represent it to K. W. as a** thing so **unknown** in these Countries, **which are Governed by** Laws, That **Fire and Sword** would sound very harshly; no such words having ever **been** heard from any of our Native Kings. This procured the mitigation **of that** order, by the Instructions of the 16th, which poured **all the Thunder** upon **Glenco;** because some **Sacrifice** must be made! **What concern'd Glenco was in the** 4th of these Instructions, and is **as follows :—**

WILLIAM R.

> *As for* MAC-IAN *of* GLENCO, *and that* TRIBE, *if they can be well distinguished from the* Rest *of the* High-Landers; *It will be proper for the Vindication* of *Publick Justice, to* EXTIRPATE *that Sett of Thieves.*
>
> W. R.

This was directed to **Sir** Thomas Levingston, and Collonel Hill. **And the Parliament has** voted that Levingston, or Hill's Orders did **not exceed these Instructions;** nor indeed could they: For what can **exceed EXTIRPATION!** And that to be Executed at the discre-

Massacre of Glencoe.

tion of Soldiers! As it is worded in the Secretary's Letter to Sir Tho. Levingston. "I am confident" (says he) "you will see there are full powers given you in very plain Terms, and yet the method left very much to your own discretion."[1]

Take Notice that these Instructions are Counter-sign'd W. R. at Bottom, as well as at Top, which is not usual: For it is the Secretary's Office to Counter-sign the King's Orders; and the Reason is, that if any thing be amiss, the Secretary must be answerable: Therefore Dalrymple had reason to waive that Ceremony, in this instance, and let his Master take all the Glory to himself. And lest this should not be sufficiently taken Notice of: and that he might have a Voucher, when time comes, he took care to inform Sir Tho. Levingston punctually of it, in the same Letter which enclosed the first most Bloody Instructions of the 11th Jan. 169½, for an Universal Massacre of All, who had not taken the Oaths. And begins in these words: "Sir, I send you the King's Instructions super and subscribed by Himself."[1] And to show how pleasing a thing Mercy was to them, and with what reluctancy they Prosecuted those who had not taken the Oaths, he says in the same Letter: "Just now Argyle tells me, That Glenco hath not taken the Oaths, at which I Rejoyce. It's a great work of Charity to be exact in Rooting out that Damnable Sect." And to shew how great this Charity was, and whence it proceeded, The Wise Secretary Blurts out these words; "I have no great kindness for Keppoch, nor Glenco, and it's well these People are in mercy." Well indeed! They were in merciful hands! Who can say they ought not to Die, for whom such a Secretary hath no GREAT Kindness! But who are they must die? ALL! ALL! Man, Woman, and Child! Massacre the Men, and Drive the Women and Children to perish more cruelly in the mountains. To which purpose, that extreme Cold Season was chosen for the Execution. "The Winter is the only Season (says the Secretary) in which we are sure the High-Landers cannot escape us, nor carry their Wives, Bairns, and Cattle to the Mountains."[2] "It's the only time they cannot Escape you; for Human Constitution cannot endure to be long out of Houses. This is the proper Season to maul them in the long cold Nights."[3] This was express'd with the Gusto of a Vulture, in expectation of a Glorious Massacre! And then how easy it would be! "I expect (says he) you will find little Resistance but from the season."[4]

---

[1] Letter 5.   [2] Letter 1.   [3] Letter 2.   [4] Letter 4.

And then what thorough work they would make? "To destroy entirely the Country of Lochaber, Lochells, Lauds, Keppoch's, Glengaries, Appin, and Glenco."¹ Here was a beautiful Feast provided! It was a Ravishing Prospect!

But O! how these Lyons were Enraged when any of their desired Prey was delivered out of their Jaws. It was in a mournful strain the Secretary tells the sad News. "We have an Account (says he) that Lochart, and Mac-naghton, Appin and Glenco took the benefit of the Indemnity at Inverary; and Keppoch, and others at Inverness:"² But after this, when Argyle told him that Glenco had not taken the Oaths; How did he Rejoyce! as above Quoted. "I am glad (says he) that Glenco did not come in within the time prescribed."³ "I am content that CLAN except itself."⁴ "For my part, I could have wished the Mac-donalds had not divided, (that is, that they had all excluded themselves from mercy) and I am sorry that Keppoch, and Mac-jan of Glenco are safe."² But it seems they were not safe. Some must be made a Sacrifice; and Glenco was pitched upon for the Victim. And the implacable Fury, which was shown against that Clan, expressed the Rage they felt, that so many had escaped them. And therefore that Clan was to be destroyed entirely. I assure you (says the Secretary to his Officers) your Power shall be full enough, and I hope the Soldiers will not trouble the Government with Prisoners."¹ "For a just Example of Vengeance, I entreat that the Thieving Tribe in Glenco may be rooted out in earnest."⁵ "I shall entreat you for a just Vengeance, and publick Example, the Thieving Tribe of Glenco may be rooted out to purpose. The Earl of Argyle and Broadalban have promised they shall have no Retreat in their Bounds; the Passes to Rannach would be secured, and the Hazard certified to the Laird of ——— to Retreat: Then in that Case Argyle's Detachment, with a Party that may be Posted in Island Stalker, must cut them off."⁶ "Pray when any thing concerning Glenco is resolved, let it be secret and sudden, otherwise the Men will shift you, and better not meddle with them than not to do it to purpose, to cut off that Nest of Robbers, who are fallen in the mercy of Law."³ "I am glad Glenco did not come in within the time Proscribed. I hope what is done there may be in earnest, since the rest are not in a

---

¹ Letter 3.   ² Letter 4.   ³ Letter 9.   ⁴ Letter 1.   ⁵ Letter 7.
⁶ Letter 8.

Condition to draw together to help. I think to herry their Cattle, or burn their Houses, is but to render them Desperate Lawless Men, to Rob their Neighbours: But I believe you will be satisfied it were a great Advantage to the Nation, That that Thieving Tribe were Rooted out, and Cut off. It must be Quietly done, otherwise they will make shift for both the Men and their Cattle. Argyle's Detachment lies in Keppoch well, to assist the Garrison to do all ON A SUDDEN." Was ever so greedy a Hunt after the Lives of a Company of Secure and Un-arm'd People, who slept fearless, and suspecting no danger, under the Protection of those who were thus Contriving to Massacre them, in the most Savage and Treacherous manner!

The Secretary tells Collonel Hill that "the Oaths are Indispensable."[1] This was a fearful Method of Imposing the Oaths upon these Highlanders, that none must live who would not take them! But were all admitted to take them? One would think so; when they were made Indispensable. Yet notwithstanding, in that same Letter, He gives these Directions to Coll. Hill. "Till we see what is done by the CHIEFS, it is not time to Receive their Tenants, or Admitting them to take the Oaths, or hoping for Pardon, 'till they give Evidence that they are willing to pay their Rents to you, and to take Tacks for their former Duties; who will not do so, and were in the Rebellion, must feel the dismal consequences of it."

Thus Naboth's Vineyard made him a Blasphemer! If the Tenants would betray the Rights of their Land-Lords to Atturn, and Pay their Rents to the Secretary, or his Governour, then, and not otherwise, They should be admitted to take the Oaths: And yet they must not live, if they did not take the Oaths: But Glenco took the Oaths; yet that sav'd not his Life, nor his Clan.

It were reasonable here to presume that K. W. did not know that they had taken the Oaths. First, If it had been so, This manner of Massacre, in Cold Blood had been a Cruelty without Precedent. Secondly, It was taking Advantage of the Time, with the Greatest Rigour. For the Time limited by the Indemnity expired but the 1st of January 169½. And the Instructions for a General Massacre were dated the 11th of the same Month, at London, which was hardly time enough to know whether he had taken the Oaths or not. But Thirdly, Here is no room left to surmise, that K. W. did not know it;

[1] Letter 7.

because **Secretary** Dalrymple (in **his Letter to Sir Thomas** Levingston, before Quoted, which is dated at **London the** 9th of January, 169½) tells him "That they had an Account that Glenco had taken the Oaths at Inverary;"[1] which was the Place where he did take them, as is told in the foregoing Narrative. And **he** tells Sir Thomas, **in the same** Letter: "I have been **with** the King. He says your Instructions shall be despatched **on Monday."** And they were so. **For that** Monday was the 11th of January, 169½ which day the Instructions do bear Date. And this **Letter** of the Secretary's was **Dated the** 9th of January 169½. which was the Saturday before. **And then** he tells Sir Thomas, "That he had the Account of Glenco's having taken the Oaths with several others; and that he had been with the King concerning it, and Instructions should be sent," &c. 'Tis true, his **Letter** of the 11th, which went with the Instructions, says, "That Argyle told him **Glenco had not taken** the Oaths."[2] But this **was no more than Hearsay;** and it was not true. For Glenco had taken the Oaths before that time; according to the Account which the Secretary own'd **was sent to him: And Argyle** was an enemy to Glenco, as appears **by what is above quoted out of Letter 7.** But this saying of Argyle's to the Secretary in London, could not be of Argyle's own Knowledge. **And one** would think that the Secretary of State should have as good **Intelligence as he.**

But, to make the **most of it, this** cou'd amount to **no more** than a Doubt. **And it was his duty** to Suspend his further Resolution, till he might have the **Certainty** from **Scotland.** But they did not stay for this. For the particular **Instructions to Massacre** Glencoe, bore Date the 16th **of January 169½, Betwixt which time and** the 11th. when Argyle told **the Secretary, as** above, "**They could** not send to Scotland, and have any **Answer back."** Now these Instructions of the 16th were no way **Conditional, to cut** off Glencoe, *if* **he had** not taken the Oaths. But **Positive, and without more ado.** When it is certain that K.W. Must, at least, Doubt whether he had **taken the** Oaths, **or** not. But it is apparent that Collonel Hill, who **had given** Glencoe his Protection, **and to whom Glencoe** came to take the **Oaths, I** say it is certain that **he, and** the other **Officers** there upon **the Place,** knew very well that **Glenco** had taken the Oaths, and submitted to the Government. Those Officers **whom he** receiv'd into his House, and quarter'd their **Soldiers among his Tenants,** upon his laying down his Arms; These

[1] Letter 4.   [2] Letter 3.

Massacre of Glencoe.

must know that he had submitted. But if notwithstanding they must Obey their Orders (as they did) if it be not permitted to Officers, so much as Rescribere, to acquaint the King with any mistake may be in his Orders; but to Execute them blindfold, and without Asking Questions, then let me lie out of the Reach of a Soldier.

The Reader must likewise know, that none of the Foresaid Instructions were communicated to the Privy Conncil of Scotland; to whom by the Constitution of that Kingdom, and Continual Custom, all the Kings Orders are directed. They knew nothing of this Matter, It was contriv'd to be Carry'd in such a Manner, as not to be prevented. And when Gallienus his Thirst of Blood is once Satisfy'd, then let Slaves Grumble, and make Inquiry! We know how to Manage them. Johnston hath undertaken it. Nay he hath done it. *Done it!* More effectually than ever was heard, or I believe, Imagin'd, in these Nations, before this Happy Revolution: For here is a Precedent made, and that by Parliament, That the King may send his Guards, and Cut any Man's Throat in the Nation in Cold Blood; Nay, he may Massacre the whole Parliament, as they are there Sitting, by the Rule that they have given; That is, To acquit Levingston and Hill; and to justify them for pursuing the King's Orders to Massacre a whole Clan, which is no more Just, or Law, than to Massacre a Parliament.

Let us Banter the World, or ourselves no more with Liberty and Laws! And when Parliaments can be brought to Approve, and to Justify all this—— Well! Johnston! Thou hast Manag'd Nobly. Thou art fit to Serve a Monarch! But not unless you bring your Monarch cleverly off in this Business; For what if you can place it upon Dalrymple; And if Dalrymple should be Hang'd for Daring to send such an Order, tho' he refus'd to Counter-sign it, What will become of Him, who both Sign'd it, and Counter-Sign'd it, and Commanded it to be Sent?

<blockquote>
If the Man such Praises have,
What must He Employs the Knave?
</blockquote>

Why! did his Master never Inquire into this Matter before? Never before the Parliament Clamour'd! And what was the Meaning of a Commission to Examine into what himself had Order'd— But *Mes James!*—And have you e'en brought your Master into this Noose! What can you expect from him but to be Glenco'd for your pains? *Qui Glencoat Glencoabitur*—You have brought all his Sins to

Remembrance. The Dewitting[1] in Holland was almost forgot.—You have pretty good Experience of his Temper, or you may have. But if he suffer you to live to see another Revolution, you may plead Merit: For all his Enemies have not render'd him so Black; so effectually Proved, and Demonstrated it to the World, as your Management has done. He is happy in his Ministers! at least very Justly serv'd by them!

He wants but a good Historian, that he may not lose his Character to after Ages. And Secretary, you cannot do better than to recommend your Uncle to that Office. He'll do it Deliciously; he'll either find or make Parallels to him out of Antient Histories (for he'll find none among the Modern, especially in these Countries.) And make him (I'll warrant you) Excel them all. And among the rest, I would recommend one to him, that fits the present case so exactly, that you would think one was copied out of the other, and it is as follows:—

"Gallienus, ut erat Nequam & Perditus; ita etiam, ubi necessitas coegisset, velox, furibundus, ferus, vehemens, Crudelis—In omnes Mesiacos tam Milites quam Cives asperime Ceviit: Nec quemquam suæ Crudelitatis exortem reliquit: Usque adeo Asper et Truculentus ut plerasq; Civitates vacuas a virili sexu relinqueret.

"Extat sane Epistola Galieni quam ad Celerem Verianum Scripsit, qua ejus Nimietas crudelitatis ostenditur: quam Ego idcirco interposui, ut omnes intelligerent, hominem Luxuriosum crudelissimum esse, si necessitas Postulet.

GALLIENUS VERIANO. "Non mihi satisfacies, si tantum Armatos occideris, quos et sors Belli interimere potuisset. Perimendus est omnis sexus Virilis, si et senes atq; impuberes sine Reprehensione nostra occidi possent. Occidendus est quicunq; malevoluit. Occidendus est quicumq; male dixit contra me, contra Valeriani filium, contra tot Principum Patrem et Fratrem. Ingenuus factus est Imperator. Lacera, occide, concide: Animum meum intelligere potes, mea Mente irascere qui hæc Manu mea scripsi." [*Trebell. Pollion. Trigint. Tyran. de Ingenuo.*]

This is the Description of Gallienus, a Cruel, and a Bloody Tyrant: And here is the Copy of some Instructions he sent to Verianus, an Officer of his, about just such another Massacre as Glenco, which he

---

[1] This word is coined as an allusion to the murder of the brothers John and Cornelius De Witt at the Hague, by the Prince of Orange's party in 1672.

Massacre of Glenco.

wrote, or Sign'd with his own Hand: Wherein he Commands him, to put all to the Sword, All that durst speak or think against him, as well Old as Young; He bid him Plunder, Kill, Tear; and that it would not please him if he Kill'd only those in Arms against him, but All of the Masculine Sex.

Here was a Great deal of Do, and many Words about it! But our Milder Order, bid only EXTIRPATE, and that not this or that Body, or making Distinctions of Old or Young, Men or Women. What need all that Cookery! But only The Whole TRIBE. That was all! He Scorn'd to Except the pitiful Women, as Gallienus did. What need They be Excepted? Why! He Excepted no Body! Short Work's best—and Few Words. And as the *Answer to Great Britain's Just Complaint*, Publish'd by Authority, 1692, says, p. 37. in Vindication of W. R. as to this of Glenco. "*A milder Order was never given.*" And he says that his Majesty has Express'd a High Displeasure at it. It was High indeed: For we never heard of it before. Nor are we like to hear of it, that I can see: For all the Officers who Commanded, or who Executed it, are still in their Respective Posts, unless Advanc'd. Nor have we heard that so much as an Ill Word has been said by Him to any one of them.

But this we know, by that *Answer to Great Britain's Just Complaint*, that W. R. cannot plead Ignorance, that there was a great Clamour about the Massacre of Glenco, Three Years ago: And that he has taken no Notice of it all this time nor Now, till it was first Started in Parliament; And that then, what he did, was, as much as he could to take it out of the hands of the Parliament, and by all his Might and Main, to Stifle, or at least to Baffle it. And it has been Baffled. And this horrible addition is thereby made to the Guilt of that Murther; That whereas none were answerable for it before, except only Gallienus and his Verianus's with their Accomplices, it is now become a National Guilt (so far as the Parliament are the Representatives of the People) by the Parliament's making GALLIENUS's Instructions sufficient to justify Verianus in his Execution of them. Whereby they justify the whole Murder, and bring it upon their own Heads, and upon the Heads of their Children. For if Gallienus had no Power by Law, to send such Instructions, they could be no Justification to Verianus: But now that Parliament has Voted that such Instructions are a Justification of Verianus; and therefore they have yielded that Gallienus has, by Law, a Power to send such

Instructions. And they ought to be Obey'd. And then? *Lord have mercy upon us!*

Nor has our Parliament in England been behind that of Scotland in Sacrificing our Laws, Lives, and Liberties to an Arbitrary and Despotick Power; and that not only to Orders Sign'd by Gallienus himself, but by Verianus, of his own head. Making us Double Distill'd Vassals; Slaves of Slaves!

And the instance which (among many others) I have to give of this, Exceeds even that of Glenco, in its having less Pretence, and acted with the greater face of Authority, and Solemnity. I mean the Prodigious unprecedented Manner of the Murther of Gaffney in Ireland by the command of the Lord Coningsby; for which he was impeached before the House of Commons in England, by Protestants of Ireland, Gentlemen of Quality and Estates; and of Publick and generous Spirits; whose noble Resentment to see their Laws so vilely trampled under foot by those whom they had Invited thither to protect them, brought them hither in Person, to demand Justice from our House of Commons against Coningsby, who was one of their Members. And that there could be nothing of Revenge in the Case, in behalf of the Person who was Murther'd, it's notorious; that Gaffney being a poor Fellow, a Servant to Sweetman (hereafter mention'd) and wholly unknown, I believe, to every one of the Gentlemen who prosecuted Coningsby; Besides, He was a Roman Catholic and one of the Native Irish, upon both of which Accounts he could have the less share of Interest with the British, and Irish Protestants, who were then not wholly come out of a most bloody War against them; for Limerick as yet held out. And therefore these worthy Patriots, who came over from Ireland hither to prosecute Coningsby, could have no other Incitement, but Love of their Country, and the Preservation of the Laws: But the Return they had, after a long and Expensive Attendance as it was, Mortifying to themselves, and sadly Instructive to others, will remain an Instance of Arbitrary Government not to be equall'd in former Ages, nor easily credible to the future. The Story, one would think, should not need being told in England, because it was brought upon the Stage, before the House of Commons, and is in their Printed Votes.

Yet, all that is not, it seems, sufficient to publish it at this time; not one in twenty of some sort of People that I meet with, having ever heard of it, or have forgot it. And (as I have told of the Story

122

of Glenco) they call it a Jacobite Invention; and will hear no more of it.

I will therefore present the Reader with the very Words of the Article concerning Gaffney, which (with several others of other Instances of High Arbitrary Government) was exhibited by the Earl of Ballimont, and other Protestants of Ireland, against the Lords Justices of Ireland (viz., The said Lord Coningsby, and Sir Charles Porter, both Members of the House of Commons in England) before the House of Commons in the Winter Session 1693. The Article concerning Gaffney is the 4th, and follows in these Words:—

"That the Lords Justices did, in Council, by word of Mouth, Order one **Gaffney** to be Hanged, without Tryal, the Courts of Justice being then open, and who was at that time an Evidence against one Sweetman for the murther of Collonel Foulk's soldiers: But the said Sweetman (giving all his real Estate to the value of £200 per Annum to Mr Culliford, besides the sum of about £500 to Mr Fielding, the said Lords Justices Secretary, for being his Bayl) was never prosecuted for the said murther; and the said Gaffney was immediately Executed according to the said verbal Order.

Now the Reader must know that every Tittle of the said Charge was proved fully, and past all Contradiction. Captain Fitz-Gerald, who is a Member of the Privy Council in Ireland, Declared that he was then sitting at the Board; and that the Council were not advised with at all in it. That Sweetman's Estate, valued at £3000, was offer'd to him [Captain Fitz-Gerald] on Condition that he would make interest to save Sweetman's Life. That Lord Coningsby, who gave the Orders for the Executing of Gaffney, was in so great haste to have him dispatch'd out of the way (for he was an Evidence against Sweetman) That he ordered a Provo, instead of any Legal Officer, to be Call'd into the Councill-Chamber where Gaffney was Examin'd: And after having asked Gaffney three or four Questions, and that he positively denied his having any Accession to the said Murther; Commanded the Provo to take him out and hang him up IMMEDIATELY: And the Provo making Answer, That it would take some time to make a Gallows; Coningsby answered sharply, "Hang him upon the Carriage of a Gun;" which was done IMMEDIATELY!

Of all this Coningsby could not deny One Word before the House of Commons: And all he said in his own Vindication was, That if he had not hang'd Gaffney so, he could not have hang'd him at all. Which was true: For there was no Evidence against him, and therefore they would give him no Tryal. But why must Gaffney then be Hang'd? Because, forsooth! Some Officers in the Army would have somebody Hang'd for the Murther of Foulk's Soldiers: And Sweetman (in whose Backside the Soldiers were buried, and their Coats found in his House) had given 500*l*. to the Lords Justices Secretary, and his Estate to another man in Power; but Gaffney was a Poor Rogue, and had nothing to give, and therefore it was fit he should be hang'd. And Hang'd as he was, or not at all. As CONINGSBY honestly, but Impudently Confessed.

But now comes the Astonishing Wonder. After all these things so plainly proved and confess'd, that the House of Commons could not frame any manner of excuse for Coningsby; but were forc'd to Vote the Execution of Gaffney without Tryal, to be Arbitrary and Illegal; Yet that considering the state of Affairs, They did not think fit to ground an Impeachment against the Lord Coningsby for the same. This is in the Printed Votes of the 29th of January, 1693. And this is an Original. What! Vote a man guilty, and yet that he shall not be prosecuted! Why pray? Because of the state of Affairs. This is very general. And such a pretence will never be wanting. But what was this State of Affairs, at that time? It was in the Winter of 1690, when all Ireland except only Limerick, was in the Obedience of K. W., when the Courts of Justice were open (as in the 'bovesaid Article against Coningsby is express'd) and the Lords Justices and Council sitting in Peace and Grandeur in Dublin. And what was it that cou'd or ought to have hindered giving that Poor Fellow a fair Tryal? Other Criminals were then Tryed, in the usual form, and why not Gaffney? How came the State of Affairs to reach him, more than any other? Unless you will say, that it did reach to many others: For it is express'd in the Printed Address of the Lords, Presented to K. W. 9 March 1692, That not only Gaffney, but several others were Executed, without any Tryal whatsoever; And that there were Exorbitant Abuses, great Mismanagement, and many Arbitrary and Illegal Proceedings there, within these four Years last past, as well since the determination of the War as before, which includes the whole Government since the Revolution, as well during the Administration of Gallienus in Person, while he was there, as of his several Verianus's in his Absence. One of whom did, in Almanzor strain, set up the High Prerogative, and Hector their Parliament in a manner unknown to former Ages: And without Precedent from any Lawful King that ever sat upon the English Throne in that Kingdom.

124

Massacre of Glencoe.

Which they have given us an Account of in Print; to try whether there was so much of the Spirit of English Liberty left in an English Parliament as to Vindicate their own Privileges, in that Breach which was made upon them, thro' the sides of the Parliament in Ireland, a Province of their own, and may be reckoned a branch of the English Empire. But all in vain! They had drunk so deep in the Cup of Slavery at Home, that they could take no notice of it Abroad. They have stopt their Ears close against all Charmers upon that Subject, Charm he never so wisely. They Call their Slavery, Liberty! And where then is the Remedy?

Thus poor Ireland was left without all hopes of Redress, to feed upon the Melancholy Reflection, that their Liberties have been much more notoriously violated by their Deliverers than by all the instances which were so much as alledg'd against their Lawful King; And thence to learn for the future, how much Rebellion is a worse Remedy, than the Disease of Tyranny (even when it is not made a pretence) and that it always ends in a Heavier Tyranny: Because there must go more Force to keep under New Acquisitions, than Old Hereditary Rights. And if all the Sacred Bonds of Natural Allegiance Fortified with the Religious Sanction of Oaths, and Taught and Inculcated upon Us, from our Infancy, as a Condition indispensable to our Salvation; if all this, and all the Honour and Reputation which the World has justly affixed to Loyalty, with the Horror and eternal Stain, upon the Name and Memory of Traytors and Rebels and all the Terrors of the Laws against Treason. If none (I say) Nor all of these Considerations, have weight enough to keep us in our Obedience to those whom God, and the Constitution of our Country, have placed over Us, by a Divine as well as a Legal Right: How should an Usurper secure our Duty, who has none of these Tyes, on his side; but All, and every One against him? How should, How can He do it, but by Corrupting our Representatives in Parliament, so as to pass all his Arbitrary Designs upon Us, in their Names; and when that fails him, by open Force? How otherwise has any one of them ever yet secured himself? Have we forgot our late Deliverers in Forty One? Will no Experience serve to make us Wise? No. Not when the Time of our Destruction is come! We shall then, as the Jews did before their Final Destruction by the Romans; we do now as they did then Obstinately refuse all offers of Mercy, for our Rebellion, and continue to Provoke a Power, which we know too strong for **Us**; and which we confess must, without a Miracle, be our Ruine: Yet **we run** on, trusting only to our Dispair! And we have not **only** Delivered up our Money **or our** Lives, without Account; but what used to be Dearer to English Men, The Honour of England! Of which take this short Instance instead of many **more.**

"**The House of** Lords made (and printed) an Address, dated the **18***th* **of** *February* **1692.** Wherein They mind their King of the **Capitulation made in the Year** 1678, by which it was agreed, **That** the English Commander and Officer, in every Degree is to **Command every other** Confederate Officer of the **same** Rank (except those of Crowned Heads) without any regard **to the** Date of their respective **Commissions.** And that the contrary was the Practice in this last **War,** to the diminution of the Honour that belongeth to the Crown of England, and **to** the general Dissatisfaction of his Majesty's **Subjects.** And desire, **That** the Chief Commander of the English **Forces under** his Majesty, should **be a** Subject born in his Majesty's **Dominions: That** no Foreigner should be **of** the Board of Ordnance, or Keeper **of the Stores in the Tower of** London: **That,** for the Encouragement **of the English, there should** not be so many strangers Employ'd in **the Office of the Ordnance.** That there hath **been** many Abuses **under Pretence of** Pressing Men for the Fleet; **And** therefore They **humbly** Advise, **That** the Offenders **should** be immediately **Cashiered, and** Prosecuted with the utmost Rigour of the **Law.**"

His Gracious Answer was, "That he would consider it." And **we may suppose, That he** is considering of it still: For he hath not **perform'd one** word **of** it: **But on** the Contrary, **to** shew the regard **he has for all** the Peers of England; and for the Honour of England; **He has acted quite** contrary to this Address, more **since,** than before: **For not only** Abroad, in Flanders, **and** in Savoy, are the English **everywhere** under Foreign Commanders-in-Chief: But, to use them **as they deserve, He** has now this last time, made a Foreigner **[Schomberg]** Commander-in-Chief **of** all **the** Forces left in England. **Let the Lords** Address again! They would if they **were** English Men! Or if he **were an** Hereditary King! But **some** will bear more Insults **from a** Mistress than **a** Wife. And **a** King **of** our own making, Costs us more than Twenty of God's sending. We think our selves bound to Acquiesce **in our own** Act and Deed!

If any of the Cursed and Rebel Parliaments could have found a

126

Massacre of Glencoe.

Gaffney or Glenco, against King Charles the First, or any of his Sons, what a Noise would they have made? How had all the World been filled with Apologies and Remonstrances! What a Dismal Idea would have been Raised of Tyranny and Arbitrary Government! In the former Reigns, how was the Nation alarm'd with what was Whispered; and not Whispered, or ever so much as thought of, in the King's Bed-Chamber; in his Closet! Of Secret Leagues, and Private Assassinations of Men that Murther'd themselves; where there was not the least Umbrage or Colour of Pretence! How Industrious was it spread and imbibed by the Mob of this Nation, That King Charles the Second and the Earl of Essex were both Murthered by the Procurement of one they had a mind to Blacken! And Forty Protestant Witnesses of the greatest Quality and Reputation, were not sufficient to make them believe a Prince of Wales; though not one Man or Woman in the Nation ever Depos'd any thing to the Contrary: Nor was there any other Argument against it, besides a few Drunken Songs. But that was enough, because it was against a Lawful King. And on the other hand, though they see their Fellow-Subjects Gaffney'd and Glenco'd before their Faces: Though it be Printed in the Gazettes and Publick Votes of the House of Commons, and that the House of Lords print their Addresses, contrary to their usual Custom, on purpose to let the Nation see.—Yet they will not see. No. All this is not NOW sufficient to imprint it one half-hour in their Memories, after Reading of the Publick Papers; they neglect it, They forget it, as not concerning them! *Non Persuadebis, etiamsi Persuaseris*, is their Resolution. And *Quos perdere vult Jupiter, Dementat*, I wish may not be their Fate.

BUT to bring our Story to an End: There is One Noble Stroke of Secretary Johnston's behind. Whereby he thinks he has wiped his Master's ancle, from all Imputation of the Massacre of Glenco; And that is, He has perswaded Lieutenant-Collonel Hamilton (whose Order to Duncanson is in the foresaid Narrative) to abscond for some time; and then to slip over to K. W. in Flanders; which he has done. This shews as if he were more Guilty than the rest. He is made the Scapegoat, and all this Sin laid upon his Head. But if Hill gave his Orders to his Lieutenant-Collonel Hamilton (which he Avers in his Order to Duncanson) Why was it more Criminal in Hamilton to hand down his Collonel's Orders to the next Subaltern?

AND why must Glen Lyon, and the others who actually Committed

30 The Clarendon Historical Society Reprints.

that Horrid **Massacre**, and are now in their Respective Commands in Flanders, **Why should these be Excused?**

O! No! They are not excused, for as in the Gazette (18*th July* 1695) the Parliament in Scotland has made **a fierce Vote** against them, viz., **That** his Majesty be Address'd to send them home **to be** prosecuted for the same, Or Not, as his Majesty shall think fit.—OR NOT! This **is as** Civil as Heart could wish! And whether this **Address was sent, or** Not; whether it was trusted to Secretary Johnston **to send it, or** Not, is all One: For instead of sending them Home to be **Tryed, Hamilton** is sent to them; And **in Justice we** are to suppose that Due Care **will be taken, That** in this Campaign, They shall either be Killed, **Taken, or Desert.** And then if we had them again, **How** we would hang the Rogues.

BUT our English Parliament was much more complaysant to their Verianus's; they did not put them to the trouble so much as of a Sham Absconding for a little time; No, nor of suffering the least Disgrace for their more Solemn and Judicial Murther: But Commanded them to take their Places again in their Senate-House; Thus doing them Honour, for their Noble Breach of our Laws; And signifying to the Nation what **Qualifications** are Expected in those whom they Choose to **Represent them**; and in whose hands they have Deposited the **Absolute and** Un-Accountable Disposal of their Estates, Lives, and Liberties! At least, it is so understood. And the Silence of the People in this Case, is taken for Consent.

Finis.

"Inter Folia Fructus."

THE

SEVERAL DECLARATIONS

MADE IN

COUNCIL

CONCERNING THE

𝔅irth of the 𝔓rince of 𝔚ales.

1688.

"History is but the Unrolled Scroll of Prophecy."

—James A. Garfield.

PRIVATELY PRINTED
FOR THE CLARENDON HISTORICAL SOCIETY.

1885.

This edition is limited to 120 *large paper and* 400 *small paper copies, for Subscribers only.*

The Several

DECLARATIONS

Together with the Several

DEPOSITIONS

MADE IN

COUNCIL

On *Monday*, the 22d of *October* 1688.

CONCERNING

The BIRTH

OF THE

PRINCE OF WALES.

N.B.—*Thofe Mark'd with this Mark* * *are* Roman Catholicks.

London: Printed, and Sold by the Bookfellers of *London* and *Weftminfter*.

AT THE COUNCIL-CHAMBER IN

WHITEHALL,

Monday the 22*th** of *October*, 1688.

THis Day an Extraordinary Council met, where were likewife Prefent, by his Majefty's Defire and Appointment, Her Majefty the Queen Dowager, and fuch of the Peers of this Kingdom, both Spiritual and Temporal, as were in Town. And alfo the Lord Mayor and Aldermen of the City of London; the Judges, and feveral of Their Majefties Council Learn'd, hereafter Named.

The King's moft Excellent Majefty.

Her Majefty the Queen Dowager in a Chair, placed on the King's Right Hand.

His R. H. Pr. George of Denmark,	Duke of Hamilton,
Lord Chancellor,	Lord Chamberlain,
Lord Prefident,	Earl of Oxford,
Lord Privy Seal,	Earl of Huntingdon,
Earl of Craven,	Earl of Peterborow,
Earl of Berkeley,	Earl of Salifbury,

* *Sic.*

Earl of Rochester,
Earl of Moray,
Earl of Middleton,
Earl of Melfort,
Earl of Caftlemain,
Vifcount Prefton,
Lord Bellafyfe,
Lord Godolphin,
Lord Dover,
Mr. Chancellor of the Exchequer,
Mafter of the Rolls,
L. Ch. Juftice Herbert,
Sir Thomas Strickland,
Sir Nicholas Butler,
Mr. Titus,
Lord A. B. of Canterbury,
Duke of Norfolk,
Duke of Grafton,
Duke of Ormond,
Duke of Northumberland,
Marquefs of Halyfax,
Earl of Pembroke,

Earl of Clarendon
Earl of Cardigan,
Earl of Ailefbury,
Earl of Burlington,
Earl of Litchfield,
Earl of Feversham,
Earl of Nottingham,
Vifcount Newport,
Vifcount Weymouth,
Bifhop of London,
Bifhop of Winchefter,
Bifhop of Rochester,
Bifhop of Chefter,
Bifhop of St. Davids,
Lord North.
Lord Chandos,
Lord Montagu,
Lord Herbert of Chirbury,
Lord Vaughan Earl of Carbery,
Lord Colepeper,
Lord Churchill,
Lord Waldegrave.

The Lord Mayor and Aldermen of the City of London.
Sir Robert Wright, Lord Chief Justice of the King's Bench.

Sir Thomas Powel,
Sir Thomas Baldock,
} Juftices of the King's Bench.

Sir Thomas Street,
Sir Edward Lutwich,
Sir Thomas Jennor,
} Juftices of the Common Pleas.

Sir Richard Heath,
Sir Charles Ingleby,
Sir John Rotheram,
} Barons of the Exchequer.

Sir John Maynard,
Sir John Holt,
Sir Ambrofe Philips,
} His Majefties Serjeants at Law.

The Birth of the Prince of Wales.

Sir Thomas Powis, His Majefty's Attorney General.
Sir William Williams, His Majefty's Solicitor General.
Sir James Butler.
Mr. North, the Queen's Attorney.
Mr. Montagu, the Queen's Solicitor.
Sir Charles Porter.

To whom His Majefty fpake to this Effect.

My Lords,

I Have called you together upon a very extraordinary Occafion; but extraordinary Difeafes muft have extraordinary Remedies. The Malicious Endeavours of my Enemies have fo poifoned the Minds of fome of my Subjects, that by the Reports I have from all hands I have Reafon to believe that very many do not think this Son with which God hath bleffed Me, to be Mine, but a Suppofed Child. But I may fay, that by particular Providence, fcarce any Prince was ever Born where there were fo many Perfons prefent.

I have taken this time to have the Matter Heard and Examined here, Expecting that the Prince of Orange, with the firft Eafterly Wind, will invade this Kingdom; and as I have often ventured My Life for the Nation before I came to the Crown fo I think My Self more obliged to do the fame, now I am KING; and do intend to go in Perfon againft him, whereby I may be expofed to Accidents, and therefore I thought it neceffary to have this now done, in order to fatiffie the minds of My Subjects, and to prevent this Kingdom's being engaged in Blood and Confufion after My Death, defiring to do always what may contribute moft to the Eafe and Quiet of my Subjects, which I have fhewed by Securing to them their Liberty of Confcience, and the Enjoyment of their Properties, which I will always preferve.

I have Defired the Queen Dowager to give Her Self the trouble to come hither, to Declare what fhe knows of the Birth of My Son, and moft of the Ladies, Lords, and other Perfons who were prefent, are ready here to Depofe upon Oath their Knowledge of this Matter.

Whereupon the Queen Dowager was pleafed to fay.

THat when the King sent for her to the Queen's Labour, fhe came as foon as fhe could, and never ftirred from her till fhe was Delivered of the Prince of Wales,   Catherine R.

And the following Depositions were all taken upon Oath.

Elizabeth Lady Marchioness of Powis, Deposeth,

That about the 29th of December last, the Queen was likely to Miscarry; whereupon she immediately went unto her, and offered her some effectual Remedies, which are made use of on the like occasion; which the Queen ordred this Deponent to acquaint the Doctors with. The day following the Queen Dowager sent this Deponent to see how the Queen did; who replied, She had a pretty good Night, and did think she had Quickned, but would not be positive till she felt it again; That after this the Deponent did frequently wait on the Queen in the Morning, and did see her Shift her several days, and generally saw the Milk, and sometimes Wet upon her Smock. That some time, after this Deponent went into the Country, and came not up till a few days before the Queen was brought to Bed; and from the time of this Deponents Return, she saw the Queen every day till she was brought to Bed, and was in the Room a Quarter of an hour before, and at the time of her Delivery of the Prince by Mrs. Wilks Her Majesty's Midwife, which this Deponent saw, and immediately went with the Prince, carried by Mrs. Delabadie into the Queen's little Bed-chamber, where she saw Sir Thomas Witherly sent for by the Midwife, who gave the Child Three Drops of something which came into the World with him, which this Deponent saw done; And this Deponent doth Aver, this Prince to be the same Child which was then Born, and that she has never been from him one day since.

* Eliz. Powis.

Anne Countess of Aran Deposeth,

That she went to the Queen from Whitehall to St. James's as soon as she heard that her Majesty was in Labour; when she came, she found the Queen in Bed, complaining of little Pains; The Lady Sunderland, Lady Roscomon, Mrs. Labadie, and the Midwife, were on that side of the Bed where the Queen lay; and this Deponent, with a great many others, stood on the other side all the time till the Queen was Delivered; As soon as her Majesty was delivered she said, *O Lord I don't hear the Child Cry*, and immediately upon that, this Deponent did hear it Cry, and saw the Midwife take the Child out of the Bed, and give it to Mrs. Labadie, who carried it into the little Bed-Chamber, where she, this Deponent, followed her, and saw that it was a Son, and that likewise she, the Deponent, hath several times seen Milk run out upon the Queen's Smock during her being with Child. A. Aran.

Penelope Countess of Peterborow Deposeth,

That she was often with the Queen, while Her Majesty was last with Child, and saw the Milk often upon her Majesty's Smock, when she, the Deponent, took it off from the Queen ; and often saw her Majesty's Belly so as it could not be otherwise but that she was with Child. That the said Deponent stood by the Bedside on the 10th of June last in the Morning, while the Queen was Delivered of the Prince of Wales. P. Peterborow.

Anne Countess of Sunderland Deposeth,

That June the 10th 1688, being Trinity Sunday, the Deponent went to St. James's Chapel at eight of the Clock in the Morning, intending to Receive the Sacrament ; but in the beginning of the Communion Service, the Man which looks to the Chappel came to the Deponent, and told her, she must come to the Queen ; The Deponent said, she would as soon as Prayers were done ; In a very little time after, another Man came up to the Altar to the Deponent, and said, the Queen was in Labour, and the Deponent must come to Her Majesty, who then went directly to the Queens Bed-Chamber. As soon as the Deponent came in, her Majesty told her, this Deponent, she believ'd she was in Labour. By this time the Bed was warmed, and the Queen went into Bed, and the King came in. The Queen asked, if he had sent for the Queen Dowager ; He said he had sent for every Body. The said Deponent stood at the Queen's Boulster, the Lady Roscommon, Mrs. Delabadie, and the Midwife on that side of the Bed, where the Queen was Delivered. After some lingring Pains, the Queen said, she feared she should not be brought to Bed a good while ; but enquiring of the Midwife, she assured her Majesty, that she wanted only one thorow Pain to bring the Child into the World ; Upon which the Queen said, It is impossible, the Child lies so high, and commanded this Deponent to lay her Hand on her Majesty's Belly, to feel how high the Child lay, which the Deponent did ; but soon after a great Pain came on at past Nine of the Clock, and the Queen was Delivered ; which the Midwife by pulling the Deponent by the Coat, assured her was a Son, it being the Sign she told the Deponent she would give her, the Queen having charged her not to let her Majesty know presently, whether it was a Son or Daughter. As soon as the Midwife had given the Deponent the Sign, the Deponent made a Sign to the King that it was a Son. When the Midwife had done her Office, she gave the Child to Mrs. Delabadie, which was a Son, and she carried it into the little Bed-chamber. A. Sunderland.

Isabella Countess of Roscommon Deposeth,

THat on the 10th of June last, she stood by the Lady Sunderland in the Queens Bed-Chamber, while the Queen was in Labour, and saw the Prince of Wales, when he was taken out of the Bed by the Midwife. L. Roscommon.

Margaret Countess of Fingall Deposeth,

THat she waited on the Queen Dowager her Mistress into the Queens Bed-Chamber at St. James's, when the Queen was in Labour, and stood by the Bed's Feet, when her Majesty was Delivered of the Prince. That the Deponent saw the Prince carried away into another Room, and soon after follow'd, and saw him in that Room.

* Marg. Fingall.

Lady Sophia Bulkeley Deposeth,

THat she was sent for on Trinity Sunday last past about Eight a Clock in the Morning to go to St. James's; for the Man that came, said the Queen was in Labour, and he, and others were sent to call every Body. That this Deponent made as much haste as she could to rise and be dress'd, but did not get to the Queen's Bed-chamber until a little after Nine a Clock, and then this Deponent found the Queen in her Bed, and the Queen Dowager there set upon a Stole, and some of the Ladies about her. After this Deponent having staid a little while, and thinking the Queen in no strong Pain, she, this Deponent, went out, and, being next to the Room where the Queens Linen was a warming, heard a noise, and look'd to see what was the matter, and finding no Body there, this Deponent ran and found the Lord Feversham in the Queen's little Bed-Chamber, who told this Deponent the Child was just born; This Deponent ask'd him, what is it? His Lordship said he could not tell. So this Deponent ran on to the Queens Bed-side, and heard the Queen say to the Midwife, Pray, Mrs. Wilks, don't part the Child (which signifies, don't cut the Navel-String, until the after-Birth is come away.) And while the

The Birth of the Prince of Wales.

Queen was with Child, this Deponent had heard her Majesty Command her Midwife not to do otherwise, it being counted much the safest way; but to what the Queen said just then (to the best of this Deponent's Remembrance) Mrs. Wilks replied, Pray Madam, give me leave, for I will do nothing, but what will be safe for your Self and Child; The Queen Answered, Do then, and then cry'd where is the King gone? His Majesty came immediately from the other side of the Bed (from just having a sight of the Child) and answered the Queen, Here I am; the Queen said, Why do you leave me now? The King kneeled on the Bed, on that side where the Deponent stood, and a little after the Midwife said, all is now come safe away; Upon that the King rose from the Bed, and said, Pray my Lords, come and see the Child: The King follow'd Mrs. Labadie, and the Lords His Majesty, into the little Bed-Chamber, where this Deponent follow'd also, and saw as well as they, that it was a Prince, and that Mrs. Wilks was in the right to desire to part the Child, For the Prince's Face, especially his Forehead was blackish, being stunn'd, as I have seen some other Children, when they have been just newly come into the World; but God be thanked, in two hours time that he was dress'd and wash'd, (which the Deponent staid by and saw done) the Prince look'd very fresh and well. This Deponent doth further add, That all the while, the Queen was with Child, this Deponent had the honour to pay her Duty very often Mornings and Nights, in waiting upon her Majesty in her Dressing Room and Bed-Chamber, and for the last three or four Months, this Deponent hath oftentimes seen the Queen's Milk, as well as when this Deponent hath had the honour to put on her Majesty's Smock.

S. Bulkely.

Susanna Lady Bellasyse Deposeth,

THat on Trinity Sunday the 10th of June last, the Deponent's Servant seeing the Queen Dowager's Coaches in St. James's at an unusual hour, went and asked the Occasion, and was told the Queen was in Labour; whereupon she came into the Deponent's Chamber, and awaked her; That the Queen having come to Lodge at St. James's but the Night before, they being in a great hurry, forgot to call the Deponent as her Majesty had ordered; That the Deponent made all the haste she could into her Majesties Bed-Chamber; and found the Queen in Bed, and Mrs. Wilks her Majesty's Midwife, sitting by the Bedside, with her hands in the Queen's Bed; The Queen asked her the said Midwife, what she thought? Mrs. Wilks assured her Majesty, that at the next great Pain the Child would be born; Whereupon the King ordered the Privy-Councellours to be called in; That this Deponent stood behind the Midwife's Chair, and immediately after the Queen's having another great Pain, the Prince was Born; That this Deponent saw the Child taken out of the Bed with the navel string hanging to its Belly; That this Deponent opened the Receiver, and saw it was a Son, and not hearing the Child cry, and seeing it a little black, she was afraid it was in a Convulsion Fit.

S. Bellasyse.

Henrietta Lady Waldgrave, Deposeth,

That she was in the Queen's Bed-Chamber a quarter of an hour before her Majesty was delivered, and standing by the Bedside, she saw the Queen in Labour, and heard her cry out much.

* Henrietta Waldgrave.

Mrs. Mary Crane one of the Gentlewomen of the Bed-Chamber to the Queen Dowager, Doposeth,

That she went with the Queen Dowager to the Queen's Labour on the 10th of June last, and never stirred out of the Room till the Queen was Delivered.

That this Deponent did not follow the Child, when it was first carried out of the Room, but staid in the Bed-Chamber, and saw all that was to be seen after the Birth of a Child. That she, the Deponent, then went to see the Prince, and found him look ill, and immediately went to the King, and told his Majesty she feared the Child was sick; that his Majesty went immediately to the Prince, and came back and said it was a mistake, the Child was very well.

* Mary Crane.

Dame Isabella Wentworth, one of the Gentlewomen of the Bed-Chamber to the Queen, Deposeth,

That she often saw the Milk of her Majesty's Breast upon her Smock, at which the Queen was troubled, it being a common saying, that it was a sign the Child would not live. And that she, the Deponent, did once feel the Child stir in the Queen's Belly while her Majesty was in Bed, and that she was present when the Child was Born, and staid till she heard it cry, and then went to fetch Vinegar for the Queen to smell to; she, the Deponent, heard the Queen command the Midwife not to tell her of what Sex it was, for

The Birth of the Prince of Wales.

fear of surprizing her Majesty: When the Deponent brought the Vinegar, she did desire to see the Child, Mrs. Delabadie having it in her Arms. The Child looked black, whereupon the Deponent desired Doctor Waldegrave to look to it, believing it was not well: That the Deponent saw the Navel-string of the Child cut, and three drops of the Blood, which came fresh out, given to him for the the Convulsion Fits.

Isabella Wentworth.

Dame Catherine Sayer, one of the Gentlewomen of the Bed Chamber to the Queen Dowager, Deposeth,

THat she waited on the Queen Dowager to the Queen's Labour, and was all the time by the Bedside, and stood there, till the Queen was Delivered, and follow'd the Child, when it was carried by Mrs. Delabadie to the Bed-Chamber, and took a warm Napkin and laid it on the Child's Breast, believing the Child was not well.

Catherine Sayer.

Dame Isabella Waldegrave, one of the Gentlewomen of the Bed-Chamber to the Queen, Deposeth,

THat she was constantly with the Queen, her Majesty was likely to miscarry, and had often seen Milk in her Majesty's Breast, and was with the Queen at the time of her Labour with the Prince, and saw the Prince taken out of the Bed, and went after Mrs. Delabadie with the Prince in her Arms into the little Bed-Chamber, and was by when the Child was shewn to the King that it was a Son; and this Deponent took the After-burden, and put it into a Bason of Water, and carried it into the Queen's Closet.

* Isabella Waldgrave.

Mrs. Margaret Dawson, one of the Gentlewomen of the Bed-Chamber to the Queen, Deposeth,

THat on the Tenth of June last, in the Morning, she was sent for by the Queen out of St. James's Chappel, where she was at Prayers, and that coming up into the Queen's Chamber, she found her sitting all alone upon a Stool by the Bed's-head, when the Queen said to her, this Deponent, she believed her self in Labour, and bid her, the Deponent, get the Pallat Bed, which stood in the next Room, to be made ready quickly for her; but that Bed having never been aired, the Deponent perswaded the Queen not to make use of it:

After which the Queen bid the Deponent make ready the Bed she came out of, which was done accordingly. The Deponent further faith, That she saw fire carried into the Queen's Room in a Warming-Pan to warm the Bed, after which the Queen went into her Bed, and that the Deponent stirred not from the Queen until her Majesty was delivered of a Son. That she the Deponent, well remembers, that on the 29th of December last her Majesty was afraid of Miscarrying, which was about the time she quickned ; and that after the Queen had gone 22 Weeks with Child, her Majesty's Milk began to run, which she the Deponent often saw upon her Smock, and that the 9th of May her Majesty apprehended miscarrying again with a Fright.

Margaret Dawson.

Mrs. Elizabeth Bromley, One of the Gentlewomen of the Bed-chamber to the Queen, deposeth,

THat she was sick all Winter, till a little before Easter last, when she the Deponent came into Waiting ; That from that Time till the Queen was brought to Bed, she the Deponent saw the Queen put on her Smock every Morning, by which means she saw the Milk constantly fall out of her Majesty's Breasts, and observed the Bigness of her Majesty's Belly, which could not be counterfeit. That the Deponent came from Whitehal to the Queen's Labour to St. James's the Tenth of June last, and remained in the room till the Queen was delivered and afterwards ; but did not follow the Child, till some time after, when she the Deponent went to see what colour'd Eyes he had.

Elizabeth Bromley.

Mrs. Peligrina Turini, One of the Gentlewomen of the Bed-chamber to the Queen, deposeth,

THat she constantly attended the Queen, when she was last with Child, and that on the Tenth of June last, she was in Waiting on her Majesty, who called her on the said Tenth of June in the Morning, and told her the Deponent, she was in Pain, and Bid her send for the Midwife, her Ladies and Servants, after which she the Deponent stay'd with the Queen during her Labour, and until she was delivered of the Prince of Wales.

⁂ The Mark of Pelegrina X Turini.

The Birth of the Prince of Wales.

Mrs. Anna Cary, One of the Gentlewomen of the Bed-chamber to the Queen Dowager, depofeth,

THat fhe waited on the Queen Dowager from Somerfet-houfe to St. James the Day the Queen was brought to Bed, and went into the Queen's Bed-chamber, where fhe this Deponent ftay'd, till the Queen was deliver'd, and faw the Prince as foon as he was born.

* Anna Cary.

Mrs. Mary Anne Delabadie, Dry Nurfe to the Prince, Depofeth,

THat she was with the Queen all the time her Majefty was with Child, and drefs'd her every Day, and in all the Nine Months did not mifs above Six Days, and that at feveral times by reafon of Sicknefs.

That on Sunday morning the 10th of June last, fhe the Deponent was fent for to the Queen, who was in Labour, That the Deponent came prefently, and was with the Queen all the Time of her Labour, and that kneeling down by the Midwife, giving her Cloaths for the Queen, the Midwife told this Deponent, that immediately on the next Pain, the Queen would be delivered, which accordingly fhe was. That this Deponent whifper'd to the Midwife, afking whether it was a Girl, fhe anfwered, No; whereupon the Midwife parted the Child, and put it into the Receiver (that the Deponent had given her) and then delivered the Child to the Deponent, and bid her go and carry it to the Fire, and take care of the Navel, which this Deponent did, and the King and Council followed her, and the King afked this Deponent, what it was, who anfwered, what he defired; the King replyed, But let me fee, whereupon the Deponent prefently fhewed his Majefty that it was a Son, and the Privy Counfellours then prefent faw it one after another. The Deponent fat with the Prince in her Lap, till the Midwife had done with the Queen, then the Midwife came and took the Prince from this Deponent, and afked for a Spoon for to give it three Drops of the Blood of the Navel-ftring, which the Midwife cut off by the Advice of the Phyficians, who said, it was good againft Fits. That the Deponent held the Spoon when the Midwife dropp'd the Blood into it, and ftirred it with a little Black Cherry Water, and then it was given to the Prince; that the Queen fent for this Deponent, and gave her the Prince to take care of him in quality of Dry Nurfe, which fhe has hitherto done; and further depofeth it to be the fame Child that was born of the Queen. And that

Mrs. Danvers, one of the Princess of Denmark's Women, and formerly Nurse to the Lady Isabella, coming to see the Prince, she told this Deponent, she was glad to see the same Marks upon his Eye, as the Queen's former Children had.

* Mary Anne Delabadie.

Mrs. Judith Wilks deposeth,

THat being the Queen's Midwife, she came often to her, especially when her Majesty was in any Danger of miscarrying, and many times felt the Child stir in her Belly, and saw the Milk run out of her Majesty's breasts; that on Trinity Sunday last in the Morning about Eight of the Clock, the Queen sent Mr. White, Page of the Back-stairs, to call her this Deponent, believing her self in Labour; when the Deponent came, she found the Queen in great Pain and Trembling; the Queen told her she feared it was her Labour, it being near the time of her first Reckoning, she the Deponent desired her Majesty not to be afraid, saying, she did not doubt that it was her full Time, and hoped her Majesty would have as good Labour as she always had; and whilst her Majesty was sitting trembling, her Water broke, and immediately she sent for the King, he being gone to his own Side, and let him know in what Condition she was, and desired him to send for whom he pleased to be present. The Queen ordered this Deponent to send for Mrs. Dawson and the rest of her Women; Mrs. Dawson came presently, and the Countess of Sunderland with her, and the rest of the Women also; that most of them saw her this Deponent make the Bed fit for the Queen to be delivered in; which when it was ready her Majesty was put into, and about Ten a Clock that Morning, the Queen was delivered of the Prince of Wales by her this Deponent's Assistance, and afterwards she the Deponent shewed the After-burthen to the Physicians, and before them the Deponent cut the Navel-string, and gave the Prince Three Drops of his Blood, to prevent Convulsion Fits, according to their Order. And this Deponent further saith, That when the Child was born, it not crying, the Queen said she thought it was dead, this Deponent assured her Majesty it was not, and desired Leave to part the Child from the After-burthen: Which the Queen was unwilling to have done, thinking it might be dangerous to her self; but the Deponent assuring her Majesty it would not, her Majesty gave Consent; whereupon the Child presently cryed, and then the Deponent gave it to Mrs. Labadie.

* Judith Wilkes.

The Birth of the Prince of Wales.

Mrs. Elizabeth Pearſe, Laundreſs to the Queen, Depoſeth,

That about Nine of the Clock on the 10th of June laſt in the Morning, ſhe came into the Bed-chamber, and heard the Queen cry out, being in great Pain, in which ſhe continued until her delivery; after which ſhe the Deponent ſaw the Prince of Wales given by the Midwife to Mrs. Labadie; that immediately after the Deponent ſaw the Midwife hold up the After-burthen, ſhewing it to the Company, and then the Deponent fetch'd her Maids, and with them took away all the foul Linnen hot as they came from the Queen; That for a Month after her Majeſty's Lying-in, the Deponent well knows by the waſhing of her Linnen, that the Queen was in the ſame Condition that all other Women uſe to be on the like Occaſion; and that ſome time after her quick'ning it appeared by her Smocks, that her Majeſty had Milk in her Breaſts, which continued until ſhe was brought to Bed, and afterwards during the uſual Time.

Elizabeth Pearſe.

Frances Dutcheſs of Richmond and Lenox, depoſeth,

That ſhe the Deponent was not at the Queen's Labour, becauſe ſhe did not know it Time enough, but as ſoon as ſhe did, ſhe made all the Haſte ſhe could to dreſs her; but the Queen was delivered before ſhe the Deponent came; And that at a Time when the Queen apprehended ſhe ſhould miſcarry, and the Phyſicians made her Majeſty keep her Bed for that Reaſon, the Deponent went one Evening to wait upon her Majeſty, and as ſhe ſtood by her Bed-ſide, her Majeſty ſaid to her, My Milk is now very troubleſome, it runs ſo much. The Deponent aſked the Queen if it uſed to do ſo; who anſwered, It uſed to run a little, but now the Fright I am in of miſcarrying, makes it run out very much, as you may ſee, throwing down the Bed Cloaths to the Middle of her Stomach, and ſhewing her Smock upon her Breaſt to the ſaid Deponent, which was very wet with her Milk.

* F. Richmond and Lenox.

Charlotte, Counteſs of Litchfield, depoſeth,

That ſhe was not at the Queen's Labour, (being in Child-bed her ſelf) but that ſhe was almoſt conſtantly with the Queen, while ſhe was with Child, and hath put on her Smock, and ſeen the Milk

run out of her Breast, and felt her Belly, so that she is sure that she could not be deceived, but that the Queen was with Child.
* C. Litchfield.

Anne Countess of Marischall, deposeth,

That she was several times in the Queen's Bed-chamber when she shifted her self and hath seen her Smock stain'd with her Milk; That she was not at the Queen's Labour, tho' sent to by One of her Ladies, being sick of a Fever; but does in her Conscience believe her Majesty was with Child, both by her Belly and her Milk.
A. Marischall.

George Lord Jeffreys, Lord Chancellour of England, deposeth,

That he being sent for to St. James's on the Tenth of June last by a Messenger that left Word the Queen was in Labour; soon after he, this Deponent, came to St. James's, and was sent for into the Queen's Bed-chamber, and to the best of his, the Deponent's Apprehension, the Queen was in Labour, and had a Pain or two to the best of his, the Deponent's Remembrance, before the rest of the Lords were called in. The Deponent stood all the time at the Queen's Bedside, and heard her cry out several Times as Women in Travail use to do, and at length after a long Pain, it was by some of the Women on the other Side of the Bed, said the Child was born. The Deponent heard the Queen say, she did not hear it cry. The Deponent immediately ask'd the Lord President what it was, he whispered that it was a Boy, which the Deponent understood he had hinted to him by the Lady Sunderland. Immediately the Deponent saw a Gentlewoman, who he had since heard her Name to be Mrs. Labadie, carry the Child into another Room, whither the Deponent followed, and saw the Child when she first opened it, and saw it was black and reeking; so that it plainly seemed to this Deponent to have been newly come from the Womb. The Deponent doth therefore depose, he doth steadfastly believe the Queen was delivered of that Child that very Morning.
Jeffreys C.

Robert Earl of Sunderland, Lord President of His Majesty's Privy Council, and Principal Secretary of State, deposeth,

That on Sunday Morning the 10th of June last, he was sent to, to come to St. James's the Queen being in Labour. The Deponent immediately went, and found many of the Council there.

The Birth of the Prince of Wales.

After having been some time in an outward Room, first the Lord Chancellour, and then the rest of the Council were called into the Queen's Bed-chamber, where in a short time her Majesty was brought to bed. The Deponent saw Mrs. Labadie carry the Child into the next Room, whither the Deponent followed, with many more, and saw it was a Son, and had the Marks of being new born.

Sunderland P.

Henry Lord Arundel of Wardour, Lord Privy Seal, deposeth,

THat on the 10th of June last, being Sunday, he had Notice given him that the Queen was in Labour, whereupon the Deponent repaired to St. James's betwixt Nine and Ten of the Clock in the Morning, where he found several Lords of the Council; in a little time after they were all called into the Queen's Bed-chamber; in less than a Quarter of an Hour after, she fell into the Sharpness of her Labour, her cries were so vehement and especially the last, that the Deponent could not forbid himself the being concern'd for her great Pain; which the Deponent expressing to the Lord Chancellour, he told the Deponent it was a Sign Her Majesty would the sooner be delivered, or Words to that Purpose, which proved very true, for presently after she was so; the Deponent heard a Whispering up and down that it was a Prince, for no Man was permitted to speak it aloud, lest the sudden Knowledge of it might have discomposed the Queen; the Deponent did not go in with some Lords when the Child was carry'd into the next Room, which was the Occasion the Deponent did not see him when he was uncovered and dress'd.

* Arundel C. P. S.

John Earl of Mulgrave, Lord Chamberlain of His Majesty's Houshold, saith, it is not to be expected one of his Sex should be able to give full Evidence in such a Matter, but deposeth,

THat he was just at the Bed's Feet, and heard the Queen cry very much, then the Deponent followed the Child into the other Room, and it seemed a little black; the Deponent also saw it was a Boy.

Mulgrave.

William Earl of Craven, deposeth,

THat he attended the King at St. James's, the 10th of June last, in the Morning, to receive the Word of his Majesty; the King had Notice brought him, that the Queen was upon the Point of falling into **Labour,** upon which the King commanded this Deponent's Stay and **Attendance;** and after the Space of One Hour and something more, **this Deponent** was, with some other Lords of his Majesty's **Privy Council,** called into the **Queen's** Great **Bed-chamber to be present at her** Delivery, and as near as this Deponent can **remember, the Queen made** Three Groans **or** Squeaks, and at the **Last of Three was delivered of** a Child ; the which was carry'd out into the **Little Bed-chamber ; and** there by the Fire this Deponent saw it cleansing : **and this Deponent** further saith, that he took that particular Mark of this Child, that **he may safely** averr, that the Prince of Wales is that very Child that **then was so brought out of the** Queen's Great Bed-chamber, where **this** Deponent and others **were present, as** aforesaid, at her Majesty's **Labour** and **Delivery.**

Craven.

Lewis Earl of Feversham, Lord Chamberlain to her Majesty
the Queen Dowager, deposeth,

THat being in Bed upon the 10th of June between 8 and **9 a** Clock in the Morning, Mr. Nicholas, One **of his Majesty's** Grooms of **his Bed-chamber,** came into this Deponent's **Room, and** told him that the **King had** sent him to tell the Queen Dowager, that the Queen was in Labour, and told him further that the Queen Dowager had given Order for her Coach, as soon as she heard **the news** of the Queen's **Labour. The** Deponent dressed himself with **all speed, and came to wait** upon the Queen Dowager, who was ready **to go into** her Coach, as she did ; the Deponent went into One of her **Coaches to** wait upon her Majesty **as** he us'd **to** do, having the Honour **to be** her **Lord** Chamberlain ; we went to St. James's, and **then** led her **Majesty into the** Queen's Bed-chamber, and finding the **Queen in Pain, the Deponent went** into the next Room, where were **several Lords of the** Privy Council, from whence the Deponent heard the Queen **cry out** several times, and a very little after the Lords of the Council were called in, and the Deponent followed them into the Bed-chamber, and a very little after the Queen cry'd louder, and then **said, Pray** do not tell me what it is yet. The Deponent went out of the Room, to tell the **News** that the Queen was brought to Bed ; and **when the Deponent** came in again, the News was, that it was a Prince ; and immediately the Deponent saw Mrs. Labadie with the Child wrapt up in her Hands, and in the Crowd ; upon which the

The Birth of the Prince of Wales. 21

Deponent defir'd to make room for the Prince, and followed her into the Little Bed-Chamber, where the Deponent faw the Prince as a Child newly-born, as he believed it.

Feverſham.

Alexander Earl of Morray, depofeth,

THat he came not to St. James's till half an Hour after the Queen was brought to bed, and only heard that her Majefty was brought to Bed of a Prince, which the Deponent verily believes, as he is alive, fhe brought into the World that very Morning, being the 10th of June laſt, 1688.

* Morray.

Charles Earl of Middleton, One of his Majefty's principal Secretaries of State, depofeth,

THat the 10th of June laſt paſt, betwixt 8 and 9 of the Clock in the Morning, he had Notice that the Queen's Majefty was in Labour, whereupon the Deponent made what Hafte he could to St. James's; the Deponent found the Earl of Craven waiting at the Queen's Bed-chamber Door towards the Drawing-room, which was then fhut; juſt after the King opened it, and called the Earl of Craven and the Deponent in; the Deponent afked his Majefty, how the Queen was? He was pleafed to anfwer the Deponent, you are a married man, and fo may know thefe Matters; the Water is broke or come away, or to that effect; and then bid the Deponent go into the Dreffing-room within the Bed-chamber, where the Deponent found feveral Perfons of Quality; above half an Hour after, to the beft of this Deponent's Memory, all the Company in that Room were called into the Bed-chamber; the Deponent ſtood near the Bed's Feet on the left Side, where he heard the Queen's Groans, and prefently after feveral loud Shrieks; the laſt, the Deponent remembers continued fo long, that he then wondred how any Body could hold their Breath fo long; prefently after the Deponent heard them fay, the Queen was delivered: whereupon the Deponent ſtepped up to the Bed fide, and faw a Woman, he fuppofes, the Midwife, kneeling at the other Side of the Bed, who had her Hands and Arms within the Bed-cloaths for a pretty while, then the Deponent faw her fpread a Cloth upon her Lap, and laid the End of it over the Bed-cloaths, and then fetch a Child (as the Deponent firmly believes, for he could not then fee it) out of the Bed into that Cloth, and give it to Mrs. Labadie, who brought it round to the Side where the Deponent ſtood, and carry'd it into a little Room, into which the Deponent immediately followed the King, and saw her sit down by the Fire, and heard her say, It is a Boy; upon which the King said, Let me see it, thereupon she laid open the Cloth, and shewed all the Child, saying, There's what you wish to see; the Deponent doth not charge his Memory with the very Words, but the Sense of what he heard. The Deponent looked upon the Child at the same time, which appeared to be very foul. This Deponent desireth Pardon if he doth not know the proper Expression, but hopes his Meaning is plain.

Middleton.

John Earl of Melfort, deposeth,

THat on Sunday the 10th of June last, betwixt 8 and 9 in the Morning, the Deponent was informed, that the Queen was in Labour; the Deponent went to St. James's and waited in the Queen's Drawing-room till some of the Gentlemen told him he might go in; the Deponent scratched at the Door of the Bed-chamber and finding no Answer, he ran down by the Garden Side and came to the Queen's Back-stairs, and finding the Dressing-room Door open, the Deponent went into the Queen's Bed-chamber, where he saw a great Number of Company, Lords and Ladies standing about the Bed: the Deponent heard the Queen cry out in great Pain, as Women use to do when they are near being brought to Bed; the Deponent heard her complain, and a Woman's Voice which the Deponent thought to be the Midwife, telling her she would be quickly well, she would be brought to Bed immediately; within a little the Deponent heard the Ladies behind the Bed say, the Queen was brought to Bed, and the Queen cry out, The Child is dead, I do not hear it cry, and immediately the Child cryed; within a little the Deponent saw a Woman bring a Child from within the Bed; the Deponent looked so earnestly at the Child, that he knew not what Woman it was; the Child was in the Condition of a new born Child, lapp'd up in loose Cloaths; the Deponent saw him carried into the Little Bed-chamber, and went about by the Dressing Room, and entred by the other Door into the Room where the Prince was, and saw him in the Condition of a new born Child; and the Deponent by the Oath he hath taken, believes him to be the Queen's Child.

* Melfort.

The Birth of the Prince of Wales.

Sidney Lord Godolphin, Lord Chamberlain to the Queen, depofeth,

THat he was called into the Queen's Bed-chamber, with the reft of the Lords of the Council, being one of the laft; and the Queen Dowager being there, and feveral Ladies, the Room was fo full that the Deponent could not get near the Bed, but ftood by the Chimney; There the Deponent heard the Queen cry out feveral times, as Women ufe to do that are in Labour: and the laft Cry that the Deponent heard, was much greater than the other; immediately upon that, the Deponent was called out of the Room, to give fome directions about the Lodgings that were preparing for the Child, which were not ready; the Deponent made haft back again, but as he was coming, he met People running with the News that the Queen was Deliver'd of a Son, whereupon the Deponent went into the little Bed-chamber, and faw the Child.

Godolphin.

Sir Stephen Fox, Knight, Depofeth,

THat on Sunday the 10th of June laft paft, about 9 of the Clock, as he came out of the Chappel at Whitehall after the firft Sermon, hearing that the Queen was in Labour, he, the Deponent, made hafte to St. James's, becaufe in waiting, as an Officer of the Green Cloth, to warn the feveral Servants below Stairs to be in their Offices, that upon that occafion there might not happen to be any thing wanting of Houfhold Provifions and Neceffaries under his, this Deponent's, Command; but firft going up by the Back-Stairs, into her Majefty's Dreffing-Room, and being there with many others, he heard her Majefty cry out very loudly; whereupon this Deponent haftned to the Green-Cloth, and ordered the feveral Servants to deliver out of their feveral Offices whatfoever fhould be called for, and as this Deponent was returning back to the Queen's faid Dreffing-Room, he was told, A Prince was born: Upon which News, He, this Deponent, went into the Queen's Little Bed-chamber, and faw the young Child before he was drefs'd.

Ste. Fox.

Lieut. Col. Edward Griffin, depofeth,

THat upon Sunday the 10th of June laft, he had the Honour to be in waiting upon the King with the Stick, and between 8 and 9 in the Morning, this Deponent was in the Queen's Dreffing Room at

St. James's, with several Lords of the Council, and after some time we were there, the King came out of the Queen's Bed-chamber, and called all the Lords in, and this Deponent went in along with them, being in waiting; immediately after the said Lords and this Deponent were in the Room; the Queen cryed out extremely, and said, Oh, I die; you kill me, you kill me: And the Midwife (as this Deponent believeth) answered, This one Pain, Madam, and 'twill be over; then presently Mrs. Dawson made this Deponent the Sign that the Child was born: Then this Deponent heard the Queen say, Don't tell me what it is yet; and Mrs. Dawson came to this Deponent, and whispered him in the Ear, 'Tis a Prince, but don't take notice of it yet. Then Mrs. Delabadie brought away the Child from the Bedside, and carry'd it into the Little Bed-chamber, and the King and the Lords of the Council went after her, but this Deponent did not follow them.

Edward Griffin.

Sir Charles Scarburgh, First Physician to the King, deposeth,

THat upon the Deponent's coming to Visit Her Majesty then lying at St. James's on Sunday the 10th of June, 1688, as the Deponent went up the Back-stairs, he heard the joyful Acclamation that a Prince of Wales was Born, upon which the Deponent hastned presently into the Little Bed-Chamber, where the Deponent found Mrs. Labadie just sitting down before the Fire, with the new born Prince wrapped in the Mantles, lying in her Lap. Then passing to the Queen in the next Bed-chamber, the Deponent congratulated the happy Birth of the Prince, and her Majesty's safe Delivery. The Queen was wearied and panting, but otherwise in good Condition: Then the Midwife brought to the Deponent the After-birth reeking warm, which Sir Thomas Witherley with the Deponent examined, and found very sound and perfect. After a while the Deponent understood that a Medicine was mentioned among the Ladies for a certain Remedy against Convulsions: It was some Drops of Blood from the Navel-string; the Deponent consulted Sir Thomas Witherly and the other Physicians; and to satisfie the Women, it was allowed of; there being, as was conceived, no Danger in the thing. Whereupon, the Midwife, with a small knife, slit the Navel-string beyond the Ligature, from which came some Drops of fresh Blood, taken in a Spoon, and given the Child, being mixed with a little Black-cherry-water. Thus much the Deponent hath to say upon her Majesty's present Delivery.

The Birth of the Prince of Wales.

Now for the Time of the Queen's Conception, she often told the Deponent and others, that she had two Reckonings; One, from Tuesday the 6th of September, when the King returned from his Progress to the Queen then at Bath; and the other, from Thursday the 6th of October, when the Queen came to the King at Windsor; but for some Reasons the Queen rather reckoned from the latter; tho' afterward it proved just to agree with the former. Moreover, her Majesty, when, according to her reckoning, she was gone with Child 12 Weeks, said, That she was quick, and perceived the Child to move; the Deponent returned no Answer to the Queen, but privately told those about her, that in truth it could not be in so short a Time. Yet the Queen was in the right, only mistook her Reckoning; for she was then full Sixteen Weeks gone with Child; about which time she usually quickned with her former Children, and accordingly was brought to Bed on the 10th of July 1688, and within Three or Four Days of full Forty Weeks.

Charles Scarburgh.

Sir Thomas Witherley, second Physician to the King, deposeth,

THat on Sunday the 10th of June, the Deponent was present in the Queen's Bed-chamber, when the Prince of Wales was born; the Deponent saw Mrs. Labadie bring the Child from the Midwife, and carry him into the next Room, whither the Deponent followed her, and saw the Child before he was cleaned; and having a Command from the Queen, that there should be Two Drops of the Blood of the After-burthen given the first Thing; we the said Deponent and the other Physicians did take Two Drops of Blood from the Navel-string which remained upon the Child, and gave it in a Spoonful of Black-cherry-water, as the Queen commanded. After this the Deponent saw (as also did the other Physicians) the After-burthen entire.

Tho. Witherley.

Sir William Waldgrave Knt. Her Majesty's first Physician, Deposeth,

THat in the Progress of Her Majesty's being with Child, the Deponent having the Honour to wait upon Her as usual, upon the 13th of February, 1687. about Ten in the Morning, she told the Deponent, she had Milk in her Breasts which dropp'd out; it was then thought the 19th week according to One Reckoning, but according to Another Reckoning, it was the One or Two and Twentieth Week; the Deponent alſo Affirmeth, That her Majeſty took ſuch Adſtringent Medicines, during the moſt part of her being with Child, in order to avoid Miſcarriage; That if ſhe had not been with Child, they muſt have been Prejudicial to her Health, and of dangerous Conſequence. Upon the 10th of June, 1688. the Deponent was called at his Lodging in Whitehall to wait upon the Queen, being told ſhe was in Labour, upon which the Deponent immediately went to St. James's, and ſo into the Queen's Bed-Chamber, and found her beginning her Labour, it being about Eight of the Clock in the Morning; The Deponent ſtirred not from thence, but to get ſuch Medicines as were fit for Her Majeſty, and then returned again, and was in the Bed-Chamber when ſhe Cried out, and was Delivered; the Deponent followed Mrs. Delabadie, who took the Prince in her Arms ſo ſoon as he was Born, and carried him into the Bed-Chamber, where the Deponent ſaw him upon her Lap, and was by when he took two or three drops of the Navel-ſtring freſh warm Blood, which was mixed with Black-Cherry-water, then returned into the great Bed-Chamber, where the Deponent ſaw the After-burthen freſh and warm.

*William Waldgrave.

Dr. Robert Brady, one of His Majeſty's Phyſicians in Ordinary, Depoſeth,

THat a little before Ten of the Clock in the Morning, on the Tenth of June 1688. the Deponent was in the Queen's little Bed-Chamber at St. James's, where the Deponent ſaw the Prince of Wales in Mrs. Labadie's Lap by the Fire ſide; the Deponent deſired to ſee the Linnen and Blankets opened in which he was wrapped; which being done, the Deponent ſaw it was a Male Child, and the Navel-ſtring hanging down to, or below the Virile parts, with a Ligature upon it, not far from the Body, but did not ſee any After-burthen hanging at, or joined to it not being at the Birth; The Deponent aſked how long he had been Born, the ſtanders by told him, At three Quarters of an Hour after Nine of the Clock, the Queen was Delivered.

Robert Brady.

James St. Amand, their Majesties Apothecary,
Deposeth,

THat from the beginning of November last, he hath generally every Day, till the 9th of June, 1688. given, by the Physicians Orders, Restringent and Corroborating Medicines to the Queen's Majesty; That on the 10th of June he was sent for in haste to come to St James's to her Majesty, who, the Messenger told him, was in Labour; That the Deponent then received a Note from the Physicians for Medicines for her Majesty, which the Deponent was obliged to stay and prepare, and so came not to St. James's till the Queen was Delivered; the Deponent meeting, just as he was going into the Bed-Chamber, Mrs. Labadie with the Young Prince in her Arms; the KING, and several of the Lords, soon after following into the little Bed-Chamber; where the Deponent saw the Child Naked, before it was Cleansed from the Impurities of his Birth; and also saw the Navel-string cut, and some Drops of Fresh Blood received into a Spoon, which the Deponent mingled with a little Black-Cherry-Water, and saw given by the Physicians' Orders to the Child; and afterwards going into the Great Bed-Chamber, where the Queen was delivered, he saw the After-burthen, &c. fresh.

Ja. St. Amand.

After these Depositions were taken, His Majesty was pleased to acquaint the Lords, That the Princess Anne of Denmark would have been present; but that she being with Child, and having not lately stirred abroad, could not come so far without hazard. Adding further,

AND now, My Lords, although I did not question but every Person here Present was satisfied before in this Matter; yet by what You have heard, You will be better able to satisfie Others. Besides, if I and the Queen could be thought so Wicked as to Endeavour to Impose a Child upon the Nation, You see how impossible it would have been; neither could I My Self be imposed upon, having constantly been with the Queen during Her being with Child, and the whole Time of Her Labour. And there is none of You but will easily believe Me, who have suffered so much for Conscience-sake, uncapable of so great a Villany, to the Prejudice of My Own Children. And I thank God, that those that know Me, know well that it is My Principle to do as I would be done by, for that is the **Law and the** Prophets : And I **would rather die a** Thousand **Deaths, than do the** least **Wrong to** any **of My Children.**

His Majesty further said,

IF **any of my Lords think it** Necessary the Queen **should be sent for, it** shall **be done. But their** Lordships **not thinking it** Necessary, Her Majesty was not sent for.

IT **is ordered** this Day **by** His Majesty in Council, **That the several** Declarations here before made by His Majesty, **and by Her** Majesty the Queen-Dowager, together with the several Depositions **here entred, be** forthwith Enrolled in **the Court of** Chancery. And the **Lord Chancellour is ordered to cause the same to be Enrolled** accordingly.

IN **Pursuance of** which **Order in Council, the Lord Chancellour on** Saturday the 27th **day of October following in** the High Court of Chancery (many of the Nobility and Lords of **his Majesty's most Honourable Privy Council being there present) caused** the aforesaid **Order in Council and** Declarations of his Majesty, **and likewise that of her Majesty the Queen** Dowager to be openly and distinctly read in **Court, as the same are** Entred in the Words aforesaid, in the **Council Book.** And the Lords **and** Ladies, and other persons who made the respective Depositions aforesaid, being present in Court, were Sworn again, and **having** heard their several Depositions distinctly Read in the Words aforesaid, and being severally Interrogated by the Court to the Truth thereof, they all upon **their Oaths** affirmed their respective Depositions to be True : and did likewise **depose** (except some few, who came in late to the **Council Chamber, or** some who stood at too great a distance) that they heard His Majesty, and Her Majesty the Queen-Dowager make the several Declarations aforesaid, and that the same as they had been **Read, were truly** Entred as they did believe, in the Council Book, according to the Sense, Intent and Meaning of what His Majesty the **King,** and Her Majesty the Queen-Dowager did then declare. And for as much as the Earl of Huntingdon and the Earl of Peterborow, who were able to depose to the Matters aforesaid, had not been Examined at the Council Board, but had brought their several Depositions in Writing, which they delivered into Court, the said **Lord** Chancellour, **after** the said Earls were severally Sworn,

156

The Birth of the Prince of Wales.

Ordered their Depositions to be openly Read in these Words following,

UPon Trinity Sunday, 10th. June, 1688. I went to St. James's House about Nine a Clock in the Morning, and followed my Lord Chancellour, through the Lodgings to the Dressing-Room, next to Queen's Bed-Chamber, where divers Lords of the Council were met upon occasion of the Queen's being in Labour, the King came several times into the Room, and amongst other things was pleased to tell us, that the Queen came exactly according to Her first Reckoning, which was from the King's Return from His Progress, to Bath in September, 1687. After this the Counsellours were ordered to come into the Bed-Chamber, and I stood on that side of the Bed, that had the Curtains drawn open, I heard Her Majesty Cry out several times. I staid in the Room during the Birth of the Prince of Wales. I saw him carried into the little Bed-Chamber, whither the King, the Lords and my self in particular did follow him.

Huntingdon.

I Had the Honour to be in the King's Chamber in the Morning, when Word was brought him, the Queen was not well, and followed him into the Dressing Room next Her Majesty's Bed-Chamber, where I staid till His Majesty called me come in, which was about the beginning of Her Pains. I Confess the Compassion I had for Her Majesty, hearing Her Cries, made my stay there very uneasy, One of the last especially seemed to me so Sharp, as it really forced me for a little Time to stop my Ears with my Fingers to avoid hearing more of the like; when setting them at Liberty, I heard no more but perceived a sudden Satisfaction in the Faces of the Assistants, several saying, that the Queen was delivered, and soon thereupon I saw the Prince brought from about the Bed, and carried into the little Bed-Chamber, whither I went afterwards, to behold him more particularly, where I saw him as a Child newly Born.

* Peterborow.

AFter which the said Earls did severally upon their Oaths affirm their Depositions to be True as they had been Read, and that they were present in Council, and heard His Majesty and Her Majesty the Queen-Dowager make the several Declarations aforesaid, and that the same were Entred in the Council Book as they did believe according to the Effect true Senfe and Meaning of what their Majefties declared in Council ; Whereupon His Majefty's Attorney General moved the Court, that the faid Declarations of his Majefty, and of Her Majefty the Queen-Dowager, and the feveral Depofitions, and the Order of Council fhould be Enrolled in the Petty-Bag Office, and in the Office of Inrolments in the Court of Chancery, for the fafe Prefervation and Cuftody of them, which the Lord Chancellour Ordered accordingly.

Finis.

"Inter Folia Fructus."

MEMOIRS

OF THE

CHEVALIER DE ST. GEORGE,

WITH

SOME PRIVATE PASSAGES

OF THE

LIFE of the late KING JAMES II.

1712.

NEVER BEFORE PUBLISHED.

"History is but the Unrolled Scroll of Prophecy."
—James A. Garfield.

PRIVATELY PRINTED
FOR THE CLARENDON HISTORICAL SOCIETY.

1885.

This edition is limited to 120 *large paper and* 400 *small paper copies, for Subscribers only.*

MEMOIRS

OF THE

Chevalier de St. GEORGE,

With some

PRIVATE PASSAGES

OF THE

LIFE

Of the late

King JAMES II.

Never before published.

LONDON:

Printed in the Year M DCC XII.
(Price One Shilling.)

MEMOIRS

OF THE

Chevalier de St. George, &c.

WHATEVER the Reader may conceive under this Romantic Title, I must ask his Pardon, for some few Pages at least, to be a little serious : As to the Original of this Young Hero, let him take it as it stands in History, without putting me to the trouble of ascertaining, that either the Chevalier De St. George is James III. or James III. Son of James II. Something therefore relative to these Memoirs, let me say of his (supposed or pretended) Father, since I shall else begin a Structure without any Foundation at all, which would seem a very Miraculous as well as Unaccountable piece of Work.

I cannot remember, that ever England had a fairer Sunshine, or Prospect of Happiness, than at the joyful Restoration of the Royal Family; when after a long and unnatural Exile, they were restored to their lawful Rights and Honours. The Reign succeeding I shall not meddle with, nor pretend to decide whether it was the Prince or the People that occasioned the domestic troubles that were then Predominant; yet this I think I am obliged to say, and which all reasonable Men will I believe own, That the Exile I have Mentioned was the grand Motive, or Foundation of the Troubles we have undergone since.

The Queen Mother, who was banished with her Children, took care to inspire them early with favorable Sentiments of her own Religion, and to dissipate the Prejudice of former Education. What effect it had on the rest, I cannot exactly say; but on the Duke of York it took such Root, that together with his Correspondence with the Catholicks in Flanders, contributed to strengthen the immoveable Impressions he had received of the Truth of the Catholic Religion.

After his Return to England, he soon made himself beloved and respected by the Nobility and Gentry; nor did he want a sufficient share of Interest in the Hearts of the Common People. He commanded the Navy against the Dutch, and in Two Engagements sufficiently raised his Reputation: But this Prosperity did not last long; for without any Eclipse of his Merit, he began to decline in the Hearts of the People; when they perceived that either he had changed his Religion, or, at least, had a mind to do it: And what added to it was the Suspicion likewise that he had converted the Dutches his First Wife, who died in the infancy of these Rumours, which therefore lessened the impression it began to make on the People. And they were yet in some hopes for the Duke himself: but he had ere this made his Abjuration to Father Simons an English Jesuit. And tho' the measures he took were always most Prudent, and he did not publicly declare himself to be a Catholic, 'twas nevertheless mighty difficult with him, not to discover to the Protestants, that he had separated from their Communion.

The Parliament took the Alarm, and from that time Measures were contrived to alter the Right of Succession. There were some Bishops of the Church of England, who, fore-seeing the Effect of so violent a Proceeding, would have stopped the Blow; to which end they addressed themselves to the Duke himself. They begged of him only to accompany the King his Brother to Chappel, when His Majesty went to the Protestant Prayers: They humbly represented to him, that such a wise Proceeding, might lay the Tempest that had been raised against him, and prevent the Bill of Exclusion from making its way thro' the Parliament. But they could not prevail with him, receiving for Answer, these Words,—"My Principles do not suffer me to dissemble my Religion after that manner; and I cannot obtain of my self to do Evil that Good may come of it."

This Constancy of the Duke's threw the King into such disorders, that he had very great need of all his Authority and Force: For as he had a tender love for him, he was moved with the Danger wherein he saw him; resolving to support him against the Torrent of his Enemies, which in the main he did; nevertheless the Duke found himself obliged to resign his Place of Grand Admiral, and his other Trusts; Those who stuck the closest to him before, removed themselves from his Person; and this unhappy Prince, who was Presumptive Heir to Three Kingdoms, and had been used to behold a Crowd of admiring Courtiers about him, was of a sudden reduced to the Condition of a Private Person, and abandoned by all the World.

Yet so far did the King's Endearments go, and the better to prevent the Alteration of the Succession to the Crown, that he of himself proposed to the Duke of York a Second Marriage. As his Majesty had no Legitimate Children, and indeed despairing of ever attaining that Blessing; he judg'd it convenient that his Brother who had but Two Daughters left, should have an Heir, who might one day sit on the Throne of England. The Princess thought on by His Majesty, was the Lady Mary d' Este, Sister to Francis, Duke of Modena, and Daughter to Alphonso D' Este, the Third of that Name, Duke of Modena, by Madam Laura Martinessi, his Wife. She was born upon the 25th of September, Anno 1658, and had not passed the 15th Year of her Age, when at Modena she was married to his Royal Highness, by his Proxy, Henry, Earl of Peterborough, who with a noble Retinue attended her Highness and the Dutchess-Dowager her Mother into France; and after having resided some time at Paris, they came to Calais, and thence to Dover, where they arrived Nov. 21st, 1673. At Dover she was received by the Duke, where the Marriage betwixt them was personately Consummated by the Right Reverend Father in God, Dr. Nathaniel Crew, Lord Bishop of Durham, and now Lord Crew.

At London they were entertained with high Respect at the Court of England, where the Dutchess-Dowager, her Mother, having continued about the space of Six Weeks, in Order for the Settlement of her Daughter, she returned to Italy, to manage Affairs in the Infancy of the Duke her Son.

This Marriage met with great Opposition on the part of the Parliament, because the Princess was a Roman Catholic, yet the King gave little regard to what was Remonstrated to him on that account. He was pleased after, that the Dutchess proved fruitful, from whence he hoped a numerous Progeny to supply the Throne, which he judged in Time would eat up and destroy all manner of Prejudice. And here I think it will not be improper to repeat the Issue she had by the Duke, before the Person I am writing of, was said to be born.

On the 10th of January, 1674, she was brought to Bed of a Daughter, at the Palace of St. James's. She was Baptised by the Name of Katherine Laura, having for Godmothers the Ladies Mary and Anne, her Half-Sisters, and the Duke of Monmouth for her

Godfather. She died the Year following, Anno. **1675, on** the 3d of October, and **was** interred in the **Vault** of Mary, Queen of Scotland.

Isabella of York, Second Daughter of His (then) Royal Highness, James, **Duke of York,** and the Lady Mary D' Este, his Second Wife, **was born at St.** James's, the 28th of August, Anno. **1676.** Her **Godmothers were the** Duchess of Monmouth and the **Countess of Peterborough, and her** Godfather, Thomas, Earl of Derby, **Lord High Treasurer of** England, now Duke of Leeds. This young Princess **died at** the Age of **3** Years 6 Months, and Odd Days, viz. the 2d. of **March,** 1680, and was privately buried in the Vault of Mary, Queen of Scots.

Charles of York, Duke of Cambridge, **first Son** of His Royal **Highness, James, Duke of** York, **by the** Lady **Mary D'** Este his **second Wife, was** born at St. James's, **the 7th of** November, Anno. **1677, and the Next Day** was **Baptised by the** Bishop of Durham ; the King his Uncle, and the Prince **of** Orange, were his Godfathers; and the **Lady Isabella his Sister his** Godmother. **He died** suddenly on the **12th of December the same Year, and was** interred privately in the **Tomb of Mary,** Queen of Scots.

Charlot* **Maria of** York, third Daughter of James, **Duke of York, by the** Lady Mary **D'** Este his second Wife, was born at St. James's, **the** 15th **of August, 1682,** and two Days after was christened by Henry, Bishop **of London.** Her Godmothers were the Countesses **of** Arundel **and** Clarendon ; and the Duke of Ormond her Godfather. **She died** the 6th **of October following, and** was interred privately in the **Vault of** Mary, Queen **of Scots.**

None of these Children **surviving** long, **gave** Wings to the **Ambition of the Duke's enemies ; but** had **a** contrary effect on the **King's Spirits, and those who had** any esteem for him. Another **thing now trumped** up, that mightily helped to overwhelm the Duke's Interest, and alleviate even **the good** Opinion the King had of him, and this was the Popish Plot, wherein the Duke was brought in. The **Accusers boldly gave out, that** they were first to have assaulted the **King's Person, and after** that to have made away with all the **Protestants. The** Parliament took the **Alarm** and encouraged the **Discovery of it ; and the** King, when he met them, told them in his **Speech : "That he had been** informed of a Design against his Person, **by the Jesuits,"** whereupon a Bill was brought in and passed into an

* *Sic.*

Act, For the more effectual preserving the King's Person and Government, by disabling Papists from sitting in either House of Parliament. Five of the Popish Lords were committed to the Tower, and impeached of High Treason, One of which was beheaded: Diligent search was made after the Priests, and the Religious, several of them were hanged up in London, and others died miserably in the Prisons they were sent to.

The King however was very unwilling to lend an ear to the Suspicions raised against his Brother, and therefore did all he could to endeavor to clear him of the Insinuations laid against him: The Duke despised the scandalous Discourses, and false Reports that were made of him: But he was little sensible of the pressing Instances, and indeed the Reproaches of his Friends, who carried them so far, as to condemn the firm Steddiness of his Mind, giving it the Name of Prejudice and Obstinacy in Opinion. They remonstrated to him, that he would be the occasion of his own, and the King's Ruin; and the utter Extinction of the Catholic Faith in England; and the Overthrow of the State. A greater Check he yet met with from the King, who urged his Reasons with great Strength, and earnestly begged him to be contented to keep his Religion within his own Breast, without discovering and giving open Proofs of it to the World; who at such a juncture would not fail to improve it to his Ruin. He likewise remonstrated to him the great Hardships they had undergone already from the implacable Temper of the English Nation, and concluded all with assuring him that he should never want his Protection, did he not put it out of his power to cherish and support him. But the Duke remained inflexible, and resolved to hazard all, rather than dissemble his Religion.

The King, on the other hand, finding something must of necessity be done to appease the Minds of the People, thought fit to have the Duke to remove to Brussels, and after some Months ordered him to pass into Scotland. He obeyed the King with an entire Submission, and instantly prepared to be gone: But it was a smart Trial with a Heart so tender as his, to take leave of the King on these Conditions.

On the other hand, he found the King softened into Tears, and the Dutchess his Consort Inconsolable on this occasion. Nevertheless he still bore up against his own Tenderness, and the violent Motions of Nature that worked so strongly on his Mind, and so without Trouble or Complaint set out as the King had commanded him.

During his residence in Scotland, he sufficiently won upon the Hearts of the People, and the Parliament there by a solemn Deputation returned their most humble Thanks to His Majesty, that he had sent them a Prince so very acceptable to them: Which favourable Account made way for his Return into England a Few Months after.

In the Year 1680, a New Parliament being called, the Commons fell into a debate of the Popish Plot, and came to several rigorous resolutions, the first of which was against the Duke of York as being a Papist; and after several speeches it was resolved that a Bill should be brought in (this was the Second Bill of Exclusion) to disable James, Duke of York, from inheriting the Imperial Crown of England, and Ireland, and the Dominions thereunto belonging: Which Bill passed the Lower House, and was carried up to the Lords by William Lord Russel, but at the second reading the Lords threw it out: and the King, upon the Warmth that grew in Parliament, found himself obliged to dissolve them.

Soon after the King calling a New Parliament to meet at Oxford, a Third Bill of Exclusion was brought in, read the first time, and ordered a Second Reading, but the King thought fit again to prorogue them. Soon after the Duke returned to England, where he was received in a very affectionate manner by the King; and the Act drawn up against him was no more talked of.

The Duke's Friends had now in their turn an Instance of Triumph, in the Discovery of the Ryehouse Plot, for which several of his most inveterate Enemies suffered Death, and others were sufficiently mortified. From whence to the death of his Brother King Charles II. and his attaining the Crown, he had a clearer sunshine of Peace, than the Foregoing Part of his Life had been acquainted with: Nor shall I omit one Passage at his Brother's Decease, which is borrowed from an Author,* who seems to be of Credit.

"As his Zeal was ever the same in Adversity, so he took care to preserve it in Prosperity: He passionately desired the King's Conversion, and found it pretty well advanced, when he came to discourse the King upon such Occasions as he thought most seasonable.

"The King gave him a Paper he had composed himself, and writ with his own Hand, which contained a Summary of the most Material

---

* Father Francis **Brettoneau's** Abridgment of the Life of King James II.

and Solid Arguments for the Truth of the Catholic Religion. In fine, Heaven gave a blessing to these good Dispositions, and the Duke had this Comfort, when he lost his Brother, to see him die in the Bosom of the True Church.

"King Charles II. fell sick, and on the 4th Day of his Illness, was by his Physicians given over: When Two Protestant Bishops came to wait on His Majesty, they began the read, as is usual, at the Bed's Feet, the Office for the Visitation of the Sick. When they came to the Place where the Sick Person is exhorted to make Auricular Confession, but at the same time is told, that there is no Command obliges him to it, and he may if he pleases dispence with it; the Bishop of Bath stepped up to the King, made him a short Exhortation, and asked him if he repented of his Sins? The King having answered, *He did so*; His Lordship pronounced the form of Absolution, after the Manner of the Church of England. When the Office was over, the Bishop returned to the King to ask him whether he was willing to receive the Sacrament; and to exhort him to it. But the King answered him not a Word. His Lordship urged, and the King was pleased to tell him he would think on it. The Bishop still insisting on it, His Majesty still evaded it.

"The Duke of York did not let slip so fine an Occasion. He ordered all those who were by the King's Bedside to withdraw; and then addressing himself to the King, he testified his Joy to see him at last (as he thought) resolved to execute what his Conscience had so often solicited him to do; and offered at the same time to call for a Priest. *For God's sake Brother*, answered the King, *go send for one. But*, added he, *Won't you expose yourself too much?* To which the Duke replied, *Sir, tho' it should cost me my Life, I will get you one.* He went out immediately, and by a particular Accident, or a very singular Providence, the First Priest he met was Father Huddlestone, a Benedictine, the same that contributed much towards the Saving the King's Life after the Battle of Worcester, when that Prince hid himself all Night in the Hollow of a Tree. Father Huddlestone was shewed up a Private pair of Stairs into a Closet near the King's Bedchamber. As soon as the King knew him, he gave order for all that were in the Chamber to retire, except his Brother.

"The Duke however had a mind that the Earl of Bath, First Gentleman of the Bedchamber, and the Earl of Feversham, Captain of the Guards, both Protestants, should stay and be Witness of what passed. This Precaution he thought necessary to prevent the malignant Consequences that his **Enemies might have** made from thence, in case the Duke had staid alone with the **King,** when His Majesty was in that weak condition.

"Father **Huddlestone** went **in,** received the **King's** Abjuration, heard his Confession, and afterwards administered him the Sacraments. There was no delaying the Matter, for a few Hours after **the** King **died.** He acknowledged upon his Death-Bed, that next to God, **he owed** the Grace of his Reconciliation to the Church, to the indefatigable Zeal and tender Affection of the Duke his Brother. Nay more, he asked his Pardon aloud for the severe Treatment he had several times given him; and testified to those who were present, in terms of Esteem, Friendship, and Tenderness not to be expressed, how much he was touched with the Resignation and Patience which the Duke had all along shewn on these Occasions."

After the **Death of** King Charles **II. the Duke of** York was proclaimed King of Great Britain, by the Name of James II. Publick Rejoicings were heard **in all** Cities; **and** the Acclamations, and Shouts of Joy, which were heard from all parts, gave occasion to hope **for** a very happy Reign both to Prince and People.

If he had followed **the** Advice **of** his Council, he would have **been a little** remiss in **the point of Religion:** They would have persuaded **him to** stay some **time before he** publicly declared himself a Catholic. **Of** this opinion were several Catholicks themselves; but all **the Reasons** they offered him, **made** no manner of impression on his Mind, and the Sunday after his accession to the Crown he heard Mass publicly.

Not fully content with this Proceeding, he designed to re-establish Liberty of Conscience in England by Act of Parliament, wherein the Catholicks should be comprehended, as well as the rest of the Nonconformists; mean time **he gave** it out beforehand, as some of the ablest Lawyers after serious Examination, assured he might by Virtue of his Prerogative Royal.

The present Juncture was favourable enough for the King to make his Orders obeyed, and execute **what** he had undertaken, as to Liberty of Conscience. One would have thought that the Defeat of **the** Duke of Monmouth, and the Earl of Argyle, who took up Arms, **one in** England, and the other in Scotland, should have confirmed his Authority. But the Prejudice to the Catholic Religion had so deeply prevailed in the Hearts of the People, that it soon raised new Troubles, and hindered the King's Intentions.

It was insinuated to the People, that the King designed to destroy the Church of England, and introduce Popery, by main Force; that their Liberties and Properties were in danger, and themselves of being oppressed by an Arbitrary Government. These Reports eat into the People's Minds, and there lay corroding; and from that time nothing but Complaints and Murmurings were heard over all the Nation: After all the most Moderate Men confessed, that excepting the Case of Religion, they could not wish for a King fitter to procure the Advantage of the Nation, both in respect to his personal Virtues, and of his great Insight in Trade and Government.

Whilst Affairs were at this Crisis, the Queen, who had already had Four Children, as we have mentioned, was now with child, and sufficient cause of Joy it was to the King's Friends, especially the Catholicks: A Proclamation was published appointing a public Day of Thanksgiving to be observed in the Cities of London and Westminster, and soon after in all other Places of the Kingdom, and a suitable Form of Prayer was likewise ordered to be prepared for that purpose.

This News caused various Reflections throughout the Nation, and instead of allaying the former heat of the People, enflamed them the more. They entertained a Prejudice, which no doubt was instilled into them, that the Queen's Big Belly was only a Feint, an artifice of the R. Catholicks, for some end or other; but yet they knew not what Name to give it. And as every thing seemed to forward the King's Misfortunes, about this Time the Bishops were sent to the Tower, a Proceeding the King was more to blame in, than the Blackest Incidents they had to charge him with.

On the 10th of June, between the Hours of 9 and 10, a Rumour spread that the Queen was in labor; the Town took the alarm, and People seemed not a little surprized. This was not only confirmed, but was soon followed with the News of her being brought to bed of a Prince, and in the Afternoon the following Account was published by Authority.

"Whitehall, June 10. This Day between 9 and 10 in the Morning, the Queen was safely delivered of a Prince at St. James's; His Majesty, the Queen-Dowager, most of the Lords of the Privy Council, and divers Ladies of Quality being by."

The Prince of Orange himself, and the States of Holland, sent to compliment the King upon this Occasion, and acknowledged the new Prince, as did almost all the Cities in the Kingdom, who thereupon sent their Addresses to His Majesty, full of Expressions that signified a most sincere Fidelity and Zeal. Notwithstanding which there was a very deep **Resentment** lay hid in the Breasts of most **People**. The Prepossession they had that the **Prince** was imposed **on them, was** agitated by other melancholy Circumstances; that the **Order of the** Church and Constitution were in danger of being totally subverted : **And this,** as **a** stronger Physic on the Mind, drove out all **lesser** Humors, and divested them even of the Respect and Allegiance they **owed to their** Sovereign. It unluckily happened too, that Five Days **after** this Account was published of the Birth of the Prince, the Bishops were brought **to** Trial, and the Army lay then encamped at Hounslow Heath: Two things which did grievously alarm and afflict the People : The former needed no Aggravation of Words to provoke them, the Trial was public, and **as** universally resented : The other **required a little Art to possess them, that it was an Irish** Catholic-**Army,** and designed to keep **a heavy** hand over the Kingdom, if they pretended to **dispute the** King's **Authority** in repealing the Tests and Penal **Laws, by** which **Method he designed to** introduce his own Religion.

This worked so effectually, that People were every where ripe for Self-Defence, **and** the King was no less than accused of imposing **a Child** for his **Lawful** Successor, **to** the Prejudice of **his own** Daughters, for whom he had always expressed all the Affection **and** Tenderness imaginable, and they to him, and paid all the Duty and Respect due to **an** indulgent Father : And notwithstanding all **the** Royal **Favors** he had bestowed, yet **he** could depend **on** nothing but his **Army ;** nor with any great Confidence on them, which made him **resolve to try how far** he might **trust** their Fidelity, and therefore endeavoured to engage **them,** both Officers and Soldiers, to sign a Writing, whereby they should promise to contribute as far as in them **lay,** towards supporting the King's Design of taking off the Test and Penal Laws. This Project was thought fit to be proposed to all the Regiments one **by** one, and the first, His Majesty's Desires were made known to, **was the Earl of** Litchfield's Regiment, who all thereupon, **both** Officers and Soldiers (Two Captains and some private Men excepted) laid down **their** Arms; at which the King being astonished, **commanded them to take up** their Arms again. This was a sufficient **Experiment of the** Temper of the Soldiers ; and His Majesty found **that nothing** but new modelling the Army would do.

Things standing in this disposition, a Memorial of the Church of
172

England was drawn up privately, and sent to the Prince and Princess of Orange, to implore their Protection, whilst many of the Nobility and Gentry joined in these Sollicitations ; and others withdrew themselves into Holland, where they gave the Prince Assurances of a sufficient Power, that would immediately join him on his landing.

In the mean time, His Majesty had resolved to call a Free Parliament, to establish an Universal Liberty of Conscience, and to remedy all the Complaints of his Subjects. The Charter of the City of London was restored, the Suspension of the Bishop of London taken off; the Deputy Lieutenants and Justices of the Peace, who had been removed for disputing His Majesty's Commands, were suffered to resume their Commissions ; and a Proclamation was published for restoring Corporations to their ancient Charters.

The Rumor of the Prince's being an Impostor began to spread with greater Warmth, and to this was added, that his true Mother was to be brought over with the Dutch Fleet : Being now about Four Months old, he received private baptism in the Chappel of St. James's, on the 15th of October, of which the Following Account was published by Authority.

"Whitehall, Oct. 15. This day in the Chappel of St. James's, His Royal Highness the Prince of Wales, being before christened, was solemnly named (amidst the Ceremonies and Rites of Baptism) James, Francis, Edward. His Holiness, represented by his Nuntio, Godfather, and the Queen-Dowager Godmother. The King and Queen assisted at the Solemnity, with a great Attendance of Nobility and Gentry, and a Concourse of People, all expressing joy and satisfaction, suitable to the Place and Occasion.

And now to stifle the Suspicion and Report, which had gained but too much credit, that the Prince was not lawfully born of the Queen's Body, the King assembled an Extraordinary Council, where the Queen Dowager, the Peers that were in Town both Spiritual and Temporal, the Lord Mayor and Aldermen, the Judges, and His Majesty's Council at Law, were present.

To whom His Majesty delivered himself in this manner,

" My Lords,

" I Have called you together upon a very extraordinary Occasion ; but extraordinary Diseases must have extraordinary Remedies. The malicious Endeavors of my Enemies have so poisoned the Minds of some of my Subjects, that by the Reports I have from all hands, I have reason to believe, that very many do not think this Son, with which it hath pleased God to bless me, to be mine, but a Supposed Child. But I may say, that by particular Providence, scarce any Child was ever born, where there were so many Persons present.

"I have taken this time to have the Matter heard and examined here, expecting that the Prince of Orange, with the first Easterly Wind will invade this Kingdom: And as I have often ventured my Life for the Nation before I came to the Crown, so I think my self more obliged to do the same now I am King; and do intend to go in person against him, whereby I may be exposed to Accidents, and therefore I thought it necessaay to have this now done, in order to satisfy the Minds of my Subjects, and to prevent this Kingdom being engaged in Blood and Confusion after my Death; desiring to do always what may contribute most to the Ease and Quiet of my People, which I have shewed by securing to them their Liberty of Conscience, and the Enjoyment of their Properties, which I will always preserve.

"I have desired the Queen-Dowager to give her self the trouble to come hither, to declare what she knows concerning the Birth of my Son; and most of the Ladies, Lords, and other Persons who were present, are ready here to depose upon Oath their knowledge of this Matter.

After His Majesty had ended his Speech, the Queen Dowager rising from her Chair, which was placed on the King's Right Hand, was pleased to declare in the manner following.

"THAT when the King sent for her to the Queen's Labor, she came as soon as she could, and never stirred from her till she was delivered of the Prince of Wales." To which she signed

"Catherina R."

The Clerk of the Council was then ordered to receive the Oaths of the Ladies, Lords, and other Persons, who had any Evidence to deliver in this Matter.

These were

THE Marchioness of Powis.
The Countess of Arran.
The Countess of Peterborow.
174

The Countess of Sunderland.
The Countess of Roscommon.
The Countess of Fingal.
The Lady Bulkley.
The Lady Belasyse.
The Lady Waldgrave.
Mrs. Mary Crane and Mrs. Anne Cary, Gentlewomen of the Bedchamber to Queen Dowager.
Mrs. Isabella Wentworth, Mrs. Catherine Sayer, Mrs. Isabella Waldgrave, Mrs. Margaret Dawson, Mrs. Eliz. Bromley, Mrs Pelegrina Turini, Gentlewomen of the Bed-chamber to the Queen.
Mrs. Mary Ann Delabadie, Dry Nurse to the Prince.
Mrs. Judith Wilkes, Her Majesty's Midwife.
Mrs. Eliz. Pearce, the Queen's Laundress.
The Dutchess of Richmond and Lenox.
The Countess of Litchfield.
The Countess of Marischal.
George, Lord Jefferies, Lord Chancellor.
Robert, Earl of Sunderland.
Henry, Lord Arundel of Wardour, Lord Privy Seal.
John, Earl of Mulgrave, Lord Chamberlain of the Household.
William, Earl of Craven.
Lewis, Earl of Feversham, Lord Chamberlain to Catherine, Queen Dowager.
Alexander, Earl of Murray.
Charles, Earl of Middleton.
John, Earl of Melfort.
Sidney, Lord Godolphin, Lord Chamberlain to the Queen.
Sir Stephen Fox. Kt.
Lieutenant Colonel Edward Griffin, afterwards Lord Griffin.
Sir Charles Scarborough, Kt. First Physician to the King.
Sir Thomas Witherley, Second Physician to the King.
Sir William Waldgrave, Kt. First Physician to Her Majesty.
Dr. Robert Brady, One of His Majesty's Physicians in Ordinary.
James St. Amand, Their Majesties' Apothecary.

All these declared, with some little Differing Circumstances, the Birth of the Prince; the greatest part, as they attested, having seen it before it was cleansed from the Impurities of its Birth, with all other infallible **Tokens** of his being **immediately born of the** Queen's **Body.**

After these Depositions were taken, the King was pleased to acquaint the Lords, that the Princess Anne of Denmark, his Daughter, would have been present, but that she being with Child, and having **not lately** stirred abroad, **could not** come so far without Hazard. "And **now, my Lords,"** adds the King, "altho' I did not question **but all here** present **were before** satisfied in this Matter; yet by what **you have** heard, **you will be** the better able to satisfy others. Besides, if **I and the** Queen could be thought so wicked as to endeavor to impose **a Child upon** the Nation, you see how impossible it would have been; neither could **I my** self be imposed upon, having constantly been with the **Queen,** during her being **with child,** and the whole time of her **Labour.** And there is **none of** you but will easily believe me, who **have suffered so much for** Conscience-sake, uncapable of so great a Villainy, to the Prejudice of my own Children. And I thank **God, that** those who know me, **know** well it is my Principle to do as **I would be done by ;** *For that is the Law and the Prophets;* And I would rather die a **Thousand** Deaths, than do the least wrong **to any of** my Children."

"If any of **my Lords think it necessary the** Queen should **be sent** for it shall be done ;" which the Lords declined, saying, **they had received** satisfaction enough from what the King had declared.

Then an **Order in Council** was made, "That the Declarations before made, by His **Majesty** and by Her Majesty the Queen Dowager; together with the several Depositions then entered, should be forthwith enrolled in the Court **of** Chancery.

In pursuance of which Order in Council, the Lord Chancellor, on **Saturday** the **28th of October** following, in the High Court of Chancery, many of the Nobility, and the Lords of His Majesty's most Honourable Privy Council, being **present,** caused the aforesaid Order **of Council, and the** Declarations of His Majesty, and the Q. Dowager, **to be openly and** distinctly read **in Court, as the** same were entered in **the Words aforesaid in** the Council **Book. And** the Lords and Ladies, **who made** the respective Depositions aforesaid, being present in Court, were **sworn** again, and having heard their Depositions distinctly read **in** the Words aforesaid, and being severally interrogated by the Court to the Truth thereof, they all upon their Oaths affirmed their respective Depositions to be true; and did likewise depose (except **some** few, who came late into the Council Chamber, or some who stood at too great a distance) that they heard His Majesty, and Her Majesty the Queen-Dowager, make the several Declarations aforesaid, and that the same, as they had been read, were truly entered into the Council Book, according to the Sense, Intent and Meaning of what His Majesty the King, and Her Majesty the Queen-Dowager did then declare. And for as much as the Earl of Huntingdon, and the Earl of Peterborow, who were able to depose to the Matters aforesaid, had not been Examined at the Council Board, but had brought their several Depositions in Writing, which they delivered into Court, and were to the same effect with the rest, the Lord Chancellor, caused them to be openly read, and examined them severally upon their Oaths to the Truth thereof. Whereupon His Majesty's Attorney General moved the Court, that the said Declarations of his Majesty, and of Her Majesty the Queen Dowager; and the several Depositions, and the Order of Council, should be enrolled in the Petty Bag Office, and in the Office of Enrolments in the Court of Chancery, for the safe Preservation and Custody of them, which the Lord Chancellor ordered accordingly.

Before this His Majesty had received the Compliments of Congratulation from most of the Princes of Europe, the Prince and Princess of Orange not excepted; and Addresses from all Parts of the Kingdom to the same purpose. And not only this, but the most Spritely and Ingenious of the Two Universities employed their Pens in celebrated Verses, to congratulate the King on this Occasion. There seemed a glorious Interval of Peace and Happiness, and a hopeful Promise of Lasting and Infinite Blessings to the Nation; but in the Mazes of Providence there is something ordained for Man not to see, and which the most glorious and fair Appearance of is only delusive. In One of those famous pieces of Poetry I have mentioned, the Author seems to have had much such another Thought, and indeed to prophesy something of Futurity.

O NCE more my Goddess, hear thy Priest,
   Indulge me, O indulge this last Request!
The Mightiest Boon thou hast in store,
I ask, but grant, and I will ask no more.

Oh let me enter to the Inmost Room,
The darken'd Retirement of Apollo's Doom.

> *The sacred Mirror there expose,*
> *The Wondrous Magic-Glass,*
> *Which from its bright reflective Face,*
> *Fate's inmost Secrets shows,*
> *And great Futurities already come to pass.*
>
> *There I would view when James shall late repair,*
> *In the first Orbs to shine a Star;*
> *And guide with guardian Rays, his People from afar.*
> *There I would view his Godlike Son*
> *With Shouts ascend his Father's Throne;*
> *And cheer, with mighty Hopes, the drooping Albion.*
>
> *Next, Goddess, I would see him reign,*
> *Crown'd and uncontrol'd, the Monarch of the Main.*
> *Whilst humble Belgians sue for Peace,*
> *And the far East and West the British Power confess.*
> *Let him next on land appear,*
> *Bold, yet cautious, open, and yet wise,*
> *Generous, and yet frugal, good without Disguise.*
> *With Justice mild, and piously severe.*
> *Shew me Goddess, shew me this,*
> *And let thy Oracles to morrow cease.*
>
> *Alas, the Muse the well meant Pray'r denies,*
> *She struts, frowns, and thus replies:*
> *"With Furious Folly, and with Zeal Profane,*
> *The uneasy Britons still would pry*
> *Into the Depths of late Futurity;*
> *Whilst Heaven showers present Blessings down in vain.*
> *What Time shall come, and what the Fates will do,*
> *Concerns not thee, O Man to know;*
> *To-day is thine, O seize the useful Now!*
> *But nothing happy, Man can please,*
> *Wanton and lawless grown, with Luxury and Ease."*

How near this Poet hit the Temper of his Countrymen, I need not shew; they were not to be pleased, Cabals were formed against the King, and an Intelligence kept with the Prince of Orange, who was invited over, and being succoured by the Hollanders, appointed a

178

numerous Fleet, with which he passed into England with an Army of 13000 Men. The King in a very indulgent manner, offered whatever his Subjects could reasonably require, if Reason and their own Interest could have reclaimed them ; but the Frenzy was grown too strong : The Prince was advancing with his Troops, and the King seeing no other means of healing this Breach, put himself at the head of his Army, and marched against the Enemy, when drawing near to them, he soon found what he had to trust to ; his Army was instantly abandoned by almost all its Officers, most of which had been gained by the Prince of Orange's Emissaries, who instead of doing their Duty to attack him, went over to him.

The Desertion in short was so general, that the King's own Creatures forsook him, and even those he had overwhelmed with his Royal Goodness were found in the Confederacy. In this Confusion of Affairs he judged it improper to continue at the head of such an Army, from whom he could promise himself no Subjection, and therefore retired again to London.

Mean time provision was to be made for the Security of the Queen, and Prince of Wales (then so called) who was now not above Six Months old, whom the King caused privately to pass into France ; and intended himself soon to follow them. At length he got out of Whitehall, parted from London, and imbarked ; but being obliged to put ashore again for Ballast, he was arrested and discovered near Feversham, where he was so rudely treated by the Mob, as very much exercised his Royal Patience ; the Dignity of his Person not being sufficient to guard him from those mean Insolencies, which but to a Private Person would have been accounted infamous Outrages. Here however he received the courtesy of having his wearing Cloaths brought him, being sent on board a Man of War then in the Hope, below Gravesend, for that purpose ; and as soon as 'twas known at London of his being stopped at Feversham, the Lords sent him his Coaches and Guards, and at the same time deputed the Earl of Feversham to go and engage him to come back.

The King had no time to deliberate, for he was no longer Master of his own Proceedings, and therefore took Coach and submitted to be conducted to London : The People, by their loud Acclamations, testifying an extraordinary Joy and entire Devotion to the King's Interest ; which was but a Transitory Comfort, for about Midnight, when the King lay fast asleep void of all Fear and Suspicion, the Lords Hallifax, De la Mere, and Shrewsbury, came to awake him, and to tell him from the Prince of Orange, that it was found necessary for him to retire from London. They offered him at the same time his choice of Hampton Court or Ham, for the Place of his Retreat, but the King desired to go to Rochester, which was granted him, and thither he was carried Prisoner.

Here he continued some few Days, always bearing in mind that he was a Christian and a King, till he met with a favorable Opportunity for his Escape. There was a Boat waited for him at the Seaside, the King passed unobserved thro' a Garden, stepped into the Boat, and set sail for France, whither in a day or two he happily arrived. He was received in France with all the Marks of Honor and Distinction suitable to his Character, and hasting to St. Germans he there found the Queen and Prince (so-called) newly arrived. And here one may pretty well judge what were the Sentiments of the Hearts of their Britannic Majesties at this afflicting, yet joyful Interview. They now saw one another again after so sorrowful a Parting, and so many Dangers they had both undergone ; but at the same time could not but reflect deeply on the Condition they were reduced to, which yet was very much alleviated by the obliging and generous Offers of the King of France, and the repeated Promises he made them, to succour and assist them with all his Power.

But this mutual Comfort of seeing one another again did not last long, the King had not been above Two Months at St. Germans, before he thought himself obliged, for the Good of his Affairs, to pass into Ireland, where the Lord Tyrconnel, at the head of the Catholics, still maintained the King's Authority. The King sailed thither, and there sustained the War against Duke Schombergh for above a Twelvemonth, till King William arriving with a numerous Force of veteran Troops, had the advantage of the King's Army, and defeated him at the Passage of the Boyne ; after which he was advised by My Lord Tyrconnel, and all the General Officers to retreat to France, where, about Two Years after, his Queen bore him a Daughter, who was born the 28th of June, 1691, and christened Louise Marie, about the time of her Father's Disappointment by the Defeat at *La Hogue* ; from which time the Residue of his Life was wholly employed in Exercises of Piety and Devotion, of which he was a very shining Example to the time of his Death.

For some time before which he made it his daily Prayer to God, that He would be pleased to take him out of this troublesome World, and on this Subject he had some conversation with the Queen, who
180

seemed very sensibly afflicted at his having so passionate a desire of Death, telling him that she looked upon the Preservation of his Person as necessary for the Good of her and her Children. But she received no other Answer but this, "That God Almighty would take care of her, and her Children, and that his Life gave him no Capacity of doing any thing for them." He would often have communication with his Children, especially the Prince of Wales (as they then called him) in whom the King was infinitely delighted, as finding in him, tho' yet very young, a Genius capable of arriving at the highest Accomplishments, which the King would passionately indulge him in, and by repeated Instructions take all imaginable care to fructify his tender Mind with the most Useful and Noble Sentiments, to which in Nature he seemed so apparently inclined.

About Midsummer, 1701, the King was seized with a dead Palsy, and grew dangerously ill upon it. The Physicians being of opinion that he might receive some benefit from the Waters of Bourbon, he went thither, and took them with some Success: But some Months after he began to spit Blood again, as he had done before his Journey to Bourbon; and on the 2d of September he was taken very ill; in which State he contiuued for Two Days, and then his Physicians began to Despair of his Life. The same Day he made a general Confession, which he had scarce finished before he was taken with such a Weakness as was followed by a Vomiting of Blood, which had like to have choaked him, however, he recovered himself a little, and called for the Prince of Wales (as then called) who immediately entered the Chamber; but it was a sad Spectacle for him to see the King covered with Blood, and half dead. He ran to embrace him, and the King held out his Arms to him himself, and embraced him with all the tenderness imaginable. He blessed him, and as he gave him his benediction, recommended to him above all things to stand fast by his Religion, and the Service of God, whatever came of it, and to have always for the Queen all the respect and submission due to the Best of Mothers. He likewise let him understand how much he was indebted to the King of France, which he charged him never to forget: What else the King had to say to him, he gave him in Writing, and bid him read it often when His Majesty was gone; a Copy of which is hereafter printed.

It was not without some Violence that the Prince was taken from him, the King would fain have held him; "Leave me my Son," said he, "let me give him my Blessing once more;" which when he had done, he **suffered** him to retire to his own Apartment. After which the King ordered the Princess his Daughter to be brought him; to whom he spoke much in the same Terms; and gave her his blessing: And the Princess, melted into Tears, gave him to understand by the Abundance of them the inward Sorrow of her Heart.

When the King had done speaking to his Children, he ordered the Protestant Lords, and his Domesticks of the same Religion, who were in his Chamber, to come near him. He exhorted them every one **in particular to embrace the** Catholic Religion, assuring them that if they followed the **Advice** he gave them, they would feel the same Consolation that he did, whenever they found themselves in the same Condition they then saw him in. Nor did he forget the Catholicks, **whom he exhorted** to live according to their Faith, and all together to pay a lasting and just obedience to the Prince.

The King of France, who had not missed One Day to inform **himself of** the state of his Health, **and** had been already twice to see **him, paid him** a third visit. **His** Most Christian Majesty went first into the Queen's Chamber, where he declared to her the Resolution he had taken, That "provided it pleased God to take the King her Husband, he would acknowledge the Prince of Wales (as **he** was then called) for King of England," Upon which the Queen sent immediately for **him,** and acquainted him with what His Most Christian Majesty designed to do in his favour; to whom the King, resuming the Discourse, said, "Sir; you are going to lose the King your Father, **but you shall** always find another in me, and I shall look **on you as** my own Child." At which **the** Prince, embracing the **King's** Knees, assured him, "That he would also have the same **respect for** his Majesty, as he had had for the King his Father. That he would never forget how much **he was** indebted to him, but preserve the Acknowledgement of it whilst he lived."

The King of **France** passed from thence into the King of England's Apartment, and went to his Bedside. The Courtiers out of Respect would have withdrawn; but His Most Christian Majesty signified to them, that he would be glad to let the World know what he had to say; then addressing himself to **the** Sick King, he repeated aloud what he had before declared to the Queen concerning the Prince, adding withal, **to the** King's Consolation; "That he perceived in him those early Appearances of Vertue **and** Honor, that could not but strengthen His Majesty in his Affection to him, besides the Obligations of Conscience and Affinity, which he had always indispensably thought himself under."

It is impossible to represent the Sentiments of the English Court upon this Occasion. Without any regard to the measures of Decency, every one was eager to testify their grateful Acknowledgements to the Most Christian King. They threw themselves at his Feet, and in Sentiments mingled with Comfort and Sorrow, made the Chamber ring with Applauses and Sighs, insomuch that the Thanks of his Brittanic Majesty could not be heard : And the Most Christian King found himself so sensibly touched, that he could scarce restrain from Tears, and therefore retired.

I shall here repeat no more of this sad Catastrophe of the English King, he lay till the 16th of September, when he resigned his Soul to God, and was with very little Pomp and Ceremony interred in the Parish Church of St. Germans, as a private Gentlemen, according to the Request of his Will, and no Epitaph on his Tomb, but these four words, "Here lies King James."

Thus I have run thro' the Life of this unfortunate King, which I shall conclude with the Instructions he left in Writing to the Prince of Wales, as he was then called : but penned some time before his Death.

"KINGS not being responsible for their Actions, but to God only, they ought to behave themselves in every thing with more circumspection than those that are of an Inferior Condition ; and if Subjects owe a faithful Obedience to their King, and his Laws, the King is likewise obliged to take a great care of them, and to love them like a Father. Then as you hold the first rank among them, and that you must be one day their King your self, I believe it to be my duty, as your King, and your Father, to give you the following advice : And I find my self yet more obliged to it, when I reflect on your Age, my own, and the present State of my Affairs.

"I. Serve God as a perfect Christian, and be a worthy Child of the Roman Church. Let no Humane Consideration, of what nature soever, be ever capable to draw you from it. Remember always that Kings and Princes, and the Great Ones of the Earth, shall give an Account of their Conduct before the Dreadful Tribunal of God, where every one shall be judged according to his Works. Consider that you are come into the World to glorify God, and not to seek your Pleasure. That it is by Him that Kings Reign ; and that without His particular Protection, nothing can prosper of all that you undertake.

Serve then the Lord in the Days of thy Youth, and you shall receive a Recompence in the Land of the Living. Begin by times, and without Delay. Never forget that there are greater things expected from Persons in High Stations, than from others: Their Example gives great impressions, and is always most followed, be it as it will.

"II. If it pleases God to re-establish me upon my Throne, I have reason to hope that I shall put things in that Condition, that it shall be more easy for you to govern my Kingdoms after me, with Security of the Monarchy, and intire Satisfaction of all the Subjects. A King cannot be happy if his Subjects be not at ease, and the Subjects also cannot securely enjoy what belongs to them if their King be not at his ease, and in capacity to protect and defend them. Therefore preserve your Prerogatives, but disquiet not your Subjects, either in their Estates or their Religion. Remember the great Precept, Do not to others what you would not have done to your self. Take great care that no body oppresses the People with Vexatious Law-Suits, or Undertakings that are chargeable to them: I told you, and it is true, that a King ought to be the Father of his People, and consequently to have a tenderness for them that is altogether fatherly.

"III. Live in peace with your Neighbors, and know that Kings and Princes may commit the same Injustice with the most notorious Robbers, that openly attack the Passengers upon the High-Ways, or the Pyrates, that take whatever they meet: Without doubt they'll be punished for it at the Judgment of God. Then suffer yourself not to be drawn away by Ambition, and the Desire of a False Glory, so far as to forget the Precept of the Law of God and Nature, which I told you but just now. Hearken not to the Counsels of those that shall persuade you to Enlarge your Estates and Dominions by Unjust Acquisitions, but be content with what is your own.

"IV. Do your endeavour to establish by a Law the Liberty of Conscience; and whatever may be represented to you about it, never leave that Design until you have compassed it. It is a grace and particnlar favor that God does them, whom he enlightens with His Knowledge, in calling them to the True Religion; and it is by Mildness, Instructions, and a good Example, that they are won, much more than by Fear or Violence.

"V. If you begin early to live well, it will be much easier to you to preserve your innocence, than to recover it after once you shall have lost it. Forget not the good Instructions that have been given you, to shun Idleness, and Bad Company. Idleness will expose you to all sorts of Temptation, and Bad Company will be a Poison to you, of which you'll hardly scape the Influences. Suffer no Persons to come near you that talk obscenely or impiously, and by their Railleries endeavor to destroy Christianity it self, and turn into ridicule the most Holy and Religious Practices.

"VI. Nothing is more fatal to Men, and to the Greater Men (I speak with a dear-bought Experience) than to be given over to the Unlawful Love of Women, which of all Vices is the most seducing, and the most difficult to be conquered, if not stifled in its Birth : It a Vice that is but too universal and too common in Young People ; there are but few that apply themselves to know the Danger of it, and are not drawn to it by Bad Example, as well as the Suggestions and Artifices of the Devil ; no body ought to be so much on guard as your self ; because it has pleased God to make you, by your Birth, what you are ; for the more Men are elevated, the more they are exposed ; especially if they live in Peace and Plenty. But what ought more to oblige you to watch over your self, is the Remembrance of the terrible Example of David ; he was hardly established in his Throne, but he forgot the great Things that God had done for him, and suffered his Eyes to dazzled by the Sight of a Woman, so far as to fall into the Sin of Adultery, and from Adultery into that of Murder. Could but all, that, with him, have had the misfortune of falling into those heinous Crimes, remember the sincere Repentance he had of them, and imitate him ; not forgetting the Chastisements and Afflictions that God sent him in this World, to save him in the next.

"VII. Master your self so much as never to be transported by Anger. That Passion offends God, and is grating to Men, and while it lasts, takes away the Reason and Judgment of him that gives himself over to it. It has been the Ruin of Several Great Men. What a King says is not easily forgot ; and there is nothing but Fear and Religion that can hinder Men from resenting it, and being revenged of it. Anger makes a Prince incapable of governing ; for how shall he rule others, when he cannot rule himself.

"VIII. Take not pleasure in feasting; but shun all sorts of Excesses that ruin Health, and makes Men unfit for Business. It is very hard to leave the Habit of them when once it is contracted. The Excess of Wine kills in a short time those that are of a Hot Constitution, and besots them that are Phlegmatic. I believe it is not necessary to enlarge upon this Point, since few Princes among the Civilized Nations are addicted to so foul a Vice.

"IX. I must yet give you warning not to suffer your self to be engaged, either by the Heat of Youth, Ambition, Interest, or flattering Councils, into an Offensive War that is not evidently just: Otherwise it would be all at once to violate the Divine and humane Laws. Kings and Princes, to come again to the Comparison which I made you, can no more justify the Injustice which they do to their Neighbors, in taking (unless it be by way of Reprisal) their Cities and Provinces, than the Highway-men and Pirates can that which they do to Private Persons, when forcibly they take away their Goods. You ought, when Necessity requires it, to preserve and defend what is lawfully your own, in taking up Arms, and repelling Force by Force. You owe that to your self; you owe it to your Subjects. But to be the Aggressor in an Unjust War, is an Undertaking of Fatal Consequence for this Life, and that to come. For in the first place, God pardons not if we make not restitution: And that Princes seldom do. In the second place, what Devastation makes not War in Provinces and whole Kingdoms, by the Ruin of so many Thousands of innocent Persons? Besides these general Rules of Conscience, a King of England ought of good Politicks to be more circumspect in this Point, than any other. For not being able, without the assistance of his People to begin and carry on a War, and the People of England never believing it their Interest to furnish Money for making conquests abroad, it follows necessarily, that the Charges of the War fall upon the King's Funds, and upon what we call the Civil List, and that so the King gets in debt.

"X. For the same reason a King of England ought to take care that in his Expences he exceeds not his Revenue, and that he applies himself to what is agreeable to the People, and tends to the Public Good. If you find any of your Ministers, or Officers, that abusing the Power with which you have trusted them with, employ it to vex and oppress your Subjects, take away their Places, and punish them your self, without giving them over to the Examination of a Parliament, who desire no better than to snatch them out of your hands, and bring them to justice themselves; which would but weaken your Authority, and discourage those that serve you faithfully.

"XI. Apply your self principally to know the Constitution of the English Government, that you may keep, both you and your Parliament, each in the due Bounds that become the one and the other. Further, be instructed concerning the Trade of the Nation, make it flourish by all Lawful Means. It is that which enriches the Kingdom, and which will make you considerable abroad. But above all, endeavour to be and to remain superior at Sea, without which England cannot be secure.

The Prince (as he was then called) was about Thirteen Years of Age at the Death of King James, fraught with the blooming Appearance of all manly Virtues, which now began to ripen in him, so as to attract the eyes of the Court of France. 'Tis true, the King's generous Design of declaring him King of England, according to the Promise he had given, did not pass uninterrupted through the Council; yet even those who disapproved it, took pride in excusing themselves from any manner of Prejudice and Disrespect, but on the contrary declared, "They should be glad of any Opportunity to serve him, whose Interest they could never think of deserting, were not that of their own Country in the Scale, the inevitable Commencement of a War depending from the express Terms of a Peace very lately concluded. And therefore if they did not think this a proper Season to proclaim his Title, they could not doubt but they should merit His Majesty's, and the Prince's Excuse in what they had said." The D—— de T——, the D——de M——, the Counts of V——e, d—' C——, M. Ch—d, and others, were of this opinion; but the King was steadfast in his Resolution, and the Dauphin, who was the last that spoke in Council, left no objection unanswered, either in respect to the King's Honor or Advantage, that did not entirely convince His Majesty of the Justice and Integrity of such a Proceeding; and of the same opinion were all the Princes of the Blood.

The King, who in his Heart was resolved before, took a great deal of pleasure in the Dauphine's Words, and immediately gave Orders for the proclaiming him King of Great Britain, &c. as soon as the Breath was out of King James's Body, and the People very willingly proclaimed their Satisfaction, by joining in it their loud and hearty Acclamations. The usual Ceremony on this Occasion being punctually observed : The Queen Mother was appointed Regent, my Lord **Middleton gave** up the Seal, all **the** Lords took the Oaths of Fidelity, the **Servants** kissed his Hand, and every thing stood as it did in **King James's Days.**

The **King of France (who** had not only Proclaimed him in his **own Dominions, but had** likewise given Orders to his Embassadors to do **the same in** all the Courts of Europe) thought it now a very great **Argument of** his Affection **to** him, to take care of his future Education : **Thus far** he had proceeded in all necessary Literature, and was ready to be initiated in **the** more Manly Exercises of Life : His most Christian Majesty therefore ordered him proper Masters at his **own Expence, to instruct him in the most** useful parts of the Mathematics, **particularly Navigation, Fortification, and** the like ; the **former of** which **(Naviga**tion) he **is said to be an** exquisite Master of, as **he is** likewise of most of the European Languages. To these more Masculine Accomplishments were added Riding, Dancing, Fencing, Shooting ; **and such like** Embellishments, **as together** made up the Character **of** the Person that the French had proclaimed him to be.

Those who have conversed **with him, allow** him to be endued with excellent Wit, and those who have seen him under the trials of it, **are of the same** opinion as to his Courage. In the Twelfth Year **of** his Age, as he was Hunting **with the** Duke of Berry and others in the Forest of St. Germain, they had a monstrous Boar in Chase, the Company were dispersed and the (pretended) Prince meeting the Boar separately, having only with him one Servant, shot him in the Body **and ended the** Pursuit. At which kind of Exercises of Shooting, **Running,** or Flying, there are few among the French, tho' they are **very Excellent** at it, that exceed him. His Dexterity in Riding and **Fencing might** likewise be **added** among these other Qualifications, **but it is enough** to say, **that there was nothing wanting** to contribute any thing to **his Education.** Thus far the Accounts of French Authors **go.** He is proclaimed there, and stiled King of England, a Detachment **of** Fifty of the French Guards appointed him, with Twelve Yeomen of the Guard, Six Guard du Corps, a proper Division of Houshold Servants, and an Allowance of 50000 Livres a Month, conveyed constantly to St. Germains in an Iron **Cart** ; together with a Private-Purse from the French Court of near as much more : And **here** we leave him a little to see how this is relished in other Places.

In England, the People seemed to be in a wonderful Surprize. For they had been taught to look on him as an Impostor, and his most Christian Majesty had, to reap the Fruits of Peace, but a little before acknowledged King William, as King of Great Britain, who being a Prince of a very great Spirit, was sufficiently rouzed by such a Proceeding. He immediately writ to the King of Sweden, as Guarantee of the Treaty of Ryswick, to give him an Account of the manifest Violation thereof, and at the same time sent an Express to the Earl of Manchester, his Ambassador at Paris, to come immediately away, without taking leave; and Monsieur Poussin, the French Secretary here had suddain Notice to depart the Kingdom, The Nation addressed the King, and agreed in an unanimous adherence to his Majesty, expressing an Abhorrence of this Action in the French King, so that many who were no Enemies to the Person proclaimed, began to fear his most Christian Majesty had proceeded a Step too far.

King William was so Active, that he immediately formed the Grand Alliance, which the French were not able to prevent, and then Dissolving the Parliament, called a new One, before whom he laid the Copies of those Treaties, which they unanimously approved; and one of the first Things transacted, was the passing an Act for the Attainder of the (Pretended) Prince of Wales. But this was hardly done before King William died; yet Matters were so far carried in Parliament, that a War was inevitable, which had been already begun in Italy, of which I have not room here to repeat any thing, if it were material, more than saying, that the French King meerly drew it on himself thro' his immovable and generous Principle of supporting the (Pretended) Prince; for he might otherwise have made very good terms for his Grandson, by a reasonable Partition, or at least have warded off the English share in it, which has been much the heaviest, and without which, this War could not in human Probability, but have proved successful on his side.

On the contrary, in the Year 1706. The most Christian King found himself under the Necessity of suing for Peace; yet it was not without severe struggles of Conscience to depart from the Promises he had made the late King James II. He consulted the Court of St. Germains, and in a private Conference with the Queen Dowager, and the (pretended) Prince at that time, "assured them that he would never depart from their Interest, tho' the present Exigency of Affairs, and the pressing Instances of his Subjects had obliged him to make some Overtures of Peace to the Enemy." They read hea his Majesty's Compliment with Sighs ; and the (pretended) Prince himself replied, "That not only his **Interest,** but even his Life it self, was too small a Consideration for his most Christian Majesty to put in Composition with the Good of his Kingdom. I am Content," says he, "to leave my Cause to Providence, being entirely assured of your Majesty's sincere Affection to me."

However, for the present, his Majesty's good Wishes for Peace were baffled, by some who thought it their Interest to carry on the War, and would be contented with nothing but the utter Ruin of the French Nation, which when the King found, he exerted himself in a very wonderful Manner ; the Offers of Peace that he had made, softned the Hearts of his Subjects, and very much helped to alleviate the Hardships they lay under, so that his Majesty, contrary to the Expectations of the Enemy, and even surpassing their Belief, was in a Capacity next Year, not only to stop the Torrent of the Confederates in Flanders, but to be victorious in Spain, at the Battle of Almanza. In Germany the Marshal de Villars likewise made a very advantageous Irruption into Germany ; and in Provence the Allies had been forced to retreat from before Toulon. As these Successes did not a little Elevate the drooping Spirits of the French Nation, so it likewise put some Life into the Court of St. Germains.

Another thing was likewise before the French Court, that promised them some Advantage. The Scotch Lords at St. Germains, had not been idle, in improving the Opportunity the Union of the two Kingdoms had given them to sound the depth of the Male-contented Party in Scotland ; and so good a Correspondence was held there, that they had the earliest notice of all that passed, and how the Nation stood affected, which was constantly communicated at Versailles. The French King, however, with his usual Caution, was not too hasty to credit the Business ; tho' it appeared to have a very good face, till a List was produced of the Names of many Leading Men in Scotland that were ready to receive (as they called it) their lawful King James VIII. The King therefore, at the repeated instances of the Scotch Lords, dispatched thither the Marquis de Nangis, by whom he sent the necessary Arms for an Expedition, and ordered him to bring back the best Intelligence possible, not only of the Truth of what had been laid before him, but what Force would be required to put it in action, and what Strength the English would be able to send thither on a sudden ; who upon his Return brought

190

the King large Assurances of having a strong Party in that Kingdom ready to join them, and all manner of reasonable Hopes of succeeding in the Enterprize.

Under these Circumstances, the Affair was dispatched to the Court of Rome, and related with such feeling Aggravation of being a great Means towards promoting the Cause of the Holy Catholic Religion ; and likewise so tenderly remonstrated by the (pretended) Prince himself in a dutiful and moving Letter to His Holiness ; that he was prevailed with to furnish a considerable Sum of Money towards so hopeful an Expedition, which he remitted to France ; And so diligent was His Most Christian Majesty in expending it in the necesrry Preparations for this Expedition, which were transacted with such Secrecy, that the Design was rather guessed at than known, and every thing got ready before the Spring.

The Chevalier de St. George (for this was the Name he had now assumed) who had had several Interviews with the French King on this Occasion, was charmed with this new Opportunity of putting himself into the World, having a secret Impulse of Glory that spurred him forwards to appear in something worthy of the Character that was given him ; and of putting in Action those Rudiments of Honor, which he had learned with so much Pleasure. He now received the compliments of the Chief of the French Nobility on his intended Expedition, who flocked to wish him good success therein : and he likewise in his turn visited the Princes and Princesses of the Blood, and if we may believe Report (for it will be no Wonder to find Love in the Breast of a sanguine Prince at the Age of 20) he paid something more than a formal visit of leave to the blooming Mademoiselle de C——, on whom he had looked for some time with passionate eyes, as made it whispered at Court, that they too apparently betrayed something more than a common Respect due to so celebrated a Beauty. Why this Affair has been no more talked of, is perhaps the Reasons of State that moved in the Necessity of dissipating such a Match ; and tho' of late, thro' the prevailing persuasions of the Queen, it has been less a Subject of Discourse at Court, yet 'tis certain he never speaks of her to this Day without discovering the tender Remains of a broken and disappointed Passion.

To return therefore to his Military Affairs ; the day before his Departure from St. Germans, the K. of France came thither to pay him a visit, and bid him adieu. He received the King in the most dutiful and affectionate Manner, having a great crowd of Courtiers about him, and began with expressing some extraordinary Sentiments of Thanks for what the King had been pleased to do for him in this Affair. The **King** told him very gayly, that he came not to receive his thanks for it, but to wish him good success, and likewise to furnish **him** with a **Sword,** which he **desired** him to wear in the Cause he went on, and **to** remember if it proved successful that it was a French **Sword. The** Chevalier returned the Compliment, by assuring His **Most Christian** Majesty, "That **if it** were his good fortune to **get** possession of the Throne of his Ancestors, he would not content himself with returning **him** Thanks **by** Letters and Embassadors, **but** would shew his Gratitude by his Actions." The King likewise asked him if he was satisfied in the choice of Officers and Servants that he had made to attend him? **To which the** Chevalier replyed, That, as in every thing else, he left it entirely at His Majesty's Disposal.

And now having taken his final leave, he set out for Dunkirk on the 8th of **March (N. S.) Nor will it be necessary to** reiterate the sad Parting between **him and the Queen;** as likewise the Princess his (supposed) Sister. **The Grief of the former was** inexpressible, unless thro' the **Multitude of Tears** which she shed, that could best delineate it; she embraced him **often, and sunk** under **a** Thousand Fears and Cares for his Safety, as **if** she seemed to doubt of ever seeing him again: The latter likewise drowned in Tears, hung about him in **a** very tender **and** affectionate Manner, and Expressed **very** dreadful Apprehensions she conceived of his Safety.

In **the** mean time, while every thing was hurrying on for **that** Expedition, **the French** King who had entertained great Hopes of its Success, thought it no longer worthy to be made a Secret, and **therefore** sent the following Circular Letter to his Ministers at Rome, **Switzerland,** and Geneva, and other Neutral Places, the very next Day after the Chevalier's Departure.

"I Have **long been of** Opinion, that the assisting the King of England to possess the Throne of his Ancestors, would be for the general Good **of** Europe **; I** believe **a** Peace would be the Consequence **of its** Success; and that this Prince's Subjects will esteem themselves equally happy to Re-establish him in the Place of **his** Predecessors, and in being themselves delivered from the continual Impositions, **wherewith they** are Over-whelmed, to maintain a War altogether Foreign **to** them.

"As the **Scots have yet** more Reason **than** the English to be

Disatisfyed with the present Government of England, it appears to me a convenient Opportunity to restore that Nation her Lawful Sovereign, and to enable the Prince to deliver it from the Oppression it has suffered since the Revolution, which happened under the late King of England James II.

"These are Reasons which have determined me to Equip a Squadron of my Ships at Dunkirk, and to furnish the King of England with a considerable Number of my Troops, to accompany him to Scotland to support those his faithful Subjects, who shall Declare for him.

"He left this Place Yesterday, to go to Dunkirk, in order to Embark and get with all Expedition to Scotland. His Intention is not to enter the Kingdom by Right of Conquest, but as Legal Possessor of it. He will behave himself in like manner with Respect to all his Dominions, who shall pay the Obedience they owe him, and his Subjects will only be distinguished according to the Zeal and Affection they shew to him, without Examining what Religion they professed in which he leaves them to their entire Liberty.

"I have not Thoughts of enlarging my Power by assisting to Re-establish this Prince. 'Tis sufficient that I do an Act of Justice in Vindicating the Honour of Crowned Heads, highly Affronted in the Person of the King his Father; and my Wishes will be entirely accomplished, if by God's Blessing on the Endeavors, the Success become the Means of procuring a lasting Peace, so necessary to all Europe.

"As this Resolution of mine will soon spread itself thro' Europe, my Will is, that you speak of it in the Manner I Direct you. Given at Versailles this Eighth of March, 1708."

His Holiness upon this appointed public Prayers, in the English, Scotch, and Irish Churches at Rome, for the Success of the Undertaking, and granted Indulgences to such as should put up those Prayers.

The Chevalier, upon his arrival at Dunkirk, found fresh Marks of the French King's Esteem. He was furnished with very Fine Tents, a Considerable Quantity of Gold and Silver Household Plate, of curious workmanship ; Cloaths for his Life-Guards, Liveries for his Household, and all other Necessaries for his Expedition. The Mottoes or Devices on his Colors and Standards were adapted to the Purpose. On some there was that of the Royal Standard of England—"*Dieu et mon droit*, God and my Right : On others, *Nil desperandum Christo Duce et Auspice Christo*, I don't despair since Christ is my Guide and Helper ; And on others, *Cui Venti et Mare obediunt, impera Domine, et fac Tranquilitatem!* O Thou whom the Winds and the Sea obey, command Lord, that it be calm." Whilst he is here, waiting only the favorable Event of Wind and Weather, let us see what is doing elsewhere.

Notwithstanding the great Secrecy with which this Expedition had been Concerted, it could not be supposed but that Time would bring about the Discovery of it. It was at first suspected in Holland, who gave intimation to Her Majesty's Minister, M. Cadogan. This Gentleman had a watchful Eye on these Preparations ; but it was not till the Chevalier came to Dunkirk that he made any real Discovery (nor even then as to the Place where they were designed) at what time he sent immediate notice to England ; where on the 4th of March (O. S.) Mr. Secretary Boyle acquainted the House of Commons, That Her Majesty had ordered him to lay before them several Advices received the Night before, and that Morning, of great Preparations that were making at Dunkirk, for an Invasion upon England by the French, and the (pretended) P. of Wales was come to Dunkirk : Which produced the following Address to Her Majesty.

" WE Your Majesty's most faithful and obedient Subjects, the Lords Spiritual and Temporal, and Commons of Great Britain in Parliament assembled, do beg leave to return our most hearty Thanks to Your Majesty, for being generously pleased to communicate to your Parliament the Intelligence you have received of an intended Invasion of this Kingdom by the pretended Prince of Wales, supported by a French Power.

"We are so sensible of the Happiness we enjoy under Your Majesty, and are so afflicted with the dangerous Consequences of such an Attempt both to your Person and Government, that with Hearts full of Concern to Your Majesty's Safety, we beseech Your Majesty that you will be pleased to take particular care of your Royal Person, and we on our parts are fully and unanimously resolved to stand by and assist Your Majesty with our Lives and Fortunes, in maintenance of your undoubted Right and Title to the Crown of these Realms against the pretended Prince of Wales, and all other your Enemies both at home and abroad.

"The care Your Majesty has taken for the defence of your

Dominions, and particularly in fitting out so great a Fleet in so short a time, gives satisfaction and encouragement to all your Good Subjects who are likewise very sensible of the Zeal the States-General have shewn upon this Occasion.

"As a farther Instance of our Duty we humbly desire that you would be pleased to order that the Laws against Papists and Nonjurors be put in Execution, and that directions be given to seize and secure such Persons, with their Horses and Arms, as Your Majesty shall have cause to suspect are disaffected to your Person and Government.

"And as we doubt not but by the Blessing of God, upon the Continuance of Your Majesty's Care, your Enemies will be put to Confusion, so we readily embrace this Opportunity to shew to Your Majesty and the whole World, that no Attempts of this kind shall deter us from supporting Your Majesty in a vigorous Prosecution of the present War against France, till the Monarchy of Spain be restored to the House of Austria, and Your Majesty have the Glory to compleat the Recovery of the Liberties of Europe.

To which the Queen replied:

"My Lords, and Gentlemen,

"I Have such entire Dependence on the Providence of God, and so much Trust in the faithful Services of my good Subjects, that I hope this Attempt will prove Dangerous only to those who undertake it.

"I am extreamly Sensible of your Concern and Affection for me and my Government, and shall have a very particular Regard to the Advice you give Me upon this Occasion.

"I am also very well pleased with the Justice you have done the States General, in taking Notice of their timely Care for our Safety, and their Readiness to give us all possible Assistance.

"The firm Resolutions which you Express upon all Occasions, of Supporting me in bringing this War to a Safe and Happy Conclusion, as it is most essentially obliging to me, so I assure my self it will mightily Dishearten our Common Enemies, and give the greatest Encouragement and Advantage to our Allies."

The Commons likewise ordered a Bill to be brought in, to empower her Majesty to secure and detain such Persons as her

Majesty should suspect were Conspiring against her Person and Government. And pursuant to the Parliaments Desire in their Address, a Proclamation was Issued, declaring the Chevalier and all his Accomplices, Adherents, and Abettors to be Traitors and Rebels. Strictly Charging all Papist Recusants, to repair to their Places of Abode, and not remove from thence above the Distance of Five Miles; and also to depart out of the Cities of London and Westminster, and from all Places within Ten Miles distance of the same.

And here it is certain, that the Catholicks in England and Scotland in many Places were great Sufferers thro' this Expedition: Who tho' they are by Principle obliged to wish the Chevalier well, yet it is thought that many of them were not over warm in this Affair, as believing if it was Unsuccessful, it would be a means of laying them under fresh Hardships.

A Bill was likewise actually brought in, and ready to pass, wherein there was a Clause, for discharging Vassals from their Allegiance to their Superiors, the Leaders or Chieftains of Clans, in case they resisted them that took part with the Chevalier. Besides the former united Address of the Lords and Commons, there were two other presented on the 13th of March, in Answer to Her Majesty's Speech of the 10th, wherein were contained very warm Expressions against the Chevalier and his Adherents.

Upon the first Notice of the French Armament at Dunkirk, Major General Cadogan had repaired to Brussels, and Concerted with Monsieur de Auverquerque, the March of the British Forces to be Shipped of for Great Britain, and how to supply their Room in their several Garrisons. From Brussels the Major General went to Ghent, and having Conferred with General Lumly the Governor of that Place, and Commander in Chief of the British Troops, Orders were given to Ten Battalions to hold themselves in a readiness to March at an Hour's Warning. This done, that General repaired to Ostend, to forward the Preparations which were making there for the Embarking of those Regiments, as soon as there should be certain Advice, that the Twelve French Battallions that were to attend the Chevalier in his intended Expedition were actually Embarked. On the other Hand, the Admiralty of Great Britain fitted out a Fleet with such incredible Diligence and Expedition, that appearing in sight of Dunkirk before it could have been expected, a Stop was put to the Embarkation of the Troops, and frequent Expressess Dispatched to Paris for new Orders. The Count de Fourbin who commanded the Squadron, having represented to the French King, That he might indeed get out of Dunkirk Harbour, and perhaps Land the Troops, but that he could not be answerable for his Majesty's Ships. Notwithstanding which, he received positive Instructions to Re-Imbark the Troops, and put to Sea with the first fair Wind. In the mean time, to cover the Reason of Dis-imbarking the Troops, it was given out that the Chevalier was indisposed of the Measles, attended with an Ague; but the last Orders coming, that pretence vanished. And Count de Fourbin having received Advice that the British Fleet, forced from their Station by the high Winds, was seen off the coast of Bretany, they began to Re-imbark the Troops, and the Wind turning fair on the 17th of March, they laid hold of that Opportunity, and sailed out of Flemish Road; but the Wind veering towards Night, forced them to anchor again in Newport Pits, where they continued till the 19th, and then sailed directly for Scotland.

In the mean time the British Fleet, under Sir George Bing, which was considerably reinforced, returning to their Station off Graveling, the next day received notice that the French Fleet was sailed, when leaving Admiral Baker with a strong Squadron, to convoy the Troops, they sailed directly after to Scotland. Besides Ten Battallions embarked at Ostend, a considerable Reinforcement was sent from England toward Scotland, consisting of Two Troops of Guards, the Duke of Northumberland's Regiment of Horse, a Squadron of Horse Grenadiers, Two Regiments of Dragoons, One Detachment of 16 Men per Company out of the Foot Guards, besides several Regiments of Foot; whom the Earl of Leven, before dispatched to Edinburgh, was to command.

On board the French Ships there was 10 Battalions (besides some Troops that were to follow them) with sufficient Stores, and 400 Non-commissioned Officers, for the raising of more Forces: The whole commanded by Count de Gace,* a Mareschal of France. The Chevalier himself was on board the Mars, with the said Mareschal de Gace, the Duke of Perth, the Lord Middleton, the Lord Galmoy; and other Officers, and Persons of Distinction. Notwithstanding the Design was given out to be on Scotland in general, yet the Castle of Edinburgh was the particular Place aimed at, the Plan of which had been laid before the Council at Versailles, where the Design was unanimously approved.

---

* *Sic.* It should be *de Grace.*

In Scotland at this time they were in the greatest Confusion; those who were Friends to the Chevalier, and wished well to the Expedition, were under various Apprehensions, and not without Fears of being seized and imprisoned, as it happened to a great many; others were in as great Pain, not only from their Apprehensions of the French Fleet, which was to invade them, but likewise of the Chevalier's Friends within, whom they expected to rise in arms in many Places of the Kingdom, which Fleet appeared on the Coast, having reached the Frith of Edinburgh the 23rd of March (N. S.) in the Morning.

Upon Sight whereof the Country was in an alarm. At Edinburgh the Magistrates assembled the Corporations, to know what assistance they could expect from them in defending themselves, and keeping the Peace of the City? Upon which it was resolved that the Freemen should keep guard by turns in their respective Halls, and be ready upon the first Notice of any Disorder.

On the other hand great Diligence was used in observing and securing several Persons, suspected either of holding correspondence with the Chevalier, or at least being inclined to favour his Design; amongst whom were the Dukes of Hamilton, Athol, and Gordon, and many other Persons of Note. As to the French Fleet, tho' they had been on the Coast a whole Day and Night, yet no body came off to them, and the English followed them so close, as wholly disappointed their Landing, and obliged them to steer out of the Frith, where they were at anchor, and to make use of the Favor of the Night and a small Breeze, to further their Escape. Of which the following Account was given by the Count de Gace, otherwise called the Mareschal de Mantignon, to M. Chamillard.

"SIR,

"I Had the Honor to acquaint you with our Embarkation at Dunkirk, the 17th past, and you shall see by the following Journal what has happened since till our Return.

"The 17th of March, at 4 in the Afternoon, the Chevalier de Fourbin set sail with the Fleet; but about 10 in the Evening the Wind proving contrary, we were obliged to cast Anchor in the Downs of Newport, where we were detained the 18th and 19th. The *Proteus*, on board of which were 400 Landmen, the *Guerrier* (or *Warrior*) and the *Barrentin* with 200 Men each, were obliged by the

198

high Winds, to put back into Dunkirk. The same day (19th) at Ten in the Evening, the Wind having chopped about, we set sail again, and having pursued our course the 20th, 21st, and 22d, with a strong Gale, we made the Frith of Edinburgh the 23d in the Morning, and in the Evening, cast anchor at the Mouth of it. The 24th in the Morning, as we made ready to enter the Frith, we discovered a great Number of Ships which we soon found to be the Enemies Squadron, to the Number of Twenty Eight Sail, who we Judged to be the same that appeared off Dunkirk, whereupon Monsieur de Fourbin resolved to bear off by the Favour of a Land Breeze, which very luckily carried us from the Enemy; The latter pursuing us very close all that Day (24) and four of their best Sailors being come up with our Sternmost Ships, the Enemy's foremost Ship attacked at four in the Afternoon, the *August* with whom she Exchanged some Shot, for some time after the English bore down upon the *Salisbury*, which was more a Stern, and Endeavoured to put her between herself and another English Ship that was coming up to her. The Fight between those two Ships and some others on both sides lasted till Night, during which time, the *Salisbury* made a great Fire with their small Arms.

"Our Fleet being dispersed, and the Enemy near us, Monsieur de Fourbin steered false during the Night, which had a good Effect, for the next Day (the 25th) we found ourselves with twenty Sail at a considerable Distance from the Enemy, whereupon I Discoursed Monsieur Fourbin, to know of him, whether having missed our Landing in the Frith of Edinburgh we might not attempt it in another Place; He proposed to me Inverness, which is a very remote Part in the North of Scotland, and we went immediately to the (pretended) King of England, who Entertained the Motion with Joy, and told us, 'We ought to Concert together the Measures that were to be taken, and he would pursue our Resolutions.'

"The Question now was to get Pilots to Conduct us thither, and give us the necessary Notice: But there being none in our Squadron that was acquainted with that Port, Monsieur de Fourbin detached a Frigate, with the Sieurs Caron and Bouyn, to fetch some from the Cape of Buccaness. All that Day (25) we steered with a pretty favourable Wind towards the North of Scotland, but about Eleven at Night, there arose a strong contrary Wind, which having continued the next Day with Violence, Monsieur de Fourbin told me, it was high time to acquaint the (pretended) King with the Inconvenience of pursuing our **Course, which were the** inevitable Dispersion **of** the Fleet, the **Danger the** Ships that should be separated would be in, either of falling into the Enemies Hands, or of Perishing **on** the Coast, **if they were** driven thither, and even the want of Provisions.

"**The impossibility** Sieurs Caron and Bouyn found of approaching **the Shoar,** by reason of the stormy Weather, and consequently of **bringing Pilots to Guide us ; the** Uneasiness and Danger of Landing in **a** Port we were Strangers to, where the Enemy might come up again with us, together with other Hazards and Difficulties, having **been** represented to the (pretended) King by Monsieur de Fourbin, **in the** presence of the Duke of Perth, my Lord Middleton, Mr. **Hamilton, my Lord** Galmay, and Messieurs de Beauharnois and d'Andrezel, the (pretended) **King of** England, with the unanimous **Advice of all** those Gentlemen resolved to return to Dunkirk, where we could not arrive before **this Day, by the** reason of the Calms and contrary **Winds.**

I am, &c.

The following Letter was likewise wrote from Dunkirk,
by an Officer of Distinction to his Friend at Paris.

Dunkirk, April 12. N.S., 1707.

"WE were in **such a Hurry on our Expedition** to Scotland, the Design being communicated to none but our Prince's Privy Council till we were on our March, that I neither could not durst say anything of it, but now we are returned I believe it won't be disagreeable to you to know the Truth of the Matter.

"When the Prince set Sail, three Battallions and some Provisions that could not be got ready to go with him, were ordered to follow him to Leith Road, which accordingly we did four Days after, in Seven Privateers, Commanded by Monsieur Zoust, and got to Leith Road without meeting any Ships in our Passage. We were much surprised to find no Ships at our Place of Rendezvous, and therefore put out Dutch Colours, and went close in with the Town of Leith, to get Intelligence. A Boat came of to us with two Pilots, who told **us, that** the French Fleet had not been there, but that Advice was **come from the English Fleet,** which lay off the Frith Mouth, that **the People on Shoar** took our Ships to be Dutch East-India Men, that they heard had been upon the Coast.

"We kept the Pilots on Board, and made all the haste we could out of the Firth, keeping close under the South Shoar, to cover us from the sight of the English, whom we saw off Fifeness, about three Leagues to the Northward of us, steering our Course North-East, we came up within two Days with the Body of the French Fleet, all scattered, and resolving homeward. I went on board the *Mars*, where I was told the Prince and Privy Council were, to receive further Orders, and to give an Account of my Expedition, and there heard of their Escape by the luckiest Accident in the World: They had got into the Firth on Friday Night, having heard nothing of the English Fleet, and anchored off Pittenweim and Creil, with Design to Land near Leith in the Morning, when in the Night they heard the English Fleet fire the Signal for their Ships to come to an Anchor. Monsieur Fourbin knowing the meaning of it, immediately sent a Boat on Board of every Ship in his Squadron, ordering them to put out their Lights, and to Sail one by one out of the Firth, and steer a North-East Course till they should come off the town of St. Andrew's, which accordingly they did, but the Wind and tide being against them, the English made them in the Morning and pursued them. In the Pursuit, which lasted three Days, they lost the *Salisbury*, the *Blackwall*, foundred since at Sea, the *Deal*, *Castle*, *Sun*, and *Squirrel* we are afraid are lost on the Coast of Holland, and the *Triumph*, which we thought also lost, is got in, but much shattered. On Thursday, put just off of Zealand, our small Squadron fell in with four English third Rates, which frighted us out of our Wits, for we were in so dismal a Condition, that we could not make any Defence, and we must have surrendered; but they knowing nothing of our Circumstances bore away from us, and we got that Afternoon into Dunkirk Road, and next Day our Prince arrived with the rest in so miserable a Condition all of us, that the Soldiers when they crept on Shoar, looked more like Rats than Men. The Prince suffered much in his Health, and what with Fatigue and Chagrin looked very thin, but to put a good Face on the Matter, Dressed himself very fine, in an Embroidered Suit, and a blue Feather in his Hat; when he went ashoar, where he was received by abundance of Ladies in their Coaches, with Looks that put me in Mind of an English Funeral. When he went off the Noise was all over, *Long live the King*; but at our return shrugging of Shoulders and shaking of Heads gave a dismal Welcome. Poor Clermont and his Brother are taken in the *Salisbury*, and my Lord Dumbarton is either with them or lost in the

Blackwall. General Dorington, **Gilmoy,** and some of our Bottle Friends, **are now very** ill at **Mr. Goff's House here, the** Macdonalds **&c. are gone up to St. Germans with the Prince."**

"**I need not tell** you that the **Foundation of our whole** Design **was the Castle of** Edinburgh, which miscarrying by **the Arrival** of the English Fleet, the Prince's Council did not think **fit to land any where** else. The **Plan** of this Castle was laid before **a Council of General Officers at Versailles, and it** was unanimously concluded, **that with the Troops,** Mortars, and Bombs, which we carried it could **not hold above 3 Days.** We designed to have made a False Attack at the **Postern Gate, while 3** Battallions should enter the Outworks that **front the City, and lodge** under their Half Moon, which would **oblige them the next day to surrender. By the** Taking of this **Castle we should have had the Regalia; and I am told,** Two Protestant **Archbishops would** have **crowned the Prince in the** High Church. **The** Equivalent from England **being also in this** Castle, would have **been** a great supply **to us for raising of Men. We have** above 400 Officers with **us for that** Purpose, **all Pretty** Fellows, that have **served in the** Wars of Italy and Spain, **and above 100** Chests of **Money.** Some were for Landing **in** Murray Firth, if it had only **been to refresh our Troops, but you** know how **nicely** the French **King's Orders are be obeyed, and** how little **Power he** gives of his **Troops to any Ally, but** always secret ones to his **own** Generals. **We** Scots and Irish might have landed, **but the French were** restrained to Musselburgh and Leith, **or no where."**

To these Accounts, we shall on the other **hand** subjoin, those that were written by **Sir** George Bing, **from on board the** *Medway*, the **13th and 15th of March, O. S. The first whereof is as follows. "According to the Opinion we had framed when we** left the Station of Dunkirk, it has proved that the Enemy was designed for Edinburgh. **This Morning we saw the French Fleet in the Mouth of the Firth, off of** which Place we anchored the Last Night, and sent a Boat **ashore to** the Isle **of** May, from whence we had **an** account that the **French** came to an Anchor yesterday in the Afternoon : They sent **one Ship** up into Leith Road, which had a Flag at the Main Topmast **Head :** They reported it **a** Blue one, but we are rather of opinion that **it is** the Standard. **The** People of the Island say, that by the time **that** Ship could **get up** before the Town, they heard several Guns fire, which were **in the** Manner of a Salute. The Ship that went up yesterday, came down this Morning, and is now within Two Leagues of us: She appears to be a Ship of 60 Guns, but has now no Flag on board. We saw this Morning, when they weighed, a Flag at the Main Top-Mast Head on board of one of their Ships. They stand from us, and we after them with all the sail we can."

The Second Letter was as follows, "We chased the Enemy to the Northward of Buchaness, sometimes with reasonable Hopes of coming up with them. The *Dover* and *Ludlow Castle* being the only Clean-Sailing Ships we had: They were the first which came up with part of the Enemy's Squadron, passing by some of the Smaller to engage some of the larger Ships, and stop them till they should be relieved. They attacked 2 or 3 of their Ships, amongst which was the *Salisbury*: They did not part with them till more of our Ships arrived, but worked their Ships in a handsome manner, to cut them off from the rest of the Fleet; but in the Darkness of the Night they all got out of our Sight, except the *Salisbury*, who falling in amongst our Headmost Ships, the *Leopard* entered Men on board her. We were informed by the Officers who were taken, that there were 12 Battallions on board their Squadron, commanded by the Count de Gace, a Marshal of France, the pretended Prince of Wales, Lord Middleton, Lord Perth, the Macdonalds, Trevanion, and several other Officers and Gentlemen on board the *Mars*, in which also was Monsieur Fourbin, who commanded the Squadron. The Number and Strength of their Ships are very near the Account we lately received from Dunkirk, nor were they joined by the Brest Men of War: And they further assure us that the Ships our out Scouts saw off of Calais, were Privateers and their Prizes going into Dunkirk. The Morning after this Chase we saw but 18 of the Enemies Ships as far as we could perceive them from the Mast-head, in the E N E of us. Having no prospect of coming up with them, we lay off and on Buccaness all day yesterday, to gather all our Ships together; and this day it blowing hard at N E with a Great Sea, judging the Enemy could not seize the Shore to make any attempt, we bore up for this Place, which was thought most reasonable, not only to secure, but to give Countenance and Spirit to Her Majesty's Faithful Subjects, and discourage those that could have Thoughts of being our Enemies."

There were taken on board the *Salisbury*, the Lords Griffin and Clermont, Colonel of a Regiment, and Son to the Earl of Middleton, with Mr. Middleton his Brother, and Colonel Francis Wauchup; together with the Marquiss de Levy, a French Lieutenant General, one aid de Camp, one Colonel, two Lieutenant Colonels, five Captains, two French Lieutenants, Fifteen Irish Lieutenants, ten Serjeants, ten Corporals, ten Lanspessades, with M. de Segent, Commissary of War; and about 180 Soldiers: Besides the Ships Company of about 300 Men, Officers included. As for the four first mentioned, as well as the fifteen Irish Lieutenants, being Subjects of Great Britain, they were brought to London, and Committed, the former to the Tower, and latter to Newgate. Many State Prisoners were likewise brought from Edinburgh to London, who had been confined in the Castle of Edinburgh, and that were admitted to Bail, except such against whom there was any particular Information, which I think was very few; not one Person having suffered on this Account. The Lord Griffin indeed was sentenced upon a former Outlawry for High Treason, a Rule of Court was made out for his Execution, and a Warrant passed for fulfilling the same, but he was reprieved the Night before the Sentence should have been Executed; and in the End died in the Tower on the 10th of November, 1710. And now Sir George Bing having continued in Leith Road, till he had Intelligence the French Fleet was returned to Dunkirk, he returned to the Downs, and thus ended this memorable Expedition, which had put Britain into a thousand Hopes and Fears. It is therefore time to pursue the Chevalier, who was by this time returned to France.

The Gentleman who wrote one of the foregoing Letters from Dunkirk, seems to be mistaken, when he says the Chevalier returned to St. Germans, for he went from Dunkirk to St. Omers, where he spent some time among the English Gentlemen there, who in the Welcome they gave him, could not but mix with sad and dejected Looks, some Sighs and affectionate Expressions of Sorrow, for the unfortunate Disappointment he had met with: But he had learned so much of the Hero, as to shew a perfect Unconcernedness at what they said, and with a becoming Serenity, very rare in one so young, turned the Discourse to other things.

The Armies being now ready to take the Field in Flanders, he besought the French King that he might serve among his Troops there, then Commanded by the Dukes of Burgundy and Vendosme which the King not only complied with, but permitted the Duke of Berry to accompany him. They arrived in the Army some Days

Memoirs of the Chevalier de St. George.

before the Battle of Audenarde, in which the Chevalier was present during the whole Action, and did the Duty of Aid de Camp to the Duke of Burgundy, whom he constantly attended during the heat of the Day. Not only the *Paris Gazette*, and other French News Papers, gave large Accounts of the intrepid Behaviour of the young Princes, but Officers who were on the Spot could not restrain speaking of it in their Letters, tho' they were writ in a very great Hurry and Perplexity; Which because they are not Foreign to the Subject of these Memoirs; as well as that they give a Concise Account of the Action, it would seem a Neglect to overlook them.

A Letter written by a French Officer the Day after the Battle of Audenarde.

"I Can only send you the unwelcome Relation of the Particulars of the Battle, which happened yesterday about two in the Afternoon near Audenarde. 'Twill prove a great Blow to France; for without Exaggerating the Matter, we had above 10000 Men killed, wounded, or taken. The Action was very ill managed on our side; for instead of attacking the Enemy when they began to pass the Schelde near Audenarde at Eleven in the Morning, we let them come over the River quietly, which they would not have adventured to do, had we in any tolerable Manner offered to dispute their Passage; but seeing us stand still, they were encouraged to prosecute their first Design, and began to pass over two Bridges which they had laid. As fast as their Horse and Foot came over, they ranged themselves in Order of Battle against us, and while our Generals were in Suspense, what Resolutions to take, whether to venture an Engagement or not, the Enemy's Army continued coming over the River, and soon possessed themselves of some Villages and Hedges; so that at last our Generals were compelled to endeavour to dislodge them. Accordingly, our Infantry advanced, and the Ground was disputed two or three Hours, with a terrible Fire and great Obstinacy on both sides; but our Foot being tired with Charging the Enemy five or six times, and disheartened to see themselves not supported by our Horse (who could not act because the Ground was so full of Inclosures) and pressed hard by the Enemy, were at length forced to retire, and quit the Ground to them. We Dragoons were obliged to endure the continual Fire of the Enemies Foot and Cannon, without daring to stir, because we were on the Right of the King's Household, who suffered as much as we. Toward the Evening, we were fallen upon by a great Number of the Enemy's Horse, to hinder us from succouring the rest, who were put to the Rout; and of Seven Regiments of Dragoons, we lost above half: At last, we saw no other Exedient, but to force our way thro' the Enemy; but first we sent to see whether we could be assisted in that Design by any of our Forces: In the mean time Night came on apace, and we were informed that the King's Household (whose Retreat was covered in some measure by us) were at too great a Distance. Things standing thus, our Resolution of breaking thro' the Enemy sunk, and some of the Enemy's Adjutants summoning us to yield our selves Prisoners of War, we submitted to it, seeing no other way to save our Lives. At least Forty of our Regiments are reduced to a wretched Condition, the greatest part of them being killed or taken, so that it will be long before they can be Re-established. Of four Regiments of the King's Household, at least half were taken Prisoners, and among them are several Persons of Note. The Chevalier de Longville, and 15 other Officers were mortally wounded, and two of them are since dead. The Regiments of Psiffer and Villars are quite ruined, and almost all their Officers are taken, with all their Baggage, &c.

"The Dukes of Burgundy, Berry, and the Chevalier de St. George, staid at the Head of the Household during the whole Action, and Retreated with them to Ghent, where we are just now told they are safe arrived. I cannot pretend to tell you yet what the Result of this Battle will be, or how our Generals will square their Motions, which we are like to have no farther Share in this Campaign."

"Yours,"

Another Letter had in it this Expression.

"That there was not wanting those, who advised the Princes to set out Post for Ipres, but this they generously refused, and staid at the Head of the Troops till the very last." And the Duke de Vendosme in his Letter to the King of France, assured him, "That the Chevalier de St. George, and the Duke de Berry, were very forward during the Battle."

The next Summer, the Chevalier made the Campaign under the Marshal de Villars, who had a particular Charge of him, and with whom during the whole time of continuing in the Field, he constantly accompanied on all Duties, and rode with him continually when he visited the Lines, or Reconnoitred the Enemy, and in the Battle of Mons; or Blaregnies, was present with him in the Heat of all the Action, as we may find by the Marshal de Bouflers Account thereof to the King, where he has these Words, in the Conclusion of his Letter, applied to the Behaviour of those that Distinguished themselves in the Battle.

"I Cannot now give your Majesty any particulars of this Action, but will endeavor to send them to morrow, or next day: I can assure Your Majesty that all the General Officers did their Duty perfectly well, and with the greatest Bravery and Skill; but Monsieur d'Artagnan, who commanded the Right of the Foot distinguished himself in a particular manner, as well by his Valor as by his good Orders: He had 3 Horses killed under him, and received 4 Blows on his Cuirass: The D. de Guiche, who was also on the Right, a little forwarder than M. D'Artagnan, behaved himself with all possible Skill and Bravery, and received a Musket Shot in his Leg: The Marquis Damfort and M. de la Frazelliere, who were also on the Right, and in M. d'Artagnan's Rear, shewed the same Valor and Capacity: M. de Gassion, who commanded the Right Wing of Horse, did Wonders at the Head of your Majesty's Household, and shewed on this Occasion his Courage and Ability, having pushed and defeated more than 2 or 3 of the Enemies Lines Sword in Hand. The Gendarmes, Light Horse, Musqueteers, and Horse Grenadiers also did wonders: The P. de Rohan, and M. de Vidame did all that could be expected from Persons of the greatest Valor: The Gendarmarie did Wonders also, and the Marquis de la Valiere was every where, and charged with all possible Bravery at all the different Charges. The Cavalry behaved themselves very well, and all the Troops, as well as the Foot, stood with incredible Firmness one of the briskest. Cannonades that ever was: All the Foot did Wonders and distinguished them.

"The Chevalier de St. George behaved himself, during the whole Action, with all possible Bravery and Vivacity. I say nothing of Your Majesty's Left, by reason I was not there, but I know that all the General Officers, and all the Troops, animated by the Mareschal de Villar's Presence and Example, behaved themselves with all possible Valor."

Upon his Return from this Campaign, the Chevalier was complimented by the Principal of the Court of France ; for the Mareschal de Villars had likewise given such **an account, as served to** heighten the public **Opinion of** him.

I am now, for want of more Room, drawing to a Conclusion of **these Memoirs.** And it may be well presumed there are many things **that will not** bear mentioning, with regard to the Strictness of Caution **we are now tied up to.** As there is no Offence designed, so **I cannot but** suppose there **will be** none taken. Were **he of no other Consideration but his adding a** Clause (and perhaps one **of the most considerable) in** the whole Articles in this memorable Treaty **of Peace, it seems** sufficient to warrant an Undertaking of this nature, **and to record a** NAME in some collected manner, that is; and indeed **but barely is, scattered and** interspersed thro' so many Scraps of History. **I shall only further remember the** Reader**, that Last** Year he made a tour thro' **the Eastern Parts of France,** while **at the same** time there **was a great Armament to Toulon** and Brest **; which** amused a **considerable part of Europe, and gave** foundation to a Surmise, that **some Expedition was to be made in his** Favor.

He had before had an interview with **the French King, who in a very solemn manner, tho' not without** Impressions **of Concern, told him, that he found himself** under **the** necessity **of** giving Peace **to his People ; and that some Overtures had** passed which gave **him hopes of obtaining that long** desired End : He proposed therefore **to him many Places for his Retreat,** which he was assured must **attend the Issue of the Affair: But** remembered to him **what** he had formerly **said on this Subject, for** which he assured him he should never alter.

He visited most of the Principal Towns of **that** Part of France, **and likewise the Army of the Duke de** Berwick : **But as** there was **a good Space of Time, in which** the Public News gave no account of his **Journey, it** comfirms **me in the** Opinion of what I have been confidently **told ;** That he **then** visited the Place of his Retreat, when he quits the **Realms of** France, and had a private interview with a certain **Prince that is to** receive him.

The beginning **of** April last, a few Days after his (supposed) Sister, **he was visited** with the Small Pox, and in great Danger of Death, **but Providence** designed to lengthen a LIFE, tho' meanly treated in **History, that has a very large** share in the most momentous Affairs that **relate to this part of** Europe, and would yet be of more Regard were **not France reduced to the** Necessity of Submitting, that the

208

Preservation of their National Religion in Britain, is the most just and reasonable part of their Government; and which to Subvert, will not only be the most difficult thing in Nature, but always preferred above the Concern for their Lives and Safety.

I Conclude all with an Account of the Death and Character of the Princess Louisa Maria Teresa, Daughter of King James II. who died of the Small Pox at St. Germains, the 18th of April, 1712. as it was said to be sent in a Letter from a Nobleman of France, to his Correspondent at Utrecht.

"My Lord,

"I Send you by these, the sad and deplorable News of the much lamented Death of the Princess Royal of England, who died of the Small-Pox, the 18th of this Month, at St. Germains, who as she was one of the greatest Ornaments of that afflicted Court, so she was the Admiration of all Europe; never Princess was so universally regretted. Her Death has filled all France with Sighs, Groans, and Tears. She was a Princess of a majestical Mien and Port; every Motion spoke Grandeur, every Action was easy and without any Affectation or Meanness, and proclaimed her a heroine descended from the long Race of so many Paternal and Maternal Heroes; Majesty sat enthroned on her Forehead, and her curious large black Eyes struck all that had the honor to approach her, with Awe and Reverence; but all her External Glories, though the greatest of her Sex, were nothing to her Internal, and she seems to have established the Opinion of Plato, who asserts, "That the Soul frames its own Habitation, and that beautiful Souls make to themselves beautiful Bodies." She had a great deal of pleasant Wit, joined with an equal Solidity of Judgment; she was Devout, without the Defects that young Aspirers to Piety are sometimes incident to; and though she complied with the Diversions of the Court, her greatest Pleasure was in pious Retirement. She was very affable, and of a sweet mild Temper, full of Pity and Compassion, which is the distinguishing Character of the Royal Family of the Stuarts. To sum up all in a few Words, she was a dutiful and obedient Daughter, an affectionate Sister, tenderly loving and beloved by the Hero her Brother. On both their Countenances were divinely mingled the noble Features and Lineaments of the Stuarts and the D'Este's, and Beauty triumphed over both, with this only Difference, That in him it was more Strong and Masculine as becoming his Sex, in her more Soft and Tender as more suiting with hers; in both, excellent and alike. She was four Years younger, as if designed by Providence to confute the black Calumny of her Brother's Birth, and her Royal Mother's Inability of having Children. To be short, in her the Distressed have lost a certain Comforter, her Servants an excellent Mistress, and the World one of its most precious Gems. She died expressing the warmest Sentiments of Piety, and the most perfect Resignation, uttering often her Royal Father's dying Words and Ejaculations, as Inheritrix of his Piety. The great Discomposure of my Mind on this sad Occasion, and my gushing Tears hinder me to add any more. Adieu."

Finis.

"Inter Folia Fructus."

A FAITHFUL

MEMORIAL

OF THAT

REMARKABLE MEETING

OF

Many Officers of the Army in England, at Windsor Castle, in the Year 1648.

1659.

"History is but the Unrolled Scroll of Prophecy."
—James A. Garfield

PRIVATELY PRINTED
FOR THE CLARENDON HISTORICAL SOCIETY.

1885.

This edition is limited to 120 *large paper and* 400 *small paper copies, for Subscribers only.*

A FAITHFUL

MEMORIAL

OF THAT
REMARKABLE MEETING
OF
Many Officers of the Army in England,
at Windsor Castle, in the Year 1648.

AS ALSO,

A DISCOVERY

OF THE

Great goodnefs of God, in his gracious meeting of them, hearing and anfwering their fuit or fupplications, while they were yet fpeaking to him.

ALL

Which is humbly prefented, as a precious Patern and Prefident unto the Officers and Souldiers of the faid Army (or elfewhere) who are or fhall be found in the like path, of following the Lord in this evil day; fearching and trying their waies, in order to a through Return and Reformation.

By William Allen, late Adjutant-General of the Army in Ireland.

Turn you at my reproof: behold I will pour out my wrath upon you, I will make known my words unto you.

LONDON,
Sold by *Strivewel Chapman*, at the Crown in *Popes-head* Alley. 1659.

To Lieutenant-General Fleetwood, and other the Officers of the Armies in England, Scotland, and Ireland, especially to such of them, who in the sence of the dangers of the day, have been of late (as is said) betaking themselves to that most necessary duty of solemn Addresses, and fervent supplications to the Lord, humbling their souls before him, in the sence of their own and others abominations abounding in this day; with unfeigned desire and endeavour to find out, and forsake them accordingly; with all others in the Armies, that are or shall be found searching and trying their waies in order to return: The following Narrative is humbly tendered by a late member of them, and now a mourner for them; yet unfeignedly desiring their prosperity in the path of repentance.

Having understood, that you have of late been much conversant in seeking the Lord, in this day of distress, and enquiring (as becomes you) into the causes of his displeasure against us (which seems to wax hot) all which if performed in a right sence, observing right rules and ends, may be of much use to help in time of need. Yet knowing the aptness of our own with others hearts to miscarry in such duties, and thereby miss of the desired success, by either setting up the stumbling-block of our iniquity before our eyes, or having any secret regard thereto in our hearts, the effect of which is to shut out Prayer; I held it my duty to contribute my mite to this work of weight, by presenting you with a president once famous amongst us, by the succefs the Lord crown'd it with, and us in that path in a day of very great diftrefs round about : and defire that fo far as you fhall fee this practife here prefented, with the method therein obferved, to agree with the revealed will of God contained in the Scripture, relating to the duty of his people, in fuch a pofture, that you will not be affraid to make it your patern, fince the Lord hath formerly born fuch a witnefs to it, and written fuch blefling upon it, as may well be fet up as a Pillar of Remembrance in the midft of us, to his praife, as well as our direction to, and in like duties in future ftreights.

In the year 47. you may remember, we in the Army were engaged in actions of a very high nature, leading us to very untroden paths, both in our contefts with the then Parliament, as alfo conferences with the King; in which great works wanting a fpirit of faith, and the fear of the Lord, and alfo unduly furprized with the fear of man, which alwaies brings a fnare ; we, to make hafte, as we thought, out of fuch perplexities, meafuring our way by a wifdom of our own, fell into Treaties with the King and his party ; which proved fuch a fnare to us, and led into fuch labyrinths by the end of that year, that the very things we thought to avoid, by the means we ufed of our own devifing, were all with many more of a far worse and more perplexing nature, brought back upon us, to the overwhelming our fpirits, weakning our hands and hearts, filling us with divifions, confufions, tumults and every evil work, and thereby endangering the ruine of that blefled caufe we had with fuch fuccefs been profpered in till this time : for now the King and his party, feeing us not anfwer their ends, began to provide for themfelves, by a Treaty with the then Parliament, fet on foot about the beginning of 48. The Parliament alfo was at the fame time highly difpleafed with us, for what we had done, both as to the King and themfelves; the good people likewife, even our most faithful friends in the Nation, beholding our turning afide from the path of fimplicity we had formerly walkt (and been bleft and thereby much endeared to their hearts, began now to turn and withdraw their affections from us in this politick path in which we had ftept, and walkt in, to our hurt, the year before. And as a farther fruit of the waies of our own backfliding hearts, we were also filled with a fpirit of great jealoufie and divifions among our felves, having left that wifdom of the word, that is firft pure, and then peaceable, that we were now fit for little but to tear and rend one another, and thereby prepare our felves, and

The Meeting at Windsor.

the work in our hands, to be ruined by the common Enemy, as thefe that were ready to fay, as many others of like fpirit in this day, of the like fad occaffions amongft us, Lo, this is the day we looked for. The King and his party prepare accordingly to ruine all, by fuddain infurrections in moft parts of the Nation, the *Scot* concurring with the fame defigns, comes in with a potent Army under Duke *Hamilton*. We in the Army in a low, weak, divided, perplext condition in all refpects, as aforefaid, fome of us judging it a duty to lay down Arms, and quit our ftations, putting ourfelves into the capacities of private men, fince what we had done, or was yet in our hearts to do, tending as we judged to the good of thefe poor Nations, was not accepted by them.

Some alfo encouraging themfelves and us to fuch a thing, by urging for fuch a practice the example of our Lord Jefus, who when he had born an eminent Teftimony, to the pleafure of his Father, in an active way, fealed to it at laft by his fufferings; which was prefented to us as our patern for imitation.

Others of us were different minded, thinking fomething of another nature might be farther yet our duty, and therefore were by joynt advice, by a good hand of the Lord led to this refult, *viz.* to go folemnly to fearch out (and humble our fouls before the Lord in the fence of) our iniquities, which we were perfwaded had provoked the Lord againft us, to bring fuch fad perplexities upon us, as at that day, out of which we faw no way elfe to extricate our felves.

Accordingly we did agree to meet at *Windfore* Caftle, about the beginning of 48. and there fpent one day together in Prayer, inquiring into the caufes of that fad difpenfation. Coming to no farther refult that day, but that it was ftill our duty to feek; and on the morrow we met again in the morning where many fpake from the Word, and Prayed; and the then Lieutenant-General Cromwell did prefs very earneftly, on all there prefent, to a thorough confideration of our actions as an Army, as well as our waies particularly, as private Chriftians, to fee if any iniquity could be found in them; and what it was, that if poffible we might find out, and fo remove the caufe of fuch fad rebukes, as were upon us by reafon of our iniquities, as we judged at that time. And the way more particularly the Lord led us to herein, was to look back, and confider what time it was that we could with joynt fatisfaction, fay to the beft of our Judgements, the prefence of the Lord was amongft us, and rebukes and judgements were not as then upon us. Which time the Lord led us joyntly to find out and agree in; and having done so, to proceed, as we then judged it our duty, to search into all our publick actions as a Army, afterwards duly weighing (as the Lord helpt us) each of them, with their Grounds, Rules, and Ends, as neer as we could; and so concluded this second day with agreeing to meet again on the morrow: which we accordingly did, upon the same occasion, reassuming the consideration of our debates the day before, and reviewing our actions again; by which means we were by a gracious hand of the Lord led to find out the very steps (as we were then all joyntly convinc'd) by which we had departed from the Lord, and provoked him to depart from us; which we found to be those cursed carnal conferences, our own wisdom, fears, and want of faith, had prompted us the year before, to entertain with the King and his party. And at this time, and on this occasion, did the then Major *Goff* (as I remember was his title) make use of that good word, *Prov.* 1. 23, *Turn you at my reproof, &c.* which (we having found out our sin) he urged as our duty from those words, and the Lord so accompanied by his Spirit, that it had a kindly effect, like a word of his, upon most of our hearts as were then present; which begot in us great sence, shame, and loathing our selves for our iniquities, and justifying the Lord as righteous in his proceedings against us: and in this path the Lord led us not only to see our sin, but also our duty; and this so unanimously set with weight upon each heart, that none was able hardly to speak a word to each other for bitter weeping, partly in the sense and shame of our iniquities of unbelief, base fear of men, and carnal consultations, (as the fear thereof) with our own wisdoms, and not with the word of the Lord, which only is a way of wisdom, strength and safety, and all besides it waies of snares: and yet were also helpt with fear and trembling, to rejoyce in the Lord, whose faithfulness and loving kindness we were made to see yet fail'd us not; but remembred us still, even in our low estate, because his mercy endures for ever. Who no sooner brought us to his feet, acknowledging him in that way of his, *viz.* searching for, being ashamed of, and willing to turn from our iniquities, but he did direct our steps, and presently we were led, and helpt to a cleer agreement amongst our selves, not any dissenting, that it was the duty of our day, with the forces we had, to go out and fight against those potent enemies, which that year in all places appeared against us, with an humble confidence in the name of the Lord only, that we should destroy them; also enabling us then, after serious seeking his face, to come

The Meeting at Windsor

to a very cleer and joynt refolution on many grounds at large then debated amongſt us, that it was our duty, if ever the Lord brought us back again in peace, to call *Charles Stewart*, that man of bloud, to an account, for that bloud he had ſhed, and miſchief he had done, to his utmoſt, againſt the Lords cauſe and people in theſe poor Nations: and how the Lord led and profpered us in all our undertakings this year, in this way, cutting his work ſhort in righteouſneſs, making it a year of mercy equal, if not tranſcendant to any ſince theſe Wars began, and making it worthy of remembrance by every gracious ſoul, who was wife to obſerve the Lord and the operations of his hands, I wiſh may never be forgotten; bringing us together again, from all parts ſhortly after, with admiration; each ones heart as it were filled with the wonders beheld, and occaſion given to all to ſay each to other, Lo, what hath God wrought! the Kings Armies in all places broken, his ſtrong holds moſt of them taken: he himſelf all that time treating with the then Parliament, and both of them deſirous to conclude; yet by an over-ruling Providence hindred, and the King ſo infatuated, as he ſtands difputing Punctilio's till he loſes all, and himſelf with it, and is fetcht away from his place of Treaty to a Priſon, in order to execution, which ſuddenly followed accordingly; and all this done within leſs then three quarters of a year, even to aſtoniſhment of our ſelves, and other beholders both at home and abroad; yea our very enemies then were made to ſay, God was amongſt us of a truth, and therefore they could not ſtand againſt us.

But alas, who would have thought that ſo few years would have worn out the memory of ſuch a not-to be-forgotten mercy, or that any of thoſe that then ſaw his works, and ſang his praiſe, ſhould ſo ſoon forget what their eyes had ſeen, as not to wait for his faithful counſel in future ſtreights! Yet behold, how ſome directly, and others confequentially are now ſaying, All theſe things were but the product of a potent politick partie fluſht with ſucceſs; and others, though more modeſt and moderate, yet it's to be feared, in too eager a purſuit of falling in with, or fear of being hurt by what is uppermoſt, if not timely complying, at once in the lump adventure to cry up abſolute obedience to the powers that are, though thereby they condemn themſelves and others, as tranſgreſſors and rebels for oppoſing thoſe that were; together with the whole ſeries of action made glorious by Gods appearances with us, beyond parallel of any late years: and thus doth the name and works of the Lord ſuffer (as Chriſt of old) between theſe two, who almoſt equally, though not alike intentionally, rob the Lord of his glory, and give great occasion to the worst of our enemies the more to blaspheme.

This is the brief, yet true account of this matter, with the blessed effects of it, as a manifestation of the Lords inclination and disposition to poor returners; who is still the same, because he hath said, and will perform it, as in *Jer.* 29. 12, 13. *Then shall ye call upon me, and ye shall go and pray unto me, and I will hearken unto you. And ye shall seek me and finde me, when ye shall search for me with all your hearts.* And I have a little hope that this precious patern, thus presented, may not be without some use to you in this day, if the Lord lead your hearts rightly to consider it. That we are a poor broken, divided, intangled, bewildered people in our publick affairs; none but they that are very great strangers in our Israel can be ignorant: for who hath known and observed former daies, when the Candle of the Lord shin'd on Tabernacles, by the light of which we walkt thorough darkness, and shall compare those daies with these four or five years past, can look upon them without a heart deeply affected, to think what once we were (when we followed the Lord, though in a land that was not sown, when we were a more plain simple-hearted people, yet prospered by the Lord to the terrour of enemies abroad and at home, through an eminent presence of God with us) and what now we are, since we have turned aside into the carnal, empty, formal shews of the Nations, admiring, (and acting by) their Policies, and saying a confederacy with them, fearing their fear, and not sanctifying the Lord in a way of believing: how are we become the tail, and not the head, a hissing, yea, a scorn to the basest of Nations! what rebukes at Sea, at Land! what disappointments of enterprizes! what stroaks on many formerly eminent publick instruments! what impoverishing of those poor Nations, by decay of Trade in all parts, to the ruine of many! what sore visitations, and of long continuance on the Nations thoroughout, by deaths, and lingering pining diseases! Yea, what heart-dividings are amongst those that have been as one stick together, used in the hand of the Lord, in his works of wonder in the midst of us, and thereby endangering the whole interest we have fought for, into the hands of such as are known enemies, or at best have been but faint friends to it and us, in daies of distress? And are not all these things worth considering and enquiring into, by every gracious heart, with the causes of them? for sure the Lord afflicts not without cause, nor grieves not the sons of men willingly.

And would you inquire aright, pursue the method laid down in the
220

Case presented; inquire when could you with joynt satisfaction, say, At such a time the presence of the Lord was with you; and these sore hands of displeasure that have of late years attended you, were not upon you, nor works in your hands as now. And if you can but find that, let me advise and beseech you, as you tender the delivery of your own souls, and good of these Nations, weigh action by action since, and see where you have gone out of that prosperous path you were formerly in, and fear not to look into any action you are, or may be concerned to look into, in which you think evil may be at the bottom; for that remaining, will cause greater shakings then the most strict enquiry you make can do: and consider what as an Army you have done, with the grounds of it, and what you have engaged before God, Angels and Men to do; and either, if it be your sin, make your repentance as publick as your evil hath been, and so clear your selves; or else up and be doing, whatever you judge your duty, in the face of whatever difficulties you meet with; and in that path doubt not of Gods being with you, while you are with him: but if you will neither pursue your duties in one respect or other, know of a certain, the Lord who is a jealous God, will not be mockt by any who is not stronger then he, but will be above men, and make them know, he will be so in those things in which they deal most proudly, and deliverance shall arise some other way, with sore rebuke to you, for your shameful neglects of duty in such a work of weight which you have been entrusted with, and must ere long be called to an account how you have discharged it.

Alas, may we not say, and shall we be afraid to say, We, our Rulers, Prophets, Armies, People, have sinn'd; yea, have grievously departed from the Lord, and help nor healing is not to be had, but in returning from what evil soever is in our hands or hearts? It is not Power, nor Policy nor Forraign confederacies; 'tis not Prayers, though frequent, or seemingly fervent, no, though attended with tears and confessions, without thorough forsakings, will be a path of safety for us, *Isa.* 58. No, the voice of the Lord is plain to Rulers, Armies, People, *Thus saith the Lord, Consider your waies: Why do we labour in the fire for very vanity?* Why is wisdom hid from the Prudent? Why do we sow much in prayers, tears, confessions, and hazardous undertakings at home and abroad, and bring in little, and what we get is as it were put into a bag with holes, and the Lord in a way of rebuke seems to blow upon it? is it not that we should consider our waies! Oh search and try, yea call in the help of God and good men in this, to see if there be any way of iniquity in your hearts or hands, and clear your selves of it, with manifesting most indignation against it. And for your help **herein**, if it may be, let me humbly caution you to take heed of advising only with such that may be most pleasing to you; self-love is apt in such cases to blind much: yea, or with such only or chiefly, that **are or may** be under the influencing power of profitable imployments, **steer'd** by the favours, or fear of the frowns of Rulers; but **rather** with such who have been persons of known integrity, and ancient constant friends to the good old cause of God, and their Country, in all its vicissitudes and lowest ebbs; not *Shimei*-like cursing and deserting in **a day of** distress, and changing their Languages when it tended to **the** change of their conditions, for **outward** advantage; but such **as have not been** pleased with their **highest, most** profitablest promotions and preferments, when they could not see the **cause of God and their** Country promoted also; and let not those names of *odium*, of dissatisfied, *&c*. (that they have been clothed with, the better to answer the evil designs of some) **affright you** in this matter: **and if** you dare **thus** pursue duty in this **path of simplicity** presented to you, without setting up the stumbling-block **of** any your iniquities before you, I am perswaded (not without many demonstrable grounds producible from the **word**) you will find it a path of peace, through the Lords blessing it; **and you, in the sincere** applying to it, will be directed and led to grounds **more cleerly** laid, for an unanimous, vigorous prosecution of the old **dying cause, by its** best and **truest** friends, then hitherto you have found; or **at least will** find it effectual to the rescue of your own souls out of paths **of** danger, which for want of **pondering** according to the Word, you may be walking in to your **great hurt**. And therefore, let me beseech you in all sincerity, as you tender your own, and these poor **Nations** welfare, apply to **it** with speed. For your betaking your selves to any other courses, will prove fruitless as aforesaid; for the Lord hath smitten, and can only **heal**; and if ever he do, he will do it in this **way**, *Hos.* 5. If what **I have** proposed, prove any way advantagious to the ends for which it is offered, *viz.* to cause you to **search**, try, and turn from the evil of your ways; **I** have my end, and let the Lord have glory: but **if** this poor means, in much faithfulness **and tenderness presented to** you, be rejected or slighted by you; I **shall, I hope, be inabled to** mourn in secret for you before the Lord: **and shall have this satisfaction, when** I shall have come to lye down **in the dust, which** how soon it may be **I** know not, that I have in some meafure delivered my own foul, and endeavour'd the like for yours ; and fhall earneftly entreat the Lord, that this poor word of warning amongft many others in this day prefented to you, may not one day meet you, as a witnefs againft you, for not regarding it : for I am well affured it fhall live, fpeak, and have its fruit, when you and I fhall ceafe to be.

William Allen.

POSTCRIPT.

THIS Paper was sent to the Press about six weeks since, to have been made publick at that time; but by an unexpected obstruction, hath hitherto been hindred: but hoping it may be yet of some use, is therefore now publisht.

April 23, 1659.

"Inter Folia Fructus."

A

DIALOGUE

BETWEEN A

Whig and a Jacobite

UPON THE SUBJECT OF THE LATE

REBELLION

AND THE EXECUTION OF THE REBEL
LORDS, ETC.

1715-16.

" History is but the Unrolled Scroll of Prophecy."
—James A. Garfield

PRIVATELY PRINTED
FOR THE CLARENDON HISTORICAL SOCIETY.

1885.

This edition is limited to **120 *large*** *paper and 400 small paper copies,*
for Subscribers only.

A

DIALOGUE

BETWEEN A

WHIG AND A JACOBITE

Upon the Subject of the late

REBELLION

And the EXECUTION of the

Rebel-Lords, &c.

OCCASION'D by

The Phœnomeon in the Skie, March 6, 1715-16.

O Ye Hypocrites, ye can discern the Face of the Skie, but can you not discern the Signs of the Times? Mat. xvi. 3.

LONDON:
Printed for J. ROBERTS, *in* Warwick Lane:
And Sold by the Book-sellers of London and Westminster. 1716.

Price Fourpence.

A

DIALOGUE

BETWEEN A

Whig and a Jacobite, Etc.

Jacobite.—SO, Neighbour, now I hope you are convinc'd: Did you observe the *Appearances* in the Skie t'other Night? The very Heavens testify against you. I must own, I did not myself see what some fancy'd resembl'd Men, whether with Heads or without; but I saw what satisfy'd me that God Almighty is displeas'd with such Proceedings, I wish the Blood of these Gentlemen don't cry for Vengeance against us. *Deus avertat Omen!* Tho' after all, God, I hope, will plead the Cause of the Church.

Whig.—You wou'd amaze me, but that I know what Company you keep, and have heard enough of such Stuff as this of late; tho' I am sorry to hear One with grey Hairs on his Head talk so extravagantly: And I must tell you, after all your Noise and Din for the Church, as if you, and the Gentlemen of your Stamp, were the only Pillars of it, you take Methods to make yourselves and the Church too ridiculous. The Blood of these Gentlemen cry for Vengeance! Pray, Sir, what can you say for these Gentlemen? If you, or any *Jacobite* in *Britain*, can offer one Word of sober Reason to justify what they have done; to excuse, or so much as palliate the Crime of their Rebellion, I'll be willing to die to atone for the Blood that's shed, and to redeem what's behind.

J.—You are warm, Neighbour; I perceive I've rais'd the Old Man in you. I hoped when God himself had taken the Work into his own Hand, you wou'd have been more soft'ned; but it seems you are the same Man still, and 'tis like your Party will pursue the same Measures, notwithstanding Heaven so openly declares against——

W.—Against what? Speak out, if you have any Thing to say: If you mean, against the Ingratitude of a stupid Nation, that have enjoy'd the Blessings of the Reformed Religion, and a free Government so long, and yet know not how to value them; If you mean against the present unnatural, unreasonable, horrid Rebellion, there's some sense in it: But, I suppose, 'tis something else you point at; *You would insinuate some extraordinary Iniquity in the present Times, that the Foundations are out of course, the Government usurped, the Administration corrupt, and, as was said, of the Old World, the Land filled with Violence;* and that all this was legible in the Face of the Skie on *Tuesday* Night.

J. Ah Sir, such Reflections are but too well grounded, tho' I know you make light of them.

W. You seem to express yourself with an Air of Concern, as if you was in earnest; and tho' I've very little Hopes of removing the obstinate Prejudices you have imbibed, yet having found you a Person of good Nature, and in other Matters not unpersuadable, I shall be willing to talk a little with you, if you please, upon the Subject you have started; and all that I shall ask of you, as a *Postulatum*, is, That you will not renounce common Sense, deny palpable Matter of Fact, and evident Reason. I shall fall directly upon the Point in Hand, and desire we may use as few Words needlesly as possible, because I have but a little Time to spend with you.

1.) Don't you think that Rebellion is a very heinous Sin?

J.—Yes certainly, the Scripture says, '*Tis as the sin of Witchcraft.*

W. You alledge the hackney Text of your Party on such Occasions; but excuse me, if I say, 'tis impertinent, it speaks of King *Saul's* Sin against God, and not of Civil Rebellion; however, it shews the Sense you have of the Thing, and that is enough for my present Purpose.

(2.) Don't you allow, if King *George* be the rightful Sovereign of these Realms, that then the present Insurrection is Rebellion, and the Gentlemen, you so tenderly sympathize with, are *Rebels?*

J. If he be? Now you make me smile; I thought you wou'd show your weak Side presently.

A Dialogue between a Whig and a Jacobite.

W. Smile! But surely it must be at your own Folly; I know Nothing else you have to smile at: I'll go further, and assert, He has as full and as just a Title to the Crown he wears, as any Prince in *Christendom* to his; and I challenge you, and all the *Jacobites* in *England*, to dispute that Point with you; and that you may not think me confident without Reason, I shall let you see the Grounds I go upon.

(1.) 'Tis certain, and even capable of Demonstration, that the Right and Title any Prince on Earth has to his Crown, or the supreme Government, depends upon the Constitution, Law, or Custom of that Country where he governs: It would be but an odd Complement to any Man's Intellectuals, to suppose he needed a formal Proof of this. I speak not here of extraordinary Cases, as a divine Appointment formerly among the *Jews*, or Conquest now: But ordinarily no Man has any Right but what the Law derives to him; which is true of all universally, from the meanest Subject, to the Sovereign upon the Throne.

Hence (2.) Look round the World, (and you'll find the Foundation or Rule of Right to the Crown or Government) is not every where *one and the same, fix'd and invariable*, but *different*, according to the different Laws and Constitutions of the several Countries: In *Poland*, 'tis the Election of the People, that gives Right according to their Constitution: In *France*, and some other Places, a Female, tho' next in blood, and the only Issue of the Prince that reigns, has no Right, being excluded by what they call the *Salique Law:* Here in *England*, the Crown is partly Hereditary, and the Right of succeeding to the Government from Birth, tho' with Limitations and a Power in the Government of setting aside the next in Succession, and fixing on another, as the Exigencies of the State are judged to require. Thus by the 13th of *Eliz.*, Cap. 1. 'tis made High-Treason to affirm, *That the Laws and Statutes do not bind the Right of the Crown, and the Descent, Limitation, Inheritance, and Government thereof.* Which is renew'd in these Terms by the 4th of Q. *Anne*, Cap. 8. *That if any shall affirm, That the Kings and Queens of England, by and with the Authority of Parliament, are not able to make Laws and Statutes of sufficient Force and Validity to limit and bind the Crown of this Realm, and the Descent thereof, every such Person shall be guilty of High-Treason; and being convicted, &c. shall suffer of Death, and all Losses and Forfeitures, as in Case of High-Treason.* So that tho' we have, to avoid the Confusion of frequent Elections, settled the Crown on Families, 'tis with Restriction, and a Power of limiting the

Succession; no Man's Birth alone makes him King, unless he has the Qualifications the Laws require: to deny this, is no less than High-Treason.

(3.) In Pursuance of this inherent, necessary Power in the Government, of providing for its own Safety, and Limiting the Succession, our States have wisely excluded all *Papists*, and made them for ever incapable of succeeding to the *British* Crown; the Words of the Act are: * *Whereas it has been found by Experience, that it is inconsistent with the* **Safety** *and welfare of this Protestant Kingdom to be govern'd by a popish* **Prince**, *or by a King or Queen marrying a Papist; Be it therefore Enacted, That all and every Person that is, or shall be reconciled to, or hold Communion with the See, or Church of* **Rome**, *or shall profess the popish Religion, or shall marry a Papist, shall be excluded, and* **be** *for ever incapable to inherit, possess, or enjoy the Crown of this Realm, or to use, or exercise any Regal Power,* &c. *And in such* **Case**, *or Cases, the People shall be, and are hereby absolv'd of their Allegiance.*

(4.) Besides this **general** Exclusion of *Papists*, your *Pretender is by Name excluded*,† and **attainted** of High Treason; nay, 'tis declar'd High-Treason, *advisedly*, **and** *directly* **to maintain and** *affirm*, *That* **the pretended P. of** Wales, *styling himself K. of* England, *by the* **name of** James **the Third, hath any** ‡ **Right or** *Title to the Crown of these* Realms. And I need not tell you, That the same Law that has put an unmovable Bar in the Way of the Pretender, has settled the Crown on King **George** and his Family, being *Protestants*, 12. *W*. Cap. 2. 5. *An* Cap. 8. And in the present *Oath of Allegiance and Abjuration*, which several of you Gentlemen have taken, you own King *George's* Title in the strongest Terms. I'll rub up your Memory, by reciting a Part of it: *I*, A. B. *do sincerely acknowledge, profess, testify, and declare in my Conscience before* **God**, *and the World, That our Sovereign Lord King* George, *is lawful and rightful King of this Realm*, **&c.** *And I do solemnly and sincerely declare in my Conscience, that* **the** *Person pretending to be* **the** *Prince of* Wales, *during the Life of the late* **K**. James, *and since his Decease taking upon himself the Style and Title of* K. *of* **England**, *&c. hath not any Right or Title whatsoever to* **the** *Crown of this* **Realm**: *And I do renounce, refuse, and abjure any Allegiance or Obedience* **to him**, &c. Now, Sir, this being the State of the Case, **this** being **the** Law and Constitution of *England*, 'tis so evident, as not to admit of Debate, That *King* George *is the only Person that hath any Right to the* British *Crown, and to whom the Subjects can with*

---

* *W*. & *M*. Sess, 2 Cap. 2. † 4 *W*. Cap. 3. ‡ 4 *An* Cap. 8.

232

a safe Conscience pay Allegiance. And I scarce need make the Inference for you, That *therefore* the *Pretender* has no Claim or Right: And again, *therefore* those concern'd in the present Insurrection, are *Rebels*.

J. You have been very particular on this Head. I am sensible where the Right is, *according to your Acts of Parliament*; But you take no Notice of *a divine Right*, which all the Acts of Parliament in the World can't affect: Kings are born to their Crowns, as other Heirs in a Family to their Estates, and their Right is divine, hereditary, and unalienable.

W. You would not be pleas'd, should I give such Talk its proper Name: However, I shall take the Freedom to tell you, That I have examin'd your Notion carefully, and am well assur'd 'tis meer Whim, and subsists no where but in the confus'd Imagination of a *Tory*. Pray, what do you found this Dream of a divine, indefeasible Right upon? Is there any Declaration from Heaven for it? When was it made, and to whom? For my Part, I have read the Bible from first to last, and can't find one Word of it; and I dare say no Body else, unless instead of seeking it there, he bring it along with him. You can't prove, nor all the *Jacobites* on Earth, that God has appointed any one particular Species of Government, as what he would have obtain universally and in every Nation: Much less has he fix'd the Right, the Manner, and Order of Succession. The *Jews* indeed, were put under Kingly Government, at their own foolish and sinful Request (after they grew weary of the Theocracy) and against the Remonstrances of God and the Prophet. Their first King (*Saul*) had a divine Right, being chosen immediately by God, as well as the People; and yet this was so far from being indefeasible and hereditary, that he forfeited the Crown by his Male-Administration, was rejected of God, and his Posterity depriv'd of the Succession. *David*, their next King, was chosen out of a mean Family, and was the youngest of all *Jesse's* Sons, (1 *Sam.* xvi. 11.) And tho' he was a good Prince, and the Crown was settled in his Family; yet so as no Way favours your Notion of hereditary Right, *Solomon*, one of his younger Sons being appointed to succeed him, to the Exclusion of *Absalom*, *Adonijah*, &c. who according to the Law of Birth-right, might claim before him: And if you pursue the Scripture History of this Matter, you'll find other Instances enow to the like Purpose. Now I ask you, Where's your divine, indefeasible, hereditary Right of Kings? You see it has no Foundation in Scripture. When God chose a King for his People the *Jews*, the first Royal Family was depriv'd of the Crown after a single Reign; the second had the Crown continu'd in a younger Branch: And are not these admirable Precedents for divine, hereditary, indefeasible Right? Or can it be imagin'd, That if there was any such Thing, these first Examples shou'd be so absolutely against it. You say, your Pretender has an hereditary Right, which no humane Laws or Settlements can make void. But whence is this Right? If you answer, Because he's of the Family of the *Stuarts*, who had a divine, indefeasible Right: I reply, *Saul* had a more divine Right than they, and yet his Children were excluded: Tho' after all, I don't suppose the Jewish Polity was design'd for a Pattern to all the World, or that these Instances absolutely bind us either in one Respect or another: However, they may serve for what we call, *Argumentum ad hominem*, and shew how lame your Plea is from Scripture in Behalf of a divine Right. Not that I deny Government in itself to be divine, and that Monarchy is an excellent Species of it, (for some Countries;) but what particular Form of Government, whether Monarchy, Aristocracy, or a Common-wealth, shall be establish'd in this or that Nation; what Persons shall be entrusted with the Administration, and how the Right of Succession shall descend; *all this is humane:* The Scripture meddles not with it: which it may be is what the Apostle *Peter* intends; when speaking of *Government, he calls it *an Ordinance of Man*, or a humane Creature. Government in general, is the Ordinance of God, as the Apostle *Paul* calls it; but the Specification of it is from Man, and humane. I might further take Notice, what Confusion your Notion would involve the World in: It would unking the greatest Part, if not all the Monarchs on Earth. And pray look over the List of our own Princes, since the *Norman* Conquest, and see what Work it wou'd make among us. What Right *William* I, whom we call, the *Conqueror*, had, I can't imagine, if your Scheme have any Sense in it; and I am sure, his Son, *William* II, had none; he being a younger Brother, and the eldest Son (*Robert*) alive when he was made King. Nor had *Henry* I, *Stephen*, *John*, *Henry* IV, *Henry* V, *Henry* VI, *Richard* III, any Right by Proximity of Blood: So that you wou'd do well to consider, that while you turn so many of our Kings into Usurpers, you turn their Laws into Nullities, undermine our Titles to our Estates, and set us together by the Ears, scuffling for them.———But I'll have done with this *Chimera*, which indeed is regarded no where, any further

---

* 1 Pet. ii. 13.

A Dialogue between a Whig and a Jacobite.

than Mens particular Interests are serv'd by it ; no, not in *France ;* Witness the *Salique Law,* mention'd before ; witness the present King of *Spain's* renouncing the Crown of *France,* for himself and Heirs ; as his Grandfather did that of *Spain,* when he marry'd the *Infanta.* 'Tis plain, they admit of no Notion of a divine Right, *but what is subject to Reasons of State,* and varies, as their Interest varies ; if they did, they wou'd not surely pretend to controul it by humane Compacts.

J. But you'll grant, if K. *James* II, had not been a *Papist,* nor his Son bred up in the Catholick Religion, he wou'd have had a Right, nor wou'd our Law-Makers have gone about to exclude him ; and is it not hard a Man shou'd lose his Birth-Right, *purely for Conscience Sake,* and on the Account of Religion ?

W. I find you take your *Pretender's* Royal Birth for granted, and 'tis like, think I do so too ; because I did not before call it in question : But I must tell you, it has so many Marks of Imposture in it, that if a Son in my Family was half so suspicious, I shou'd not esteem it honourable to make him my Heir, and bestow my Estate upon him. And since, without Design, I have fallen upon this Subject, I shall mention to you some Circumstances of his Birth, which you may find more at large in the *Memorial* of the *English Protestants* to the Prince and Princess of *Orange.* They take Notice, "That the Custom in *England,* of Notifying to the next Heir the approaching Delivery of the Queen, was omitted. Her Breasts never swell'd, nor was any Milk ever seen in them. The Queen, contrary to her former Custom, withdrew into a private Room, when she chang'd her Linnen, and wou'd never suffer any Protestant Lady to be by. The Place of her pretended Lying-in was so variously reported, that the Ladies most concern'd knew not how to prepare for Attendance : Her Royal Highness, the Princess of *Denmark,* was kept at the *Bath* till the Time was over : The Queen was late at Cards on *Saturday* Night, very well ; and on a sudden said, she wou'd Lie-in at St. *James's* : She cry'd-out the very next Day about Ten a Clock, when most of the Protestants Ladies were at Church. In the Room where the Queen lay, there was a private Door within the Rail of the Bed into another Room, from whence a Child might be convey'd into the Queen's Bed unseen. Three popish Confidents, the Midwife, Mrs. *Labadie,* and Mrs. *Tourain,* pass'd thro' that secret Door backward and forward, none of the Lords of the Council being able to see any Thing that was done ; only they were seen in the Bed-Chamber with the King, that their Names might be publish'd to the People. The

Queen was Deliver'd in a very little Time. No Signs of Her Majesty's known Weakness in the Pangs of Birth appear'd; but all was suddenly dispatch'd, and the Midwife delivering something close cover'd to Mrs. *Labadie*, they went both thro' the private Door in so great haste as to leave her Majesty in those Moments, when her (the Midwife's) Assistance was most wanted; and as none saw what was taken out of the Bed, none heard any Child Cry in it." Now considering the violent Suspicion of the Nation of a Cheat, in so much that the Queen's great Belly was ridicul'd in Lampoons, that flew even about *Whitehall* itself, 'tis strange, to Amazement, that no more Care was taken to give the Publick Satisfaction. ' I remember, that 'tis said of the Empress *Constantia*, Wife to *Henry* IV, Emperor of *Germany*, That being in Years, and the People suspecting she was past Child-bearing, she prepar'd a Place in publick, where she remain'd till her Labour, with Keepers, that no Suppositious Child might possibly be convey'd to her; and there, in the Sight of the Citizens, she brought forth a Prince, who was afterwards *Frederick* II. But here, all Things are huddl'd up in Darkness; and so manag'd, that if the Birth was real, 'tis impossible for an unprejudic'd Person, not to question it.

It increases the Suspicion, that the *Papists*, (who knew their Cause was like to be ruin'd, if K. *James* died without an Heir Male, that might exclude his *Protestant* Daughters) were so mightily solicitous in the Affair; which no doubt would set their Heads at Work: And tho' at the Time of the Birth, many of them call'd it miraculous, yet they spoke of it before with strange Assurance, That the Queen would have a Child, *and that it would be a Son*. When the Earl of *Castlemain* was sent Ambassador to the Pope by K. *James*, the *Jesuits* shew'd one of his Retinue a Device, signifying their Expectation and Confidence with Reference to this Matter, and implying, as one wou'd think, that they were let into the Secret: The Device was a Lilly, from whose Leaves distill'd some drops of Water, which, as *Naturalists* say, becomes the Seeds of new Lillies; and the *Motto* was, *Lachrymor in prolem*, I weep for a Child; and underneath was this *Distich:*

> *Pro Natis,* Jacobe gemis, *Flos candide Regum;*
> *Hos Natura tibi si neget Astra dabunt.*

" O *James*, thou best of Kings, dost thou weep for Children, if Nature denies, Heaven will grant the Blessing." But that neither Nature, nor the Stars gave K. *James* this Son, *but that he was the Birth of a*

A Dialogue between a Whig and a Jacobite.

popish Juggle, and Imposture, the Circumstances before-mention'd render it at least grosly suspicious. So that I must tell you, had I as great an Opinion as you, of Nearness and Relation of Blood, I should prefer, on that very Account, the Title of King *George* (in whom the Royal Families of *Plantaginet* and *Stuart* are united) to that of the *Pretender*, whom no Body knows (except a Few in the Secret) *whence he is*.

And besides, when you talk so much of his Right, and his Birth-Right, you should call to Mind, that the good People of *England* have their Birth-Rights as well as your *Pretender*; even tho' his Birth was unquestionably Royal. We have all of us a Birth-Right to our Estates, Religion and Liberties: And pray how comes his Right *to supersede and null all our Rights?* Who gave him, or any One else, a Right to ruin Mankind? to trample on the Necks of Millions of People, and tear out their Bowels? which must be the Consequence of owning the Right of a *Papist*, and submitting to the *Pretender*: For my Part, as the Law has made me free (the Law of God has left me so, the Law of Nature, and the Law of the Land has made me so) I'm resolv'd to stand fast in my Liberty, as long as I can, and never sacrifice the Blessings of my Birth and dear Country, to the Lust of your Sham-Sovereign.

J. This is all Exclamation: Can you imagine, we desire to be undone any more than you? We are not for parting with our Religion, or Liberties either; but expect to have them better secur'd, by that Sovereign you speak of, with so much Contempt, *under whom we may be all happy.*

W. Better secur'd! Why; were they ever safer than under the present Administration? or humanely speaking, is it possible they should? But suppose, that really your Religion and Liberties were in Danger, where lies the Wisdom of seeking to a popish *Pretender* to rescue them? If you knew what Popery is; if you knew the Conscience of a popish Prince; you wou'd never wish to see a Protestant Church under his Protection; which is just the same Thing, *as for a Flock of Sheep to choose a Wolf for their Shepherd.* The *Pretender* is a Wolf by Principle, whatever he is by natural Inclination: As a pupil of *France*, bred up in the Maxims of arbitrary Government, he's taught to destroy our Civil Liberties; and as a *Papist*, he's sworn to destroy our Religious. Methinks, you cannot but reflect upon his refusing just now the Coronation-Oath in *Scotland;* which must be because he wou'd not come under any Obligations to favour your Heresy; nor have his Oaths cast up at every Turn by you, and thrown in his Way, while he was accomplishing the Work he has undertaken: And for the same Reason, no Question, 'tis, that he does not so much as promise to support our Church and Religion, in his Declaration, Dated from *Commercy*. He says indeed, *Let the Religious Right of all our Subjects receive a Confirmation in a Free Parliament; let Consciences truly tender, be indulged.* But he promises Nothing. Which I mention, not to his Reproach at all; for I look upon this plain Dealing, to be the most honourable Thing I ever heard of him. In the mean time, 'tis no small Reproach to you, who call yourselves Protestants, that you thus stickle for one that does not so much as speak you fair, nor give you any Assurances for the Security of your Religion: It shews your Credulity, the Grossness of the Infatuation you are under; and I must needs say, looks like a Judgment of God upon us, who for our Sins has given up so great a Body of Unthinking People to strong Delusions: I wish it be not to theirs, and all our *Ruin*.

I know but one Thing you can suggest against what I have been hinting; I don't say one Thing, which has any Weight in it; for that it has not, but with which you can possibly cheat yourselves into a Confidence in the *Pretender;* and that is, That tho' he has been a little upon the Reserve with you; yet his known Goodness, the Obligations he'll be under to you for his Advancement, and even his own Interest will oblige him to be kind to the Church of *England*, and protect you in all your Privileges both Civil and Religious. To this I answer (1.) That you have a Prince upon the Throne from whom you may justly expect all this: I would not lessen the great King *George* so far as to compare him with your *Pretender;* but surely it must argue Distraction in a Church of *England*-Man to think himself and Religion Safer, under such a Tool as the St. *German's* Pupil, than under a stanch Protestant, *The wisest and bravest Prince in Christendom.* Pretender designs you no such Favour as you expect, *from his saying Nothing of it,* when it might have serv'd his Interest with some of you at least; tho' others are resolv'd to espouse him upon any Terms, and to run all Hazards for him, without so much as looking before them or asking Questions. (3.) I add, should his Inclinations be never so kind to you, (and I believe he never intends you the Honour of Martyrdom if you don't prevent him by your Apostacy) nay, should he promise and swear by all that's sacred to maintain your Establishment, *'tis what he can't do:* Principle would controul Nature, and the prior and superior Obligations of Conscience cancel the most solemn

238

Stipulations with *Protestants*. The religion he has learnt teaches him, That *Faith is not to be kept with Hereticks*. He's bound on Penalty of Depofition and Damnation, to deftroy them out of his Dominions. The Decrees of two General Councils (*Conftance* and *Lateran*) hang over his Head, arm'd with the moft terrible *Anathema's* in Cafe he fhould be remifs in the Difcharge of his Duty, and fhew Mercy to Hereticks contrary to his Vows. I'll give you the Words of the Council of *Lateran:* * *If the Temporal Governour, being requir'd and admonifhed, fhall neglect to purge his Country of Herefy, let this be fignify'd to the Pope, that from henceforth he may declare his Subjects free from their Allegiance.* Nay, Pope *Martin* V, went fo far as to tell the Duke of *Lithuania*, That he Sin'd mortally if he kept his Oath with Hereticks. So that fhould this Youngfter you dote on, give you the Security of Promifes and Oaths, he would regard them no more than his pretended Father did, who, you know, made all the hafte poffible to break them: Nay, fhould he be touch'd with Compaffion, with a Senfe of Honour and Gratitude towards a Company of Mad-men, that were willing to ruin themfelves and Pofterity to ferve him; yet the Terrors of the holy Father's Rod, the *Anathema's* of the Church, the Dread of a future Purgatory, and Hell, would force him thro' thefe leffer Reftraints: *He muft perfecute and deftroy you whether he would or not;* the fame Argument would urge him to it, that one of the *Popifh* Lords is faid to make ufe of when he engag'd in this Rebellion, *viz. his Salvation lay at Stake.*

J. But still, methinks, 'tis a little harfh, that a man who has done Nothing to forfeit it, fhould lofe his Right, *purely on the Account of his Religion.*

W. Harfh! Not at all, when what you call his Right would be the Ruin of the Community, as in this Cafe, I have undeniably prov'd it would; fo that I do and muft maintain, was his Birth lefs fufpected and abfolutely neceffary for the Safety of the State, (*Proteftant;*) nor would you yourfelf think it any greater Hardfhip (had you not loft the Power of fober Cofideration) than 'tis *to deprive a Lunatick of his Eftate,* and difpofe of it to the next Heir of a fober Mind: For who fees not that a *Papift* is far more unfit to be entrufted with the Government of a *Proteftant* Kingdom, than a Lunatick with a private Eftate; the one would only injure a particular Family, the other deftroy a Community. Pray reflect on the Practice and Conduct of the *Papifts*

---

* Sub. *Innocent.* III. An. 1215 Can 3.

in this Matter, of whom of late you begin to fpeak fo favourably ; Do they allow *Proteftants* any Right to Crowns among 'em ? 'Tis their avow'd Doctrine, That Herefy in a Prince is an univerfal Forfeiture of his Crown, his Life, and All: accordingly their Church deprives, depofe, excommunicates heretical Kings, and leaves them to the Mercy of Ruffians, who may murder them and be guiltlefs. You remember the Fate of *Henry* IV, of *France*, who was forc'd to declare himfelf a *Papift* before he could fit quietly on his Throne ; and being afterwards fufpected to incline too much to the *Hugonots*, *Ravilliac* was imploy'd to affaffinate him. Now pray, my good Neighbour, can you give me any Reafon why we in *England* fhould not exclude a *Papift*, as well as the *Papifts* every where exclude *Proteftants;* efpecially when the Religion of the latter includes, as its effential Principles, univerfal Love, Charity, and Compaffion ; and the Religion of the former breathes nothing but Fire and Faggot, Defolation and Slaughter.

J. You're a warm Advocate for your Cause ; and I muft confefs have offer'd more for it than I expected could have been faid ; But you muft grant the prefent Government has not taken the moft proper Methods, to reconcile its Enemies, and recommend it felf to the Nation: Our Church can go as far as any Society in the World in true Loyalty ; but has not loft the Senfe of Feeling ; *Oppreffion will make a wife Man mad.*

W. I am glad you have mention'd this ; it being the common Topick your Party infifts upon to afperfe the prefent Government, and fpread their Venom among the People ; but really 'tis the moft unreafonable and impudent Slander, that ever was invented: Full two Years are not expir'd fince his Majefty's happy Acceffion ; 'tis easy to look back upon the Occurrences of fo fhort a Reign ; and to recount the feveral Tranfactions thereof ; which furely muft be frefh in their Memories, that cry out fo loudly of Oppreffion, as to take up Arms, and attempt to dethrone their lawful Sovereign on that Account: Now Sir, we'll bring this Matter to a fpeedy Iffue. I have only one Thing to demand of you, than which Nothing can be more reafonable, *viz.* That if neither you nor any of your Party throughout *Britain*, can produce a Single Inftance of Injuftice, Tyranny, or Oppreffion, in his Majefty's whole Adminiftration hithero ; that you'll then grant the Clamour raifed againft the King, muft be Nothing but Malice, and the Contrivance of a bafe Faction, that have vile Ends to ferve thereby. This, Sir, is what I ask of you, and if after all your

Noife you can alledge Nothing in the Government *that has so much as the Appearance of Tyranny in it*, and I challenge Malice itfelf to do its worſt; then I expect you'l defert your Party, and be aſhamed of your Cauſe and Company for the future.

J. You come clofe now, and think to pinch me: I own I have not been fo bufie in Politicks, as to be able to anfwer you fully in this Matter; but I have heard feveral Complaints, that I can't think are wholly groundlefs: You may be fure we can't but with Concern fee the Friends of the Church all turn'd out of Place and in Difgrace: If a Man fpeaks a word amifs, he's prefently bound over and hal'd to Prifon: The *Habeas Corpus Act*, the greateſt Relief of the oppreffed Subject, is now fufpended, that no Man can have the Benefit of that Law; nor is this the worſt of it, a ſtanding Army is kept up to awe the Subject, and terrify the Nation.

W. You need not plead Infufficiency; you underſtand well enough the *Shibboleth of your Party*, and have alledg'd all that ever I heard from any of them; and how perfectly nothing 'tis, I ſhall ſhew you in a few Words. Your *firſt* Complaint, that the Church has fuffer'd, and is in Danger, by the Change of the Miniſtry, is odd enough at this Time a Day. I'm fatify'd many who once fell in with that Cry, are now aſham'd of it, when they fee what Courfe fome of thofe Gentlemen were ſteering; and indeed if your difgrac'd Friends are neceffary to the Safety of the Church, you muſt mean the *Pretender* is fo too, (for thither they were carrying you); which is fo fenfelefs a Sham, that I leave you to bluſh at it when you become capable of calm Reflection: I might further re-mind you, that They in Place now, are all Church-Men; yea, better Church-men than thofe that are turned out: Nor has there been one Act of Injuſtice or Unkindnefs done to the Church, fince the Change you make fuch a Stir about. What you talk of a Standing-Army is moſt abfurd, when you your felves have occafion'd it by your Confpiracies and Rebellion; nor have you any Thing after all to fear from this Standing Army. The King was Abfolute in his own Country, and had an arm'd Force ready to execute his Pleafure at any Time, and yet none ever heard the leaſt Attempt or Inclination to Opprefs any of his Subjects there. Befides, you ſhou'd confider this ſtanding Force is judg'd neceffary by the Government; is rais'd and continued by Confent of the Parliament, and will you call this Oppreſſion and Tyranny, &c. efpecially when the Neceſſity is from your felves? As for what you fay of Perfons being taken up and imprifon'd for a Word &c. 'tis a poor Pretence, I hardly believe you can think the Government ought to pafs by fuch Infults as are offered it, without fhewing its Refentment; and indeed you might as well defire the King to refign all at once, and leave you *Tories* and *Jacobites* to fill his Throne as you pleafe, and trample upon his faithful Subjects. The Sufpenfion of the *Habeas Corpus* Act may appear to fome a more ferious Matter, and look like an Hardfhip; but really is no fuch Thing: This Act was made in the 31ft Year of K. *Charles* II: In the 1ft Year of K. *William* and Q. *Mary*, two Acts pafs'd to fufpend it, *i.e.* to enable their Majefty's to Apprehend, Detain, and Commit without Bail, fuch Perfons as they fhould find juft Caufe to fufpect were confpiring againft the Government, which was thought in that Time of Confufion, neceffary for the common Safety. At the Time of the horrid Affaffination-Plot, in the 7th and 8th Year of K. *William*, the like Act pafs'd; and upon the *Pretender's* attempting to Land in *Scotland* in the 6th of Q. *Anne*, the fame Power was given Her Majefty by Parliament, to Apprehend and Detain fuch Perfons, as Her Majefty fhould fufpect were confpiring againft her Perfon and Government; and now on Occafion of the prefent Rebellion, which makes the Reafon and Neceffity as urgent as in any of the former Inftances, the fame Power is granted his Majefty; and pray what is there amifs in this? Where lies the Oppreffion of it? The King does not difpenfe with the Law by his own abfolute Authority, as you know the Prince did whom your *Pretender* calls Father; but 'tis done by the Legiflature, *pro re natâ*, for a limited Time only, and to anfwer a prefent Neceffity.

J. But fure you can't juftify the Severities us'd of late: *Never was there fuch Slaughtering before*; you may well imagine it will occafion Murmuring and Uneafinefs among the People, to fee fo much noble Blood attainted, and fo many Lives taken away for I know not what: Read all our Hiftories, and I don't believe you'll be able to parallel this in any Reign fince the Reformation, nay fince the Conqueft: Mercy and Goodnefs is the Glory of a Prince; and methinks a Government that *owes its Being to a Pretence of fecuring us from Tyranny and Cruelty*, fhou'd not lay its Foundation in *thofe very Crimes*.

W. I know the poor Sots, that range about the Streets, between Drunk and Sober, talk at this Rate; but I'm forry the Infection fhou'd reach above the Mob. However, fince you have efpoufed this Notion, weak as it is, and own it as one of your Prejudices againft the Prefent Government, I fhall debate the Matter a little with you,

242

A Dialogue between a Whig and a Jacobite.

and so take Leave. It may be necessary to put you in Mind (for I see you have very mistaken Apprehensions of governing Mercy) that when God himself was pleas'd to do the Part of a Sovereign Magistrate (as I may express it) and take the Administration of Government into his own Hand more immediately, as in the Jewish Theocracy, he appointed Capital Punishments for Offenders against the State; and you know, or may know, that when these Criminals were conniv'd at, and exempted from Punishment in such Instances as the Law requir'd it, the Land was esteem'd polluted, as by the Execution of Justice it was esteem'd cleansed, and the political Guilt expiated: *Now shall Man be more Righteous or more merciful than God?* Or shall that be call'd unmerciful in an earthly Sovereign, which the God of Heaven, when he stood in the Relation of a King to his People, so strictly requir'd and executed: I grant that Mercy is the Excellency of a Governor, and shou'd triumph when there's Room for it, and it may consist with the publick Safety; but in many Cases, what some call Mercy, is not Mercy but foolish Compassion; and the Exercise of it argues such Weakness in the Prince, as would expose his Government to Contempt and Ruin.

But to come directly to the Point in Hand, *viz:* the Rebellion and Sufferings of the Rebels: I find you make light of the former, and strangely aggravate the latter: Let me ask you one plain Question: You know that in the Reigns of K. *Charles* II, and K. *James* II, several took up Arms against the Government, at first under more obscure Leaders; the second Time under the Dukes of *Monmouth* and *Argyle*, and were proceeded against with Rigour: Now I ask what you think of this? Were these Insurrections, Rebellion; and the Executions done upon those concern'd in them, just and necessary; or were they Acts of Tyranny and Unmercifulness in the Government?

J. No Man of Sense and Loyalty ever thought other, but that these Insurrections were *an hellish Rebellion*, and the Government acted honourably in prosecuting the Rebels in the Manner they did. *Those Fanaticks deserv'd ten times more!*

W. Very well, then I hope you'll grant that if the present Insurrection your Friends engag'd in, hath more of the horrid Nature of Rebellion in it, and many Aggravations, the former had not; and if the Proceedings of the Government against the Rebels of that Time, were more severe than his present Majesty's against the Rebels of this Day, then you'll grant I say, *Your Clamours against King* George *on this*

Head are unreasonable, and must acquit the present Government, or condemn the former you so much applaud.

J. **If** and *If:* This *If* spoils all: **If you can prove** what you suppose, I'll grant you all you **ask**; but I defy you.

W. I shall prove it presently; and defy you and all your Party to object one Word of Reason against what I say. The Thing I have to do, is to shew that the present Rebellion is *worse* than **that under** King *Charles* and King *James* the II; and yet the Sufferings **of the** Rebels *less*: In order to which, I shall compare the one with the Other, with respect both to the *Crime and Punishment*. I shall begin with the Crime, the Rebellion it self.

(1.) **In the** former Rebellion, there **was** *a Papist* at one Time near the Throne, at another Time, (as in *Monmouth's* Rebellion) actually upon it; whom they consider'd as bound to destroy them and their **Religion, as** they knew he intended it. In this Rebellion here's a Protestant upon the **Throne**; whose Family has been celebrated for their **Steadiness to the Protestant** Interest; and his present Majesty is not a **Whit** behind his **Illustrious Ancestors in this** Respect: So that *They* took up Arms against **a** *Papist* ready to devour them; *your Friends* join with *Papists* against a *Protestant*, Zealous to Defend **and Protect** them.

(2.) **In the former** Rebellions they had the *utmost Provocation given them.* **They** did not fright themselves with Imaginary Evils; but saw their Religion **and** Liberties invaded; felt themselves almost **undone** by continued Acts **of Violence** against and contrary to Law. I can't pretend **at** this Time to **enumerate** all the Oppressions of those Reigns; they would fill a Volume. But since **you seem** quite to have forgot these Things, I shall a little refresh your **Memory.** In *Scotland* the poor People were almost harrassed out of their Lives. *Lauderdale,* **the** Tool of the Court at that Time, obtained an Act of Parliament declaring; *That by* ***virtue*** *of the King's Supremacy, the ordering of the Government of the Church do's properly belong* **to** *his Majesty; and that he may Enact and Emit such Orders and Constitutions, concerning Church-Administrations, Persons employ'd in the same, and* **all** *Eccleßiastical Meetings,* &c. *as he shall think* ***fit,*** &c. In **Purfuit** of this, to force the People to Conformity, and to comply with the King's Will in Matters of Churchgovernment and Religion, *high Commission-Courts* were set up, (too like the **Spanish** Inquisition) and several severe Orders were made. It was requir'd of the People to give Bond for themselves, Wives, Children, and **Servants, to** frequent **the** Parish-Church, never to go to the

244

Worship of the *Presbyterians* in their Field-meetings whither they were driven; Nay an Oath was put upon them to difcover all they knew that reforted to thefe Meetings, and deliver up all Vagrant Preachers. Thefe Orders were executed by Dragoons, who exacted the aforefaid Bond, which if any refus'd, they had 10 or 12 Soldiers quarter'd upon them, and Sums of Money demanded befides the Free-Quarters. And when they had drain'd the poor People to that degree, they had Nothing left to anfwer the Soldiers Demands, they were tied Hand and Foot, and dragg'd to Prifon like Beafts. At laft thefe Methods not prevailing to fupprefs their Meetings as they defir'd, Orders were given for the Soldiers to Attack the People wherever they were affembled for Worfhip, which they often did, *mingling their Blood with their Sacrifices.* Now it was upon fuch Oppreffions as thefe, that they took up Arms; firft at *Pentland-hills*, and afterwards at *Bothwell-bridge* in 1679. How the Cafe was in *England*, I need not tell you; all the World faw King *James* aim'd at nothing lefs than the utter Subverfion of the Government and Proteftant Religion; the preventing of which was the Occafion of *Monmouth's* Infurrection, as he owns in his Declaration. "Unlefs, *says he*, we could be contented to fee the Reformed Religion and fuch as profefs it, extirpated; Popifh Idolatry establifh'd, the Laws of the Land trampled under Foot, and all that is facred and civil violated: And unlefs we could be willing to be Slaves as well as *Papifts*, and forget the Example of our noble Anceftors, who convey'd our Privileges to us at the Expence of their Blood and Treafure; and withal be unmindful of our Duty to God, our Country, and Pofterity; deaf to the Cries of our opprefs'd Friends; and be content not only to fee them and ourfelves imprifon'd, robb'd, and murder'd, but the *Proteftant* Intereft throughout the World betray'd to *France* and *Rome*; We are bound as Men and Chriftians to betake ourfelves to Arms, *&c.*"

(3.) They were depriv'd of all Profpect of Relief, and Hopes of Redrefs: In *Scotland* the Law was over-ruled, and fufpended in a great meafure: And in *England* all Methods imaginable were us'd, to fubject the Law, and both the Makers and Interpreters of it to the Will of the Prince. The Declaration mention'd before takes notice, "That perjur'd Judges were fuborn'd to declare for the King's *difpenfing Power:* That fuch were advanc'd to the Bench that were the Scandal of the Bar: That by packing Juries, by falfe Returns, new illegal Charters, and other corrupt Means, they were depriv'd of all Expectation of Succour where their Anceftors us'd to find it; fo that, say they, that which ought to be the Peoples Fence againſt Tyranny, is become the Means of eſtabliſhing arbitrary Power, and confirming their Thraldom." Thus Matters were circumſtanc'd with them; They were undone, *without any Remedy*, unleſs what the Sword brought, which they look'd upon as their laſt Reſort, and only poſſible Means of Safety: How far this is your Caſe, I leave the moſt harden'd *Jacobite* among you to conſider; and only deſire you to reflect upon one Particular relating to the Judges: That now they not only hold, *quam diu bene ſe geſſerint*, but his preſent Majeſty has generouſly increas'd their Sallaries, that they might be more above Temptation, whereas before they were not only Cloſetted, but to render 'em more obſequious, their Patents ran *durante Beneplacito*. Upon the Whole. (4.) 'Tis evident thoſe Rebels fought for their Religion, Laws, Liberties, againſt Oppreſſion, Popery, and Tyranny: 'Tis as Evident you are Free, and fight for Slavery: are at Liberty, and ſeek for Chains: Both your Religion and Eſtates are Safe, and have, it may be, the beſt Guardian of any Proteſtant Church or Nation in the World; and yet Nothing will ſerve you but *a raw Youth, a Dependant on France, and Tool of Rome*, that hates both you and your Profeſſion. Bluſh O ye Heavens at the Stupidity and Folly of theſe Men! Don't miſtake me, I'm not vindicating the former Inſurrections headed by *Monmouth* and others, that's none of my Buſineſs; but 'tis as clear as the Sun at Noon-day, that your's is a black Crime compared with Theirs: If they were Offenders, *you are Sinners before the Lord exceedingly*, as was ſaid of the Men of *Sodom;* And if you'll allow me to ſpeak my Thoughts freely, I muſt ſay the preſent Rebellion is the moſt Complicated Villany that ever was acted among Mankind, ſince *Abſalom* drew the Sword againſt his own Father.

J. I'm a little ſurpriz'd, I confeſs, at your Diſcourſe; I did not imagine Things had been thus: I muſt own if what you ſay be true; they had far more Cauſe to complain than we have: But do you ſay *they ſuffer'd more*, if you can make that out, you'll ſilence me for ever.

W. I ſhall make it out preſently: I'm glad 'tis with any Proſpect of Succeſs with you. A few Remarks upon the Methods taken with the Rebels then, compar'd with what you ſo much complain of now, will be ſufficient for your Conviction.

(1.) The Number of Sufferers at that Time was conſiderable. In *Scotland* They were driven *like Sheep to the Slaughter*. Both the Noblemen that led the Parties, *Monmouth* and *Argyle*, loſt their Heads: *Jefferies* condemned above 500 Perſons in two Places only, *Taunton*

A Dialogue between a Whig and a Jacobite.

and *Wells;* whereof 239 were executed; besides what were dispatch'd at *Dorchester, Exeter,* and *Winchester;* so that he had some Grounds for his brutish Boast, when he return'd from the West, *(viz.) That he had hang'd more Men than all the Judges of* England *since* William *the Conqueror.* Nor would so many have escap'd as did, had not the Judge's Covetousness pleaded stronger than the King's Mercy for their Lives: Pardons were sold at all Prices, from 10 *l.* to 14000 Guineas: and those that had no Money rarely found any Mercy.

(2.) Several suffer'd without any Legal Trial and Conviction: Which was common in *Scotland;* where the Soldiers, being impower'd by the Council, us'd to tender an Oath to such as they suspected, and if they did not answer to Satisfaction, *they shot or stabbed them upon the Spot.* There were near 100 sacrificed to the Rage of the Soldiers in this manner: And if they desir'd *Time* to recommend themselves to God, they were answer'd with a Scoff: *What the Devil have you been doing so many Years; han't you had Time enough to pray in the Caves and Mountains?*

(3.) When they allow'd them the Formality of a Trial, the Injustice and Tyranny appear'd as flagrant in perverting the Law, as when they set it wholly aside. They would try Prisoners without either Accusers or Libel, requiring them to answer *super Inquirendis,* to any Questions that should be put; And some times they would offer them such Oaths as they knew they would not take, and then proceed against them without any more ado: And if in some notorious Cases the Jury scrupled to bring in the Person Guilty, the King's Advocate by Threatnings forc'd them to it; as did *Jefferies* in the Case of Mrs. *Lisle* whom the Jury brought in 3 Times, *not Guilty,* but were so Hector'd by the Judge, that they were forc'd to comply and cry *Guilty.*

(4.) A Variety of Arts were us'd to trick People out of their Lives, and involve them in the Guilt of Rebellion against whom they had no Proof at all. Witness the State-Questions in *Scotland,* invented to insnare such as they had a Mind to destroy: *As what they thought of the Rising at Bothwell-Bridge, and of the Death of the Bishop of St.* Andrew's, whether the one was Rebellion, and the other Murther? Many were imprison'd for a Year together, and never told for what; and not having sufficient Matter of Accusation against them, Spies were sent in among them under the Pretence of being Prisoners, who by conversing with them might fish out something which their Enemies might make an Handle of to condemn them. Nay, those that were never concern'd in their Insurrections, if they gave a Night's Lodging to any of the Rebels, or a Meal of Meat, it wou'd be made a Sort of Treason, and cost them their Necks. *Jefferies* trapan'd a great many out of their Lives, by telling them, "If they pleaded *not Guilty*, and were found so, they should have little Time to live; but if they expected Favour, *they must plead Guilty.*" By which Eighty Persons were deluded and immediately condemn'd and executed. Mrs. *Lisle*, mention'd before, a Woman of extreme Age, suffer'd for High Treason, upon *Jefferies's* Sentence, for only harbouring a Non-Conformist Minister, tho' in no Proclamation.

(5.) Their Manner of Proceeding against the Criminals, either upon their Trials, or at their Executions, was barbarous to the last Degree. The *Bothwell-Bridge* Prisoners were brought to *Edinburgh* and kept in an open Church-yard, for Days and Nights, without any Thing to shelter them from the Cold or Rain: Sometimes a Number of them were cram'd into the same Room, and so wedg'd together, that they could not stoop but their Excrements went from them standing: Some of them by Boots and Thumkins had the Marrow squeez'd out of their Legs and Thumbs, to make them confess: Others, when under Examination, were kept waking by the Soldiers eight or ten Nights together till they were almost distracted, and ready to say any Thing their Enemies would have them. And when they came to execute any of them, they generally put off all Humanity: Often the Sufferers might not have Leave to speak a Word at their Death, in Vindication of themselves, but were hurried out of the World; or at least the Drums were kept beating, *&c.* that they could not be heard. Some had their Ears cut off upon one Sentence, and were hang'd upon another: Some were tied to a Stake within the Sea-Mark, and there left to perish leisurely by the increasing Waves: Others had their Hands and Privy Members cut off, and their Heart pluckt out and thrown into the Fire before their Face.

In *England* Matters were carried much after the same sort. To say nothing of *Jefferies*, whose very Name is Infamous, and gives a Sort of Horror and Indignation, especially in the *West*, Collonel *Kirk* acted the Butcher beyond most you have heard of: He caus'd Ninety wounded Men at *Taunton* to be hang'd, not only without permitting their Relations to speak to them, but with Pipes playing, Drums beating, Trumpets sounding, and all other Military Rejoycings. At another Time he invited his Officers to Dinner, near the Place where some of the condemn'd Prisoners were to be executed, and order'd

A Dialogue between a Whig and a Jacobite.

Ten of 'em to be turn'd off with a Health to the King, Ten with an Health to the Queen, and Ten more with a Health to *Jefferies:* But nothing is more Infamous in the Brute, than his Decoying a fair Virgin to his Embraces, with the promise of saving her Brother's Life; and when he had gratify'd his vile Inclinations, hang'd the Man on the Sign of the House before the abus'd Damsel's Face.

(6.) I shall only further observe, that great Numbers were made Criminals, Indicted, Imprison'd and Punish'd even to Death (some of 'em) *for slight Offences:* Much less than many of your Party are guilty of every Day. I could give you the Names of Scores that were Fin'd and Whip'd for speaking against the Government, and complaining of Oppression: The *Taunton* Girls were Fin'd Forty and Fifty Pound a Piece for flourishing *Monmouth's* Colours: Nay, a Constable was hang'd for executing *Monmouth's* Warrant; and 'tis said another poor Man met with the same Fate, for the horrid Treason of *Three Pennyworth of Hay for his Horse.*

And now, Sir, I leave it to your own Ingenuity and Conscience, to determine the Case between the Sufferers, (the former and present Sufferers.) Can you find any Passages in the Proceedings of the Government against the present Rebels, that answer the strange Inhumanities I have been speaking of? Is there as much Blood-shed now as there was then? Tho' the Crime of this Rebellion is a Thousand Times greater, and many Thousand Times more have espous'd it directly or indirectly. Are any executed now without a Trial, or condemn'd without Evidence? Do you know of Arts us'd to trick Men out of their Lives, or to involve innocent Persons in the Guilt of such Crimes they have never been concern'd in? Are any Prosecuted or Hang'd for harbouring Rebels, or giving them a small Relief, when almost ready to famish for Want? Is every Word spoke against the Government made criminal, as heretofore? If so, the Women and Girls durst not talk so much saucy Treason at their Tea-Tables as they do, but would be taken up, and whipp'd for it, as indeed they well deserve. Act impartially, Sir, as becomes an honest Man, and then I need say no more, but refer the Matter wholly to your self: Only I must tell you what I expect from you, unless you can except against what has been said; *viz.* That you'll never after this pretend to excuse the present most unreasonable Rebellion: That instead of reproaching his Majesty's Government your self, you'll Rebuke such as do: And that as an *English-*Man and *Protestant,* you'll shew your Gratitude; That those unhappy Men, whom you're now convinc'd you have thought too well of, have not been able to ruin themselves, their King and Country, as they attempted

J. Sir I thank you for your free Conversation: I shall endeavour to recollect what you have said, and impartially consider it: I hope it will at least have this Effect, that I shan't be so easily impos'd upon, and carried away with every foolish Prejudice, as I perceive I have too much been heretofore. But pray, Sir, what do you think after all, of the *odd Appearances* the other Night?

W. We have spent too much of our Time in Politicks to enter upon Philosophy now. They might proceed from a Natural Cause, and be no more Monitory and Ominous than the Moon-shine. However let them signify what they will, I'm sure They can't signify *God's Approbation of the horrid Enterprize of these Rebels,* or his Displeasure at the Punishment that has overtaken them. 'Tis no less than Blasphemy thus to interest Heaven in so great a Villany. I think the Country-man put a far better Sense upon the *Phænomenon*, (viz.) *That it was an Illumination and publick Rejoycings in the Heavens, for the Defeat of King* GEORGE's *Enemies.*

"Inter Folia Fructus."

THE

EXECUTION

OF

MARY, QUEEN OF SCOTS.

" History is but the Unrolled Scroll of Prophecy."
—James A. Garfield.

PRIVATELY PRINTED
FOR THE CLARENDON HISTORICAL SOCIETY.

1886.

This edition is limited to 120 *large* **paper** *and* 400 *small paper copies, for Subscribers only.*

AN ACCOUNT

OF THE

EXECUTION

OF

Mary, Queen of Scots,

NOT HITHERTO PUBLISHED.

Being a Letter from

Robert Wyngfield, *Esq; to Lord Treasurer* Cecil.

LONDON:

Printed for and sold by JAMES CROCKATT, in Prujeian Court, over against Surgeon's-hall, in the Old-Bailey. MDCCLII.

A CIRCUMSTANTIAL ACCOUNT

OF THE

EXECUTION

OF

MARY, QUEEN OF SCOTS.

By ROBERT WYNGFIELD, Esq.

IT maye pleafe your good Lordfhipp, to be advertifed, that according as your Honour gave me in command, I have heer fett downe in writting the trew Order and Manner of the Execution of the Lady *Mary* laft Queen of *Scots*, the 8th of *February* laft, in the great Hall within the Caftle of *Fotheringtray*, togither with relation of all fuch Speeches and Actions fpoken, and done by the fayde Queen, or any others, and all other Circumftances and Proceedings concerning the fame, from and after the Delivery of the faid *Scottifh* Queen, to *Thomas Andrews*, Efq; high Sherife for hir Majeftyes County of *Norfolk*, vnto the End of the fayde Execution, as followeth :

It being certyfied the 6th of *February* laft, to the fayde Queen, by the Right Honourable the Earl of *Kent*, the Earl of *Shrewsberry*, and also by Sir *Amias Pawlet*, and Sir *Drue Drurie*, hir Governors, that shee was to prepare hirself to die the 8th of *February* next, she seemed not to be in any Terror, for ought that appered by any of hir outward Gesture or Behaviour, (other than marvelling shee should die) but rather with smiling Cheer and pleasing Countenance digested and accepted the sayde Admonition of Preparation to hir (as she sayde) unexpected Execution; saying that hir Death should be welcome unto hir, seeing hir Majestie was so resolved, and that that Soule were too too farr vnworthye the Fruition of the Joyes of Heaven for ever, whose Bodye would not in this World be content to endure the Stroake of the Executioner for a Moment. And that spoken, shee wept bitterlye and became silent.

The sayde 8th Day of *February* being come, and Tyme and Place appointed for the Execution, the Queen being of Stature tall, of Bodye corpulent, rownde shouldered, hir Face fat, and broade, double chinned, and hazell-eyed, hir borrowed Hair aborne; her attyre was this, on hir Head shee had a dressing of Lawne edged with Bone-lace, a Pomander Chayne, and an *Agnus Dei* about hir Neck, a Crucifix in hir Hande, a Payre of Beades att hir Girdle, with a golden Crofs at the End of them, a Vale of Lawne fastened to hir Caule, bowed out with Wyer and edged round about with Bone-lace; hir Gowne was of black Sattin printed, with a Trayne and long Sleeves to the Grounde, with Acorn Buttons of Tett, trymmed with Pearle, and shorte Sleeves of Sattyin black Cutt, with a Pair of Sleeves of purple Velvet whole under them, hir Kirtle whole of figured black Sattin, and hir Petticoate Skirts of crimson Velvet, hir Shoes of Spanish Leather with the rough Side outward, a Payre of green Silk Garters, hir nether Stockings worsted colour watchett, clocked with Silver, and edged on the Topp with Silver, and next hir Leg a payre of Jarsye Hose white, *&c.* Thus appareled she departed hir Chamber, and willinglye bended hir Stepps towards the Place of Execution.

As the Commissioners, and divers other Knights, were meeting the Queen coming forthe, one of hir Servants called *Melvin*, kneeling on his Knees to his Queen and Mistress, wringing Handes and shedding Tears, used these Words unto hir: "Ah! Madam, unhappy me, what Man on Earth was ever before the Messenger of so important Sorrow and Heaviness as I shall be, when I shall Reporte that my good and gracious Queen and Mistress is behedded in *England?*" This sayde, Tears prevented him of any further speaking; whereupon the sayde Queen powring forth hir dying Tears, thus answered him, "My good

Servant, ceafe to lament, for thou haſt Caufe rather to joye than to mourne, for now ſhall thou fee *Mary Stewarde's* Troubles receive their longe expected End, and Determination, for know (fayde ſhee) good Servant, all the World is but Vanity, and fubject ſtill to more Sorrow, than a whole Ocean of Tears can bewayle. But I pray thee (fayde ſhee) carry this Meſſage from me, that I dye a trewe Woman to my Religion, and like a trewe Queen of *Scotland* and *France*, but God forgive them (sayde ſhee) that have longe defired my End, and thirſted for my Blood, as the Harte doth for the Water Brookes. Oh! God (fayde ſhee) ſhow thou art the Anchor of Truthe, and Truthe itfelfe, knoweſt the inward Chambar of my Thought, how that I was ever willing that *England* and *Scotland* ſhould be vnited togither. Well, (sayde ſhee) commend me to my Sonne, and tell him, that I have not done any Thinge preiudiciall to the State and Kingdome of *Scotland;*" and fo refolving hirfelfe agayne into Tears, fayde, " good *Meluin* farewell," and with weeping Eyes, and hir Cheekes all befprinkled with Tears, as they were, kiſſed him, saying once againe farewell, good *Meluin*, and praye for thy Miſtris and Queen." And then ſhe turned hirfelf unto the Lordes, and told them ſhee had certayne Requeſts to make vnto them. One was, for certayne Monye to be payde to *Curle* hir Servant ; Sir *Amias Pawlet*, knowing of that Monye, anfwered to this Effect, It ſhoulde : " Next, that hir poor Servants might have that with quietneſs which ſhee had given them by hir Will, and that they might be favourably intreated, and to fend them fafely into their Countries," to this (fayde ſhee) " I conjure you laſt, that it would pleaſe the Lordes, to permitt hir poor diſtreſſed Servants to be prefent about hir at hir Death, that their Eyes and Harts maye fee and witneſs how patiently their Queen and Miſtriſs would endure hir Execution, and fo make Relation when they came into their Country, that ſhee dyed a trewe conſtant Catholique to hir Religion," Then the Earle of *Kent*, did anfwer thus. " Madam, that which you have defired, cannot conveniently be granted, for if it ſhould, it weare to be feared, leaſt fomme of them, with Speeches or other Behaviour, would bothe be grevous to your Grace, and troublefome and vnpleafing to vs and our Companye, whereof we have had fomme Experience, they would not ſticke to putt fomme fuperſtitious Trumpery in practife, and if it were but in dipping their Handkerchieffs in your Grace's Blood, whereof it were very vnmeet for vs to give Allowance."

" My Lords, (fayde the Queen of *Scots*) I will give my Worde although it be but dead, that they **shall not** deserve any blame in any the Actions **you** have named, but **alas (poore** Soules) it would doe them **good to bidd their** Miſtris **farewell ; and I** hope your Miſtris (meaning the Queen) being **a Mayden** Queen, will vouchſafe, in **Regard of** Woman-hood, that **I ſhall** have ſomme of my own People about me att my deathe, and I know hir Majeſtie hath **not given you any** ſuch ſtreight Charge or Commiſſion, but that you might grant **me a** Requeſt of farr greater Courteſie than this is, if I were a Woman of farr meaner Calling than the Queen of *Scots*." And then perceiving that ſhee **could** not obtayne her Requeſt without ſome Difficultye, burſt out into Tears, ſaying,

 "I am Coſen to your Queen, and diſcended from the Blood Royal of *Henry* the VIIth. and a **marryed** Queen of *Fraunce*, and an annoynted **Queen of** *Scotland*." **Then** upon great Conſultation had betwixte the **two Earles, and the others** in Commiſſion, it was granted to hir, what **ſhee** inſtantly **before** earneſtly **intreated, and deſired** hir to make **Choice of ſix** of her **beſt beloved Men and** Women. Then of hir **Men** ſhee choſe *Melvin*, hir Apothecary, hir Surgion, and one old Man more, and **of** hir **Women,** thoſe two which did **lye in** hir Chamber. Then with **an** unappalled Countenance, without any Terror of the **Place, the** Perſons, or the Preparations, ſhee came **out of** the Entrye **into the** Hall, ſtept upp **to the** Scaffold, being two Foote high, and **twelve** Foote broade, **with** Rayles round about, hanged and covered with black, with a lowe Stoole, longe fayre Cuſhion, and **a Blocke** covered alſo with blacke. The Stoole brought her, ſhee ſat downe ; the **Earle of** *Kent* ſtood **on the** Right Hande, and the Earle of *Shrewsbery* on the other ; **other** Knights and Gentlemen ſtoode about the Rayles : The Commiſſion for hir Execution was redd (after ſilence made) by Mr. *Beale*, Clark of the Counſell, which done, the People with a loude Voice ſayde, God ſave the Queen. During the reading of this Commiſſion, the ſayde Queen **was** very ſilent, liſtning vnto it with ſo careleſs a Regard, **as** if it had not concerned hir at all nay, rather with ſo merry **and** cheerfull a Countenance, as if it had been a Pardon from hir Majeſtie for hir Life, and with all uſed ſuch a ſtrangneſs in **her** Wordes, as if ſhee had not knowne any of the Aſſembly, nor had been **any** Thing ſeene in the *Engliſh* Tongue.

 Then Mr. Doctor *Fletcher*, Deane of *Peterborough*, ſtanding directly before hir without the **Rayles,** bending his Bodye with great reverence, vttered this Exhortation followinge.

 "**Madame, the Queen's** Moſt Excellent Majeſtie (whom God

preferve longe to reigne over us,) havinge (notwithftanding this Preparation for the Execution of Juftice juftly to be done vpon you, for your many Trefpaffes against hir Sacred Perfon, State, and Government) a tender Care over your Sowle, which prefently departing out of your Bodie, muft either be feperated in the trew Fayth in Chrifte, or perifh for ever, doth for Jefus Chrifte offer vnto you the comfortable Promifes of God, wherein I befeech your Grace, even in the Bowells of Jefus Chrifte to confider thefe three Thinges.

"Firft, your State pafte, and tranfitory glorie: Secondly, your Condition prefent of deathe: Thirdly, your Eftate to comme, eyther in everlafting Happinefs, or perpetuall infelicitye. For the firft, lett me speake to your Grace, with *David* the King, forgett (Madam) yourfelfe, and your owne People, and your Father's House; forgett your natural Birthe, your royal and princely Dignitie, fo fhall the King of Kings have Pleasure in your spirituall bewtye, &c.

"Madam, even now, Madam, doth God Almightye open yow a Doare into a heavenly Kingdom; fhutt not therefore this Paffage by the hardening of your Hart, and grieve not the Spirit of God, which may feale your Hope to a Day of Redemption."

The Queen 3 or 4 tymes fayde unto him, "Mr. *Deane*, trouble not yourfelf nor me; for know that I am fettled in the auncient Catholique and *Romaine* Religion, and in Defence thereof, by God's Grace I minde to fpend my Bloud."

"Then," faid Mr. *Deane*, "Madam, change your Opinion, and repent you of your former Wickednes: Settle your Faythe only upon this Grounde, that in *Chrift Jefus* yow hope to be faved." She anfwered agayne and agayne, with great Earneftnefs, "Good Mr. *Deane*, trouble not yourfelf any more about this Matter; for I was borne in this Religion, have lived in this Religion, and am refolved to die in this Religion."

Then the Earles, when they faw how farr unconformable fhe was to hear Mr. *Deane's* good Exhortations, fayde, "Madam, we will praye for your Grace with Mr. *Deane*, that you may have your Minde lightned with the trew Knowledge of God and his Worde."

"My Lordes," anfwered the Queen, "if yow will praye with me, I will even from my Harte thanke you, and think myfelfe greatly favoured by you; but to joyne in prayer with you in your Manner, who are not of one Religion with me, it were a Sinne, and I will not."

Then the Lordes called Mr. *Deane* agayne, and badd him faye on, or what he thought good els: The Deane kneeled and prayed, as follows: *Oh moſt gracious God*, &c.

All the Aſſembly, ſave the Queen and her Servants, ſayde the Prayer after Mr. *Deane* as he ſpake it, during which Prayer, the Queen ſat upon her Stoole, having her *Agnus Dei*, Crucifix, Beades, and an Office in Lattyn. Thus furniſhed with ſuperſtitious **Trumpery**, not regarding what Mr. *Deane* ſayde, ſhe began very faſtly with Teares and a lowde **Voice** to pray in *Lattin*, and in the Midſt of hir **Prayers**, with over much **Weeping** and Mourning ſlipt off hir Stoole, and kneeling preſently ſayde divers other *Lattin* Prayers. Then ſhe, roſe and kneeled down **agayne**, praying in *Engliſh* for Chriſt's afflicted **Church**, an end of hir **Troubles**, for hir Sonne, and for the Queen's Majeſtye, to God for Forgivenes of the Sinnes of them in this Iſlande: She forgave hir Enemyes with all her Harte, that had longe ſought hir Bloud. This done ſhe deſired all Saints to make Interceſſion for hir to the Saviour of the World, *Jeſus Chriſt*. Then ſhe began to kiſs hir Crucifix, and to Croſs herſelf, ſaying theſe Wordes: "Even as thy Arms, oh *Jeſu Chriſt*, were ſpread here upon the Croſs, ſo receive me, ſo receive me into the Armes of Mercy."

Then the 2 Executioners kneeled downe unto hir, defiring hir to forgive them hir Death: Shee anſwered, "I forgive you with all my Harte; for I hope this Death ſhall give an end to all my Troubles."

They, with her 2 Weomen helping, began to diſroabe hir, and then ſhe layde the Crucifix upon the Stoole. One of the Executioners, took from her Neck the *Agnus Dei*, and ſhe layde hold of it, ſaying, ſhe would give it to one of hir Weomen, and withall told the Executioner that he ſhould have Monye for it. Then they took off her Chayne, ſhe made herſelf unready with a kind of Gladneſs, and ſmiling, putting on a payre of Sleeves with her owne Handes, which the twoo Executioners before had rudely put off, and with ſuch Speed, as if ſhee had longed to be gone out of the Worlde.

During the Diſroabing of this Queen ſhe never altred hir Countenance; but ſmiling, ſaid, ſhe never had ſuch Groomes before to make hir unreadye, nor ever did putt off hir clothes before ſuch Company, At lengthe unattyred and unapparelled to hir Petticoate and Kirtle, the 2 Women burſt out into a great and pittifull Shrieking, crying, and lamentation, croſſed themſelues, and prayed in Lattine. The Queen turned towardes them, embraced them, and ſayed theſe Words in *French*, *Ne cry vous j'ay praye pur vous*, and ſo croſſed, and kiſſed them, and bad them praye for her.

Execution of Mary, Queen of Scots.

Then with a smiling Countenance she turned to her Men Servants, *Meluin*, and the rest, crossed them, bad them farewell, and pray for hir to the last.

One of the Weomen having a *Corpus Christi* Cloathe, lapped it up three Corner wise, and kissed it, and put it over the Face of the Queen, and pynned it fast vpon the Caule of hir Head. Then the 2 Weomen departed. The Queen kneeled downe on the Cushion resolutely, and without any Token of Fear of Death, sayde allowde in Lattine, the Psalme, *In te domine confido:* Then groaping for the block, shee layde down hir Head, putting hir cheane over hir backe with bothe hir hands, which holding there still, had been cut off, had they not been espyed. Then she laid hirself upon the blocke most quietly, and stretching out hir Armes and Leggs, cryed out, *In Manus tuas, Domine, commendo Spiritum meum*, 3 or 4 times.

Att last while one of the Executioners held hir streightly with one of his Hands, the other gave two Stroakes with an Axe before he did cut off hir Head, and yet left a little grisle behinde.

She made very small Noyse, no Part stirred from the Place where shee laye. The Executioners lifted upp the Head, and bad *God save the Queen*. Then her dressing of Lawne fell from hir Head, which appeared as graye as if she had been threescore and ten Years olde, powled very shorte, her Face much altred, her Lippes stirred upp and downe almost a Quarter of an Hower after hir Head was cutt off. Then said Mr. *Deane, So perish all the Queenes Enemyes*. The Erle of *Kent* came to the dead Body, and with a lower Voice sayde, *Such end happen to all the Queenes and Gospells Ennemyes*.

One of the Executioners plucking off her Garters, espyed her little Dogg, which was crept vnder her Cloathes, which would not be gotten forth but with Force; and afterwards would not departe from the dead Corps, but came and layde between hir Head and Shoulders, a Thing much noted. The Dogg, embrewed in her Bloud, was carryed awaye and washed, as all things else were that had any Bloud, save those Things which were burned.

The Executioners were sent awaye with Money for their Fees, not having any one thing that belonged vnto her.

Afterwards every one was commanded forth of the Hall, saving the Sheriff and his Men, who carryed hir upp into a great Chamber, made ready for the Surgeons to embalme hir, and there she was embalmed.

And thus, I hope, (my very good Lord) I have certifyed your

Honour of all Actions, Matters, and Circumstances, as did proceed from hir, or any other att hir Death: Wherein I dare promise vnto your good Lordship (if not in some better or worse Wordes then were spoken I am somewhat miftaken) in matter, I have not any Whitt offended: Howbeit, I will not so juftifye my Duties herein, but that many things might well have been omitted, as not worthy notinge. Yet, becaufe it is your Lordship's Faulte to defire to know all, and so I have certyfied all, it is an Offence pardonable, so refting at your Honors further Commandment, I take my leave this 11th of *February*, 1586.

Your Honour's, in all humble Service to **Command**.

R. W.

"Inter Folia Fructus."

Twenty Lookes

OVER ALL THE

ROUND-HEADS

That ever lived in the World.

"History is but the Unrolled Scroll of Prophecy."
—James A. Garfield.

PRIVATELY PRINTED
FOR THE CLARENDON HISTORICAL SOCIETY.

1886.

This edition is limited to 120 *large paper and* 400 *small paper copies, for Subscribers only.*

TVVENTY
LOOKES
Over all the
ROVND-HEADS
that ever lived in the World.

1. Heathenish Round-heads.
2. Round-head Vowers.
3. Aged Round-heads.
4. Davids Round-heads.
5. Round-head Mourners.
6. Ifraelitish Round-heads.
7. Round-head Corinths.
8. Golgothan Round Heads.
9. Feminish Round-Heads.
10. Oxford Round-heads.
11. English Round-heads.
12. Effex Round-heads.
13. Women Round-head.
14. Court Round-heads.
15. Round-head Cat.
16. Round-head Friers.
17. Round-head Citizens.
18. Strange Round-heads.
19. Round-head Seperatists.
20. Round-heads of the time.

TIME.   REFORMATION.   1643.   SUPERSTITION.

TWENTY LOOKES

OVER ALL THE

ROUNDHEADS

IN THE WORLD.

1. *Heathenish Round-heads.*

THE firſt Round-heads that I have read of, were the Heathen in the land of Canaan, whoſe manner was, to cut their locks round, as ſome doe now, hanging equally to one proportion about their heads: but the Lord commanded the Iſraelites, that they ſhould not transforme nature, but cut their haire according to the faſhion that God had made it to grow; and therefore charged them not to round their heads, nor ſhave off their muchatoes, Lev. 19. 27. By theſe Round-heads is meant such as is when the lockes are cut round, as *Tindall* tranſlates it.

2. *Round-head Vowers.*

There was a cuſtome in the old Law, to dedicate a mans ſelfe to God by a vow for a certaine time; and whoſoever did cut and trim the haire of their head in pride, during the time of that vow, were termed Round-heads; and therefore the Lord forbad them ſo to doe. Num. 6. 5. The Lord forbad them to cut their lockes during the time of the vow.

3. *Aged Round-heads.*

Sometimes the crowne of the head is bare by reason of age, when the haires of the gray head fall off, and ſo leave a round baldneſſe on the top of the head, as *Elias* his head was, by reason of which a company of unruly boyes mocked him, and called him Round-head, or bald-pate.

But we may read in 2 Kings 2. at the latter end, immediately two and fourty of thofe boyes were torne in peeces by two beares which God fent amongft them out of the wood, which could not chufe but bee a heavie fpectacle to their parents and friends when they came and faw their children torne in peeces, and pulled into morfels bit by bit by the cruell beares.

4. *Davids Round-heads.*

The messengers of *David*, that were sent to *Hanun* King of Ammon, were fhaven and made Round-heads: for the Kings Counfel had perfwaded him to deride them in great fcorne of the children of Ifrael the people of God, when as they were fent from *David* with an intent to prepare a way for *David* to doe good to the children of Ammon; which by reafon of this their derifion of the people of God, it brought upon them a great overthrow, when *David* was hereby ftirred up to come againft them, as it is 1. Chron. 19. These had their haire fhaved off quite round.

5. *Round-head Mourners.*

There was a cuftome in the Judaicall Law to fhave the crowne of the head in time of mourning, as the Friers doe now; which ceremony is at this time fuperftitious. Thus did *Job* round his head when he faw himfelf in that fudden great affliction, Job. 1. 20.

6. *Israelitifh Round-heads.*

The Prophet *Efay* told the Ifraelites, that God would make them round-heads by fhaving all the haire off from their heads, &c. Ifai. 7. 20. They had highly offended God, and therefore this judgement was denounced againft them, meaning the taking away of their nobles and rulers by the fhaving of the head.

7. *Round-head Corinths.*

There is a decent wearing of fhort haire, fuch as Citizens and civill men weare, which was derided and fcorned of fome fhag-hair'd Ruffians amongft the Corinthians; which *Paul* reproves them for fo deriding the decent wearing of the haire, and exhorts thofe that fcorne them for it, to cut their haire fhort alfo, as it is 1 Cor. 11. at the beginning. I wonder how fuch fhag Ruffians dare now fcorne at the decent wearing of haire, when indeed themfelves are the *Abfolonians* that provoke the Lord to curse the land for their foolish pride, and wanton wearing of love-lockes and unseemly haire, (I had almost said periwig.)

8. *Golgotha Round-heads.*

In the Gospel we find a place called Golgotha, that is, dead mens sculls, the round sculls of dead men, Joh. 19. 17, whither our blessed Lord and Saviour was led to be crucified; and happy are those round-heads that receive the benefit of his bloud, and rise to glory by the vertue of his resurrection.

9. *Feminish Round-heads.*

In the reigne of *Henry* 1. the Englishmen shaved off their beards, and made their faces smooth like women, and let their haire grow round their heads in its full length, wherein they gloried, contending with women who should bee the most absolute feminine Round-head. *Lib. Dunelm.*

10. *The Oxford Round-heads.*

In the reigne of *Henry* 3, King of England, there were divers Oxford schollars who slew their chiefe cooke at Osney Abbey: for which fact 12. of them went bare-head from *Pauls* Church in London to the Abbey to doe penance, for which they were derided a long time after. *Mat. Par. Ypodigm.* These were called the Round-heads of Oxford. *L.D.*

11. *English Round-heads.*

In the reigne of *Edward* 3. the English men used to weare their haire cut short, round their heads: but after that King *Iohn* of France was taken and brought over into England, it grew a fashion (in a short time) for men to weare long haire over their shoulders, and those that went after the old English decent manner, were called Round-heads. *Stow.*

12. *Essex Round-heads.*

In the dayes of *Richard* 2. the heads of the Jurors in Essex were chopped off by the countrey that rose against them in that rebellion, *Chro. Ma. Lo.* but some of them were executed for their labours, as traytors.

13. *Women Round-heads.*

About this time also those women were derided as much as men are now by the name of Round-heads, except they wore, as the fashion then was, high attire on their heads, picked like hornes. *Stow.*

14. *Court Round-heads.*

In the dayes of *Henry* 8. it being a fashion to weare long haire, and for men to shave their beards quite off, King *Henry* therefore commanded all about this Court to weare their hair short. And to give them an example, he caused his owne head to be polled, and from thenceforth his beard to be notted, and no more shaven. *Chro.* 1. *Brist.*

15. *Round-head Cat.*

In the Reigne of Queene *Mary* (at which time popery was greatly exalted) then was Round-heads so odious by them, that in derision of them was a Cat taken on the sabbath day, with her head shorne, and the likenesse of a vestment cast over her, with her feet tied together, and a round piece of paper like a singing cake betwixt them; and thus was she hanged on the gallows in Cheapeside, neere to the Crosse, in the Parish of Saint *Mathew;* which Cat being taken downe, was carried to the Bishop of London, and he very reverendly sent it to Doctor *Pendleton* (who then was preaching at Pauls Crosse) for a present, commanding it by him to bee showne to the congregation. *Row. Lea.* The Round-head Fryers cannot abide to heare of this Cat.

16. *Round-head Fryers.*

About the same time, there was a company of Round-head Fryers, in London, who had plotted a notable peece of knavery, and had got one *Elizabeth Crofts*, a maid about 18. years of age, to counterfeit certaine speeches in a wall of an house, without Alderfgate, where they had made her a convenient place for performing that falacy, through the which the people of the City were wonderfully molested, for that all men might heare the voyce, but not see her person; some said it was an Angell, and a voice from heaven; some said it was the holy Ghost, &c. This was called the spirit in the wall; she lay there playing in a strange whistle, made for that purpose, which was by them given to her: *idem*, and they forged constructions of her voyce, which was at last found out, and she confest it openly at *Pauls* Crosse.

17. *Round-head Citizens.*

In these latter times, the shagge head Cavalliers, wearing all long haire, and the Citizens of London cutting their haire short round about their heads, there being so great a controversie between the

Cavalliers and the Citizens, to the end that they might make the Citizens ominous, they branded them, with a refolution among themfelves to ftrive that they might every where be called Round-heads, and therefore fpread an univerfall tearme and appellation on all that cut their haire fhort, to bee called Round-heads, which quickly was every where fpread up and downe the Country.

18. *Strange Round-heads.*

This terme of Round-heads became fo great a name on a fuddaine here in England, that the Kingdome (in moft part) and indeed every where moft people, wondred what thefe Roundheads fhould be; imagining that they were fome new fect that was fprung up.

19. *Round-head Seperatifts.*

People paufing, and imagining what thefe Round-heads were, in the end it was taken for granted, that Brownifts, Anabaptifts, &c. and fuch like, whofe braines fay they run round from one fchifmaticall opinion to another, and is never fixed, are the Round-heads.

20. *The Round-heads of the time.*

But now if a man have any religion in him, then (fay they) he is a Round-head, if he profeffe the truth heartily, then hee is branded for a Round-head; he that is no fwearer, curfer, cheater, drunkard, whooremafter, quarreller, he is fcandalized with the name of a Round-head; he that abhorreth Atheifme, hates idolatry, ufeth only yea, and nay, in his communication, keepes the Sabbath, loves the King, and Parliament, and is courteous, charitable, chaft and modeft; thefe are the men whom the blades of our time braid with the name of Round-heads, and indeed every honeft man is now call'd Round-head.

As Papifts call us Hereticks, fo Atheifts Round-heads make us,
Let them joy in their Periwigs, for Rome fhall never take us.

"Inter Folia Fructus."

THE
Memoirs
OF
GEORGE LEYBURN.

BEING

A JOURNAL OF HIS AGENCY FOR PRINCE
CHARLES IN IRELAND IN THE YEAR
1647.

"HISTORY IS BUT THE UNROLLED SCROLL OF PROPHECY."
—JAMES A. GARFIELD.

PRIVATELY PRINTED
FOR THE CLARENDON HISTORICAL SOCIETY.

1886.

*This edition is **limited** to 120 large paper, and 400 small paper copies, **for** Subscribers only.*

THE

MEMOIRS

OF

GEORGE LEYBURN.

Doctor of Divinity, Chaplain to *Henrietta Maria*
QUEEN of *ENGLAND.*

BEING

A Journal of his Agency for Prince *CHARLES* in *Ireland* in the
Year 1647.

Accompanied with Original Instructions and Letters to
the Author, from Prince *Charles*, Queen-Mother, the Duke of
Ormond, Lord *Digby*, Lord *Clanriccard*, the Pope's Nuncio, &c.

---

*Publish'd without the least Alteration from the Original in the Author's
own Hand.*

To which is prefix'd,

An Account of the Author's Life, with his Remarkable
Prediction concerning General *Monck*, and the Restoration of
King *CHARLES* the Second, mention'd by Dr. *Thomas Gumble*,
in the LIFE of that great General.

L O N D O N: Printed for W. L E W I S near the *Piazza* in *Covent Garden.*
MDCCXXII.

An Account of the Author's Life.

DR. *George Leyburn* was born in *Westmoreland* of a very ancient Family, known in those Parts a confiderable time before the Conqueft, and which afterwards was diftinguifh'd by feveral honourable Alliances, efpecially with the *Dacre's* and *Norfolk's*. The Eftate belonging to the Family was formerly very confiderable, but by Degrees much impair'd by Heireffes; and in Queen *Elizabeth's* Days it was ftill more reduced, by the unfortunate Circumftances of *James Leyburn*, Efq; who was executed at *Lancafter March* 22, 1583. *George Leyburn* was Born in the Year 1597, and fent very young to Study in the *English* College in *Doway*, where he was enter'd a Member of that Houfe *March* 13. 1617, under the Name of *George Bradley*. He made a confiderable Progrefs in all Sorts of Learning, and *June* 12. 1618, anfwer'd to his two Years Labour in Philofophical Studies, under the celebrated Profeffor *Thomas White*, otherwife *Blackloe*. Having run thro' two Years of Theological Learning, he undertook to teach a Leffon of Humanity, which Employment he began in *October* 1620, and having perform'd it fome Years with fingular Applaufe, he reaffum'd his Theological Studies and compleated 'em; during which Time he receiv'd the Order of Priefthood, *viz. August* 5. 1625. In 1627, having laid in a good Stock of Divine Learning, he was defirous to polifh it, and improve himfelf fomewhat farther in the famous Univerfity of *Paris*, for which Place he fet out from *Doway*, *November* 3, the Year above-mention'd. Here he remain'd two or three Years, and became a noted Tutor in *Arras* College. Afterwards being invited over into *England*, he took *Doway* in his

Way, and began his Journey from thence *August* 29, 1630. **He was soon** admitted to the Queen's * Presence, made one of her Chaplains and Favourites. Some Disturbances happening in the Queen's Family **on Account of** Religion, the *English* Chaplains were obliged to abscond. **It was** Mr. *Leyburn's* Misfortune to be apprehended and **confin'd.** He was design'd to be prosecuted, but by **the** Queen's **Means** it was exchanged into Banishment. And **now he** was again resolved to make a further **Progress in** Theological Studies, and setling at *Doway*, he spent **some Years in** teaching Philosophy and **Divinity.** It was during this Time **that he** took a Journey to the **University of** *Rheims*, where **he compleated** the Degree of Doctor of **Divinity, and was invited by the Arch-Bishop, at** the Head of a **Provincial Synod**, to answer to his **Act in their Presence,** which Piece of **Honour he refus'd** with remarkable **Modesty. Desiring** soon after to **return into** *England*, which was about **the breaking out of** the Civil **Wars, he found every** Thing in great Confusion ; and had not been **there long before he was** taken up and **committed to** the Tower. It **was about** 1644, when he became acquainted with Colonel *Monck*, **then a Prisoner in the same Place for** adhering to the Royal Cause. **I must not omit some remarkable** Passages which happen'd **between** these two, and which are related by Dr. *Thomas Gumble* † **in his Life of** General *Monck*, *Page* 119. Take 'em in the Author's own **words.** "*I must here crave leave to tell you a Story, and because none may believe it forg'd, for this Relator hath heard it above fifteen Years ago, and is able to bring good Testimony thereof; while General* Monck *was in the* Tower, *one Dr.* Leyburn, *a Professor in Divinity, and a Romish Priest, came often to see the General in the* Tower, *and it was upon some little Acquaintance which he had with him in the Company of* Sir **Thomas** Cademan, *the late Queen's Physician; some Friends of his ask'd this* Leyburn *(if I do not mistake his Name) why he gave himself the Trouble to visit this* Monck *so often. He replies, that within some Years that Person shou'd* **be the greatest** *Person of the three Nations, (and so he was for some Time before the* **King's** *Return) ; and long afterwards the same Person being at Supper with the General and other* **Friends, *a little before*** *his Expedition into* Scotland *with* Cromwel, *he publickly asserted at the Table, that he shou'd within* **six** *Months, or there-*

---

* Henrietta Maria.
† Thomas Gumble, D.D., Chaplain to General Monck. "The Life of Gen. Monck, Duke of Albemarle, London, 1671, 8vo." In French, 1672, 12mo.—The London Retrospective Review (xiii., 265-277 ; and xiv., 153-179) says : " Curious as a specimen of the Tory or Royalist mode of writing History which prevailed during the period immediately following the Restoration."

278

abouts, be a General in the North, and within some Years shou'd command the three Nations. This indeed prov'd true, but by what Means this Leyburn pretended this Fore-knowledge I cannot imagine; I do not remember that he ever cast his Nativity; but some think that he took this up, from secret Lines and Marks in his Face; which wou'd render the Story very incredible, tho' the General had a Soldier-like and Majestick Countenance: But this is certain, that Leyburn came out of the Spanish Netherlands after his Majesty's Restoration, and visited the General; and also, that he did Prophecy of this long before: Now that such a vain Prediction should have any Influence upon the General's Faith, is to me very doubtful. I know he never listen'd to such vain Prognosticks. He told me this Story himself in Scotland." Thus far Dr. *Gumble*, who doubts not of the Fact, but is puzzl'd about the Manner. I have been assur'd by some, who were personally acquainted with Dr. *Leyburn*, that he was a Person of such extraordinary Piety and Regularity in his Conduct, that few were better intitl'd to the Secrets of Divine Providence, and it seems as much for the Credit of the Royal Cause to make Heaven busie on this Occasion, as to draw unaccountable Inferences from the Lines of the Face. But to proceed, when Dr. *Leyburn* had obtain'd his Liberty, he went over into *France*, where he was very serviceable to the Suffering Party. In the Year 1647, Prince *Charles* and Queen Mother engaged him to go over into *Ireland*, and report the real Grounds of the Misunderstandings between the two Confederate Roman Catholick Armies. This Journey being over, he drew up the Particulars of his Agency, to give the Prince and Queen a true Idea of their Affairs in *Ireland*. In 1648, *Richard Smith*, Bishop of *Calcedon*, residing then in *Paris*, appointed Dr. *Leyburn* to be his Vicar General in *England*, jointly with *Mark Harrington* alias *Drury*, Batchelor of *Sorbon*. Afterwards, upon the Decease of Dr. *William Hyde*, President of *Doway* College, our Author was install'd in that Place *June* 24, 1652, which he enjoy'd above eighteen Years, and resign'd to his Nephew *John Leyburn*, about the Middle of 1670, being at that time call'd up to *Rome*. He remain'd at *Rome* about a Year and a half, then returning into *England*, after having setled some Domestick Affairs, he took his leave of it, and spent the Remainder of his Days at *Chaalons* in *Champaign*, where he gave up his last Breath *December* the 29th, 1677, leaving behind him a Character becoming the Primitive Ages; and the Inhabitants of *Chaalons* to this Day pay a Respect to his Memory, little inferior to that of a canonized Saint. He was Doctor of Divinity of the University of *Rheims*, President of *Doway* College, Chaplain to the

Queen of *England*, Vicar General to the Bishop of *Calcedon*, and Agent to Prince *Charles* in *Ireland*. He was learned, pious, and warm with Zeal, both in Publick and Domestick Concerns. He had been twice a Prisoner, and as often Banish'd. His Life was attended with several Controversies, and Contradictions, which he always made a Hand of to his Improvement in Virtue, and the worst Part of his Character was that of being obstinately Good. Tho' he did not affect appearing in Print, yet he has left some Instances of his Abilities in that Way, *viz.*

1. An Encyclical Epistle to his Brethren.
2. Holy Characters.
3. As to the present Performance it has been reserv'd in Manuscript ever since 1648; now what Credit may be given to him in Regard of the Subject he treats of, may be learnt from these Words of the Lord *Clanriccard* in *Ireland*, to Sir *John Winter* the Queen's Secretary at *Paris*. "*From this worthy Bearer you may be pleas'd to receive a very clear and perfect Account, both of Persons and Actions here; and his known Piety, and setl'd Zeal to the Service of their Majesties, does most justly deserve a special favourable Regard and firm Belief.*" This Letter of Credence was written by Lord *Clanriccard*, General of the Confederate Catholicks in *Ireland* for the King, and brought over by Dr. *Leyburn*, the Original whereof is in my Custody. And what Character is here given of our Author, I believe the History it self will make good, to which I remit the Reader.*

---

* Of the 3 works here named, only the last is mentioned by Alibone.

A Preface.

IN this following Difcourfe, being accidentally and haftily written for my own Inftruction, and the Satisfaction of thofe, who in that Imployment had Authority to take an Account and judge of my Actions; I have willingly omitted all Circumftances whatfoever, that did not precifely tend to thofe Ends; fetting down nothing but Matters of Fact. But now that I meet with fome Friends, who having heard of this Manufcript, defire to fee it, willing, as it feems, to be guided out of thofe Mazes, into which the Difcourfes and Reports of feveral Factions have engaged them, concerning the Paffages and Tranfactions of Things in the Kingdom of *Ireland*, I have thought fit, as well as my Memory will permit me, by way of Preface, to fet down fo much of the State of that Country, at my Arrival thither, as may ferve for the better Underftanding of this following Relation; which, when all is done, whether or no it will give them the Satisfaction they defire, I know not; and if in the Computations of fome Things, as Places, Numbers of Men, or the like, I fhall be 'miftaken, they muft pardon me; for I undertake no exact Defcription, but only to fay fo much, as may give a Reader the better means to judge of the whole Matter, and neither indeed at my being there, did I clog my Memory with the Obfervation of fuch Things, being more intent on the Bufinefs I had then in Hand, then on the Confideration of Matters not fo neceffary.

Ireland, which I judge to be, at leaft, as great as *England*, take off *Wales* and *Cornwall*, is divided into four Provinces, *Leinfter*,* *Munfter*,

---

* This, throughout the original, is spelt *Leimster*.

H

Connaught, and *Ulster*: In the whole, there were three Parties openly declared against each other, in this manner commanded. The first, by my Lord Marquiss of *Ormond*, Governor of the Kingdom for **the King, under the Title** of Lord Lieutenant. The second, by **that which they called the Supreme Counsel of** the Confederate Catholicks. **The third, by those three** (as I conceive, independant of each other) **the Lord of** *Insequeen*, Sir *Charles Coute*, and Colonel *Monroe*, all under the *English* Parliament, **though the** last had a more immediate Relation to his Country-men the *Scotts*. The Lord Lieutenant was possess'd in *Leinster* of *Dublin*, the principal City of the Kingdom (and equal to any other I have seen in *England*, except *London*) with the adjacent Territory, some ways twenty, some ways thirty Miles about it; in which he had all the Sea Ports on that Coast, with divers Garrisons, as *Tredaugh*, *Trim*, *Carlow*, and others, out of which he could draw some 2000 Foot, whereof, **as I** believe, the most part **were** Catholicks, **and some** 400 Horse, most Protestants, and the Commanders, for the greater part, if not all Protestants, *English* or *Scotts*. Besides those, he had then received from the Parliament of *England*, as I take it, three **Regiments of Foot,** whereof **there** were two quartered in *Dublin*, the third in *Trim* and *Tredaugh*; as also some Quantity of Ammunition.

The Supreme **Council of the** Confederate Catholicks were possess'd of **all the rest of** *Leinster*, in Quantity of Ground, **as I guess, three parts of four,** wherein *Wexford*, *Rose*, and *Kilkenny*, were the **most considerable** places; **with** all the Ports, but **those in** my Lord of *Ormond's* Quarters. I think likewise, they had much about the same Proportion in *Munster*, with **those chief Towns** *Waterford*, *Limerick*, and *Clonmell*; with many **other Towns and Castles**; all the Ports up to *Youghall*: They were likewise possess'd of *almost* all *Connaught*, with *Galloway* the principal Town **and** Haven, and all the others except *Sligo*. In *Ulster*, the greatest Province in *Ireland*, they had few **Places, except** *Charlamont*, and some Castles **on** the Borders of *Connaught*, though from thence came most **of their** best **Foot** under *Oneale* their General for that Province. They had, not long after my coming thither, on foot those **Forces,** under Preston their General for **Leinster,** betwixt **six** or **seven** thousand Foot, and one thousand Horse, as **I** verily believe **by the Poll.** In *Munster*, under my Lord of *Worcester*, **who** commanded with the King's Commission, though **with** their Consent, against my Lord *Insequeen*, five or six thousand **Foot,** and near one thousand Horse: In *Ulster*, and upon the Borders of *Leinſter* and *Connaught* under *Oneale*, nine or ten thouſand Foot and Horſe.

My Lord of *Inſequeen*, by the Parliament made Preſident of *Munſter*, was in that Province poſſeſs'd of *Youghall*, *Kinſale*, and *Corke*, with ſome other places adjoining; and about as much Territory (as I can gueſs, having never been there) as my Lord of *Ormond* had in *Leinſter:* He was able, out of his Garriſons, to draw into the Field ſome 5000 Foot, almoſt all *Engliſh;* and ſome eight hundred or a thouſand Horſe, *Engliſh*.

Sir *Charles Coote*, by the Parliament made Preſident of *Connaught*, was poſſeſs'd in that Province of *Sligo* a Port Town, and *Coleraine*, otherwiſe called *Londonderry*, with ſome places on the Borders of *Ulſter*. He could make two or three thouſand Foot *Engliſh* and *Iriſh*, and ſome two hundred ill Horſe.

Colonel *Monroe* commanded in *Ulſter* for the Parliament, and was in that Province poſſeſs'd of *Knockfergus*, *Carickfergus*, and divers others Places: He could draw into the Field three or four thouſand Foot, all *Scotts* or *Scottiſh Iriſh*, of which there are many Inhabitants of that Country, and ſome two or three hundred Horſe. Thoſe were the ſeveral Parties, or Factions, with their Leaders: Theſe the Places, Territories, and Quarters of which they ſtood ſeverally poſſeſs'd; and theſe the Forces, they could upon Occaſion draw into the Field, at my Arrival in *Ireland*.

And now for the Reader's better underſtanding, it remains that I briefly, and hiſtorically ſay ſomething of every one of them. And firſt, of the Marquiſs of *Ormond*. He, one of the nobleſt of the old *Engliſh* Families, and by King *James* his Command, taken from his Father, brought into *England* young, under *Abbots*, Biſhop of Canterbury bred a Proteſtant, after returned into *Ireland*, and there ſettled, was by the late King *Charles*, about the Year 1645, made Lord Lieutenant of *Ireland;* that Kingdom, during the Interval from my Lord of *Strafford's* Death, having been governed by Commiſſioners, and Thoſe managing things there totally according to the Parliament Intereſt, gave the King cauſe to remove them, placing my Lord of *Ormond* in that Government, who receiving the Command of the *Engliſh* Army, made War for ſome time ſharply and ſucceſsfully on his Countrymen, the *Iriſh* Confederate Catholicks, until the Civil War broke out in *England*, between the King and his Parliament. The King finding on the one ſide that the Money he had confented ſhould be raiſed for the War of *Ireland*, was imployed againſt himſelf;

and on the other, needing the **Affiftance of that** Army, caufed my Lord Lieutenant to make a Ceffation with the *Irifh*, and fo drew all, or the greateft Part, of thofe Forces over to him. After which, the **Ceffations were** continued from time to time, until (after the Battle of *Nasby*, where **the Blow was** fo fatal, **as the** King could no longer make Head againft the Parliament) a Peace **was** concluded between **my Lord** Lieutenant **of** the **one** Part for the King, and four or five Commiffioners on the other Part for the *Irifh*; Which Peace was no fooner made than broken; the Nuncio, then refiding there for the Pope, with the Clergy, protefting againft it, and excommunicating all the Adhearers to it, with whom in time joined all the confiderable Towns **and** Caftles **in** *Ireland*, that were not actually in the Poffeffion of the Lord Lieutenant, **or** the Parliament; and generally fpeaking, all the **People Catholick, who were** not otherwife overawed by living within **the Quarters of one, or the** other; only fome **of the** Nobility and Gentry, **as alfo of** the Clergy excepted, induced thereunto, either by their Allegiance **to** the King, my Lord of *Ormond's* Intereft in the Nation, or laftly, **Averfion to,** and Fear of *Oneale* **and the old** *Irifh;* fo as **my** Lord Lieutenant's Heralds, fent to Proclaim the Peace, were at *Limerick*, the principal Town of *Munfter*, **beaten and wounded; and** himfelf, attended with **fome** two **thoufand Foot, and four hundred Horfe,** thinking by his Authority, fo accompanied, **to make good the** Peace, was, by the Appearance of *MacThomas*, **at a diftance, in** the head of the *Leinfter* Horfe (from **whom he received no** fatisfactory Anfwer) and the notice of *Oneale's* march **towards him with his Army,** forced in great **Trouble** and Diforder to make **his Retreat to** *Dublin;* where, expecting **a** Siege, he prefently endeavoured **to** ftrengthen himfelf, **within by** Fortifications, without by deftroying the Country towards the Confederate Quarters, which the *Irifh*, by their flow Proceedings, gave him Opportunity enough to do; who fome three or four Months after, in the middle of Winter, **approached** *Dublin* with two Armies under **the** Commands of *Oneale* **and** *Prefton*, **independant of each other; when** the Marquifs of *Clanrichard*, a Catholick, and the greateft Perfon **of** *Ireland*, after the Lord Lieutenant, with whom he **was then in** *Dublin*, offered to treat, which **accepted** by *Prefton* **and his Officers, an** Agreement was made and Sworn **to, but not perfected by** prefent Execution of the Things agreed, **fo that it** came to nothing; for which my **Lord** Lieutenant accufed *Prefton* of too little Care of his Word, and too much Fear of the Nuncio and Clergy; and he again, my Lord, of Subtilty, in fetting Division amongst them, and Delay in performing Things to be done on his Part; whereby, through the Unseasonableness of the Weather, and Want of all things, he was forced to retreat, his Army dissolving of it self. And now the King having put himself into the *Scotts* Hands, with whom he treated, my Lord of *Ormond* did so too; for surrendring up his Authority, and those Places under his Command into the Power of the *English* Parliament of the same Faction; during the time of which Negotiation, he was content, for his better Defence against the *Irish*, to receive some Number of Parliament Foot into his Garisons, with certain Quantities of Ammunition, for which, and for Performance of Articles agreed on, or to be agreed on, he delivered his Son, my Lord of *Ossory*, as a Hostage. Thus much concerning my Lord of *Ormond*.

And now to say something of the Supreme Counsel, or the Confederate Catholicks, I must draw a little higher towards the Spring that so the Reader may the better judge of the whole. The predominant Faction in the *English* Parliament, knowing no so likely Impediment to the Designs they had in hand, as that which might proceed from the Catholick Party, which though not very great in *England*, in respect of their Numbers, yet was numerous in *Ireland*, the Hundredth *Irish* Man not being a Protestant, and abominating all of that Religion, had no so good Way to affright the King from making use of that Assistance, as by all Means they could possible, to thrust the *Irish* into Rebellion, and then to accuse the King, the Queen being a Catholick, as the Author of it; from whence divers Things would follow. First, that they should, with the help of their *Scottish* Friends, have a good Occasion to destroy and extirpate that People, possessing themselves and their Party of their Lands; as also, the Catholick Religion in the three Nations. Secondly, the King having this Principle infused into him, that Nothing was so necessary to his Safety, as the clearing himself and the Queen from that Imputation, would be so far from seeking Assistance that Way, as he should not dare to refuse joining with them, in such Acts of Parliament as they should propose to him, for the better perfecting those Designs; provided, the Pretence were the repressing or punishing of that Rebellion, by which it would come to pass, that they would levy what Forces, or raise what Monies they pleased, which afterwards they might convert to what Use they thought fit; and all this, as Things were disposed, was no hard Matter to compass: For, the *Irish* had not enjoyed such a pleasant Bondage under the *English*, but that they had contracted Ill-will enough against their Masters, besides which, other Things contributed. First, The Example of the *Scotts* then marched into *England* against the King with an Army; the manifest Combination with them of the *English* Puritans, then highly Predominant, by Reason of other Circumstances, in the two Houses of Parliament; which, if prevailing, the Destruction of the *Irish* and Catholick Religion must follow. And as those Things, with other Circumstances, might give the most Reasonable amongst them Cause enough to be troubled; so wanted They no Provocation from Those, who sate then at the Helm of the Government, and were totally of the Parliament Faction. But as there is no Cruelty like that of Slaves, when they get the upper Hand; of which we have divers Examples, both *Roman*, *Grecian* and *Carthaginian*, so those People had no sooner shaken off their Fetters, but they did run hastily and furiously to all kind of bloody Executions; and as their Rebellion was without Order, so were their Actions without Measure; none that was called *English*, and was within Reach, escaping their Fury; nor in this first Heat was the Name of Catholick a Protection, but all went together; so that in *Ulster*, *Connaught*, some Part of *Munster*, and generally all Places without the *English* Pale, they either killed the *English*, or forced them to forsake their Habitations: After getting into Bodies, they assailed the Castles and Houses of such of their Catholick Country-men (which were in great Numbers) as would fain have been Quiet, and continued their Obedience to the *English* Government: Those petitioned the Council at *Dublin*, either to be protected, or to have Arms given them, whereby they might protect themselves; but being neglected, both in the one, and in the other, and fearing that the Faults of a Part, would be imputed to the Whole, and consequently the Innocent suffer with the Guilty; made thus desperate, they did for the most part join with the rest, as well those of *English* as *Irish* Extraction, amongst whom were many of very good Quality; and getting into some Form, raised Something like an Army, but were from time to time beaten by the *English*, though in far less Numbers, partly for Want of Arms and Ammunition, of which they were exceedingly destitute; partly, that they trusted more to their Heels than their Hands, which last may proceed of several Causes: As that no Servile Nation were ever good Soldiers, until Custom and Success had given them Spirit; that they are (it may be) the best Footmen in the World; that they have so many Boggs and Fastnesses well known unto them, by which they hope to escape; but whatsoever the Reason was, they had almost ever the Worst of the *English*, even when they were better Officer'd, and wanted neither Ammunition nor Arms, until the King (as hath been formerly mentioned) called away that Army, which had, with his Consent, been employed against them by the Parliament; and which had more than sufficiently revenged all the Evils committed even by the most Guilty, leaving nothing of Cruelty, either on their Bodies, or Estates, unexecuted; this being the Difference, that the one was done by a rude headless Multitude; the other, by Soldiers under Order and Command. From the Beginning they had endeavoured to put themselves into a kind of Government, by assembling the Nation together, according to the Form before used in their Parliaments, brought in by the *English*, consisting of the Nobility, Clergy, and Commons; chusing Knights and Burgesses out of such Places as were of their Party, or not in the actual Possession of their Enemies: This Assembly made divers Acts or Ordinances, causing a Declaration to be printed, expressing the Motives of their taking Arms, wherein they mention the principal to be the Defence of the Catholick Religion, the King's just Prerogatives, his Person, and the Queen's, with their Liberties, &c. against the Puritans and Sectarists, &c. as may appear in their Declaration, set out in *May* 1642. To which was added, an Oath for all People to take to the same Purpose. They also formed that Body, which they called the Supreme Council of the Confederates, consisting of some of every State, Nobility, Clergy, and Commons, about four and twenty in Number, which during the Intervals of the Assemblies, had a kind of limited Government and Power, to call the Assembly on Occasion: In the mean time, as hath been said, their Armies had commonly the Worst; yet, my Lord of *Castlehaven*, their General for *Munster*, did them some good Services; as also, *Preston* their General for *Leinster*, though the latter was overthrown by my Lord of *Ormond* in a great Battel near *Rosse*; which Misfortune, it may be, made them first think of employing *Oneale*, who before had been seen walking up and down *Kilkenny* alone and unconsidered; for even then the Supreme Council, whereof the major Part were old *English* Men of States and Fortunes, gotten by their Ancestors from the *Irish*, had no Mind that *Oneale*, or any of the ancient Possessors, should get into Command; but now, Necessity inforcing to make use of all Hands, and almost ashamed to deny him, who, beside the Antiquity of his Extraction, had the Fame of a very good Soldier, as having long served under the *Spaniard*, in Places of considerable Command; they made him their General of *Ulster*, then wholly possefs'd by the *Scotts* and **English**, except *Charlemont*, which Sir *Philome Oneale*, in the Beginning of their Rebellion, had furprized and fortified. Notwithftanding which, he foon got an Army out of that Province, and fome other Places; very many of the old *Irish*, ranging themfelves under him, and became fo confiderable, as **not** long after **he** durft **encounter** **Monroe,** General for the Parliament of that Province, and **in a great** Battel overthrew him, with very great Slaughter of his Men, and the taking all his Baggage. Not long before this, while thefe Things were in Agitation; of the one Side a **Nuncio** was come from the Pope, who to that Purpose had been petitioned, by the whole Catholick Party of the Nation; and on the other Side, the then Earl of Glamorgan, now Marquifs of Worcefter, with Commiffion **and** Inftructions **from the** King, to advance and conclude a Peace with the *Irish*, with whom my Lord of *Ormond* had **from** time to time continued Ceffations: Accordingly my Lord of *Worcefter* proceeded fo **far,** as he, for the King, and certain Commiffioners appointed for that Purpofe **by the** *Irish*, concluded a Peace; **whereby on** the one Part, there **was** convenient Provifion made for **Catholick** Religion, and Indemnity of the Nation: And on the other, **an Army of** *Irish* was to be levied, and fent **for the King's** Affiftance **into** *England*; **the** Conditions **of which** Peace were to be concealed; **the King, it feems, fearing that** their untimely Revealing, might **Prejudice him with his Proteftant** Subjects; fo that very few Copies **of the Original** being difperfed, yet it fo happened, that one of them **was found (as it was faid) in the** Archbifhop of *Thune* his Pocket, flain **by the** *Scottish* **Forces, and fent** to the Parliament of *England*; which **coming** to my Lord **Lieutenant's** Knowledge, **the** Earl of *Worcefter*, **ignorant** of the **Matter,** was, by Letters, **invited to** *Dublin*; where, **accufed** by my Lord *Digby*, the King's principal Secretary, and then prefent, of having concluded that Peace without fufficient Authority, he was made Prifoner in the **Caftle of** *Dublin*, and not long after releas'd upon a Bail of 40000*l.* to appear and anfwer the Accufation, whenfoever he fhould be called; the King in the mean Time, by his Declaration, difclaiming my Lord of *Worcefter's* **Act.** After which **the** Ceffations **being** continued from time to time, and certain **Conditions** for a Peace offered by my Lord of *Ormond*, an Affembly was **called,** where the greater Part of the Laity was for accepting thofe Conditions, though thereby Catholick Religion was not fo provided for, as in the Peace made with my Lord of *Worcefter*; and though oppofed by the

Nuncio, and moſt of the Clergy, yet was it carried in the Affirmative, that the Temporal Part of the Peace being Satisfactory, there ſhould be no Mention of the Spiritual, but they would truſt the King's Goodneſs; rather making Choice of that, than to have the Abolition only of the Penal Laws expreſſed, which by the Lord Lieutenant was, in the King's Name offered; and ſo ſome Plenipotentiary Commiſſioners were authorized to conclude, which the Nuncio finding himſelf not able to hinder, all he could obtain was, a Delay of the Signing and Sealing until *May*; pretending that there was an Agreement made by the Pope, with the Queen of *England's* conſent at *Rome*, which he hoped would be ſent to him before that time, wherein the Splendor and Safety of Catholick Religion was more amply provided for, than it had been with the Concluſion made with the Earl of *Worceſter*. But the Time prefix'd being come, and no News of the other Agreement from *Rome*, the Commiſſioners did Sign and Seal the Peace; and all that followed thereon I mentioned before, this only excepted, that not long after, the Commiſſioners, who had ſigned the Peace, were accuſed of not having done their Duty, nor diſcharged their Truſt, and therefore impriſoned; and an Aſſembly being called, the Acts done by the Eccleſiaſtical Authority were confirmed, and the Peace voted invalid; though at the ſame Time the impriſoned Commiſſioners were ſet at Liberty, and declared Innocent.

But now methinks the Reader ſhould wonder at all thoſe ſtrange Turns; nor will I undertake to ſatisfy him, in giving my Judgment of the Reaſons, having reſolved in the ſhorteſt Method I could, to ſet down only Matters of Fact; from which yet, my hope is, I ſhall not be thought to vary, if I here relate, what I have heard the Nuncio, and thoſe of his Party ſay, in their Juſtification: For, what hath been ſaid on the other Side is in Print, lately written, as it is reported, by one Doctor *Calligan*, eloquently, and in very good Latin.

Firſt, the Nuncio ſays, that the Pope, though he was from time to time informed of the mercileſs Proceedings of the *Engliſh* Parliament againſt the whole *Iriſh* Nation, for the tumultuous Rebellion of a Part; thereby demonſtrating, it was not ſo much their Fault, as their Religion, which they meant to puniſh; yet he had no Intention otherwiſe to meddle in the Buſineſs, than by his Prayers for them, until his Aid and Aſſiſtance was importuned by the Vote of the whole Nation Catholick, which, as the Common Father of the Church, he could not deny.

That himself being chosen to this Imployment, all the Inftructions he had from the Pope, tended to those two Ends: First, the Prefervation and Increafe of Catholick Religion; then, the fettling the *Irish* Nation in their due Obedience to the King. Concerning which two Inftructions, there was no Prudent Man, let him be of what Religion he will, but muft believe the Pope did intend, the firft fhould be firft done.

That at his coming into *Ireland*, he found the *Irish* generally inclining to a Peace with the Royal Party; of which fome confidered the Intereft of Religion more, and fome lefs.

That for his Part, none defired that Peace more than he, being a main Part of his Inftructions, provided that Religion were firft provided for. That it was true, he had to the uttermoft of his Power, together with the Clergy, oppofed the Conclufion of that Peace, agitated in the Affembly of the *Irish*, *January* 1646, becaufe by it there was no Provifion at all for Religion, nor the Church; as alfo, that when he could not hinder the Vote made for it, he procured a Delay of the Signing and Sealing, until *May* following, and of the Publication until *July*, in Hopes that before that time, he fhould hear of fome Agreement made between the Queen of *England*, and his Holinefs at *Rome*, where it was then in Agitation, as he could make appear.

That my Lord Lieutenant being not to be perfwaded from publifhing the Peace, and attempting to fecond the Publication with Force, he had proceeded to Excommunication of all the Adherers to it, and oppofed Force with Force.

That he was fo far from denying or extenuating any Thing he had done, as he fhould neither have performed the Truft repofed in him, nor his Duty to the Pope and Catholick Religion, if he had done otherwife; to which, befides many other Reafons, thofe which principally induced him were,

That it was apparent to all fuch as had fought to inform their Underftandings, concerning the modern Differences amongft Chriftians, that of all the Sects in Rebellion againft the Government of the *Roman* Church, none hath been tranfported with fo much Rancour and Malice to Catholicks and Catholick Religion, as thofe, to whofe Herefies, *Calvin* gave a Beginning.

That the whole *Scottish* Nation, to fpeak generally, and the governing Part in the *English* Parliament, who at this Day both drive one and the fame Intereft, confift totally and abfolutely of thofe Sectarifts.

That the King hath always feconded his Hopes of being reftored to his Rights, rather on an Agreement and Accord to be made with them, than either, Conquering or Beating them into their Duties ; as may appear by all his Proclamations, Declarations, and Meffages fo often fent for Treaties, and in the Treaties themfelves.

That in all the Declarations and Meffages fent from the Parliament, and in all thofe Treaties had been with the King, this Demand was principally infifted on, *viz.* the Diftinction of Catholicks, and Catholick Religion, in *England* and *Ireland*, and in the laft, under the Name of Rebels, in which, generally fpeaking, they would have included all the Catholick Natives, the Extirpation of the Nation : That as the Recovery of his Crown and Dignity, with the Prefervation of his Church, was the King's principal Intereft, fo was he not to hope his attaining in any Degree to both, or either, by any Accord to be made with thofe Sectaries, but by confenting to divers their Demands, though never fo much contrary to his Inclination and Juftice; of which, one and the principal, on which they did and would ftill infift, was the laft above-mentioned concerning Catholicks.

That thefe Premiffes had been fo well known to the King and his Minifters, as it had been the true Reafon, why he would never treat of any Peace with his *Irish* Subjects, until the defperate Condition of his Affairs compelled him : Neither then would he treat or conclude with them in avowed or exprefs Terms, concerning the Particular of Religion ; becaufe he would not do, what he fhould again be forced to undo : And therefore did he fend the Earl of *Worcefter*, a great Nobleman of *England*, and a Catholick, into *Ireland*, with private Commiffions and Inftructions, authorizing him to make a Clandeftine Peace with the *Irish*, therein including their Satisfaction concerning Religion ; which if difcovered, he might, at his Pleafure, difavow, as after it came to pafs, when by the Accident of finding the Copy of that Peace in the Bifhop of *Thume's* Pocket, (if at leaft that Story be true) it came to his Parliament's Knowledge.

That this Means having failed, and his Affairs in *England* ftill preffing more and more, he made ufe of my Lord of *Ormond's* Power and Faction in the Kingdom, to force thofe that would not affent to fuch a Peace as he would have : Which Game my Lord of *Ormond* play'd fo dexteroufly, efpecially, in making ufe of the Divifions, betwixt the Old and New *Irish*, thereby fetting Catholick againft Catholick, many preferring that Intereft, before the Splendor and Dignity of their Religion, as that fhameful Peace (to ufe his own

291

Words) was at laſt concluded, himſelf and the Clergy in vain oppoſing; beſides a great Number of the Laity: Wherein, what ſhuffling, Breach of Promiſe, and Betraying of Truſt had been uſed, would be too long to ſpeak of. That the Motive, which had induced ſo many of the *Iriſh* Nobility and Gentry to vote that Peace, and which the Principal of that Faction uſed to perſwade the others, was, that the King would make good thoſe Conditions granted by the Earl of *Worceſter*, with his Commiſſions and Authority, however he had been forced, for the Satisfaction of his other Proteſtant Subjects, openly to diſavow them; and which was ſecretly implied by thoſe Words in the Peace, of referring Conditions for Religion unto the King's good Will and Pleaſure.

That before the Sealing, and long before the Publication of the Peace, the King had voluntarily caſt himſelf into the Power and Mercy of the *Scottiſh* Army, where he was detained as a Priſoner, and thereby rendered uncapable of the Power, if he had the Will, ever to satisfy that Expectation. To conclude, the Catholick *Iriſh*, that were a hundred for one Proteſtant, had always been ſo deſirous of uniting themſelves under the Royal Authority, as if his Majeſty would in any Time, being at Liberty, and *Sui Juris*, have given his Royal Aſſent to their juſt Petitions and Demands for Religion, and their Churches, with what belonged unto them, they had ſo much Confidence in his Juſtice and Goodneſs, as they would have inſiſted on no other Security for the Thing granted, than his Royal Word and Promiſe: But now, that he had put himſelf into the Power of his, and their mortal Enemies, where he was Priſoner, and conſequently unable to Protect them, and out of whoſe Hands he ſhould never get, but by a Compoſition made to their Deſtruction; there was left no imaginable Way to ſecure any Accord ſhould be made, but by giving them a Catholick Governor; ſuch a one, as he himſelf ſhould have juſt Reaſon to truſt; of which he had many Noble *Engliſh* Men, and of them they would refuſe none. For, as for my Lord of *Ormond*, they neither would, nor ever could think themſelves ſecure under him; who if he were ſo valuable, as to be eſteemed more than the Union of all that Nation under his Obedience; if through that, there came Inconvenience to his Affairs; it was not their Fault, the Law of God in Conſervation of their Religion, not a Religion founded but Yeſterday, in the Opinion of particular Men, but a Religion they had received from their Anceſtors Time out of Mind; and the Law of Nature in preſerving their Throats from Cutting, being above all other Laws whatsoever. To all this my felf did then make such **Objections, as** I could remember: As, that it was **no** Wonder, if the King were backward in relying or trufting on them, who had not only rebelled, but in their Rebellion had proceeded with such Cruelty against his *Englifh* Proteftant Subjects amongft them.

That the King, and all **other** *English*, had Cause to fufpect General *Oneale*, and those that adhered to him, to have Defign for Extirpation of the *English*, fhaking off the Government, **and drawing in** the *Spaniard*.

That the King was no Enemy to Catholicks; but being to rely upon his Proteftant Subjects for Re-eftablifhment into his Throne he durft not feem to favour them, but was forced to pretend to the Contrary.

That the Church of *England* purely confidered, and abftracted from thofe other Sects, did agree in that which was Effential to *Catholick* Religion, in moft of their Tenets, and did acknowledge herfelf to be defcended from the *Catholicks*, and from them to have received both the Scriptures, and their Ordination of Bifhops and Priefts.

That it was not to be wonder'd at, if **the** King fought an Agreement with his Parliament, rather than to continue a Civil War, which muft deftroy fo many of his Subjects, **and of** which the Event is always doubtful.

That concerning the King's Declaration againft, and difavowing his Commiffions given to the **Earl of** *Worcefter;* Firft, it was but a bare Affirmation of the Earl's, that the Commiffions were fuch; the Bufinefs paffing only between the King and him. Secondly, those Commiffions, were either all, or for the moft Part, Blanks; which if the Earl did fill up otherwife than **he fhould, the** King was not bound to juftifie; and as the principal **Reafon that** moved **the** King, **to** fend him into *Ireland*, **was, to appear in granting fuch Things** concerning Religion, wherein my Lord of *Ormond* **would not;** fo was he not to do any Thing **therein**, but with my **Lord of** *Ormond's* Knowledge and Confent.

That it **was** not ftrange, if when the King thought fit **to make a** Peace with the *Irifh*, he ought to make fuch a one, as he thought might conduce, and be moft advantageous to him, in the prefent Condition wherein **he** was, to which the Grants of their Demands for Religion in that Conjuncture **of** Time, had been as **he** conceived, **fo** deftructive, as it would **have** made his other *Proteftant* Subjects, fall from his Obedience, and leave to affift him in the Recovery of his

Regal Power, and Authority ; and therefore he made use of my Lord of *Ormond*, his Governor of that Kingdom, to produce such a Peace, as he might justifie : In contriving of which, by all such Means, as his Interest in that Kingdom gave him, my Lord of *Ormond* had done but his Duty to the King in obeying his Orders and Commands, and to his own Conscience, being a *Protestant*, not to give his Consent, that the *Roman* Bishops and Clergy should be possest of the Churches, and Church Livings in *Ireland;* and consequently, his own Bishops and Clergy excluded ; which was also the King's Care.

That the late Peace, advantageous, or disadvantageous, or however it was brought to pass, was on the one Side concluded by Authority of the great Seal of *England;* and on the other, by the Assent of the major Part of the Votes, orderly taken in an Assembly of the *Irish* Nation, according to their own Constitutions ; by which, Power was given to those Commissioners of their own Choice, to conclude a Peace ; who according to the Commissions given them (which were extant) had proceeded ; which Peace so made, no after Accidents could invalidate, for so all Agreements, and Contracts made in the World, would be little to the Purpose : And therefore, the Allegations made of the King's putting himself into the Power of the *Scott's*, and the Consequences like to grow thereby, were not effectual.

That if they thought themselves unsecure under the Government of my Lord of *Ormond*, because he was a *Protestant*, which Objection might also be made against the King himself, how much more Cause had the King to doubt his own Security, being now in the Hands of his Parliament, if he should avowably give them a *Catholick* Governor? And therefore they should do well, not to exact any such Thing from him, which he could not do, either with the Safety of his Crown or Person.

To all this it was replied, that as no Rebellion is justifiable, so was there never any more excusable than that of the *Irish*, for the Matter, though not for the Manner ; for their Rebellion was not against the King, but against their Fellow Subjects, and mortal Enemies to them, and to their Religion, who under the Name of a Parliament, had then actually in their Pay, an Army of *Scottish* Rebels ; by the Terror of which, they did as it were, hold a Dagger at the King's Throat, forcing his Consent to such pernicious Demands as they suggested to him : And for the Manner, as it was not defensible, so was it that, which all Governors must expect from Those, whom they hold in the

Nature of Slaves, and not of Subjects, which was the *Irish* Condition; which reckoning yet they had paid to the uttermost Farthing, the *English* Army sent thither by the Parliament, not only exceeding them in all inhuman Acts of Cruelty, but indeed all others that we have heard, or read of.

That General *Oneale* his Power, was wholly derived from the Nuncio and Clergy, from whom he principally received the Means of levying and paying his Men, who if they were satisfied in their Demands for Religion, he would yield to reasonable Conditions. And concerning that of bringing in the *Spaniard*, it was a Bugbear to affright Children; all wise Men being too well acquainted with the *Spanish* Condition at that Time, who had too much on his Hands already, to embroil himself with a new War; that being an Invention of the *French* Agents in the Kingdom of *Ireland*, who sought all they might to divert the King from putting himself on the Assistance of his *Catholick* Subjects, but rather to embrace that of the *Scotts*, their ancient Allies; as also, out of this Supposition, that the *Irish* and *English* Catholicks are more affected to the *Spaniards* than to the *French*; and consequently, if the King should be by their Means re-established, his Inclinations would lead that Way.

That, how the King's Affections to *Catholicks* stood, they did not know, but this was manifest, that if he could have compounded with his Parliament, he would have sacrificed them all.

That they could not distinguish the Church of *England* from the Rest, neither by their Writings, nor Actions; for out of no Country, since the Beginning of these modern Heresies, had issued Books more virulent against the Pope, and Catholick Religion, written by Bishops and Doctors of that Church; neither was there any Place in the World, where such cruel Laws had been made, and put in Execution against Priests, and Catholicks of the same Nation, as those made by Men living in, and under the Government and Communion of that Church.

That no Man can doubt, but my Lord of *Worcester's* Commissions were real, all signed with the King's Hand and Seal, in which he promised on the Word of a King, to make good whatsoever he should conclude; and that my Lord of *Worcester* was ready to justifie, that he had exactly followed his Instructions; and particularly, that concerning my Lord Lieutenant, whom he had made acquainted with all, that he transacted with the *Irish*, of which he could produce Proof.

That not only in his Opinion, but in the Opinion of others as wife, and who wifhed the King's Re-eftablifhment as much as any; the fureft Way to that Re-eftablifhment had been, by granting their juft Demands for Religion, to rely on the Affiftance of his *Catholick* Subjects, which Demands only extended to a Toleration in *England*, and the Face of the Church fettled in *Ireland*, without impofing any Thing on himfelf, or *Proteftant* Subjects, who fhould be as free amongft them, as themfelves; nor refufing to joyn with any his other Subjects of what Religion foever, in his Affiftance for Recovery of his Authority, and all thofe Prerogatives enjoy'd by his Anceftors; which Affiftance as it was more certain, being to come from People in Union; fo was it more powerful, not only confifting in *Ireland*; which if the King had been pleafed to take a Courfe accordingly, would foon in Spight of all his Enemies and theirs, have been united in his Obedience; but alfo in the Pope, who in his Particular, would have contributed much himfelf; and both would and could in that, have joined all the Clergy, in all the Chriftian Countries.

That as the King's Counfels and theirs, on whom he rely'd, have always gone upon contrary Principles, the Effects of which have been, that he is now fain to fubmit himfelf to the Mercy, and throw himfelf, as it were, at the Feet of thofe, who had been the Beginners and Contrivers of all his Misfortunes; who had branded his Perfon and Family with the bafeft Slanders; and being his Enemies, and the Enemies of his Church, were alfo the moft mortal and irreconcileable Enemies of Catholicks and Catholick Religion. So no Body muft think it ftrange, that now he had left himfelf in a State, no longer to be able to Protect them, if they fought their own Prefervation, which could not be, but by having a Catholick Governor.

Thefe Reafons, with others to the fame purpofe, I heard fometimes from the Nuncio, fometimes from the Bifhop of *Clohar*, efteemed one of the ableft Men of that Nation; which how effectual they are, I leave to the Reader's Confideration; who out of them may poffibly draw fomething, which may the better make him to judge of the whole Matter. And now to fay fomething briefly of my Lord of *Infequeen*, who being of that ancient Family of the *Obrians*, a Young Man of Spirit and Courage; when the *Englifh* Army fent by the King and Parliament firft came over, had raifed a very good Regiment, and done confiderable Service againft his Countrymen: After, when that Army was recalled, he in Perfon came into *England*, together with his Regiment, intending, as it feems, to ferve the King; but whether diftafted for being refufed, the Prefidentfhip of *Munfter* being, as I have heard, promised to the Earl of *Portland;* or inclinable to the Presbyterian Faction, which is no impossible Supposition, having been bred under Sir *William St. Leger,* President of *Munster,* whose Daughter he Married ; whatsoever the Cause was, he returned into his Country, and there took up Arms for the Parliament, by whom he was made their President of Munster. And having, with the Help of the Lord *Brohill,* Son to the Earl of *Corke,* possess'd himself of *Yoghall, Kingsale* and *Corke,* whereof two are Haven Towns, all considerable in *Munster,* he did, with Assistance of Men and Money from the *English* Parliament, make War on the Confederates, who lay nearest in his Way, prevailing often upon them, and taking divers Towns and Castles, whilst I was there. And after the Surrender of *Dublin,* and before my coming away, in a pitch'd Battle, being given by Consent of both Sides in mutual Letters, overthrew my Lord *Taste,* then General for the Confederates, with his Army, killing many, amongst the rest, that famous *Alexander Macdonnel,* otherwise *Coll-kito,* and taking many Prisoners, with much Baggage, and in that Victory, breaking the very Heart of the Confederates Affairs : This falling out not long after *Preston's* Overthrow by *Jones,* which I mention, because there is nothing of it in the Discourse before, to which it was not pertinent.

And now for Sir *Charles Coote* and *Monroe,* I shall not need to say much more of them, than I have already, more than the first was the Son of that Sir *Charles Coote,* Provost Marshal of *Ireland,* of whom it is said, that he would bid his *Irish* Prisoners blow in his Pistol, and then would discharge it. *Monroe,* an *Irish Scot,* as I think was he, to whom the Faction in the *English* Parliament would willingly have consigned the Command of the Army, sent over against the *Irish;* but that being opposed by the rest, it was carried for *Parsons,* and *Borlacie,* their then Commissioners for the Government of *Ireland;* which in Effect was all one, as to their Purpose.

A DISCOURSE

OF

MY JOURNEY INTO IRELAND,

AND MY EMPLOYMENT THERE.

HIS Majesty, the late King my Master, being a Prisoner at Holmby, and all Negotiations for his Deliverance and Re-establishment being rendred fruitless; it was thought fit by the Queen, and Prince of Wales, with their Council, that some Body should be sent into Ireland, with Letters and Instructions to my Lord of Ormond, for the Settling of a Peace in that Kingdom; and for that Purpose, I was by her Majesty chosen, and accordingly received these Instructions following, signed by the Queen.

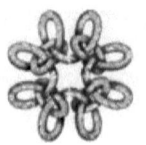

Her Majesty's Instructions.

I. YOU shall with all convenient Speed imbark your self for the Kingdom of Ireland; and after your Arrival there, you shall with all possible Speed repair to the Place, where you shall understand the Lord Lieutenant and Lord Digby to be, and to them you shall deliver all such Letters, as are directed to them from Us and the Prince.

II. You shall inform the said Lord Lieutenant, how sensible We and the Prince are of the present Troubles of that Kingdom, as well in Consideration of the King's Affairs in general, as particularly out of the Apprehension of the great and imminent Danger, that may thereby happen to those, which yet remain under the Obedience of him the said Lord Lieutenant; and how desirous We and the Prince are, to contribute all that is in our Power, to reconcile the Things in Question, between the said Lord Lieutenant, and the Confederate

Catholick Subjects in Ireland; whereby all of them may be firmly united under the Authority of our dearest Lord the King; and thereby enabled to defend themselves against the Common Enemy, and seasonably assist the King in his other Dominions.

III. You shall shew unto the Lord Lieutenant all the Papers and Dispatches wherewith you are charged, and particularly our Letter to the Nuncio now in Ireland, and the Clergy; as likewise, these your Instructions: And you shall, from Us and the Prince, acquaint the Lord Lieutenant, that these Preparations, as likewise all that is hereafter mentioned to be agitated by you with the Nuncio, Clergy and Confederate Catholick Subjects of that Kingdom, are not intended as any conclusive Opinions from hence; much less, as any positive Directions from Us and the Prince; but are only propounded by Us to the Lord Lieutenant, as probable Expedients to be considered of, resolved, varied, used or rejected by the Lord Lieutenant, as he upon the Place (best able to judge) shall think fit.

IV. You shall likewise acquaint the said Lord Lieutenant from Us, and from the Prince, that if he shall think fit to make use of any of these Expedients, before, or hereafter mentioned; or to direct the

Delivery of any of the said Letters or Dispatches; or to appoint you to pursue all or any of these Instructions, or any others, that the said Lord Lieutenant shall give you in their stead; that then both We and the Prince will always avow and justify the same, as Our Advice and Directions, in such Manner as the said Lord Lieutenant shall propound, and think proper for the Service.

V. When the said Lord Lieutenant shall have read and considered of the said Letters and Dispatches, you shall either deliver them according to their Addresses, or suppress them as he, the Lord Lieutenant shall think fit; and you shall in Our Name, and the Name of the Prince, deliver Civilities to any Person, or Persons, according as he, the said Lord Lieutenant, shall advise you: As likewise, you shall vary from, and pursue the rest of your Instructions in such Manner, as the Lord Lieutenant shall think fit; and in all other Things, you shall govern your self according to the Advice and Orders of the said Lord Lieutenant.

VI. If he, the said Lord Lieutenant, shall direct you to repair to the Nuncio, or the Assembly of the Clergy, or to the Supreme Council of the Irish, or to their General Assembly now met at Kilkenny, you shall, upon all Occasions, when your Discretion shall think fit, publish, avow, and declare, the great Inclinations, which We and the Prince have, to contribute effectually all that shall be proper for Us and Him, to the speedy concluding a happy Peace in Ireland; and how willing and desirous We and the Prince are to advance that good Work, as well by Our Mediation with the King in their Behalf (as there shall be Cause) as otherways in what We may.

VII. You shall further let them know, how seasonable to the King's Affairs, a good Conclusion of a Peace in Ireland would be; as also, upon all fit Occasions you shall press and insist upon the Necessity of it, with Relation to themselves, and the great Honour and Advantage, which the whole Irish Nation will have by such a Peace; and on the contrary, what Use the Common Enemy will make of the Continuance of these Distractions, even to the endangering of the whole Nation and Catholick Religion there.

VIII. You shall apply your self, as you shall see Cause, to such Persons amongst the Irish, as you shall find to have Credit and Power amongst them, and Inclination to conclude a Peace upon more moderate

Conditions; and shall let them know from Us and the Prince, how acceptable to the King, Our Self, and the Prince, such their Endeavours are, and will be; and how ready We will be, really to express Our good Acceptance of their Service therein, by such Marks of Our Favours, as shall be most suitable to their Condition, and most proper for them to receive.

H. R.

These were one Sort of Instructions I received, which were not to be kept so private, but that they were in some Cases communicable. Those that follow were not so.

Private Instructions.

I. YOU shall deliver to the Lord Lieutenant of Ireland, Fourteen Blanks now given into your Possession by Us and the Prince; Six others are Signed by Us alone, and the other Six by the Prince alone.

II. You shall acquaint the Lord Lieutenant, that We and the Prince do authorize and appoint him, to fill up all the said Blanks in such Manner, and to such Purpose, and with such Contents, as he shall think most proper for the Service of our dearest Lord the King in his Irish Affairs: And you shall assure him, the said Lord Lieutenant, that as We and the Prince repose this Trust and Confidence in him, that he shall make such Use of them, as he shall think fit, for the Advancement of the Peace in Ireland; so will both of

Us at all Times avow and justify those Instruments so to be filled up by him, as Our own Acts, and as done by Our particular Directions and Command.

III. You shall more particularly acquaint the Lord Lieutenant from Us and the Prince, that if in the Treaty of the Peace, or in the Conclusion thereof, he desires to be assisted with any further Authority, grounded upon any Letters sent to him from the King, or otherwise in Our Power, then We desire him, the said Lord Lieutenant, to fill up the Blanks Signed by Us or the Prince, or any other of the said Blanks Signed either by Us or the Prince, with such Authority from Us, or from Us and the Prince, or from the Prince only, in such Manner as he shall find most proper and conducing to such a Peace.

IV. You shall likewise particularly acquaint him, the Lord Lieutenant, that if he shall think it proper for the Advancement of the Peace there, that your self, or your self with any others now in Ireland, should in Our Name and authorized by Us, repair to the General Assembly now held at Kilkenny, or the Supreme Council of the Irish, or to any other Body, or Persons, with the Overtures of a Treaty, or any Particulars, i order to, concerning or conducing to the same, Our Desire is, and We hereby authorize him the said Lord Lieutenant accordingly, that he should fill up one or more of the said Blanks signed by Us, in the Nature of a Commission, Letters or Instructions, with such Authority from Us, and in such Manner, as he shall think fit; and that he would accordingly, insert the Name of such Person, or Persons, as he shall think fit to be joyned with you, in this Employment from Us.

V. You shall acquaint the Lord Lieutenant, that upon Advertisement of the Restraint made on the Person of the King at Newcastle, We enter'd into a serious Debate of his Affairs; and particularly considering of the Proposition made to Us formerly by the Lord Digby, when he came from Ireland; and that thereupon, both We, and the Prince do much incline to the Opinion then delivered to Us by the Lord Digby; That after a Peace made in Ireland, it will be fit for the Prince in Person to repair to Ireland; and there, by his Presence, to unite that Nation under the King's Authority, and imploy Forces from thence for his Assistance, as his Affairs in England and Scotland shall require. Therein you are to desire the Lord Digby from Us, and from the Prince, to send Us speedily his Opinion and Advice: And if he shall approve those Propositions, that he order his Business accordingly.

VI. You are to acquaint the Lord Lieutenant with the Proposition made to Us by the Earl of Craford in the Name of the Marquis of Montross himself, and many other Persons of Quality and Condition in the Highlands of Scotland; [and shall thereupon assure him, that Our Zeal to serve the King in the Recovery of his Liberty, and Defence of his Crown, now in Hazard, is such, that if the Design (after the Peace shall be made in Ireland, and that Nation shall appear in Arms for the King's Assistance) shall be approved by his Judgment, as the most probable to attain the End aforesaid; We shall be willing to give Our Consent to the pious Inclinations and Desires of the Prince, to expose his person to all the Danger and Accidents, that are to be expected in such an Attempt, in hope thereby, to bring real Succours to the Distresses of the King his Father: In the mean Time you are to propound to the Lord Digby Our Opinion; that the Irish should be encouraged all that may be, to send such sufficient Succours to the Earl of Antrim in Scotland, as may continue a Footing there, and so confirm the King's Party in that Kingdom, as to render that Design practicable, when it shall be proper to attempt it.

VII. These Particulars you are to communicate to none but the Lord Digby, and Lord Clanriccard; unless the Lord Lieutenant shall think fit to give you other Orders concerning the same.

H. R.

Then follows the Prince's Approbation of all the Instructions of both Sorts; with his Command to put them in Execution, in these Words.

Charles, Pr.

We have perused, and do fully approve of your Instructions, bearing Date herewith, and signed by our Royal Mother; and do appoint and authorize you, so far as you shall find Us named therein, to put the same in Execution.

Charles, Pr.

We have perused, and do fully approve of your private Instructions, bearing Date herewith, signed by our Royal Mother; and do hereby appoint and authorize you, so far as you shall find Us named therein, to put the same in Execution.

With these Instructions, and many Letters, not only to my Lord Lieutenant, Lord Clanriccard, and Lord Digby; but also from the Queen to the Nuncio, and Clergy, to Oneale and Preston, with all the considerable Persons then amongst the Irish, I parted from Paris about he 16th of March, 1647, in Company of my Lord of Craford mentioned in the Instructions. At Orleans finding by Letters, as also by the Print from London sent after me, that my Lord of Ormond was deepiy engaged in a Treaty with the Parliament, so as possible I might not be able to come to him at all, if Dublin were surrendred before my Arrival; and in that Case having Nothing in my Instructions, I took the Boldness to write to her Majesty, desiring to know what it was her Pleasure I should then do, if that should so fall out, to which at Nantz, I received this Answer.

TRusty and well Beloved We greet you well; upon Consideration of what you writ unto Us since your Departure, We have thought fit hereby to signify unto you, that at your Arrival in Ireland, if you find the City of Dublin besieged in such Sort, as you cannot have Access to Our Right Trusty, and entirely Beloved Cousin, the Marquis of Ormond, or that it be surrendred to the Rebels; in such Case, you forbear not the present Delivery of your Letters to the Nuncio, and Confederate Catholicks of Ireland, to whom We have written by you; and you are to assure them from Us, that as the Consideration of the Service of our dearest Lord the King, and the Interest of Catholick Religion, hath continually inclined Us, most passionately to desire the Peace of that Kingdom; so is there nothing that may conduce therein to their Satisfaction and Security, wherein We will not contribute Our best and promptest Assistance. You shall not fail before long, to receive further Directions from Us; in the mean Time you are to pursue those We have already given you, and execute the same with all possible Diligence; whereof, We remain Confident: And so We commit you to the Protection of the Almighty. From the Lovre at Paris, March the 19th, 1647.

With this Letter I received another from the Secretary as follows:

SIR,

I send you herewith an Answer of your Letter to her Majesty, whereby you will receive full Light and Satisfaction of what you write: And by her Special Command I am to advise you, to make all fitting Application both to the Nuncio, and Others the most considerable Persons amongst the Clergy, to possess them with a real Belief of her Majesty's Cordial and Affectionate Intentions to comply with and further on her Part, whatsoever may set forward the happy Settlement of that Kingdom, to their Satisfaction and Security in Point of Religion; which being her chiefest Aim, and sufficiently provided for, her Majesty expects in the winding up of that Bottom, those fitting Regards towards his Majesty's Affairs, and present Condition, as may justify to her and the World, the Merits of their publick Professions and Proceedings. Her Majesty will be very sensible of particular Deservings in this Kind, and resent them with the uttermost Effects of her Favour, or Mediation for their Desires, &c. March the 19th, Lovre.

It was about the latter End of March, that we parted from Nants, (for, no sooner could we find a Passage) in an Irish Merchant's Vessel of some 200 Ton, heavily laden, and without any considerable Danger, more than being very much affrighted, got into Ireland about six or seven Days after at Waterford, and yet so unluckily, as the Assembly at Kilkenny, after it had resolved Things as opposite to the Means of attaining those Ends for which I was come thither, as could be, broke up that Night at Ten of the Clock, which they would not have done, had they first heard of my Landing, for so Mr. Baron, who had been Agent here in France for the Confederate Irish, and to whom I sent a Post so soon as I was in Waterford, writ back to me. Indeed, I was very Unfortunate, for the Assembly had both Power and Means to do or undo what they had done, to the Prejudice of a Treaty, which the Supreme Council, limited within Bounds by the Assembly, afterward had not. At Waterford I had Notice that my Lord Digby, with my Lord of Castlehaven, lay secretly within a Mile or two of the Town, ready to set Sail for France; to my Lord Digby I sent presently, and had Answer, that Mr. Slingsby, his Secretary, would be with me the next Morning, which he was, and told me, that he looked for my Lord very soon. I stayed from Sunday until Wednesday, in that Expectation, at Waterford, which is but twenty Miles from Kilkenny; but then fearing to give the Council Jealousy, who at that Time beheld my Lord Digby as their Enemy, and who was come secretly into their Quarters without a Pass, I parted toward Kilkenny, my Lord of Craford being gone before, where the next Morning I was, by Mr. Baron, brought to the Council; to whom (after they had caused me to sit in a Chair, not far from my Lord of Antrim their President, nor would they hear me until I had done so) I delivered the Cause of my Coming thither, which was, the Queen and Prince's Desire of a Peace in that Kingdom; and for the Queen, she was not only moved to it for the King's Interest, but also by her Zeal to the Catholick Religion, and Good of the People; that for the Catholick Religion, she did not conceive (abstracting from miraculous Providence) how it could be preserved from Ruin, but by a Peace; to which End her Majesty had made Choice of me, a Catholick, before any other, to send thither with Instructions and Letters to my Lord of Ormond, who was the Kings Lieutenant over that Country, to whom I was first to make my Address: And therefore I had for the present, no other Particulars to communicate with them, more than desire their Pass, with a Warrant for Post-Horses, and Convoy for my Safety to the Borders of their Quarters. After this, being so advised by Master Baron, I did rise and go out, and not long after had Orders for what I desired, and the next day parted for Dublin, being fifty Miles, whither I came the Day after, and was that night brought to my Lord of Ormond, to whom I delivered such Letters as were for him; and then said, "That I was sure those Letters expressed Civilities from the Queen and Prince, much better than I could; and that therefore I had nothing more now to say, until I had deciphered such Instructions as I had, which were many, and would take up some good Time; and by which his Lordship would find the Confidence her Majesty and the Prince had in him, which was great, as no Reports could shake, though we had Weekly News of Treaties with the Parliament, for the Delivery up of those Places under his Command." To which his Lordship Replyed, "That Confidence shall never deceive them; and, that he, who had ventured himself, his Wife, and all his Children in the King's Service, would make no Scruple of venturing or casting away one Son, when there shall be Cause (this he spake because his Son was then Hostage with the Parliament) yet if there be Necessity, he should give up those Places under his Command rather to the English Rebels than the Irish Rebels, of which Opinion he thought every good English Man was." To this I replied nothing, but after some Questions and Answers concerning Things in France, parted from his Lordship to my Lodging; and after two Days (for so long it was before I could decipher my Instructions, a Work to which I had not been accustomed) I returned to his Lordship with them, written out in mine own Hand, which having read unto him, I gave them, together with the fourteen Blanks, into his Lordship's Possession, and so returned towards my Lodging; where, by the Way, I met with my Lord Digby newly alighted, who told me he had neglected his Voyage at the present for France, desirous to see what Fruits my coming thither would produce; and, after I had given him Letters, we parted. The next Day being Wednesday, I intended to wait on my Lord of Ormond at Dinner; but at Eleven of the Clock, I was sent for by my Lord Digby, and told by him, that it was my Lord of Ormond's Pleasure I should forthwith go to Kilkenny, and move the Council for renewing the Cessation (which would expire on Saturday following at Twelve of the Clock) for three Weeks longer, which Order I obeyed; and

317

in the Afternoon, coming to receive my Lord Lieutenant's further Commands, he delivered me the Cessation signed on his Part. I desired to know what I should say, in Case they should object that my Lord did it, but to gain Time, that he might receive more Forces from the Parliament. He answered, I should receive Orders for that on the Way, if, on Consideration, there were Cause. I desired to know his Lordship's Pleasure, what I should do with those Letters I had to the Nuncio, Clergy and Others, with the Confederates; he told me I should follow my Lord Digby's Directions. So I parted that Night with my Lord Digby to Leslip: and there my Lord Digby thought fit I should deliver all those Letters. The next Day, on the Way, a Post overtook me from my Lord Lieutenant, with these Letters from his Lordship.

SIR,

ON further Consideration of the Discourse we had Yesterday touching a Cessation, I think fit to give you Power, to undertake to the Confederate Party, that if a Cessation be agreed on, I will not receive, into the Garrisons under my Command, Forces from the Parliament, during three Weeks, to begin from Saturday next the 17th of this Month, the Cessation being agreed upon until then: But you are desired to use your uttermost Endeavour to procure a Cessation without this Condition, or at leas that it be kept private; which last you are to engage them in, before you consent to the said Condition. And so I rest your Affectionate Friend, Ormond. Dublin Castle the 15th of April, 1647.

On Friday I came to Kilkenny and after Discourse had with the French Agents, Monsieur du Moullin, Monsieur de la Monerie, and Monsieur Tallon, whose Advise I was to receive in it; the next Day in the Morning I moved the Council, from whom I had Answer to this Purpose: That their Army was well advanced on its March to Carlogh, (a strong Castle in my Lord's Quarters) and that they did not know what to do with it for Three Weeks, but must so long keep their Army on Foot to no Purpose. But if my Lord would have a Cessation for six Months, on the terms agreed upon by them, they would agree. The Propositions themselves were as follow.

Ouertures for an Accommodation delivered by Doctor Gerard Fennel, and Geofrie Baron, Esquire, from the General Assembly of the Confederate Catholicks, the 3d of March 1646.

I. THAT each Party should continue their respective Governments independent of each other, within such Quarters as by the Accommodation shall be agreed on, until a Peace.

II. That both should join in a War both by Sea and Land, against the Enemies of his Majesty and this Nation; and that neither Party shall make Peace, Cessation, or other agreement, or enter into any Commerce or Traffick with the said Enemies, without the Consent of the other, until a Peace.

III. That Dublin and the other Garrisons within your Lordship's Quarters, may be secured against the said Enemies.

IV. That the Confederate Catholicks within the Quarters that shall be agreed on by this Accommodation to be left to your Lordship, shall be secured of the free enjoying of their Religion, Lives, Estates and Liberties.

V. The like for all other Catholicks in the said Quarters.

VI. That your Lordship shall suffer none to live within your Quarters, but such as shall Swear the Performance of the Accomodation.

VII. That your Lordship shall enjoy the Profit of your **Estate** in the Quarters of the Confederate Catholicks, paying such Contributions out of it, as the **Confederates** shall do out of theirs.

VIII. That the **Confederates** will contribute to the Maintenance of your **Lordship's** Charge in a competent Way.

IX. That during the Accommodation, no Outlawries be prejudicial.

With the Paper above-mentioned, relating to these Propositions, I departed from Kilkenny towards Leslip Castle, Sir Nicholas White's House, six Miles from Dublin, where my Lord Digby was; to him I delivered it, who two Days after returning from my Lord Lieutenant with this following Answer, but not signed, my Lord Lieutenant giving the Reason, because the Propositions sent before from the Assembly to him, were not signed.

Answers to the Overtures from the Confederate Catholicks, sent by Gerrard Fennell and Geofrie Baron, Esquires; and likewise, to the last Paper of the 10th of May, 1647, sent by relative to the former.

THE two first Propositions are such, as appear fitter to be treated in a League Offensive and Defensive between neighbouring Princes, than between his Majesty's Governor of a Kingdom, and his subjects of the same, declined from their Obedience, with whom it is inconsistent with his Majesty's Lieutenant to join, otherwise than by their Return to their Obedience, and Submission to his Majesty's Authority.

To the 3d, when they are thus returned to their Obedience, and have submitted to his Majesty's Authority, it will be then seasonable to consider of securing the Garrisons in this Article mentioned, against all Enemies of his Majesty and the Nation.

That the five other Propositions are such, as may be fit to be considered in case of a Cessation, which when they shall propose unto us, we shall take into Consideration, and give such Answer thereunto as shall be reasonable.

That since in their last Paper they declare, that they resolve to insist positively upon the Votes of the late Assembly, which, as we understand them, are inconsistent with those Grounds, on which there can be any Hope of ever settling any Peace in this Kingdom. If they have any real Desire of the same, they will take the Course to be freed from their Obligation of insisting upon those Votes, if any such be upon them ; and to be invested with Power to propose such Things, as may with Honour and Safety be hearkened unto.

This last my Lord added, because of their Votes in the Assembly against the last Peace, without Recalling of which, and Submission to the said Peace, my Lord Lieutenant was resolved not to treat with them, on any Terms ; and this my Lord Digby told me, of whom when I demanded, why my Lord Lieutenant would do nothing in order to those instructions, with so many Blanks signed by the Queen and Prince, as I had brought him ; his Lordship's Reply was, that my Lord Lieutenant was wiser. If I shall deliver my Opinion, it is, that my Lord Lieutenant having received a legal Commission from the King to conclude a Peace, and that Peace concluded and broken by the Irish, he did not think it safe, without a new Authority, as legally founded, to make another Peace, and therefore it was, that my Lord Digby answered me he was wiser. I then desired of my Lord Digby to know what it was, that my Lord Lieutenant would have ; and that he would draw up something for me to carry to the Conncil, by Way of Proposition to them ; to which my Lord consented, and presently writ out a Paper and gave me ; but the next Morning, before my Departure, called for it back, saying he was fearful I might be surprized by some Horse on the Way ; and therefore I must find some Way to preserve it in my Remembrance, without the Writing ; whereupon I was forced to set down two or three words only in the Beginning of a Line, so to help my Memory, and parted towards Kilkenny, and the third Day came to Clonmell in Munster, whither the Council were removed ; there I gave them my Lord Lieutenant's Answer, and desired that a Committee might be appointed to speak with me, which was done ; and soon after the Bishop of Limerick, my Lord Muscrey, and Mr. Nicholas Pluncket, appointed for that Purpose, met me ; to whom, after some Discourse, I delivered in this Paper, which I had, as well as my Memory would serve me, drawn up according to my Lord Digby's Sense.

324

Propositions made by me to the Committee, about the 18th of May, 1647.

I. IF you do intend a Submission of the whole Catholick Party to his Majesty's Authority.

II. If you intend to do it by going on the Foot of the former Peace, the only Way which in Possibility is left, either for your Security, or any Body's else, that is to deal with you; the King's Condition being such as it is.

III. If for such other Agreements, as either are in the Marquiss of Clanriccard's Engagement, or such further Advantages as may be obtain'd from the Queen and Prince, you will take such Security as may be reasonably devised, and will give the like for what concerneth you.

IV. If you be not enabled of your selves to go thro' with a Peace, you will, when it shall be seasonably proposed, accord to the Calling of an Assembly.

V. If you will presently in Order to this, send to obtain a Cessation from Month to Month for six Months, one Month only to be known, on reasonable Conditions for both Parties; one whereof I suppose on my Lord's Part will be, such an Enlargement of his Quarters, as may serve for the reasonable Maintenance of his Men, in Case there be a Breach with the Parliament; which Quarters shall be secured to be restored if there be Cause; during which Cessation, Things may be negociated in France, with the Queen and Prince; mutual Securities agreed on, and my Lord have Time to disengage himself.

VI. If you will trust me, and some one or two Persons more, that you shall think fit, with the Entrance into the Manage of this Business, as long as there shall be Reason to keep it secret.

VII. Lastly, if you will proceed on these Grounds speaking generally; then I will do my best to bring all This to pass, and have Reason to be Confident I shall perform it.

After this was read, Mr Plunckct objected, that the Foundation of all my Propositions was impossible to be laid; and that was, the Proceeding on the last Peace, which had been voted against by the Assembly, and all the Adherents to it excommunicated by the Nuncio. I replied, that what one Assembly had voted, another might unvote, if they should see Cause; that the Nuncio's Excommunication against the Adherers to the Peace, was not, that there was any Thing evil in that Peace, in which there were many excellent Provisions for the Benefit of the Nation; but that there was not so much Good, in it for the Securing of Catholick Religion, as he thought necessary; and when he should see that reasonably secured any other Way, it would be all one to him, and the Excommunication might be recalled: After some other Discourse, we parted, they promising to render an Account of the Thing to me speedily. Three or four Days after, the Council sent for me, and did speak to this Purpose; That though it was a very unusual Thing to treat with a Person that shewed no Kind of Commission or Authority, yet they were so Confident of me on the one Part, and so desirous on the other, to lay hold on any Thing might tend to a Peace, as they had taken my Propositions into Consideration, and had agreed concerning an Answer, which for the present I could not receive, but was desired to go along with the Bishop of Clohar, to Kilkenny, some 20 Miles off, where the Nuncio then was, and there I should have it. So the Bishop and I parted together, who by the Way told me, that when we had been at Kilkenny, we must go to General Oneale, that lay with his Army some 30 Miles beyond. After we had been some two Hours in Kilkenny, the Bishop found me out, and told me that my Lord Nuncio he feared would be some Stop to our Proceedings; and that I should do well my self to speak with him, which I presently did, my Lord of Clohar being Interpreter. The Nuncio began, saying, that he would willingly consent to the making of a Peace, but not a Cessation, for that, Cessations had been the Reason why the Irish Affairs had no better Progress; and that my Lord of Ormond did it, but to gain Time, that so he might receive more Forces from the Parliament. I reply'd, that now there could be nothing possible done without a Cessation, the Additions for Religion being to be transacted into France and back again : As also a new Assembly was to be called for Confirmation of Things agreed on. And as for the Landing of Parliament Forces, I did not doubt, but the Council had sufficiently provided for that, in the Conditions of the Cessation, which once signed by my Lord Lieutenant, would be infallibly kept. He answered, that my Lord Lieutenant had deceived him, and he durst not trust him. And after some other Discourse, in which I could see he was not my Lord Lieutenant's Friend, in the End I wished him to be advised what he did, in hindring of an Act decreed by the Supreme Council, that gave so great Hopes of a Future Peace, whereof if Ill should come, it would be attributed to him. He desired me to rest satisfied untill to Morrow, when he would again speak with me; in the mean Time he would write to the Council. The next Day he came to my Chamber and told me, that the Council had by their Letters signified their Consent to his Desire; which was, that it might be deferred untill Friday come Fortnight, when he would call a Convocation of all the Clergy of Limerick; alledging to me how much better it would be, that it were done by the Council and Congregation together, than by the Council alone; desiring me that I would signify as much to Dublin : I reply'd, I feared that Delay might prove fatal, for that I was most assured, the Parliament Commissioners with good Forces and Instructions to satisfy my Lord of Ormond in all his Demands, lay at the Waterside, expecting nothing but a Wind; who, if they arrived in the Interim, it would be too late afterwards to talk of any Agreement. What the Nuncio's Reason was for this Delay, I cannot certainly tell; whether he really intended, not to have a Thing of so great Consequence done without the Consent of the Clergy of the Kingdom; or whether having no Intention to conclude with my Lord of Ormond on any Terms, he had no other Way to break off the

Council's Decree, to which Oneale himself, had been consenting, I know not; but this I believe, that this Delay, was the Cause that rendered all my Labours fruitless: For, the Council and Oneale, of whose Intentions I was advertised by David Oneale, having agreed to the Cessation, as was desired, by which the Parliament Forces would have been excluded from Landing, all the Rest would have followed. My Opinion is, that the Latter was the Cause, and that he and the Bishop of Clohar would run any Hazard rather than accord with my Lord of Ormond; against whose Person, I found in the Nuncio, great Animosity; my Lord of Clohar being a better Hider of his Thoughts. Soon after I signify'd what had been done, by an Express, to my Lord Digby, and with my Letters, sent a Copy of the Propositions I made to the Council: From whom not long after, I received this Answer.

SIR,

YOURS of the 27th May I received not until Yesterday Night, and whenever it had come unto my Hands, you may be sure I should have hasten'd my Answer to you, since here is nothing that possesseth me more, then the importance of this Business we have in Hand, concerning which you have collected, and represented very rightly my Sence in the Paper you sent me; unto which upon further Thought I can add nothing, but that I daily grow more confident of my being able to do good, if in any Time these People you have to deal with, will enable me in any proportion of reasonableness. I am very glad of the Assembly of the Clergy at Limerick, and should be gladder of a general Assembly; for I can never hope to extract any Usefulness out of this Kingdom, but by an unanimous and entire Consent of the Catholick Party, to whatsoever settlement shall be made. I expect with impatience the the Result of the Assembly at Limerick, in Way of Answer to the Propositions, of which I am sure you will not be slow to advertise me. As for Daniel Oneale's Proposition, if it be meant for all the

Accommodation, is for the present aimed at, without Relation to the former Peace, is ridiculous; but if there be intended by it, that the former Peace stand valid, and unusually submitted to, such a Kind of Government Assistant to their Quarters, may be continued till they be secured in the conditional Concessions that shall be agreed on, the Proposition in that Sense may not be very unreasonable; but this you must lay as a Ground, that without preserving good the former Peace, (I mean, without Prejudice to any Additionals) not my self, much less my Lord Lieutenant, can meddle at all in any Conjunction with them, since it is that alone, that can restore them to the Quality of such Subjects, as the King's Lord Lieutenant can joyn with. I shall add nothing at this present, but only desire you to hasten unto me, if possible, Security for Repair, and Residence in their Quarters, and the Transportation mentioned to you; since, if this Traffick between us should take vent, I do not know how soon I might run Hazard in these Parts; when as, if once I have my Retreat secure, I shall be bold: besides that there may be suddenly such an Opportunity of drawing Men away from the Parliament, as if once lost, cannot be recovered. God send you in your Endeavours, the Success that is wished by your affectionate Servant,

GEORGE DIGBY.

Leslip, June
3d, 1647.

That which I observe in this Letter is, that my Lord acknowledgeth me to have rightly digested his Sense into Propositions. Secondly, whereas he mentioneth a Proposition made by Daniel Oneale (not spoken of before, and which I have not by me) it was something of a joint Government, as one may perceive by the Letter, whereby my Lord Lieutenant should have governed by Assistance of the Confederate Council in their Quarters, until the Peace had been perfect. With his Uncle Owen Oneale's Consent, Daniel Oneale came on Purpose with it to Clomell, with Intention to propose it to the Council,

330

where he was made Prisoner for coming without a Pass. To me he gave it, when I came to see him, and I to the Council; to which nothing was said, because the other Propositions were then on Foot; how ever it was, and what soever it had been, there was nothing to be done without recalling the former Peace, as is Thirdly to be observed in my Lord's Letter; a Thing very difficult, if not impossible, for a new Assembly must be called to unvote, and the Nuncio perswaded to recall his Excommunication; all which did not dishearten me so, but that I still had hopes, until I received this second Letter from my Lord Digby, which was as followeth:

SIR,

YESTERDAY the Parliament Commissioners landed with 600 Horse, and 8 or 900 Foot; they hastily and infinitely press my Lord Lieutenant's Performance of Conditions and Surrender of the Places, with as much Eagerness, as if they feared something might thwart them out of England. If I receive not from you within five Days, positive and reasonable Resolutions unto what I proposed, it will be too late to hope any Good in the Main; besides, this Place will grow too hot for me: I do therefore desire you to hasten unto me a safe Conduct from the Irish, to pass and embark in their Quarters; and to reside for a while, and embark such men as I can draw away from hence; which if they will presently allow, I am confident I can in a short Time draw away the better Part of the Parliament Forces, and if I might secretly lye for some Time, in some private Place, in their Quarters to confer with you and them, they would not repent it. I have nothing more to add, but to desire you to hasten an Answer to your Affectionate Servant,

GEORGE DIGBY.

P.S. If you find them likely to be reasonable, send me Word in what Condition their Armies are, to march suddenly, if Occasion should be. June the 8th, 1647.

I was, two or three Days before the Receipt of this Letter, come to Clomell, to attend the Resolutions of that Congregation the Nuncio had called, intended at Limerick, but by Accident transferred to Clomell, and so longer deferred, than was at first spoken of by the Nuncio, to me; sent for by the Nuncio and Clergy, they had made some Objections to me concerning the Propositions, but insisted especially on the Impossibility of having any Thing to do with the former Peace, which had been condemned by the Clergy and People of the whole Nation; and no wonder (to use their own Words) since whatsoever Provision had been made for the Temporal Part, there had been so little for Religion, as that God was not once named in it. My Reply was something long, but resolved into these two Heads, that my Lord Lieutenant neither would or could treat on any other Foundation, the King's Condition being as it was; That all the Peace being good for the Nation, the Defects in securing Religion might be provided for some other Way, to their Contentment.

Being returned to my Lodging, I received these Letters from my Lord Digby above-mentioned, with which I went presently to the Council; and having told them that was come to pass, which I had so long feared, and which they did enough believe: I read such part of my Lord Digby's Letter to them as I thought fit, and then spoke to this Effect:—"That there was now no longer time for Delay, near two Days of the five limited in the Letter being expired; that if they would delay to do, he would no longer delay to speak freely to them, though I had little Hope that should prevail, if their own imminent Danger, in the Loss of those Places under my Lord Lieutenant's Power, to the Parliament, did not move them: That the King my Master being in that Condition, as they did well know, had given the Queen and Prince of Wales Power to treat and conclude in the Business of Ireland; who accordingly had been pleased, not only to send me with Letters and Instructions to my Lord Lieutenant; but also with Letters to all the principal Persons and Corporate Towns amongst them; whereby they might see the real Intentions of the Queen and Prince, to contribute all that lay in their Power to such a Peace as might be for the King's Service, and Good of the Nation, and particularly of the Queen, for Advantage of Catholick Religion : That I had now been in the Kingdom more than two Months, and seen very little Effects of those Protestations they had entered into, of their Obedience to the King, which they could not otherwise shew now (especially in the present Conjuncture of Things) but by Demonstration of their Desire to return under the Authority of his principal Governor my Lord Lieutenant: That my Commands being to come back so soon as I should see no Hopes of their Union with my Lord Lieutenant, I was resolved very soon to return and give an Account according to the best of my Understanding of the Irish Affairs, which had not been the less Cause of my Sending thither; the Queen having been pleased (though unworthy) to make Choice of me, not only as an honest Man, but as a Catholick, who therefore was not likely to give a worfe Colour to the Proceedings of the Confederates than they deserved ; but that as yet I could say Little for their Advantage, unless they did, in this Instant of Time, do Something that might alter my judgment in their Favour."

After this I withdrew ; and two Hours after my Lord Muscrey, and another, whose name I have forgotten, were sent to me with these Answers to my Propositions.

I. TO the first we do intend it.

II. When we understand the Matter, and Assurance of the Additionals to the late Peace, we shall then call an Assembly, who only have Power to proceed upon the Foot of the late Peace, and to conclude therein, as they shall find Cause.

III. We intend to take and give such Security for the additional Advantages, as shall be agreed upon until a Settlement in Parliament.

IV. We will, when it shall be seasonable, call an Assembly.

333

V. We will agree to a Cessation for two Months, the one visible, the other secret, until the Expiration of the first; and in Case there be a clear Resolution of a Breach with the Parliament, we shall then treat upon Enlargement of Quarters, or other Consideration for Maintenance of those of his Lordships Soldiers, as adhere to the King, upon Security of Restitution as is offered. We also agree to mutual Security during the Cessation and Negotiation with the Queen and Prince.

VI. We agree to this.

VII. Needs no Answer. June the 11th.

With these I received the Copy of a Cessation, importing three Things; First, a Cessation from all Hostility, according to the usual Manner in such Cases. Secondly, obliging my Lord, during the Time, to receive no more Forces from England or Scotland into any of his Ports, Cities, or Garrisons. Thirdly, That my Lord should not, during the Time, assist the Enemies of the Confederates in Ulster or elsewhere in Ireland, nor receive Forces from them.

With these Papers I presently departed, and came the next Night to Ballisonnon, the Castle of Mac Thomas, fifty Miles from Clomell, and twenty from Dublin, the outermost Garrison of the Confederates, which I thought the fittest Place for me to lye in, for the hearing from both Parties. From whence I sent away, by Sir Richard Barnnel, the Answers to the Propositions, with the Cessation to my Lord Digby, with so much Speed, as it came within the Time he had limited; which Messenger was no sooner parted, but I had a Letter from my Lord Digby's Secretary, in which, amongst many others, were these Words.

MY Lord Lieutenant hath written to my Lord yesterday, that all his Conditions were fully assented unto by the Parliament; and that if he heard not from the Irish on Tuesday or Wednesday at Night, he would put it past Recovery, &c.

334

And again, Nothing is more certain, than that my Lord Lieutenant will put himself and all his Party into their Hands, if now they give him not such an Answer as may in Security and Honour invite him to treat with the Irish, whereby the Law will be in their own Hands. Leslip, 12th of June, 1647.

Soon after I received another from the same Hand, wherein, after he had informed me of Fairfax his taking the King from Holmby, he concludes with these Words: For God's sake make haste to come or write to us your Irish Decrees: now they make themselves and us happy if they will but comply a little. Leslip, the 15th of June, 1647. A Day or two after I received these,

SIR,

UPON Tuesday last, the Lord Lieutenant being fiercely press'd by the Commissioners to Surrender, and both needing and desiring the Assistance of his best Friends, with Hazard in the doing, and with great Disturbance since, I got into the Castle at Night, where I now am, and where I received Yesterday your Dispatch of the 14th, unto which, in Regard of our present Distractions, I can return at this Time but a very short Answer; which is, that the Answer you sent carries a Shew of so much more reasonable Disposition in the Council there, than I have met with heretofore, that I shall willingly engage my self to deal with you farther upon it, and I will hazard my Life, or secure such a Suspence in the Lord Lieutenant's giving up the Government, as shall allow Time to see whether it may be brought to good Effect; and I conjure you be not disturbed with any Thing you shall hear from any Body but my self, for the Matter here is exactly secret, pray God it be so there, or else all will be undone; it will be impossible, without ruining all, for me to come into those Quarters, and to return to these; but by that Time you shall have sent me the Pass I desired for my self and the Gentleman depending upon me, to Leslip, I am confident I shall have settled the Business of the Cessation, and be ready to come thither for good and all, till I pass into France to perfect all Things. Whatever the Event be, be assured of the clear and faithful Endeavour of your affectionate humble Servant,

GEORGE DIGBY.

P.S. I pray be sure, whatsoever you direct to me, to send it by safe Hands, and carefully writ in Cypher. If the Irish Forces could suddenly press us at Trim, or any where but here, it would help us much, but let them beware coming near Dublin. June 17, 1647.

I think after this Letter (though Matters in Dublin were brought to that narrow Straight) yet I had not Cause utterly to despair of Success to my Endeavours: I did not know that the Face of Things in England were changed; the King in a Kind of Liberty at Hampton Court; the Parliament, which had been hitherto Presbyterian, and with which my Lord Lieutenant had held his Treaty, was become now Independent, quite another Thing; so that I was confident my Lord of Ormond would be very wary of parting easily from his Government, without fresh Commands from the King, which, whatsoever they were, I was contented. Full of these Hopes, I presently writ to the Council for my Lord Digby's Pass, and his other Desires; as also letting them know, I doubted not of good Success; desiring that their Army under General Preston, might with all speed, be put into a Posture of marching, for that I thought we should have sudden Occasion to use them; from whom some two Days after, I received Answer, that it should be done. About the same Time this Letter came to me from my Lord Digby's Secretary.

SIR,

TAKE all the Speed that can be, in procuring the Lord Digby's Pass and Desires, for till that come he will not stir; and the whole Business runs a great Hazard by Delay. You must also make it your Business to draw the Irish

Forces to Trim, or some other Garrison (Dublin excepted) immediately; If these Things be effected speedily and well, doubt not at all of the Success of the Matter in the End. I rest, Yours, &c.

Friday Noon, Leslip.

P.S. Send all your Dispatches hither to me upon all Occasions: Let me hear speedily of your Receipt of this, and what you intend to do in the whole Matter. Deal both with Preston and Oneale; hasten Oneale to Trim, and Preston to the Nas, and Minouth; but let him there stop and come no nearer Dublin. This will be well done whatsoever be the Event, and 'tis great Weakness to neglect it. This Letter was presently seconded by an other from the same Hand.

SIR,

THIS Morning yours of the 19th, came to my Hands, I am glad to hear of General Preston's Resolution; but all will yet be nothing, unless Oneale also do his Part: Therefore, make it your Business, and let the Irish look upon it as theirs, to see it done out of Hand; Let no private Animosities, or particular Interest or Design, divert Oneale from the Work, nay, nor delay him; for if this Moment of Time be lost, it will be for ever irremediable: Therefore do you, and let the Council lay all their Strength to perswade him to it; if he refuse, the Ruin and Desolation of Ireland, and his Nation will be his Guilt. This is the Place where the Parliament will lay the Ground of the War, and it will prove an irresistible Torrent, to drown the Kingdom without Remedy, unless they be weeded out now presently. If these Garrisons were taken in, and the Irish Armies lodged in these Quarters, the Parliament would soon be starved, and reduced to Nothing that Way, if neither the Peace took, nor Dublin were taken. These Parliament Ambassadors have already sent into Denmark for 40000 Barrels of

Rye, and intend to block the Irish Harbours out of Hand, to prevent all Supply of Ammunition from them: They may here perceive how great a Storm hangs over them; yet, if they will but engage their two Armies together in the Work, and resolve secondly, and heartily to embrace the Means, with its Appendances; and if they will send a full, and unquestionable Pass speedily, all will yet do well; that otherwise, any of that trifling will make fall to Nothing. Be not startled at any Thing you shall hear of the Lord Lieutenant, who hath given them the Power of the Army, and keeps the Sword and Castle for five weeks; in which Time and less, all must be done that will be, with and by the Irish. I rest, Yours, &c. The inclosed is for General Preston; let me hear what you have done, and hope from Oneale. Leslip Jun. 20th, 1647.

The next Day after my Receipt of his Letter, arrives the Writer himself, and shews me a Letter of Credit from my Lord Digby, written in Limons, not to be read untill it was warm, in these Words; Least outward Appearance should beget Distrust, I have thought fit to send this Bearer unto you, to acquaint you at large with the Grounds of every Thing; I pray you give him full Credit, from your affectionate Servant, George Digby, 21st of June, 1647. He made a long Narration to me, which I thought fit, in a Business of so great Concernment, to make him set down in Writing; which he did under his own Hand, and is as followeth, Word for Word.

"That the Commissioners being landed before any Return to the Propositions came, and possess'd of Dublin, and all other Garrisons, with Master Powers, they having Store of money, and the Marquis of Ormond none at all, with which to feed the Soldier; and lastly, having brought him a full Performance of all Conditions, even of those, whereon he did most ground the Hope of an Evasion; and now being fiercely press'd to a Surrender on his Part, was resolved to perform his Engagement immediately, and writ so to the Lord Digby; who had in several Letters perswaded his Delay, to see if yet any good might possible be done: But now finding nothing but a

338

personal Interview, and most serious Conference able to hinder the Marquis of Ormond any longer from accomplishing the Work, he notwithstanding the most imminent Hazard of the Attempt, ventured by Night, to steal into Dublin Castle, to prevent the Surrender the next Day intended; where, upon his Arrival, (which procured a very great Disturbance) he wrought so effectually upon the Marquis of Ormond, that he brought him the next Day to declare to the Commissioners (under Pretence of doubting the Authenticalness of their Powers, and of Expectation of the Parliaments solemn Engagements of the Faith of both Houses, for the Security of himself, and all his Party, whether perhaps excepted or not excepted) that unless they would yet give him five Week's Time to hold the Sword and Castle in order to his Satisfaction in these Particulars, he would rather die in the Gate with a Halbred in his Hand, than give it up. In which Resolution the Commissioners finding him positive, at last assented, that if he would surrender into their Hands the Militia forthwith, they would permit him the Sword and Castle, together with any three Companies he should chuse for his Guard for the fore-mentioned Time. This was all that could possibly be done in order to a Suspence, they having already, by Reason of their Money, and overpowering Number, all Things else in their Hands. The Answers to the Propositions intervening, have given good Hopes by the reasonable Face of them, that the Irish may, yet upon Terms, be brought yet to his Majesty's Obedience, and so both serve him, and preserve themselves; of which, whilst the Marquis of Ormond can in Reason cherish a Thought, he will not willingly run on in this extreme Course, which the former Proceedings of the Irish did necessitate him unto; and that so far, that they suffered him to engage almost beyond Recovery, before they did make any Overture of any better Disposition. Now, the only remaining Ways of effecting this are; First, That if in this Time the Distractions in England grow to that height, that the Parliament Party here, may see themselves deprived of Hopes of Supply, and unable to subsist, should court the Marquis of Ormond to continue here, and so both reduce

339

the Power into his Hands, and give him Time to treat and perfect a happy Accomodation. Secondly, That if, in this Time, Monsieur Tallon come back from France, furnished so with Monies and other Things, which the Marquis of Ormond verily expects, he shall soon be able to regain his own old Forces, and ruin theirs, who are far more amenable than his, having most of them served the King in his Armies in England; and so by this Means re-investing himself both in the Military and Civil Government, give both Power and Time to make a Peace. Thirdly, if in this Time, he can work either upon any of the Commissioners, or Chief Commanders of their Forces, and so reduce both them and the Power into his own Hands. Fourthly, And indeed, of all the Rest the most present and certain, if in this Time, the Irish can march into these Quarters so strong and considerable, as to take the Out-Garrisons (of all which the Marquis of Ormond wishes they could possess themselves) and distress Dublin so, as to make the Commissioners desire a Cessation, which the Irish refusing to Assent unto, unless the Marquis of Ormond would take it upon himself the visible Power, and give him Time, according to the Length of the Cessation, more or less, to continue and perfect the desired Union, and re-establish the King's Government: Now in Order to bringing this last Means about, you are desired to let the Council know, the unavoidable Danger that hangs over them, and their Nation, if they lay not immediately aside, all by Ends and private Interests and Animosity, to attend this Business, to make them sensible that the other Forces of Ulster, Munster, and Connaught will only be kept a Foot, by the Parliament to divert and distract their Powers; but that here, in Leinster, they intend to lay the great Foundation of a War; here to keep their grand Army; here to place their Government; and here to erect their Magazines of Ammunition and Victual. You are desired to inform them, how that they have already sent into Denmark for huge Provisions of Corn; how 30000l. per Month, is set aside of Contribution in England for the War of Ireland; how the Parliament intends to endeavour the blocking up of all their Harbours. Hereby you

340

will do well to let them see, that this is the only and last Opportunity, that ever will be offered them to make their own Preservation, by killing the Disease in the Beginning, before it grow too strong; and before, by the Marquis of Ormond's quitting, a Peace with the King become impossible. You will also let them know, how certainly the Parliament is like to grow to an irresistable Strength, if this Occasion be let slip, and how easily they might now distress and destroy them, before great Forces, and those great Provisions they expect, come. It were fit they did know, that supposing their Armies come down considerably strong, how much Master they must needs be of these, who cannot possibly make above 6000 Foot, and 1000 Horse; and what certain Advantages they will be sure to get by taking all the adjacent Garrisons, and possessing the English Quarters: But you are, if possible, to engage them, that they will grant a Cessation whensoever the Marquis of Ormond shall think it necessary; and if a Cessation be demanded by the Parliament, they will not accept it, but by his appearing in it, likewise to oblige them, that without the Marquis of Ormond's Permission (unless by a Siege, or some other Accident, he be reduced unto a Condition, that is not possible to be known) they will make no Attempt upon Dublin; and to prevent the Worst in such a Case, as that he should be necessitated to call them to that Work; or they, seeing an Opportunity, should, contrary to their Ingagement, and his Desire, lay hold of it; that you would, after you have set their Armies forward (which must be done in the first Place) descend to Particulars with them concerning Additionals to the Peace to be made as reasonable as you can, and to engage them under their Hands, that with those Additionals under such Security, they will entertain the Peace, acknowledge the King's Government, and admit the Marquis of Ormond for the King's Lieutenant, whensoever he shall assent unto them, notwithstanding, that in the mean Time, those Holds should come into their Possession.

"It is requisite that you press all that may be possible, to bring Owen Roe, as well as General Preston, to the Work, that with more

Speed and Security it may be performed. If this cannot be effected, that General Preston may, if possible, be made up 10000 **Foot**, and **2000 Horse, or near** unto it; and without Delay, by special Order directed thither, and instructed in all reasonable Things, to follow **the** Advice of the Marquis of Ormond and the Lord Digby. Lastly, a main part of your work must be to create a confidence in them of the Marquis of Ormond and the Lord Digby's good Intentions to **them,** which both of them, and especially the latter, with **so much** personal Hazard hath made appear. Instruct them also to let the Marquis of Ormond and **Lord** Digby see they have a Confidence in them, and assure them it is the best Way to do their Work, and all they wish for will, beyond **Expectation,** be done to their Hands, if with a generous Resignation they will cast themselves and their Business upon them. You must needs procure a full, free and indefinite Pass for the Lord **Digby in** his publick Capacity to come to their Quarters, **with a competent** Number of Attendants, and to embark for France, **or** what Place he please, without **Interruption** under what **Pretence soever.** I need not tell **you how** you are **to** inculcate Secrecy **unto them, nor to** warn you to **give in no Paper** concerning it, with the Marquis of Ormond, or Lord Digby, expresly named in it: If they make Scruple how he can, in Respect of his Hostage, go thro' here with them, you can satisfy them in that Particular, what Way he hath left to **do it.**"

These were the Instructions given me by the Secretary, grounded upon his Letter of Credit from my **Lord** Digby, and indeed **very** contrary to my Expectation, considering the Letters **I had** from his Lordship but three days before, of the 17th, wherein he **made** no Doubt of concluding the Cessation, which also **I** had written to the Council, as also **for** a Pass for him **as** he desir'd; and I do wonder how they should think that I, who had never shewed any Commission from the **Queen, or** Prince, nor was so much as **to** use either **of their** Names, **how or** from whence the Credit should come, that must support me, not only to treat with, but to manage the Council in such **a** Line of Method **as was** given me by these direc-

342

tions, on which I will forbear to comment, my meaning being to write here only Matter of Fact. Well, I shrunk up my Shoulders, and presently departed from Ballisonon towards Kilkenny, whither the Council were now come from Clomell; where, about the 25th of June, I arrived; and the Council not being all come together, it was the 28th, before I could move them, which then I did in all the Particulars before mentioned, of which, after I had spoken, I gave them in a Paper abbreviated as I thought fit; to which, the next Day, they replyed, that General Preston should, within ten Days, be ready to March so strong, as there should be no Need of General Oneale, with other Things, magnifying their own Army, and despising the Parliament Forces. I then, after I had been with several particular Persons, went again to the Council, earnestly importuning Oneale's coming, insisting principally on these two Reasons; first that a Business that so much concerned them, could never be done too surely; that I conceived there was great Danger in the English Horse, though against double their Number. Secondly, that my Lord Lieutenant would never think himself sure enough; for, whensoever he should stir, if he made it not good, no less than his Life would pay for it. But all would not do, so much did their Hatred, for to nothing else can I ascribe it, to the old Irish, over-ballance their Reason. As for the Nuncio, however possibly he might be content the Parliament should rather have those Places, than my Lord of Ormond stay in the Kingdom, which yet I do not aver for a Truth, howbeit, most certainly he was very willing that Oneale should have his Part of the Enterprize; who himself was so desirous (of which I am most certain) as he forbore proceeding on his Design against Sligo, in Expectation to be summoned to that Business, then lying idle in Connaught, with an Army of 10000 Horse and Foot. Indeed I was press'd by some Gentlemen of good Quality in that Country, to write myself to Oneale, they assuring me he would March on my Letter; whether it were so or no I know not, but I thought it not fit to try, nor durst I offend the Council. In this Interim I received a Letter from General Preston as followeth.

343

SIR,

I RECEIVED yours of the 21st, and do expect such a Number of Forces, as I shall go without any great Danger to effect any Thing I take in Hand. I understand General Oneale's Forces are advanced into Connaught, and himself at Athlone; whether he will return or not, is yet unknown to me. My Army is daily mustering, and will, God willing, suddenly be in a Body; if then any Occasion, with Assurance, shall be offered, I shall be ready to answer it, or any other Service that may tend to his Majesty's Advantage, and the Good of this Nation. In the mean time you shall have timely Notice before I move, who am your humble Servant. Camp 21st of June.

And not long after, another written to him by my Lord Digby's Secretary, in which he desires him, after his reading it, to send it to me, it seems for the News sake; for there he tells him, that "the King was come to London, &c. And then, I send you this to rejoice, for I know you love the King, and all that love him, in our Nation. The Commissioners in Dublin sate all Night, admitting no Access unto them." And this in Cypher, "Make haste in your Business, and lose no Time in your March to these Parts, but come as well accoutred as you can. This is the Scene, &c. July the 1st, 1647."

Another of the 3d to me, from the same Hand.

SIR,

I WONDER exceedingly I have not heard from you all this Time, you knowing to how short a Limit we are confined: The Distractions in England are grown to so great a Perfection, that it is believed really the King is in London, and the Parliament dissolving. I beseech you press the Irish to be quick in

244

the whole Business; principally their Advance, and the Pass; at least, let us know speedily the Result of their Councils. My Lord is affectionately yours, and commands it to be signified by your, &c. July the 3d, 1647.

Then another.

SIR,

I RECEIVED just now, yours of the last of June, and thank you for it. The Mutiny the other day at Dublin, may sufficiently let you see the Importance of the Irish Advance into these Parts; for had they been within eight miles of Dublin, ready to march at an hour's Warning, I do not know why much of that we aim at, might not then have been compassed; but I make no question, if they be at that Distance suddenly, nearer than which they must not come yet, unless they mean to unite them all, and make them attempt the Destruction of those, on whom our Hopes depend: Such Opportunities will daily be offered, but I fear the Delays: for a little more Force will make us loose them all, &c. July the 4th, 1647.

About the 13th of July, General Preston sent me this Copy of a Letter he had received from the fore-mentioned Secretary, with another Copy of a Letter to be signed and written by him to my Lord Lieutenant, of which I was to have the Council's Approbation, and had it; being drawn by the said Secretary. Take this first to Preston. "If there was not a Fate of Distruction hung over this Kingdom, it were impossible that your Army could have stayed so long out of these Quarters, into which, if you had briskly advanced, you might infallibly e'er this, have had most of the Garrisons but Dublin, or have forced the Commissioners to have put back all theirs, into the Marquis of Ormond's Hands, and enabled him and others to haue compassed that Good for the Kingdom which they most heartily desire: And yet, if they advance a good Way the next Week, it is probable, that our End may be compassed of preserving this Nation; but I fear I shall find it their Fate, that they must not contribute unto the re-establishing of his Majesty's Authority so much as here; but that on the contrary, when the Affairs of England shall have re-settled my Lord Lieutenant here, without your Help, which is confidently believed before the Time prefix'd for his quitting will be; then your Armies will be ready to March and make War upon him, however that you see Things now omitted here, that might enable us to preserve Ireland from Calamities that threaten it. The Pressures for your Advance are renewed now in the only Minute of Time for you to advantage your selves, and to merit from the King at one Time. The inclosed Draught of a Letter is offered unto you, as very requisite to be sent by you to the Marquis of Ormond. When you are upon your March, you will do well to send the copy of it to   and the Council, that it may be dispersed in Print, soon after you have sent the Letters to Dublin. I pray you also send to   a Copy of this my Letter to you, to peruse privately. The Affairs of England go on well. Your most faithful humble Servant, &c.

"P.S. Lose no Time, I conjure you; will further you in all Things; there can nothing be thought of so advantageous to your Business, nor so plausible to the World, as your sending this Letter when you come, than this, which Preston was, upon his March, to send to my Lord Lieutenant."

(*Enclosed Draught.*)

My LORD,

BEING now upon my March with an Army beyond the Limits of the Confederate Catholick Quarters; I have thought it my Duty to his Majesty, and your Excellency his Lieutenant, to declare unto you, that the Ground of my Advance into these Quarters, is my Understanding that the Power and Command in them is no longer in your Excellency, nor in any deriving Authority from his Majesty, but on the contrary, in the Hands of Parliamentary Rebels, the Supplanters of his Power in the three Kingdoms; that as we think our selves bound, both by Allegiance, in Relation to our Sovereign, by Conscience in Relation to our Religion, and by the Law of Nature for Self-Preservation, to prosecute War against them to the uttermost of our Lives and Fortunes, which by the Grace of God we shall do, renouncing all Treaty or Correspondency with such: So on the other side, I do sincerely profess unto your Excellency that I, and all under my Command, are so sensible of the most unhappy Misunderstanding, since the last Peace, and so passionately desirous, if possible, of redeeming the said Misfortune, that could I be so happy as to receive from your Excellency any Assurance, that yet the Power and Authority from his Majesty remains in you, and that there might be any Hope of our being admitted to his Service upon such Terms, as may be consistent with our Religion, and natural Freedom of Subjects, that I should be so far from proceeding a Step in any Act of Hostility, that on the contrary I shall most gladly embrace any Way of Treaty or Cessation, that may tend to that blessed End (and for which alone we will ever fight) of settling a happy Peace in this Kingdom, in perfect Obedience to his Majesty; which shall be testified to the World by the Actions of your Excellencies most humble Servant, &c."

About the 15th of July, General Preston having sent this Letter by

347

a Trumpet, advanced into the English Quarters with an Army consisting by the Pole, of between 7 and 8000 Foot, and about 1100 Horse; the Foot, as lusty appearing Men, and as well accoutred with Arms and Cloaths, as ever I did see ; and the Horse in Appearance equal to our ordinary Troops in England ; and hearing that the Enemies Horse were advanced to the Nas, a Garrison of theirs some 8 Miles, as I remember, from Dublin, marched towards them; the Enemy drawing out their Horse, which were presently charged by the Irish Horse, and after some Time forced back into the Town ; which the Irish entring with them, they quit, as their Foot had done before, and so retreated towards Dublin, Preston having much ado to restrain his Horse from the Pursuit; who it seems feared their whole Armies being drawn out to second them, his Foot being not yet come up : But it was not so, for the English Horse despising the Irish, had some 4 or 500 of them drawn out from the Rest of their Strength, and had paid dearly for their Bravado, if Preston had not been too wise : However this gave more Wisdom to the English, and more Folly to the Irish ; The First not so confident as before ; the Latter more confident after, than there was Reason. In the mean Time I received this Letter from the Secretary.

SIR,

Had yours of the 8th, the Time prefix'd, for my Lord's Surrender of the Sword and Castle draws so near, that if by fair Means we cannot compass our Ends, we must try it by Force; but to this there is something absolutely necessary ; to wit, that you have a positive Assurance from the Council, that if the Power shall be again recovered into my Lord Lieutenant's Hands, that we shall be sure of a present Cessation for 3 or 4 Months, in which to procure from the King the Powers and Conditions for a Peace; for this, that you have a solemn Engagement under their Hands, we expect to be suddenly certified ; without which, we shall not venture on any Act of Violence, to recover the Power; the Irish

348

are not wise if they stick at any Thing. Let me have your Answer speedily; there is no fresh News out of England; we have Reason to be confident, that by this Time, Things are at a good Issue there. July the 15th.

In the mean Time it seems the Council had Notice by some coming out of Dublin, that my Lord was not Master of the Castle, into which, as those informed, he had admitted some Companies of Parliament Foot; so that when I came to move them about th Assureance demanded in the last Letter from the Secretary; they told me of their Informations; as also, that my Lord had never meant in good Earnest, but that I had been deceived; which, however they seemed to believe I was not willingly; nor meant I to deceive them. Soon after which, they sent me a Paper by the Bishop of Limerick in Answer to those Assurances, and other Things I demanded of them, which what they were, may be collected out of the former Instructions and Letters; which Paper I have lost: But by the Copy of a Letter of mine, the Substance may be guess'd at; my Letter was thus to the Secretary.

SIR,

THE Copy of the Letter I received in yours, is consented unto, and dispatched away. In mine of the 8th, I gave you Reasons for the Council's Delay in returning me Answer to those your Desires, by me proposed to them; as also, that they had now promised me a speedy Resolution, in Order to which, Yesterday my Lord of Limerick gave me a Paper; the Substance of which was, that as they had hasten'd their Army's Advance to those Ends and Purposes desired, all that might be, so was it now well forward on its March, so strong as they doubted not at all, it would be able to do the Work, without the Help of General Oneale; that as for those other Things desired, which were of Substance to the main Business in Hand (and what those Things are, I doubt not but **you** can easily collect) the general **Face of** Affairs had received great Alteration since my Delivery of these last Propositions in two Things, which were not then **known.** The First, that my Lord had not only divested himself of the Power of the Militia, but also, that he was not at all Master of the Castle; **of** which last, they **were** most certainly informed by the Examination **of Divers,** that **they were** lately **come out** of the Castle, and Town of Dublin, tho' they did believe I did not **know** it, when I gave in the Propositions. The Second was, the late Alteration of his Majesty's Condition, whose Orders they did not know, my Lord Lieutenant in this Vacation **of** Time, would not be slack to send for, and being come, would do his best to obey them, what Obligation **soever** of doing, or not doing, this, or that; **in the mean Time they should** put on themselves; and that therefore, it should **be great** Imprudence in them, to oblige themselves to any Thing further than the present Condition of their Affairs required, untill such Time as some Person interested would **appear**; and be likewise, as there should be Cause, obliged. That they had already given great Testimony of their good Desires, and Intentions **to do any** Thing, tending to their Submission **to his** Majesty's Authority, in their Answers given **to my** Propositions; which altho' authorized by no Body that appeared, nor undertaken by me further than *His Verbis:* I would do my **best** Endeavour to bring them **to** pass; **yet** they had in **a** full Council and Congregarion assembled, answered fully **to** every one of them. That howsoever, when it should appear to them, that my Lord was re-invested with his former Power, to which End he should command the Assistance **of their Army** when he pleased, **they** would be ready to do any Thing, **in Order to the making good of** those Answers, they had given to my first Propositions. Lastly, concerning the desired Pass for my Lord Digby, as they **had** much Expectation of the good Offices his Lordship might do in these Businesses, being in a Place so near my Lord Lieutenant, **so were** they loth to give him any Encouragement **to come** away, **before** they might see what Issue

350

Things would have, which had been the true Reason of delaying it so long. But if that, by any Accident, he should be in the mean Time occasioned to come into their Quarters, he should not doubt of finding Safety and Protection there, for him and his, and Permission to go to Sea, when and whither he would. Kilkenny, July 18th.

This Answer of the Council was not without Grounds; nor their Information of Things in the Castle of Dublin false, though as then I would not believe it: But within 3 or 4 Days I was put out of my Doubt by this Letter from my Lord Digby, which should have come 3 Days sooner.

SIR,

Having received certain Information of the State of Affairs in England, from one employed thither by me, who hath had Access to the King himself; and finding Things there, tending to sudden and entire Settlement, but so much to the King's Advantage as was hoped: And the Discovery to the Parliament Commissioners out of the Irish Quarters of all Things formerly in Transaction between us; I hold it absolutely necessary that I should confer with you, to let you see the true State of every Thing, and to new mould our Business, that no Accident may raise a Suspicion of your not being dealt sincerely with: You are conjured to hasten hither to Leslip, in which there cannot be the least Danger for you, the Parliament Army lying as it doth, or advancing nearer as it intends this Day. Leslip, July 19th, 1647.

That Day I received this Letter, being the 23d, I parted from Kilkenny, and the next arrived to my Lord Digby, from whom I had this: "That the Commissioners having Notice, from I know not whom, of our Intelligence, had seized Colonel Barie, and my Lord Taffe in the Town, and had gone presently to my Lord in the

Castle, letting him know their Suspicion, demanding Assurance by Permission of some Companies of their Soldiers to enter the Castle, which my Lord had accorded to them, resolved now to proceed in his Agreement with the Parliament. And the 28th of July, the Day prefix'd, to deliver the Sword and Castle into their Power; that yet for all this I could not be troubled, for he had notwithstanding my Lord's Departure, great Hopes nevertheless of doing the Business." I replied, "That I could not chuse but be troubled, yet must be contented whether I would or not; that I was of his Opinion, there was yet much Good to be done, of which I was glad his Lordship did not Despair; but yet, that would now prove difficult, which before had been easy. From Leslip I went to Preston's Army, who after taking the Nas, leaving there a Garrison, marched to Minouth, a Castle of my Lord of Kildare's, I think not above 4 or 5 Miles from Dublin; and after 2 or 3 Days, took that by Assault; there likewise leaving some Men, he went and sate down before Trim: where I found him much troubled at my Lord of Ormond's Surrender, and very little confident of any Thing I could say to him, though I informed him of what Numbers about Dublin consisted; that they intended to march to him, so soon as the Scots were come to them, whom they expected every Day, being 2000 Horse and Foot; that I did yet hope we should find some Means or other to introduce the King's Authority amongst them on Conditions to their liking." He answered, "He should be very glad of it, and that there was nothing he and that Army could do should be wanting." I told him likewise, "That my Lord Digby would be accountable for Leslip, which he had forborn to take in, upon my Lord's undertaking that Charge." From thence I went with Monsieur Monerie the French Agent, who was likewise there, to a Knight's House, who was Brother in law to my Lord Lieutenant, whose Name I cannot remember, Ten Miles off, where, by Appointment, we were to meet my Lord Digby, and my Lord Taffe, who both accordingly came thither. The next Day my Lord Digby desired me to return to the Army, and if it might be, to procure a meeting between the Bishop of Ferne, with Mr. Plunkett, then Commissioners from the Council with the Army, and my Lord Digby and my self, about laying a new Foundation of our Business; I found them very incredulous and backward; yet they agreed, upon my Importunity, to meet the next Day at a certain Place, whither my Lord Digby, my Lord Taffe, and I, were no sooner come, but we had Notice that Jones was drawn out of Dublin with his Army marching behind us; and soon after a Note from the two Commissioners, that they could not come for the said Reason. So we parted, my Lord Digby to Leslip, my Lord Taffe and I towards Kilkenny, all of us expecting the Event of that Battel, which all of us feared was towards; I say feared, for we had done our endeavour to disswade Preston from fighting, both my Lord Taffe and I alledging, the Danger of the English Horse, as also the Coming up of the Scots the Night before. But my Lord of Ormond's Action had rendred Preston and the rest so distrustful, as they believed every Thing the less, because it came from any they conceived to have been of the Party; but it had been better for them they had believed; for within five Days after Preston was Overthrown, and 4000 Men killed on the Place, and almost all his Commanders Prisoners, he himself escaping very hardly: and with the Ruin of this Army were all my Hopes, as to the doing any further good in Ireland, likewise ruined; for that I resolved, although I had received no new Order from the Queen, with next Conveniency to depart for France. But my Lord Digby, for the whom I had, notwithstanding all this, procured a Pass to come to Kilkenny, though with much ado, desired me not to stir untill I heard from him out of France; alledging that there was no Body but my self left to do the King's Business there, whatever Resolution should be taken. I told my Lord, I would not stay at any Desire, but if he would Command me, I would Obey, being so tied by my Instructions. He did so, with promise to recommend my good Endeavours to the Queen and Prince, and that I should soon hear from him, and so we parted, he to Sea, and I, not long after, to Galloway, where then my Lord Clanriccard was, who invited me so kindly, as from that Time, which might be about the End of August,

I never left him until March, that I set Sail to France. At my Lord Clanriccard's, about the Beginning of November, I received a Command from the Queen for my Return, whose Date was more than three Months old, which I did not presently obey, expecting to hear from my Lord Digby, which I did about February, to this purpose: "That he did see no farther Occasion for my Stay in Ireland, and that I might come when I pleas'd." And about the latter end of March following, in the soonest Passage from Galloway I could find, in Company of my Lord of Worcester and my Lady, we set Sail, arriving at Havre de Grace in five Days.

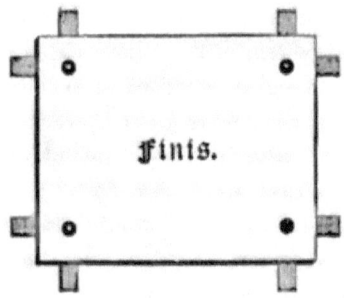

Finis.

"Inter Folia Fructus."

THE CHARACTER

OF A

MODERN WHIG,

OR

An Alamode True Loyal Protestant.

(1681.)

"HISTORY IS BUT THE UNROLLED SCROLL OF PROPHECY."
—JAMES A. GARFIELD.

PRIVATELY PRINTED
FOR THE CLARENDON HISTORICAL SOCIETY.

1886.

This edition is limited to 120 *large paper, and* 400 *small paper copies,
for Subscribers only.*

The Character of a Modern Whig,

OR

AN ALAMODE TRUE LOYAL PROTESTANT.

HE is a Certain Insect bred in the Corruption of the late Rebellion, and is (for the most part) a Traytor *Ex traduce*.

At his Majesties happy Restauration he lay stupified without Sense or Motion, but began by little and little to crawl with new life in the warmth of the Act of Oblivion, and afterwards wantonly basked himself in the Rays of Royal Indulgence and Toleration, till the old Poisonous Ferment began to work and float afresh, and furnished him with Vigour, and Insolence sufficient to hiss Venom in the Sacred Face of his Great and Gracious Preserver. And though he be sufficiently Conscious of the black Ingratitude, and repeated Provocations, with which he hath all-along abused and affronted the King's God-like Patience and Forbearance, yet the Fool hath had the Impudence to flatter himself with *Agag*, and say, *Surely the bitterness of Death is past;* little thinking that he is still reserved to be hewed in pieces before the Lord.

357

His Aspect is generally Meagre and Malicious, as representing on the one side the Puritanical Fool, on the other the Political Knave. His Profession (I cannot call it Religion) is of the *Geneva*-Stamp; not that his Conscience, or Prudence ever engaged him in a judicious Inquest, or sober Tryal of this or any other; or that his Wit and Judgment were ever capable Rationally to discern and choose, (for in Speculations of this kind, Nature and his Education have removed him but one degree from an Idiot) but his Father begetting him in the hot Zeal of this Persuasion, and his Dam all that while fixing her teeming Fancy with Adulterous lust on their able Holder-forth, he was moulded a strong *Presbyterian* in the very Womb, and so proves a rank Phanatick by the Pure force of Imagination and Extract: Nor hath he himself been since wanting to improve these natural Dispositions, and Exalt the Rebellious Genius he derived from his Sire and Dam; for observing (or rather being told) that the *Presbyterian* Principles stood in the greatest Opposition to the Established Government, he hath with irreversible Obstinancy Espoused the good Old Cause, and with the Sacred Solemnity of a Sacramental Vow hath devoted himself, Life, and Fortune, to the utter Extirpation of Prelacy, and the Royal Race of the *Stuarts*.

To effect all which, and that he may the more safely, and indiscernibly accomplish his prefidious Designs, he lies perdue in the unsuspected Covert of a *Protestant;* and though that word for ought he knows of the rise and reason of it, may be *Hebrew* for a Baboon, yet he assumes and affects it upon all occasions, because he fancies that it denotes, and signifies distinction and opposition; and he loves all things, and terms of Separation and Contradiction at his very heart. But farther observing that many wise and honest men have plainly discover'd that this Religion of his, and as he manages it, proves in the consequence of Affairs no better than an Antimonarchick-Heresie, therefore the better to supply all its defects, and answer all objections against it, he Palliates its apparent Falshood and Treachery with the specious Epithets of Truth and Loyalty, and

The Character of a Modern Whig.

with unparallel'd Impudence he once for all roundly stiles himself, a true Loyal *Protestant*. He hath been hatching Rebellion, and working under-ground the Subversion of Church and State for these many years past, but hath bestir'd himself with all imaginable Application since the breaking out of the horrid *Popish*-Plot; as imagining that he might with more Success and Safety spring his own Mines (which he had carried on to the very Foundations of the Government) at a time when we were wholly taken up in detecting the Trains and Treacheries of the *Romish* Pioneers: And this hath afore-time in all Ages since the Reformation been his Usage, then more especially to disturb and divert his Governours with Petitions, Grievances, Toleration, Comprehension, and a thousand Tricks and Artifices, when he hath seen their Endeavours and Intentions bent and busied another way, and engaged in Rescuing us from the Imminent Dangers of our *Popish* Adversaries.

The Plot, Party, and Arbitrary Government is his dayly Out-cry, the Common place and burden of his Seditious noise and clamour, and the Pretences of his impertinent Fears and Jealousies; whatever his Factious humour dislikes is *Popish*, and where the Case will not admit of a positive direct Plea, then *Popishly* affected doth the business; and any thing that bridles and restrains his Licentious Insolence, and Seditious Practices is Arbitrary, and Tyrannical. But for all the loud Hue and Cry he makes after the Plot, himself hath proved the chiefest hinderer of its full and home discovery, so that 'tis now almost quite spent and lost in running down a Channel of almost three years distance from its first Spring and Fountain. He plainly foresaw that 'twould thwart and prevent his Designs, if it had forthwith been Traced to the Fountain-head, and there stopt and ended presently (as it might very easily have been) when we were at the near distance of 78, and 79; he rather Chose to Wire-draw it at length with Tricks and Finesses, as having many Stages of devices that were to run parallel with it, and many Plots and Stratagems of his own that he cou'd never Accomplish without this Pretence and

Exclamation, that, there hath been, and is still a horrid *Popish* Plot, *&c.* That, is Still, doth his business.

And thus he hath kept the Plot at Bay for these three years to amuse and divert us, whilst all the while he is in the hot and eager Pursuit of other Game.

He endeavours to Poison the people, and Scare the Nation into Rebellion by Libelling the best King and Government in the world; insinuating malicious and groundless Suggestions of imminent *Popery* and Tyranny, by horrid Stories of *Smithfield* Flames, *Irish* Massacres, *&c.* by the Villanous Prints of *Carr, Curtiss*, and a whole Pack of scurrilous Scoundrels, and by a Thousand Artifices dayly hammer'd out on the Forge of *Faction* by Republican Operators in their respective Cabals: In a word he hath done all he can to reduce the State of these Kingdoms to present Blood-shed and Desolation, hoping thereby to make his own Markets, purchase his Revenges, and glut his Malice, or at least hide his abominable Head (due long since to Publick Justice) in the general Confusion. Again, our true Loyal *Protestant* to shew how highly he Values his Sovereigns Content and Quiet, is frequently tormenting him with his impertinent Petitions, and that about things as much beyond the reach and judgment, as they are beside the duty and proper business of the Sawcy Petitioner; especially since he knows how that his Majesty hath Proclaimed not an Aversion only, but a general Prohibition to such Dangerous and Seditious Muster-Rolls, and Factious Pragmatical intermedlings: But his greatest Artifice and the Court Bugbear as he thinks, is the perpetually making the King's Ears ring with Clamours about the Succession; so that instead of a Joyful and Dutiful Exclamation of *Vive le Roy*, he is dayly Saluting him with a *Memento mori:* This was so harsh and grating to Queen *Elizabeth*, that she returned a sharp *Reprimende* to such as motion'd it, telling them besides, That it was to dig her Grave before she was Dead. Our Modern *Whig*, I say, would lay these Kingdoms in

Blood and present Desolation, the better forsooth to prevent the imaginary Evils of a (pretended) *Popish* Successor, and such *Chimæras* as his factious Fancy only hath Conceived in the Womb of Futurity and bare Possibility. His tender Conscience can easily dispense with Disinheriting a Royal Prince of his undoubted Right to three Crowns, upon a supposition only of being of an Opinion different from himself; and yet nothing can serve his own turn, but Repealing Acts of Parliament to indemnifie his Scismatical Separation, and that he may neglect the Service of God, and break the Laws of the Land with absolute Impunity: This he prettily Stiles, Uniting his Majesties *Protestant* Subjects, though in effect and intent 'tis no better than admitting the *Trojan* Horse (a Magazine of mischiefs) within the Walls, and we should quickly find that a *Ruit alto a Calmine* would be the Fatal Consequence in our Church. He knows well enough that he hath Blasphemed his *R. H.* beyond all hopes of Pardon, and therefore his *All* is at Stake, there is now no Retreat, his Case is desperate, and he must now push it home in his own Defence.

This is our True *Protestants* Loyal Behaviour towards the Children of that Royal Father who was so lately Murdered by his Faction whereas if he had but the least Grain of his so much boasted Loyalty, or indeed of Christianity, he would strive to Expiate that loud-Crying-Guilt, and shew his deep aborrence of that Fact, by paying strict Allegiance to the present Possessor of the Throne, though he were the worst of Tyrants, and by not opposing his *R. H.* the rightful Successor, though he were a profest *Mahometan*.

He hath along Danced to the *Jesuits* Pipe, and steer'd by his Compass we know, but of late he hath openly profest, and avowed such Doctrines as these: That 'tis lawful to take any Oath whatsoever with a Mental *Salvo* for the sake of the good Old Cause. That no Faith is to be kept with the *Tory-Party*. That the selfsame Evidence in one Case is Truth and very Oracle, in another Perjury, and Subornation; and, that Truth, and Justice may *Salvâ Conscientiâ* be nipt in the bud by *Ignoramus*, when *Billa Vera* wou'd be in an ill President, prove prejudicial to the Cause, and of bad Consequence when his nearer and dearer Friends turn comes to be Concerned, &c.

To Conclude, a Modern *Whig* is the very Spawn of *Antichrist*, the Counterpart to *Popery*, the *Jesuits* Burn-Crack, the Shame of the Reformation, and the Scandal of Christianity.

"Inter Folia Fructus."

A LETTER

FROM

His Excellencie the Lord General Monck,

AND THE OFFICERS UNDER HIS COMMAND,

TO THE

PARLIAMENT

IN THE NAME OF THEMSELVES AND
THE SOULDIERS UNDER THEM.

1659.

"HISTORY IS BUT THE UNROLLED SCROLL OF PROPHECY."
—JAMES A. GARFIELD

PRIVATELY PRINTED
FOR THE CLARENDON HISTORICAL SOCIETY.

1886.

This edition is limited to 120 large paper, and 400 small paper copies, for Subscribers only.

A
LETTER
From His
EXCELLENCIE
THE
LORD GENERAL MONCK,

And the Officers under his Command,

TO THE

In the Name of Themselves and the Souldiers under Them.

LONDON:
Printed by John Macock. 1660.

A Letter of His Excellency and his Officers, &c.

Mr. Speaker,

E cannot but with thankfulness acknowledge the wonderful Goodness of God to you, in your Return to the Discharge of your remaining Trust; and to ourselves, and your Forces under our Commands, (after some difficulties) in bringing of us, by a tedious March, in such safety to this place, to wait upon you in asserting the Freedoms of our Native Country: and being here, (as we have to our utmost Hazard and Power been instrumental in your Return, so) we shall be still ready to pursue your Commands so far as possibly we may. To evidence which, we have observed and executed your late Orders in relation to the Chains, Posts, and Gates of the City; which was something grievous to Us, and to the Officers and Souldiers under our Commands; and that because we do not remember any such thing was acted upon this City in all these Wars; and we fear that many sober people are much grieved at it, and apprehend further force to be offered to them, while they seem principally to desire the speedy filling up of the House, which you have declared for, as well as we have express'd our just desires of; and are apt to doubt, lest, what we have done, may be so far from answering the expected end, as

that it may encrease the discomposure of mens spirits in the Nation. Upon this occasion, it comes fresh into our minds, that when by the treachery of some Officers of the Army you were interrupted, we declared to the world, That *the Ground of our undertaking was not onely your return to your Trust*, but also, *the Vindication of the Liberties of the People, and the Preservation of the Rights of our Country, the Protection and encouragement of the Godly and Faithful therein, as the establishment of the Peace of these Nations*. Which Declarations made before the Lord, Angels and Men, in the day of our Extremity, we (as we expect the blessing of the Lord upon our future Undertakings) cannot but still own, and stand by.

We finde that the asserting of the just Liberties of the People, is that which the generality of the Nation is much in expectation of; and that many sober people (together with our selves) are under fears lest this great price that God hath put into your and our hands, (as your Servants) should not be improved, but that we shall run in Confusion again. Therefore we humbly crave leave to present before you, some Grounds of our Fears: We are affraid that the late wonderful and unparallell'd Deliverance, is not so publickly and solemnly acknowledged as it might be, that the Lord (who wrought so stupendiously) may have the Glory of all: We are troubled that some as yet do sit in the House, who are impeached of Treason: We cannot but observe that divers Members of your House, (who contrary to their Trust, acted in that Illegal and Tyrannical Committee of Safety) are not actually disabled from sitting there: notwithstanding Colonel *Lambert* hath onely the Vote of Indemnity to secure him from as High Crimes as have been committed in this Nation, and is not obedient to your Orders, yet he seemeth to be winked at. We understand that Sir *Henry Vane* upon bare pretence is permitted to stay about the City, to the great Dissatisfaction of your best Friends; that there are dangerous Consultations, and that of those who had a chief hand in your late Interruption, and the hazarding of the whole Nations, contrary to our Expectation. VVe find continued in the Army some Persons of dangerous Principles, and such who were active enough in the late Defection. Though we are far from wishing the ruine of any, yet we could desire that your signal Indulgence to late Notorious Offenders, did meet with that Candid Reception from them as to be so much the more ingenious in their professed Repentance: but we observe that many of them do seek to justifie themselves, and are not without their Agents in print to palliate their foul enormities; which maketh us yet to suspect that we are in some danger of returning into the late distempers that You and the Nation are but newly delivered from.

We are not ignorant, that there are those who lately struck at the Root of *English Parliaments* in Practise and Design, thereby have inflamed the Nation, and given great advantage to the Common Enemy, yet they are not without a strange confidence to precipitate men into a belief, that they are the only Persons against the One, and for the Other. With grief of heart we do remember and would lament over the too palpable Breach of Engagements in this Nation; Therefore we should think it a duty rather to mourn over the same, than to promote any new Oath to be taken at this time: Yet we perceive that there is a design to provoke the Parliament to enforce an Oath upon the Nation, and do take notice, that amongst others, there are some who are most forward to promote the said design, who have made the least (if any) Conscience in keeping Engagements already taken. Here we must not silence our deep resentment of a bold Petition, and of dangerous consequence, which was lately presented to You, the consequence whereof (if You should an answer their desires) would be to exclude many of the most conscientious and sober sort of men from serving under You in Civil and Military Imployments, who have and would prove themselves most faithful; and a door would be opened in design to retrive the Interest of those who have (by the just Hand of our Gracious God) made themselves so apparently obnoxious. Moreover (which is not the least part of the Venome of that Petition) we clearly see the same Spirit, which of late would have **pull'd away the by-you-declared-just Maintenance from Ministers, would now** provoke You by an **Oath to** endanger the forcing away of many of the most Godly **from their** maintenance. In urging our fears from the **premises** that concerns some of different principles from us, we would not be thought to (as we do not) design any thing that may incur the censure **of** unjust rigidity. We freely profess our desires, that tenderness of Conscience may have its full just liberty, but we cannot in judgement, accompt that tenderness of Conscience which will not scruple at **treachery it self, or any** Unrighteousness to carry on corrupt Designs.

Having presented You with our fears, we shall adde our Resolution, That by the help of God we shall stand by You in the pursuance of **what we have** declared for; And therefore do make this humble Request to You: We could desire, That whilst **You** sit, Your utmost endeavours may be **to** manifest your affectionate desires **for** the Publique Good of these **Nations;** Our further desire **is, That those** Regiments under your consideration (whose Officers are **not) may be** speedily **pass'd.** And in regard we find that the Grand **Cause of the** present Heats and Dis-satisfactions in the Nation **is,** because they **are not fully Represented** in Parliament, and seeing **no other** probable Expedient whereby **to** keep the **Nation in peace,** then by filling up your Number; We must therefore **make this our** main desire, upon which **we cannot** but insist, that you would proceed to Issue forth Writts in Order to Elections: **For the** better effecting whereof we **entreat, That You** would conclude upon due and full Qualifications, that not only those **who have** been actually in Arms against the Parliament **may** be excluded, but also such who in the late **Wars** betwixt King and Parliament have declared their dis-affection to **the** Parliament: And because the distracted condition of this Nation is at **this** hour so evident and pressing, we are constrained for the just maintenance of Your Authority and the satisfaction of all true English Men, earnestly to desire, That all **the** Writts may be Issued forth by Friday next, returnable at the usual and legal time; For we think it convenient to acquaint you, that to pacifie the minds of this Great City, in the prosecution of your late Commands, the Chief of Us did give an assurance thereof.

And we must not forget to remember you, that the time hastens wherein you have declared your intended Dissolution; which the People and our selves desire you would be punctual in. Hereby the Suspition of your Perpetuation will be taken away, and the People will have assurance that they shall have a Succession of Parliaments of their own Election; which is the undoubted Right of the English Nation: You have promised and declared no less: Both the People and your Armies do live in the Hope and Expectation of it. That we may the better wait, for your full and free Concurrence to these just Desires on the Nations behalf, upon Mature Deliberation, we have thought it our duty as to continue the usual Guards for the safety of your sitting, so for the present to draw the rest of the Forces under our Command into the City, that we may have the better opportunity to compose spirits and beget a good understanding in that great City, formerly renowned for their resolute adhering to Parliamentary Authority, and we hope that the same spirit will be found still to breath amongst the best, most considerable, and interested persons there. This Action of ours, as we hope it will (through the blessing of God) be of good use for the present peace, and future settlement of these Nations. These are our thoughts which we communicate to you, in the Names of our selves, and the Officers and Souldiers under our Commands,

We are,

Your Honors most humble Servants,

White-hal
Feb. 11. 1659.

George Monck.

Tho. Sanders. Tho. Read.
Leon. Litcot. Ra. Knight.
Jo. Clobery. Dan. Redman.
Jo. Hublethorne.
} Colonels.

Ethelbert Morgan, Lievt. Coll.

Nathaniel Barton, Major.

Tho. Johnson.
Jer. Smith.
Tho. **Pryme.**
Fran. Nichols.
Peter Banister.
} Majors.

The End.

EXPLANATORY NOTES

OF

A PACK OF

Cavalier Playing Cards

TEMP. CHARLES II.

FORMING

A COMPLETE POLITICAL SATIRE

OF

THE COMMONWEALTH.

BY

EDMUND GOLDSMID, F.R.H.S.,

F.S.A. (Scot).

Edinburgh:
E. & G. GOLDSMID.
1886.

Introduction.

THROUGH the courtesy of Lord Nelson, the very curious Pack of Cards here presented in *facsimile* was placed at the disposal of the AUNGERVYLE SOCIETY OF EDINBURGH. The Committee of this Society were very anxious to reproduce these extremely quaint memorials of a by-gone age, but on enquiry it was found that the cost of re-engraving the fifty-two cards on copper, the only really satisfactory method, would be far beyond the means of a Society then barely numbering 120 members. Being Honorary Secretary both the Aungervyle and Clarendon Historical Societies, I suggested that the work should be undertaken at the joint expense of the two Societies. This was rather outside the plans of the Clarendon, but the Committee at length agreed to provide a portion of the necessary funds on condition that after the fifty-two cards had been re-produced in thirteen plates, accompanied by a small explanatory pamphlet, a second series of the Cards, the precise *fac-simile* of the originals, should be presented to each member of the two Societies. There still remained, however, a considerable sum to be raised. I thereupon proposed, after satisfying the above conditions, to purchase the plates from the Societies. These are now in my possession. The work, executed by the firm of Murdoch and Son, of this City, is perfect in every detail, and heavy though the cost has been, I feel sure that in this case at any rate, the object aimed at has been fully attained. Not a line, not a stroke of the original, but appears in exact counterpart in the reprint.

INTRODUCTION.

Lord Nelson, unfortunately, had lost, or never had in his possession, two Cards, the ace and three of hearts. After much trouble, these have been supplied from another source, and, with the exception that the figures of Cromwell and Fairfax in the latter are on a somewhat smaller scale than those on the threes of the other suits, it would be difficult to suspect that they did not belong to the original pack.

In the following notes, I have merely attempted to explain the allusions contained in the Cards. A few however remain riddles to me.

EDMUND GOLDSMID.

EDINBURGH, 12*th October* 1885.

A PACK OF CAVALIER PLAYING CARDS.

(Circa 1660.)

◆◆◆◆◆

1. Ace of Hearts.

Cromwell, Ireton and Hudson all in y^e same boate.

In 1650, Cromwell was named Commander-in-Chief in Ireland; Ireton, his son-in-law, his deputy; and Hewson or Huson (here misprinted Hudson) governor of Dublin. In the plate they are sailing away from the sun of loyalty towards the night of treason. The portrait of Cromwell at the stern is not to be mistaken. Next to him is Hewson distinguished from Ireton by his older features.

2. Ace of Clubs.

A Free State or a Toleration for all sorts of Villany.

In the *Mystery of the Good Old Cause** (London 1660) a Royalist attack on the leading members of the Long Parliament, the author says of the Roundheads, "Their pretences were no doubt the most specious and plausible that could be imagined, ... but, alas! never were these things more pretended to, and less in reality

---

* Reprinted by the Aungervyle Society. Second Series.

designed; greatness, wealth and command were the inducements of the most hypocritical persons in the world to profane the name of God . . . . to murder many innocent persons . . . . to ruin many noble families, etc., ... but let destruction be the reward of our destroyers, let the prey be torn out of their teeth, let the blood they have shed fall upon their own heads, and let their names be detested and infamous to all posterity!"

3. Ace of Spades.

Bradshaw, the jaylor and y^e *hangman, keepers of the liberty of England.*

Bradshaw was appointed president of the High Court of Justice in 1648, a year "of reproach and infamy above all years which had passed before it; a year of the highest dissimulation and hypocrisy, of the deepest villany and most bloody treasons, that any nation was ever cursed with or under: a year, in which the memory of all transactions ought to be erased from all records, lest, by the success of it, atheism, infidelity and rebellion, should be propagated in the world." (*Clarendon's History of the Rebellion*, vol. iii. p. 154, Oxford 1726, folio). He was born in 1586, died in 1659, and his body exhumed and hung in chains at the Restoration. He was a cousin of Milton, who has written a Eulogy of him in his *Second Defense of the People of England*.

4. Ace of Diamonds.

The High Court of Justice or Oliver's Slaughter-House.

"The charge and accusation, upon which they resolved to proceed against the King, being thus settled and agreed upon, they began to consider in what manner and form to proceed, that there might be some appearance of justice. . . . A new form they did erect never before heard of. They constituted and erected a Court that should be called the High Court of Justice. The number of the Judges named was about an hundred and fifty . . . . Bradshaw . . . . was named president . . . . and with great humility accepted the office, which he administered with all the pride, impudence, and superciliousness imaginable."—(*Clarendon's History of the Rebellion*, vol. iii. p. 138-139).

5. II of Hearts.

Onsley. Father and Sonne.

This is evidently a misprint for Onslow. Sir Richard Onslow, Kt., "of the old stamp, a gentleman of Surrey, of good parts and considerable revenue," successfully weathered the tempests of the period. He was commander at the siege of Basing House, was driven from the House of Commons by Pride's Purge, and was afterwards at the head of a Surrey regiment at Worcester. He spoke strongly in favour of Cromwell's becoming king. Later he became a member of the Convention Parliament which restored Charles II..

6. II of Clubs.

Lenthall. Father and Sonn.

William Lenthall, of Lincoln's Inn, a Counsellor at Law, and Speaker of the House of Commons. "Oliver (Cromwell) once made a spunge of him, and squeezed him out of £15,000. Who turning him and his tribe out of doors, he veered about to save himself and his great offices; and he that had been so long bell-weather in the Commons House, was thought, for his compliance and his money, to deserve to be one of the herd of Lords in the Other House," (*Mystery of the Good Old Cause*.) John Lenthall, son of the speaker, was knighted by Oliver Cromwell, made a Colonel of foot, and governor of Windsor Castle.

7. II of Spades.
Parry.   Father and Sonne.

Query, Sir George Parry, one of the Commissioners for Dorsetshire, who with those of Somerset and Cornwall, met Prince Rupert at Bridgewater shortly before the Battle of Naseby?—(*Clarendon's History of the Rebellion*, vol. ii. p. 393).

8. II of Diamonds.
Vane.   Father and Sonne.

"Sir Henry Vane was of very ordinary parts by Nature, and had not cultivated them at all by art, for he was illiterate. But being of a stirring and boisterous disposition, very industrious and very bold, he still wrought himself into some employment. . . . . . His malice to the Earl of Strafford transported him to all imaginable thoughts of revenge, ... and that disposed him to sacrifice his honour and faith and his Master's interest, that he might ruin the Earl, and was buried himself in the same ruin; for which, being justly chastised by the King and being turned out of his service, he was left to his own despair. . . . . He grew into the hatred and contempt of those who had made most use of him; and dyed in universal reproach, and not more contemn'd by any of his enemies than by his own son; who had been his principal conductor to destruction."—(*Clarendon's History of the Rebellion*, vol. ii., p. 132).

Sir Harry Vane, the younger, "was a man of extraordinary parts. . . . . He was chosen to cozen a whole nation which was thought to excel in craft and cunning,* which he did with notable pregnancy and dexterity."—(*Clarendon's History of the Rebellion*, vol. ii., p. 233). "He totally ousted Sir William Russel. He was a discontent during all Oliver's and Richard's government. He is, no doubt, a man of much religion, and would have become one of the rulers in Israel, if the intended match between his son and Lambert's daughter had not been spoiled by the restitution of the Rump."—(*Mystery of the Good Old Cause.*)

---
* The Scots.

9. III of Hearts.

"*Cromwell pypeth unto Fairfax.*"

Cromwell is here represented playing the pipe and tabor to Fairfax, who is performing a Morris dance. This dance was brought to England in the reign of Edward III., it is said by John of Gaunt. It was originally a military dance, in which bells were jingled, and swords clashed. The word *Morris* is a corruption of *Moorish*. In ancient times it used to be danced by five men and a boy, but in the reign of Elizabeth, we have an instance of Kempe, one of Shakespeare's colleagues at the Globe Theatre, having danced alone all the way from London to Norwich.—(*Kemp's nine daies wonder*, reprinted in Goldsmid's *Collectanea Adamantæa*, No. 29). Thomas, Lord Fairfax, warmly espoused the cause of the Parliament when the rupture with the King took place. He was, however, opposed to the execution of the King, and became a warm advocate of the Restoration. He died in 1671.

10. III of Clubs.

"*Bulstrod and Whitlock present to Oliver the instrument of Government.*"

On the 26th of June, 1657, the ceremony of conferring the protectorate on Cromwell took place. "After a short speech, ... Withrington, the Speaker, with the Earl of Warwick and Whitlock, vested him with a rich purple velvet robe lined with ermines; . . . . then the Speaker presented him with a fair Bible of the largest edition, richly bound; then he, in the name of all the people, girded a sword about him; and lastly, presented him with a sceptre of gold, which he put in his hand, and made him a large discourse of those emblems of government and authority. Upon the close of which, there being little wanting to a perfect formal Coronation but a crown and an Archbishop, he took his oath, administered to him by the Speaker.—(*Clarendon's History of the Rebellion*, Vol. III., page 343.) Bulstrode and Whitlock spoken of as two men on the Card, are one and the same. "Bulstrode Whitlocke, ... before the troubles was an intimate friend to Sir Richard Lane, who, going to Oxford, entrusted him with his chambers in the Temple; of which, with all the goods and an excellent library, he hath kept possession ever since; and would not own that ever he knew such a man, when Sir Richard's son was brought to wait upon him in his greatness .... Under Dick he was made Commissioner of the Seal; and, he being discarded, wheeled about and worshipped the Rump. . . . He hath a good fleece, and heir to Lilly the Astrologer."—(*Mystery of the Good Old Cause*).

11. III of Spades.

"*H. Martin defends Ralph, who design'd to kill the King.*"

"Henry Martin, colonel of a regiment of horse and a regiment of whores. He had given him £3000 at one time, to put him upon the Holy Sisters, and take off from the Levellers. He had the reputation of a precious saint from his youth, in reference to all kinds of debauchery, uncleanness, and fraud, having sold his estate three times over."—(*Mystery of the Good Old Cause*).

12. III of Diamonds.

"*Simonias sland'ring ye High Priest to get his place.*"

One of the riddles I have spoken of in the Introduction, unless it refers to Cromwell having urged the trial of the King.

13. IV of Hearts.

"*The Rump roasted salt it well it stinks exceedingly.*"

The long parliament, not proving itself sufficiently complacent,

CAVALIER PLAYING CARDS. 11

Colonel Pride entered the House with two regiments of soldiers, imprisoned 60 members, drove 160 into the streets, and left only 60. These were called the Rump. The name was revived in the Protectorate of Richard Cromwell, and to distinguish the two, the former was called the *Bloody Rump*, and the latter the ***Rump of a*** *Rump*.

" The few,
Because they're wasted to the stumps,
Are represented best by rumps."

(Butler's *Hudibras*, Part iii).

14. IV of Clubs.

"*A Covenanting Scot and an English Independent differ about ye things of this world.*"

"There was a wonderful difference, throughout their whole proceedings, between the heads of those who were thought to sway the Presbyterian Counsels, and those who govern'd the Independents, though they were equally masters of dissimulation, and had equally malice and wickedness in their intentions, though not of the same kind . . . . The Presbyterians submitted to their senseless and wretched clergy; whose infectious breath corrupted, and govern'd the People, and whose authority was prevalent upon their own wives, and in their domestic affairs in order to corrupt and seduce them. . . whereas Cromwell and the Independents . . . . considered what was necessary to their main end; and then, whether it were right or wrong, made all other means subservient to it; couzen'd and deceiv'd men as long as they could induce them to contribute to what they desired; and when they would keep company with them no longer, compelled them by force to submit to what they should not be able to oppose: and so the one resolv'd, only to do what they believ'd the People would like and approve; and the other, that the People should like and approve what they had resolv'd." (*Clarendon's History of the Rebellion*, vol. iii., pp. 63-64).

15. IV of Spades.

"*Argyle a muckle Scotch knaue in gude faith Sir.*"

Archibald Campbell, Marquis of Argyle, a zealous partisan of the Covenanters, and the opponent of Montrose. Born in 1598 he succeeded to his fathers titles in 1638. In the same year he was called to London with other Scotch Nobles, and advised the abolition of Episcopacy in Scotland. In 1641 he was created Marquis. He acquiesced in the Protectorate of Cromwell, and for this at the restoration he was committed to the Tower. In 1661 he was sent to Scotland, tried for high treason and beheaded.

---

16. IV of Diamonds.

"*Laird of Warriston an arrant knaue An my Soul man.*"

"It was agreed that the committee of safety should consist of three-and-twenty persons, ... men try'd, and faithful to the public interest . . . . besides three or four others who had been the kings judges, with Warreston, Vane, Steel, and Whitlock."—*Clarendon's History of the Rebellion*, vol. iii. p. 402).

---

17. V of Hearts.

"*The E. of Pem.: in ye H. of Com. thanks ye Speaker for his Admission.*"

On the 29th of January 1643, a letter was addressed by Members of both Houses at Oxford to the Earl of Essex. Clarendon observes "This letter was subscribed by His Highness the Prince, the Duke of York, and three-and-forty Dukes, Marquises, Earls, Viscounts, and Barons, and 118 Members of the House of Commons; . . . so that the numbers at London were very thin; for there were not above two-and-twenty peers, who either sat in the Parliament, or were engaged in their party; that is to say, the Earls of Northumberland, Pembroke, Essex, etc."—(*Clarendon's History of the Rebellion*, vol. ii. p. 274).

According to Clarendon, vol. ii. pp. 127-128, the Earl of Pembroke was a weak man with a great sense of his own importance, whom disappointed ambition "Got into actual rebellion, which he never intended to do."

18. V of Clubs.

"*Sir H. Mildmay beaten by a foot boy, a great breach of privilege.*"

It is said that in the year 1642, Sir H. Mildmay got mixed up in a brawl in Fleet Street. Whether this Card alludes to that fact or not, I cannot tell. Clarendon states that Sir John Danvers and Sir H. Mildmay were the only two members of the High Court of Justice, whom the King knew besides the officers in the army.— (*Clarendon's History of the Rebellion*, vol. iii, p. 144).

19. V of Spades.

"*Nye and Godwin, Oliver's Confessors.*"

In "*an ordinance appointing Commissioners for approbation of Publique Preachers*," printed by "William Du Gard and Henry Hills printers to His Highness the Lord Protector" 1653, appear the names of Dr. Thomas Goodwin and Mr. Philip Ny as Commissioners for such approbation. A copy of the pamphlet is in my possession, and it will be reprinted by the Clarendon Historical Society at an early date.

20. V of Diamonds.

"*Sir W. Waller looses two armys yet getts by ye bargaine.*"

Sir William Waller was defeated at the battle of Roundway Down by Lord Wilmot, losing 600 killed, 900 prisoners, all their cannon, arms, ammunition and baggage. He was again defeated at Cropredy

Bridge, by the army under the **King in person, when he** again lost all his artillery. He was however, subsequently named Lieutenant of Ireland.—(*Clarendon's History of the Rebellion*, vol. ii. p. 179; p. 311; and vol. iii. p. 70).

21. VI of Hearts.

"*Worsley an Inckle Weaver A man of personal valor.*"

Worsley, one of Cromwell's Major-Generals, and a most dear friend of his, was the first M.P. for Manchester, and his **statue is in** the Town Hall. . . . The *incles* were tapes; and the word **comes into** Shakespeare's *Winter's Tale*. The word is now very little known, except in a proverb, "As thick (*i.e.* as intimate) as Incle-weavers." I do not see this pack mentioned in the History of Playing Cards. Can the date of publication be proved? It looks as if they were intended to keep up the spirit of the Cavaliers in depressed times.— *Communicated by John Bailey, Esq., F.S.A., Manchester.*

22. VI of Clubs.

"*Desbrow Olivers Champion haueing a cannon in each pocket.*"

With reference to the proposal in Parliament to elect Cromwell King, Clarendon observes: "That which put an end to the present debate was that some of his own family who had grown up under him, **and had** their whole dependance upon him, as Desborough, Fleetwood, Whaley, **and** others, passionately contradicted the motion.' —*(Clarendon's History of the Rebellion*, vol. iii., page 339.)

23. VI of Spades.

"*Skippon a waggoner to S^r. F. Vere one of Olivers Hectors.*"

Major-General Skippon was left in charge of the Army by the

Earl of Essex, when the latter fled from Fowey to Plymouth. Skippon surrendered all his Artillery, 100 barrels of powder, and about 6000 arms (muskets) on condition that the officers should be convoyed in safety to Poole or Southampton. Skippon was originally a waggoner, as stated in the Card.—(*Clarendon's History of Rebellion*, vol. ii., page 327.)

24. VI of Diamonds.

"*Kelsey, a sneeking Bodice maker a gifted Brother.*"

On October 17th, 1645, a "summons to surrender was sent to the Garrison (of Langford House, near Salisbury) and *fair and equal conditions* were speedily agreed upon, Lieutenant Colonel Hewson and Major Kelsey being deputed to act for Cromwell."—(Godwin's *Civil War in Hampshire*, page 248.) This is probably the individual alluded to.

25. VII of Hearts.

"*Nathaniel Fines whereby hangs a tale.*"

"Colonel Nathaniel Fiennes, brother of Lord Say and Sele, who had been educated at Winchester College, and had been admitted to a Fellowship at New College, Oxford, in quality of Founder's kin, surrendered Bristol to Prince Rupert on 26 July (1643.) and on the last day of the same month reached Southampton, at the head of 80 horse, each of whom had a woman riding behind him."—*Mercurius Aulicus*, August 5th, 1643.) This, I presume, is the tale alluded to.

26. VII of Clubs.

"*Harrison the Carpenter cutting down ye horne of ye beast in Daniel.*"

Harrison was the son of a butcher near Nantwich, in Cheshire, and he it was who, with Ireton, succceded in bringing the King before the High Court of Justice.—(*Clarendon's History of the Rebellion*, vol. iii., page 141.) Of the beast in Daniel, it is said, "I beheld, and the same horn made war with the Saints . . . . but the judgment shall sit, and they shall take away his dominion, to consume and to destroy it unto the end."—(Daniel, chap. vii., verses 21 and 26.)

27. VII of Spades.
"*Feek the seer.*"

Feek was one of Cromwell's officers, who at the celebrated meeting at Windsor, in 1648, declared that in a vision the Almighty had appeared to him and announced that Monarchy should never more prevail in England.—(*The Saints Triumph*, 1648, page 3.

28. VII of Diamonds.
"*Marshall curseing Mevoz.*"

At Edgehill, "the reverend and renowned Master Marshall, Master Ask, Master Mourton, Masters Obadiah and John Sedgwick and Master Wilkins, and divers others, eminently pious and learned pastors rode up and down the army through the thickest dangers and in much personal hazard most faithfully and courageously exhorting and encouraging the soldiers to fight valiantly and not to fly, but now, if ever, to stand to it and fight for their religion and laws."— (*Jehovah Jirah*, by John Vicars, p. 200.)

29. VIII of Hearts.
"*Lambert Kt. of y*ᵉ *golden Tulip.*"

When Lambert was cashiered by Parliament, he and eight other officers of the Army conspired to wrest the power from Parliament. The badge adopted by the conspirators was a yellow tulip.

30. VIII of Clubs.
"*Pride Oliver's drayman.*"

Parliament not proving willing to condemn Charles I., was *purged* of its unruly members by Colonel Pride, (who was said to have been originally a drayman) who entered the house and drove 160 members into the streets, leaving 60 of the *faithful* to govern the kingdom and murder their monarch.—(Imprisonment and death of King Charles I., Aungervyle Society reprint, p. 58).

31. VIII of Spades.
"*Scot Oliver's clerk or tallyman.*"

Scott was one of the members of the long parliament, and with Robinson was sent to Monk to "give some check to that license of addresses and resort of malignants."—*Clarendon's Rebellion*, vol. iii. p. 410.

32. VIII of Diamonds.
"*Don Haselrigg Kt. of ye codled braine.*"

"Haselrigg was of a rude, and stubborn nature, and of a weak understanding."—(*Clarendon's Rebellion*, vol. iii. p. 401).

33. IX of Hearts.
"*Huson the cobler entring London.*"

Hewson, who had originally been a cobbler, became Lt.-Col. of Cromwell's Ironsides.

34. IX of Clubs.

"*The army entring the city persuing the apprentices.*"

Parliament had voted that "the militia of the city of London should be put into such hands as the army should desire. Many thousands, apprentices and young citizens, brought petitions to parliament" in opposition. Parliament "durst not deny concurrence, the apprentices behaving themselves so insolently, that **they** would scarce suffer the **door** of the House of Commons to be shut."—(*Clarendon's* **Rebellion**, vol. iii. p. 36). The army assembled at Hounslow Heath, and Colonel Rainsborough having seized **in the** night the defences of **London** Bridge, "the army of horse, foot and cannon marched next day through the city."—(*Clarendon's Rebellion*, **vol. iii. p. 39**).

35. IX of Spades.

"*A Committee at Derby House to continue the **warr**.*"

Parliament had **appointed a** committee "for the raising of men . . and listing in all places, companies of volunteers" which met at Derby House.

36. IX of Diamonds.

"*Lenthall runs away with his mace to the army.*"

The **Army having** declared against the Committee of Safety, Lenthall the Speaker recovered his spirit and went into the **city** uniting with the army against the committee.—(*Clarendon's Rebellion*, vol. iii., p. 407.)

37. X of Hearts.

"The Rump and dreggs of the house of Com. remaining after the good Members were purged out."

The explanation of this Card will be found above. (See VIII of Clubs.)

38. X of Clubs.

"Oliver seeking God while the K. is murthered by his order."

Cromwell who signed the warrant for the Execution of Charles I., is said to have spent the night of the 29th of January, 1648, in prayer, and to have taken good care to let his fanatic followers know it.

39. X of Spades.

"A comitte at Haberdashers hall to spoyle the caualeers, as the Jews did the Egyptians."

Parliament, after the battle of Edgehill appointed a committee to sit at Haberdashers Hall to consider the fines to be imposed upon those of the King's adherents who had been taken prisoners there.

40. X of Diamonds.

"A comittee for plundered ministers, Miles Corbet in the chaire."

This card speaks for itself.

41. Knave of Hearts.

"Hugh Peters shews the bodkins and thimbles giuen by the wives of Wappin for the good old cause."

Hugh Peters was born at Fowey, publicly whipped and expelled from the University of Cambridge, and obliged to leave England for adultery. After some years spent in Holland and America, he returned in 1641, and became chaplain to Lord Brooke's regiment. He was a most burlesque preacher, and actually performed the act stated on the card. He styled the king Barabbas and compared the army to Christ. He advised the destruction of Stonehenge. Clarendon calls him the "ungodly confessor" who contrived the tragedy of the two Hothams (*Rebellion*, vol. ii. p. 383). He is said to have been one of the masked executioners of Charles I. He was beheaded October 16th 1660, and certainly deserved his fate if any of the Regicides did.

42. Knave of Clubs.

"*Ireton holds that saints may pass through all forms to obtain his ends.*"

Ireton was born in 1610, and commanded the left wing of the Parliamentarians at Naseby. He married a daughter of Oliver Cromwell, whom he succeeded as Commander-in-Chief in Ireland, where he died in 1651.

43. Knave of Spades.

"*Sir H. Vane finds a distinction betwixt a Legal and an Evangelical Conscience.*"

Vane was the principal mover of the Solemn League and Covenant, but did not sit on the King's trial.

44. Knave of Diamonds.

"*H. Martin moues ye House that ye King may take the Covenant.*"

Martin, Vane and Hazelrigg were the principal supporters of the self-denying Ordinance.

46. Queen of Hearts.

"*The damnable engagement to be true and faithfull.*"

The taking of the Holy League and Covenant. (See Queen of Diamonds)

47. Queen of Clubs.

"*Joane hold my staff Lady Protectoresse.*"

Another riddle. Cromwell's wife's name was Elizabeth. *Query*, what was Lady Lambert's name? (*See next card*).

48. Queen of Spades.

"*The lady Lambert and Oliver under a strong conflict.*"

It was said that an improper intimacy existed between Cromwell and Lambert's wife, but although the Protector is known to have been somewhat profligate in his youth, this charge seems to be mere calumny.

49. Queen of Diamonds.

"*The Takeing of the Holy League and Covenant.*"

The Holy League and Covenant between England and Scotland was solemnly adopted by Parliament on the 16th of November 1643. It was accepted by Charles II. in 1650, but repudiated by him at his Restoration, and declared to be illegal by Parliament.—(*Clarendon's Rebellion*, vol. ii. p. 229).

50. King of Hearts.

"*The saints think it meet that the Rump make a league with Oneale.*"

Lord Broghill, president of Munster, and Sir Charles Coote, president of Connaught had shewn enmity to the Rump, who thereupon coquetted with the Irish party.—(*Clarendon's Rebellion*, vol. iii. p. 434).

51. King of Clubs.

"*Oliver declars himself, and the Rebells to be the Gadly party.*"

This card needs no explanation.

52. King of Spades.

"*Bradshaw in ye High Court of Justice insulting of the King.*"

"The King demanded by what authority they brought him thither, the President answered that they derived their authority from an act made by the Commons . . . The King demurred to the jurisdiction of the Court, but the President overruled this." When the iniquitous sentence was read, "The King would have spoken something before he was withdrawn, but being accounted dead in law immediately after sentence was pronounced, it was not permitted."—(*Ludlow's* Imprisonment and Death of Charles I.—Aungervyle Soc. Rep. pp. 62-65).

53. King of Diamonds.

"Sir H. Mildmay solicits a Cityzen's wife, for which his owne corrects him."

On September 9, 1641, the House of Commons appointed Pym, St. John, Sir H. Mildmay, Sir H. Vane, and others (six to form a quorum), as a Committee, with extraordinary powers, to act during the recess, "To draw resort and reverence to them from almost all sorts of men." Mildmay is said to have used his political power to further his own projects of lust and greed.—(*Clarendon's Rebellion*, vol. i., pp. 168 *et seq.*).

Finis.

Cromwell, Ireton, and Hudson, all in y^e same Boate.

A Free state or a tolleration for all sort of Villany.

Bradsh^w, the Iaylor, and y^e Hangman keepers of the Liberty of England.

The High Court of Iustice or Olivers slaughter house.

Onsley Father and Sonne

Lenthall Father and Sonn.

Parry Father and Sonne

Vane Father and Sonne.

Cromwell pypeth unto Fairfax.

Bulstrod and Whitlock present to Oliver the Instruments of Governm.

H. Martin defend^d Ralph who design'd to kill the King.

Simon as slandring y^e High Preist to get his Place.

The Rump roasted salt it well it stinks exceedingly.

A Covenanting Scot & an English Independent differ about y things of this world

Argyle a muckle Scotch Knaue in gude faith Sir.

Laird of Warreston an arrant Knaue Au my Saul man.

The E. of Pem: in ye H. of Com: thanks ye Speaker for his Admission.

Sr H. Mildmay beaten by a foot: boy a great breach of Priviledg

Nye and Godwin Olivers Confessors.

Sr W. Waller looses two Armys yet getts by ye bargaine.

orsley an Inckle Weaver a
man of Personal Valor.

Shippon a Waggoner to S.ʳ F. Vere
one of Oliuers Hectors.

Nathaniel Fines whereby hangs a tale.

Harrison the Carpenter cutting down ye horne of ye Beast in Daniel

Feek the Seer.

Marshall curseing Mevoz.

Lambert K⁰ of yͤ Golden Tulip.

Pride Olivers Drayman

Scot Olivers Clerk or Tally man.

Don Haselrigg K⁰ of yͤ Codled braine.

Huſon the Cobler entring London.

The Army entring the City perſuing the Apprentices.

A Comittee at Derby houſe to continue the Warr.

Lenthall runns away With his Mace to the Army.

No. VIII.
CIRCONIUS.

The Rump and droggs of the house of Com. remaining after the good members were purged out.

Oliver seeking God while the K. is murthered by his order.

A Comitte at Haberdashers Hall to spoyle the Caualeers, as the Iews did the Egyptians.

A Comittee for Plundered Ministers Miles Corbet in the Chaire.

The Damnable engagement to be true and Faithfull.

Ioane hold my Staff Lady Protectoresse.

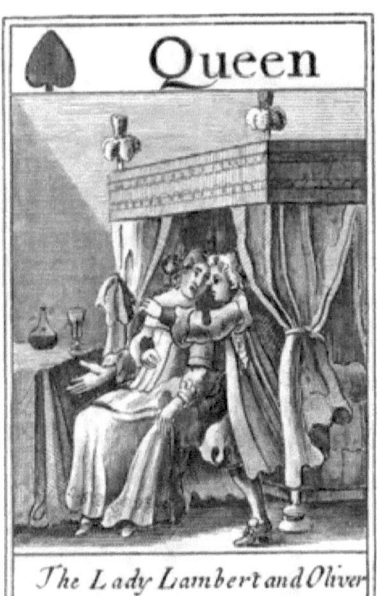

The Lady Lambert and Oliver under a strong Conflict.

The takeing of the Holy League and Covenant.

The Saints think it meet that the Rump make a League wth Oneale

Oliver declares himself and the Rebells to be the Godly Party

Bradshaw in y^e High Court of Iustice insulting of the King.

Sr H. Milmay solicits a Citizens wife for wch his owne Corrects him

www.ingramcontent.com/pod-product-compliance
Lightning Source LLC
Chambersburg PA
CBHW030542300426
44111CB00009B/827